Lecture Notes in Artificial Intelligence 6188

Edited by R. Goebel, J. Siekmann, and W. Wahlster

Subseries of Lecture Notes in Computer Science

FoLLI Publications on Logic, Language and Information

Anuj Dawar   Ruy de Queiroz (Eds.)

Logic, Language, Information and Computation

17th International Workshop, WoLLIC 2010
Brasilia, Brazil, July 6-9, 2010
Proceedings

 Springer

Series Editors

Randy Goebel, University of Alberta, Edmonton, Canada
Jörg Siekmann, University of Saarland, Saarbrücken, Germany
Wolfgang Wahlster, DFKI and University of Saarland, Saarbrücken, Germany

Volume Editors

Anuj Dawar
University of Cambridge
Computer Laboratory
J.J. Thomson Avenue
Cambridge, CB3 0FD, UK
E-mail: anuj.dawar@cl.cam.ac.uk

Ruy de Queiroz
Universidade Federal de Pernambuco
Centro de Informática
Avenida Prof Luis Freire s/n
Cidade Universitária
50740-540 Recife, PE, Brazil
E-mail: ruy@cin.ufpe.br

Library of Congress Control Number: 2010928907

CR Subject Classification (1998): F.4.1, F.3, F.4, I.2.3, G.2, I.1

LNCS Sublibrary: SL 7 – Artificial Intelligence

ISSN   0302-9743
ISBN-10   3-642-13823-3 Springer Berlin Heidelberg New York
ISBN-13   978-3-642-13823-2 Springer Berlin Heidelberg New York

springer.com

© Springer-Verlag Berlin Heidelberg 2010

Typesetting: Camera-ready by author, data conversion by Scientific Publishing Services, Chennai, India
Printed on acid-free paper   06/3180   5 4 3 2 1 0

Preface

This volume contains the papers presented at WoLLIC 2010: 17th Workshop on Logic, Language, Information and Computation held during July 6–9, 2010, on the campus of Universidade de Brasília (UnB), Brazil.

The Workshop on Logic, Language, Information and Computation (WoLLIC) is an annual event, meeting every year since 1994, which aims at fostering interdisciplinary research in pure and applied logic. The idea is to have a forum which is large enough in the number of possible interactions between logic and the sciences related to information and computation, and yet is small enough to allow for concrete and useful interaction among participants.

The present volume contains 13 contributed papers that were selected from among 32 submissions after a rigorous review by the Program Committee. Each submission was reviewed by at least two, and on average three, Program Committee members.

This volume also contains papers or abstracts that relate to the seven invited talks presented at the workshop. Between them, these papers give a snapshot of some fascinating work taking place at the frontiers between computation, logic, and linguistics.

We are grateful to all the people who made this meeting possible and are responsible for its success: the members of the Program Committee and the external reviewers, the invited speakers, the contributors, and the people who were involved in organizing the workshop.

On behalf of the entire WoLLIC community, we would also like to express our gratitude to our institutional sponsors and supporters. WoLLIC 2010 was sponsored by the Association for Symbolic Logic (ASL), the Interest Group in Pure and Applied Logics (IGPL), the Association for Logic, Language and Information (FoLLI), the European Association for Theoretical Computer Science (EATCS), the Sociedade Brasileira de Computação (SBC), and the Sociedade Brasileira de Lógica (SBL). We expect to receive financial support from the Brazilian government (through CAPES, grant PAEP-2759/2010-85), Universidade de Brasília (UnB), CNPq and FAPDF.

The reviewing for the workshop and the preparation of the proceedings were prepared with the assistance of the EasyChair conference management system, for which we wish to express our gratitude to its main developer, Andrei Voronkov.

April 2010

Anuj Dawar
Ruy de Queiroz

Organization

Program Chair

Anuj Dawar   Cambridge

Program Committee

Veronica Becher	Buenos Aires
Raffaella Bernardi	Bolzano
Ricardo Bianconi	São Paulo
Vasco Brattka	Cape Town
Bob Coecke	Oxford
Adriana Compagnoni	Stevens
Marcelo Coniglio	Campinas
Valentin Goranko	Copenhagen
Rosalie Iemhoff	Utrecth
Makoto Kanazawa	National Institute of Informatics, Japan
Giuseppe Longo	CNRS & ENS, Paris
Hasegawa Masahito	Kyoto U, Japan
Michael Mislove	Tulane
Michael Norrish	NICTA, Canberra
Bart Selman	Cornell
Scott Weinstein	Pennsylvania
Balder ten Cate	ENS, Cachan

Steering Committee

Samson Abramsky
Johan van Benthem
Joe Halpern
Wilfrid Hodges
Daniel Leivant
Angus Macintyre
Grigori Mints
Hiroakira Ono
Ruy de Queiroz

Local Organization

Mauricio Ayala-Rincon	University of Brasilia, Brazil (Co-chair)
Flavio L. C. Moura	University of Brasilia, Brazil

Claudia Nalon   University of Brasilia, Brazil
Anjolina G. de Oliveira   Federal University of Pernambuco, Brazil
Ruy de Queiroz   Federal University of Pernambuco, Brazil
                                   (Co-chair)

External Reviewers

Romain Beauxis
Arnold Beckmann
Dietmar Berwanger
Will Brian
Diego Calvanese
Sergio Daicz
Joerg Flum
Birte Glimm
Healfdene Goguen
Joos Heintz
Neil Immerman
Bruce Kapron
Roman Kuznets
Catherine Meadows
Mariano Moscato
Hans de Nivelle
Dusko Pavlovic
Mariano Rodriguez
Vladimir Rybakov
Mehroosh Sadrzadeh
Robert Seely
Inanc Seylan
Benjamin Spector
Cristoph Sticksel
Alwen Tiu
Clint Van Alten

Table of Contents

Entailment Multipliers: An Algebraic Characterization of Validity for Classical and Modal Logics

Marcelo Finger* and Mauricio S.C. Hernandes**

Department of Computer Science
Institute of Mathematics and Statistics
University of Sao Paulo
mfinger@ime.usp.br, mauhcs@gmail.com

Abstract. We propose a novel algebraic characterisation of the classical notion of validity in terms of boolean rings, called *entailment multipliers*. We demonstrate the existence of such multipliers and show how they can be used to derive stronger entailment statements. An interesting property of multipliers lies in their behaviour as invariants in a proof, a fact that is used to show how several inference systems can be employed to compute entailment multipliers. A similar characterisation of validity for modal logics is presented.

1 Introduction

The notions of logical consequence and logical validity have been explored under several points of view, mostly in terms of proof-theory and semantic entailment relations, but also in algebraic terms. In this work we propose an algebraic characterisation of the notion of logical validity, and study its relationship with proof-theoretical and semantic approaches.

Algebraic formulation of logics is usually presented in terms of boolean algebras and lattices. Here, however, we use as an underlying structure a *boolean ring*; the main motivation for the use of such structure comes from the work of Carnielli [6]. As usual, formulas can be represented algebraically as terms, and ring properties allow us to represent formulas in a more compact way.

Classical validity statements presented in terms of semantic entailment expressions or proof-theoretical sequents can be expressed as polynomials over boolean rings, where variables are inserted as *multipliers* of terms obtained from the algebraic translation of formulas in the validity statements. The main result of this work claims that such a statement is classically *valid* iff the corresponding polynomial has roots when equated to the unit (the *1-roots*).

On a different perspective, an application of this result can be seen as follows. It is quite widespread the opinion that proving a mathematical statement is

---

* Partly supported by CNPq grant PQ 301294/2004-6 and FAPESP project 2008/03995-5.
** Partly supported by CNPq grant 131263/2008-0.

A. Dawar and R. de Queiroz (Eds.): WoLLIC 2010, LNAI 6188, pp. 1–18, 2010.

more than knowing its validity. Proving brings *insight*, which may lead to a generalisation of the original statement.

The existence of entailment multipliers allows us to make such opinion formal, that is, we show how, given proof of a theorem, one can employ the *entailment multipliers* (that is, the 1-roots of the polynomial associated to the validity expression) to effectively compute a generalisation of the original theorem.

In this setting, given a proof of a validity statement $\mathcal{S}$:

$$A_1, \ldots, A_n \models B_1, \ldots, B_m$$

we compute another validity statement $\mathcal{S}'$

$$A_1', \ldots, A_n' \models B_1', \ldots, B_m'$$

that is stronger than $\mathcal{S}$, $\mathcal{S}' \geq \mathcal{S}$, in the sense that:

- $A_i \models A_i'$, $1 \leq i \leq n$; and
- $B_j' \models B_j$, $1 \leq j \leq m$

That is, both $\mathcal{S}$ and $\mathcal{S}'$ are valid, and $\mathcal{S}'$ has a weaker antecedent or a stronger conclusion, or both. Clearly, $\geq$ is a partial order. For example, from a Modus Ponens statement $\mathcal{S}_{MP} = A \rightarrow B, A \models B$, with the aid of entailment multipliers we can compute a stronger $\mathcal{S}_{MP}' = A \rightarrow B, A \vee B \models B$. Several methods of computing the entailment multipliers are analysed associated to several proof methods.

1.1   Comparisons with the Literature

The method in the literature that best approaches ours is the use of Hilbert Nullstellensatz for propositional refutations, which was initially suggested by Lovász [12] and was independently proposed again in [1] and later developed in a series of works on what has bee termed the *algebraic propositional proof system* [13, 5, 2, 4].

In this approach, formulas are transformed into polynomials over a fixed algebraically closed field F. Satisfiability of a formula A is mapped as an equation $Q_A(\bar{x}) = 0$, where $Q_A(\bar{x})$ is the translation of the formula A as a polynomial over variables $\bar{x}$. Extra equations of the form $x_i^2 + x_i = 0$ are needed to ensure that each $x_i \in \bar{x}$ takes only values 0 or 1. Theorem proving is made by refutation, trying to show that a set of formulas is unsatisfiable. In such setting, one can apply Hilbert's (weak) Nullstellensatz, that states that a set a system of equations $Q_i(\bar{x}) = 0$ does not have a solution in F iff there are polynomials $P_i(\bar{x})$ such that $\sum_i P_i(\bar{x}) Q_i(\bar{x}) = 1$.

Although there is a similarity between this approach and ours, the main difference lies in the fact that it deals with fields, so that variables can take any variables over a field. This makes the translation of a polynomial back into a formula somewhat different. By using boolean rings, the translation back into formulas is immediate, and this fact will be used to proof-theoretical applications

1.2 Organisation of the Paper

The rest of the paper develops as follows. After introducing some definitions and notation, Section 2 introduces boolean rings and proves the existence of entailment multipliers for valid statements. In Section 2.1 we show how the existence of "small multipliers" is related to the problem NP=coNP, and in Section 2.2 we show how entailment multipliers can be used to generate stronger entailment statements. In Section 3 we show how to compute entailment multipliers along the proof constructions using the inference systems of Resolution and Gentzen Sequent Calculus. We then show how the idea of multipliers generalises to extensions of propositional classical logics, such as Normal Modal Logics in Section 4. The paper concludes with some remarks and proposals of future work.

Notation

We consider formulas built over a countable set of propositional atoms $\mathcal{P} = \{p_0, p_1, \ldots\}$ and connectives $\neg$, $\wedge$, $\vee$ and $\rightarrow$. We represent formulas by upper case Latin letters: A, B, C, etc. We represent sets or multisets of formulas by upper case Greek letters, such as Γ, Δ, Φ and Ψ. A valuation is a function that maps each atomic symbol in $\mathcal{P}$ in $\{0, 1\}$, which is then generalised to formulas in the usual way; a valuation v is said to satisfy formula A if $v(A) = 1$. A set of formulas Γ is *satisfiable* if there is a v such that for every $A \in \Gamma$, $v(A) = 1$.

An *entailment statement* is an expression of the form $\Gamma \models \Delta$; such a statement is *valid* if every valuation that satisfies every $A \in \Gamma$ also satisfies some $B \in \Delta$. The proof-theoretic counterpart of entailment statements are *sequents*, which are expressions of the form $\Gamma \vdash \Delta$, where Γ is the sequent's antecedent and Δ its consequent. A sequent may be proven using several distinct *inference systems*, represented by $\vdash_I$; such a system is sound and complete with respect to the semantic entailment iff $\Gamma \models \Delta$ iff $\Gamma \vdash_I \Delta$.

Algebraic terms are represented by lower case Latin letters: a, b, c, etc. Algebraic variables are represented by x, y, z, etc. All representations may be subscripted or superscripted.

2 Entailment Multipliers

For the purposes of this paper, a *ring* is an algebraic structure $\mathfrak{R} = \langle \mathcal{R}, \cdot, +, 0, 1 \rangle$ where $\mathcal{R}$ is a set, $0, 1 \in \mathcal{R}$ and for every $a, b, c \in \mathcal{R}$ the following holds:

(r_1) $(a + b) + c = a + (b + c)$;
(r_2) $0 + a = a + 0 = a$;
(r_3) there is $-a \in \mathcal{R}$ such that $a + (-a) = (-a) + a = 0$;
(r_4) $a + b = b + a$;
(r_5) $(a \cdot b) \cdot c = a \cdot (b \cdot c)$;
(r_6) $a \cdot b = b \cdot a$;
(r_7) $1 \cdot a = a \cdot 1 = a$;
(r_8) $a \cdot (b + c) = a \cdot b + a \cdot c$.

A *boolean ring* $\mathfrak{B} = \langle \mathcal{B}, \cdot, +, 0, 1 \rangle$ is a ring subjected to the conditions, for every $a \in \mathcal{B}$:

(b_1) $a \cdot a = a$;
(b_2) $a + a = 0$

In a boolean ring, the structure $\cdot$ is interpreted as conjunction, $+$ is exclusive-or, 0 is the bottom and 1 is the top. Note that every element is its own inverse, $x + x = 0$ (that is, $(\mathcal{B}, +, 0)$ is an Abelian group of order 2). Also note that the power of any variable is at most 1. As 0 is defined by (b_2), a boolean ring is sometimes represented as $\mathfrak{B} = \langle \mathcal{B}, \cdot, +, 1 \rangle$. The *degree* of the term is defined as usual, namely, $degree(0) = degree(1) = 0$, $degree(x_i) = 1$, $degree(a + b) = \max\{degree(a), degree(b)\}$, $degree(a \cdot b) = degree(a) + degree(b)$. As usual, we sometimes write ab for $a \cdot b$.

For every propositional formula A, let A^t be its standard translation as a term of $\mathfrak{A}$; similarly, let if a is a term of $\mathfrak{A}$, a^φ is its formula translation. The *term* and *formula translations* are defined as follows.

$$
\begin{array}{ll}
\top^t = 1 & 1^\varphi = \top \\
\bot^t = 0 & 0^\varphi = \bot \\
p_i^t = x_i & x_i^\varphi = p_i \\
(\neg A)^t = A^t + 1 & (a \cdot b)^\varphi = a^\varphi \wedge b^\varphi \\
(A \wedge B)^t = A^t \cdot B^t & \\
(A \vee B)^t = (A^t + 1) \cdot (B^t + 1) + 1 & (a+b)^\varphi = \begin{cases} \neg a^\varphi & , b = 1 \\ (a^\varphi \wedge \neg b^\varphi) \vee & \\ (\neg a^\varphi \wedge b^\varphi) & , b \neq 1 \end{cases} \\
(A \rightarrow B)^t = A^t \cdot (B^t + 1) + 1 &
\end{array}
$$

It is immediate that $a = (a^\varphi)^t$ and that $A \equiv (A^t)^\varphi$.

The relationship between boolean rings and sequents is established by the following result.

Proposition 2.1. *The statement* $A_1, \ldots, A_n \models B_1, \ldots, B_m$ *is valid iff*

$$
\left(\prod_{i=1}^{n} A_i^t \right) \cdot \left(\prod_{j=1}^{m} (B_j^t + 1) \right) = 0 \tag{1}
$$

Lemma 2.2. *Suppose* $\{A_1, \ldots, A_n\}$ *is an unsatisfiable set of propositional formulas. Then there are terms* $a_1, \ldots, a_n$ *such that*

$$
\sum_{i=1}^{n} a_i \cdot (A_i^t + 1) = 1. \tag{2}
$$

Proof. By induction on n. For the base case, consider $n = 1$, so that A_1 is an inconsistent formula. As a result $A_1^t = 0$, and take $a_1 = 1$. Then $a_1 \cdot (A_1^t + 1) = 1 \cdot (0 + 1) = 1$.

Suppose the set $\{A_1, \ldots, A_{n+1}\}$ with $n + 1$ elements is inconsistent; then the set $\{A_1, \ldots, A_n \wedge A_{n+1}\}$ with n elements is clearly inconsistent, and we can apply the induction hypothesis, so there are $a_1, \ldots, a_n$ such that

$$
\left(\sum_{i=1}^{n-1} a_i \cdot (A_i^t + 1) \right) + a_n \cdot (A_n^t \cdot A_{n+1}^t + 1) = 1. \tag{3}
$$

To solve (3), it suffices to provide a'_n, a'_{n+1} such that

$$a'_n \cdot (A^t_n + 1) + a'_{n+1} \cdot (A^t_{n+1} + 1) = a_n \cdot (A^t_n \cdot A^t_{n+1} + 1). \tag{4}$$

There are many possible solutions to (4). One could make $a'_n = a_n \cdot A^t_{n+1}$ and $a'_{n+1} = a_n$; or $a'_n = a_n \cdot (A^t_n \cdot A^t_{n+1} + 1)$ and $a'_{n+1} = a_n \cdot A^t_n$. In either case, we have a set of multipliers for $\{A_1, \ldots, A_{n+1}\}$. □

Note that the possible multipliers for a given inconsistent set are not unique. In fact, in the proof above, the inductive case can generate a potentially different set of multipliers for every pair of formulas chosen in $\{A_1, \ldots, A_{n+1}\}$. The sum is called a *1-sum*.

Example 2.3. Consider the inconsistent set of formulas $A, C \rightarrow \neg A, B \rightarrow C, B$. It is easy to verify that

$$1 \cdot (a + 1) + 1 \cdot (ca) + a \cdot (b(c + 1)) + a(c + 1) \cdot (b + 1) = 1 \tag{5}$$

so a possible attribution of multipliers to this set is $1, 1, a, a(c + 1)$. □

The converse of Lemma 2.2 also holds.

Lemma 2.4. Let $\Gamma = \{A_1, \ldots, A_n\}$ be a set of formulas such that $\sum^n_{i=1} a_i \cdot (A^t_i + 1) = 1$ for terms $a_1, \ldots, a_n$. Then Γ is unsatisfiable.

Proof. We prove by induction on n. For the base case $n = 1$, so $a_1 \cdot (A^t_1 + 1) = 1$, which holds iff $a_1 = A^t_1 + 1 = 1$. So $A^t = 0$ and Γ is inconsistent.

Consider now $\sum^n_{i=1} a_i \cdot (A^t_i + 1) = 1$. By multiplying both sides by $A^t_1 \cdot A^t_2$ the first two terms of the sum are cancelled and after some regrouping we obtain

$$\sum^n_{i=3} (A^t_1 \cdot A^t_2 \cdot a_i) \cdot (A^t_i + 1) = A^t_1 \cdot A^t_2. \tag{6}$$

Adding $A^t_1 \cdot A^t_2 + 1$ to both sides of (6) yields

$$\left(\sum^n_{i=3} (A^t_1 \cdot A^t_2 \cdot a_i) \cdot (A^t_i + 1) \right) + (A^t_1 \cdot A^t_2 + 1) = 1 \tag{7}$$

The left hand side of (7) is a sum of $n - 1$ terms, where the multiplier of the last term is 1. By the induction hypothesis, we obtain that the set $\{A_1 \wedge A_2, A_3, \ldots, A_n\}$ is unsatisfiable, so Γ is unsatisfiable. □

Definition 2.5 (Characteristic Polynomial). Given an entailment statement $S = A_1, \ldots, A_n \models B_1, \ldots, B_m$, its *characteristic polynomial* over variables $x_1, \ldots, x_n, y_1, \ldots, y_m$ is $cp(S) = x_1 \cdot (A^t_1 + 1) + \ldots + x_n \cdot (A^t_n + 1) + y_1 \cdot B^t_1 + \ldots + y_m \cdot B^t_m$.

The characteristic polynomial has *1-roots* if there are terms $a_1, \ldots, a_n$, $b_1, \ldots, b_m$ such that

$$\sum^n_{i=1} a_i \cdot (A^t_i + 1) + \sum^m_{j=1} b_j \cdot B^t_j = 1. \tag{1-roots}$$

Theorem 2.6 (Entailment Multipliers). *A classical entailment statement S is valid iff its characteristic polynomial $cp(S)$ has 1-roots.*

Proof. If $A_1, \ldots, A_n \models B_1, \ldots, B_m$ then the set $\{A_1, \ldots, A_n, \neg B_1, \ldots, \neg B_m\}$ is unsatisfiable. So, by applying Lemma 2.2, the 1-roots are obtained.

Conversely, if $cp(S)$ has 1-roots, by Lemma 2.4, $\{A_1, \ldots, A_n, \neg B_1, \ldots, \neg B_m\}$ is an unsatisfiable set, so $A_1, \ldots, A_n \models B_1, \ldots, B_m$ holds.   □

We use the notation of Labelled Deduction System (LDS) [10] to designate a formula and its corresponding entailment multiplier as the label. So a statement is now represented as:

$$x_1 : A_1, \ldots, x_n : A_n \models y_1 : B_1, \ldots, y_m : B_m$$

to indicate that the statement $A_1, \ldots, A_n \models B_1, \ldots, B_m$ is valid with the corresponding 1-roots.

Example 2.7. Consider the statement $A, C \to \neg A, B \to C, B \models (A \lor B) \land C$. As its antecedent is the unsatisfiable set of Example 2.3, we obtain the following multiplier labelled sequent:

$$1 : A, 1 : C \to \neg A, a : B \to C, a(c+1) : B \models 0 : (A \lor B) \land C$$

Note that 0-labelled formulas play no part in the validity of the statement.   □

There is a naive way to compute multipliers. Let $A_1, \ldots, A_n$ be a set of inconsistent formulas, then we we compute multipliers $a_1, \ldots, a_n$ by making $a_1 = 1$ and for $2 \leq i \leq n$

$$a_i = \prod_{j=1}^{i-1} A_j^t \tag{8}$$

that is, $a_2 = A_1^t$, $a_3 = A_1^t \cdot A_2^t$, ..., $a_n = A_1^t \cdots A_{n-1}^t$. This is a direct consequence of the equation

$$\sum_{i=1}^{n} \left(\prod_{j=1}^{i-1} A_j^t \right) \cdot (A_i^t + 1) = 1, \tag{9}$$

which can be easily verified.

It is important to note that the multipliers computed by (8) depends on the order of the formulas. It is also possible to simplify those multipliers.

Example 2.8. Consider again the set of inconsistent formulas in Example 2.3. By applying equation 9 we obtain the multipliers:

$$1 : A, a : C \to \neg A, a(ca+1) : B \to C, a(ca+1)(b(c+1)+1) : B$$

On the other hand, by considering the same set in reverse order we obtain

$$b(b(c+1)+1)(ca+1) : A, b(b(c+1)+1) : C \to \neg A, b : B \to C, 1 : B$$

or

$$bc : A, b : C \to \neg A, 1 : B \to C, 1 : B$$

after some simplification.   □

In this method, prior to simplification, the degree of the last multiplier is $n-1$, which indicates that this may not be a good way to obtain small multipliers. Section 3 presents other ways of computing entailment multipliers, which are associated to proof systems.

2.1   Multipliers and the NP = coNP Problem

There is a basic asymmetry between NP-complete problems and coNP-complete problems, which is reflected in logic as well. If a set of formulas is satisfiable, it suffices to provide a valuation to have a polynomial-time computable witness of satisfiability. No such tractable witness is known to exist for unsatisfiability (or validity).

Here, we propose that entailment multipliers as a candidate for validity witness. The complexity of the verification is the number of operations (sums, products, fatorings or other forms of term simplification) to transform the left-hand side of the 1-sum to 1.

In this case, a *small witness* for the validity of a sequent would be a set of entailment multipliers such that the number of operations to verify the 1-sum is bounded by a polynomial on the number of distinct atomic formulas in the sequent. However, it is not clear that such a set of multipliers always exists.

Lemma 2.9. *If every valid sequent has a small witness set of entailment multipliers, then NP=coNP.*

Proof. The existence of a small witness set of entailment multipliers provides an NP algorithm for deciding classical propositional validity, which is a coNP problem. This implies NP=coNP [11].   □

The search space of multipliers for a given entailment can be quite big, as the set of multipliers for a given entailment is far from unique. In fact, each proof method may compute a different set of multipliers, which we investigate in Section 3.

2.2   Strengthening Entailment Expressions

The use of entailment multipliers suggests a way to strengthen entailment expressions.

Theorem 2.10 (Stronger Entailment). *Let $\mathcal{S} = A_1, \ldots, A_n \models B_1, \ldots, B_m$ be a valid statement with multipliers $a_1, \ldots, a_n, b_1, \ldots, b_m$. Then:*

(a) *For $1 \leq k \leq n$, the statement $\mathcal{S}' = A_1, \ldots, (\neg a_k^\varphi) \vee A_k, \ldots, A_n \models B_1, \ldots, B_m$ is valid with multipliers $a_1, \ldots, a_{k-1}, 1, a_{k+1}, \ldots, a_n, b_1, \ldots, b_m$, such that $\mathcal{S}' \geq \mathcal{S}$.*

(b) *For $1 \leq l \leq m$, the statement $\mathcal{S}'' = A_1, \ldots, A_n \models B_1, \ldots, b_l^\varphi \wedge B_l, \ldots, B_m$ is valid with multipliers $a_1, \ldots, a_n, b_1, b_{j-1}, 1, b_{j+1}, \ldots, \ldots, b_m$, such that $\mathcal{S}'' \geq \mathcal{S}$.*

Proof. From the fact that $\mathcal{S}$ is valid with multipliers $a_1, \ldots, a_n, b_1, \ldots, b_m$ we have that

$$\sum_{i=1}^{n} a_i \cdot (A_i^t + 1) + \sum_{j=1}^{m} b_j \cdot B_j^t = 1. \tag{10}$$

Then:

(a) The term translation $[(\neg a_k^\varphi) \vee A_k]^t = ((a_k+1)+1)(A_k^t+1)+1 = a_k(A_k^t+1)+1$, such that (10) can be rewritten as

$$\left(\sum_{i=1, i \neq k}^{n} a_i \cdot (A_i^t + 1) + \sum_{j=1}^{m} b_j \cdot B_j^t \right) + 1 \cdot (a_k(A_k^t + 1) + 1 + 1) = 1. \tag{11}$$

By Theorem 2.6 we have that $\mathcal{S}'$ is valid with multipliers $a_1, \ldots, a_{k-1}, 1$, $a_{k+1}, \ldots, a_n, b_1, \ldots, b_m$. We also have that $A_i = A_i'$ for $1 \leq i \neq k \leq n$, $B_j = B_j'$ for $1 \leq j \leq m$ and $A_k \models (\neg a_k^\varphi) \vee A_k$, so $\mathcal{S}' \geq \mathcal{S}$.

(b) Totally analogous. □

Theorem 2.10 implies that, if we start with a valid statements $\mathcal{S}$ we "incorporate" one of its multipliers into new a statement $\mathcal{S}' \geq \mathcal{S}$; clearly, $\mathcal{S}'$ is strictly stronger than $\mathcal{S}$ when the multiplier is not 1. But then we can again apply Theorem 2.10 to $\mathcal{S}'$, choosing a different non-unit multiplier, obtaining an even stronger valid statement. This process can be iterated until we obtain a statement whose multipliers are all 1.

Corollary 2.11. *Given a valid entailment statement $\mathcal{S}$*

$$\mathcal{S} = a_1 : A_1, \ldots, a_n : A_n \models b_1 : B_1, \ldots, b_m : B_m$$

we can build a lattice of valid entailment statements $(\mathbb{S}, \Gamma)$ where the elements of $\mathbb{S}$ are valid statements obtained by applying Theorem 2.10 to every subset of formulas in $\mathcal{S}$. The statement $\mathcal{S}$ is the bottom of the lattice and the top statement is $\mathcal{S}^\top$:

$$\neg a_1^\varphi \vee A_1, \ldots, \neg a_n^\varphi \vee A_n \models b_1^\varphi \wedge B_1, \ldots, b_m^\varphi \wedge B_m$$

3 Computing Entailment Multipliers

The naive method to compute entailment multipliers has a series of inconveniences. It may take an exponential number of steps, which may even lead to the storage of an exponential number of terms. As a result, the multipliers may use exponential space.

However, we believe that each kind of inference system may provide at least one method of computing entailment multipliers. In fact, each sound inference method consists of a set of transformations that preserve the validity, or the truth value, such that at each step the 1-sum is an invariant. Therefore, at each transformation step one can compute new multipliers from previous ones. We now investigate this statement for two proof methods: resolution and Gentzen Sequent Calculus.

3.1   Resolution

Propositional resolution is a refutation method in which one shows the inconsistency of a set of formulas in clausal form by deriving $\perp$ from it. The main inference step is the resolution rule

$$\frac{A \vee p_i \quad \neg p_i \vee B}{A \vee B}$$

This inference step can be simulated as an algebraic operation. Note that $(x_i + 1)$ is a factor of $(A \vee p_i)^t + 1$, and similarly, x_i is a factor of $(\neg p_i \vee B)^t + 1$. We can construct multipliers m_A and m_B for the resolvents such that $m_A \cdot ((A \vee p_i)^t + 1) = y \cdot (x_i + 1)$ and $m_B \cdot ((\neg p_i \vee B)^t + 1) = y \cdot x_i$. In this case, the resolution step can be simulated by the algebraic operation

$$y \cdot (x_i + 1) + y \cdot x_i = y \tag{12}$$

The multipliers for an original formula is the multiplication of all those factors that label the path from the formula to the final contradiction, $\perp$; if more than one path exists, take the sum of them. This method is better understood by means of an example.

Example 3.1.   The set of formulas $\{\neg s \vee q, \neg p \vee q, p \vee s, \neg q\}$, is inconsistent. This can be shown by a labeled resolution graph in Figure 1, in which each edge is labeled with the term corresponding to the negation of the resolved literal.

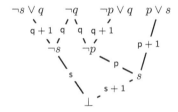

Fig. 1. Edge-labeled resolution graph

The term corresponding to a path going from a top formula to $\perp$ is the product of all labels. The multiplier of a top formula is the sum of all path terms. In this way, we compute the multipliers for each formula:

$$(\mathsf{q} + 1)\mathsf{s} : \neg s \vee q, \quad \mathsf{qs} + \mathsf{qp}(\mathsf{s} + 1) : \neg q,$$
$$(\mathsf{q} + 1)\mathsf{p}(\mathsf{s} + 1) : \neg p \vee q, \quad (\mathsf{p} + 1)(\mathsf{s} + 1) : p \vee s$$

The multipliers a of $a : A$ can be simplified by deleting from it the factors occurring in $A^t + 1$, so we end up with

$$1 : \neg s \vee q, \quad \mathsf{s} + \mathsf{p}(\mathsf{s} + 1) : \neg q,$$
$$(\mathsf{s} + 1) : \neg p \vee q, \qquad 1 : p \vee s$$

Finally, we note that the verification of the 1-sum is isomorphic to the resolution graph, as shown in Figure 2; each transformation step is an application of (12). In this sense, we can say that resolution is simulated by algebraic methods.   □

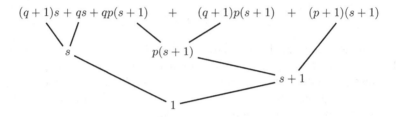

Fig. 2. Reduction of 1-sum isomorphic to resolution graph in Figure 1

Formally, define an *edge-labeled resolution graph* as a resolution graph in which edges are labeled with a term $(\neg p)^t$, where p is the reduced literal. This is the input for Algorithm 1 computing entailment multipliers.

Algorithm 1. Resolution-based computation of entailment multipliers

---

Input: an edge-labeled resolution graph G.
Output: entailment multipliers for the top nodes of G.

Let $A_1, \ldots, A_n$ be the top nodes of G, an inconsistent set of formulas.
for each path P from a top node to $\bot$ **do**
    $\text{term}(P) = \prod \{l | l \text{ is a label in } P\}$
end for
for $i = 1$ to n **do**
    $a_i = \sum \{\text{term}(P) | P \text{ starts at } A_i\}$
    delete from a_i factors occurring in $(A_i^t + 1)$
end for
return the set $\{a_i : A_i | 1 \leq i \leq n\}$

Theorem 3.2. *Algorithm 1 computes a set of multipliers such that the verification of the 1-sum as a set of applications of (12) is isomorphic to the input edge-labeled resolution graph.*   □

3.2   Sequent Calculus

There are many presentations of the sequent calculus. As our interest lies in calculi that promote the use of non-analytic cuts, we present a *cut-based* sequent calculus, in which the cut rule is *not* eliminable, and is in fact the only branching rule [9]. This version of the sequent calculus is closely related to KE tableau [8], which is a decision procedure for full propositional classical logic.

In the sequent calculus, the 1-sum is seen as an *invariant* over each deduction step, such that every rule that transforms a provable sequent into another provable sequent has to preserve it. In this way, the multipliers of a sequent rule's conclusion will be described as a combination of the multipliers of the rule's premises.

So in this presentation formulas are labeled with entailment multiplier, and in a sequent $\Gamma \vdash \Delta$, the antecedent Γ and the consequent Δ are *multisets* of term labeled formulas of the form $a : A$; if $\Gamma = a_1 : A_1, \ldots, a_n : A_n$, by $b : \Gamma$ we mean $b \cdot a_1 : A_1, \ldots, b \cdot a_n : A_n$.

$$\frac{\Gamma, a : A, b : B \vdash \Delta}{\Gamma, a(A^t + 1) + b(B^t + 1) : A \wedge B \vdash \Delta}(\wedge \vdash)$$

$$\frac{\Gamma \vdash \Delta, a : A}{\Gamma, aA^t : B \vdash \Delta, a : A \wedge B}(\vdash \wedge_1) \qquad \frac{\Gamma \vdash \Delta, a : A}{\Gamma, aA^t : B \vdash \Delta, a : B \wedge A}(\vdash \wedge_2)$$

$$\frac{\Gamma \vdash \Delta, a : A, b : B}{\Gamma \vdash \Delta, aA^t + bB^t : A \vee B}(\vdash \vee)$$

$$\frac{\Gamma, a : A \vdash \Delta}{\Gamma, a : A \vee B \vdash \Delta, a(A^t + 1) : B}(\vee \vdash_1) \qquad \frac{\Gamma, a : A \vdash \Delta}{\Gamma, a : B \vee A \vdash \Delta, a(A^t + 1) : B}(\vee \vdash_2)$$

$$\frac{\Gamma, a : A \vdash \Delta, b : B}{\Gamma \vdash \Delta, a(A^t + 1) + bB^t : A \rightarrow B}(\vdash \rightarrow)$$

$$\frac{\Gamma, b : B \vdash \Delta}{\Gamma, b : A \rightarrow B, b(B^t + 1) : A \vdash \Delta}(\rightarrow \vdash_1) \qquad \frac{\Gamma \vdash a : A, \Delta}{\Gamma, a : A \rightarrow B \vdash \Delta, aA^t : B}(\rightarrow \vdash_2)$$

$$\frac{\Gamma \vdash \Delta, a : A}{\Gamma, a : \neg A \vdash \Delta}(\neg \vdash) \qquad \frac{\Gamma, a : A \vdash \Delta}{\Gamma \vdash \Delta, a : \neg A}(\vdash \neg)$$

Fig. 3. Connective rules propagating multipliers from premiss to conclusion

As usual in sequent presentation, there are *connective rules* and *structural rules*, and the 1-sum invariant must be kept in all of them. Figure 3 presents the connective rules for cut-based sequent propositional inferences and the structural rules are presented in Figure 4. If labels are omitted from Figures 3 and 4, one obtains the cut-based rules of [9].

Structural rules have several peculiarities. The cut rule affects all multipliers in the sequent; in all other rules, only a restricted set of multipliers are affected. As we are dealing with multisets, there is no need to define structural rules for commutativity and associativity. We deal with multisets instead of sets to deal properly with the right and left contraction rules, in which the multipliers of contracted formulas have to be added. The *weakening* structural rule (also called *monotonicity*) is taken care of by the presence of Γ and Δ in the Axiom rule; Γ and Δ may be empty, or they may contain formulas which are irrelevant to the deduction, and are thus 0-labeled. The Axiom rule has no premiss and produces a 1-label to the relevant formulas.

$$\frac{}{0:\Gamma,1:A\vdash 1:A,0:\Delta}\,(\text{Axiom})\qquad \frac{\Gamma_1\vdash \Delta_1,a_1:A \quad a_2:A,\Gamma_2\vdash \Delta_2}{A^t+1:\Gamma_1,A^t:\Gamma_2\vdash A^t+1:\Delta_1,A^t:\Delta_2}\,(\text{Cut})$$

$$\frac{\Gamma,a_1:A,a_2:A\vdash \Delta}{\Gamma,(a_1+a_2):A\vdash \Delta}\,(\text{Contract}\vdash)\qquad \frac{\Gamma\vdash \Delta,a_1:A,a_2:A}{\Gamma\vdash \Delta,(a_1+a_2):A}\,(\vdash \text{Contract})$$

Fig. 4. Structural rules propagating multipliers

A *sequent proof tree* is a tree whose leaves are instantiations of Axiom, and whose internal nodes are sequents obtained by the application of some connective or structural rule. A sequent $\mathcal{S}$ is *provable* if there is a sequent proof tree with $\mathcal{S}$ at its root.

Example 3.3.   As an example, consider the proof, of $A\to B, C\to A\vdash C\to B$:

$$\frac{\dfrac{\dfrac{1:B\vdash 1:B}{1:A\to B,b+1:A\vdash 1:B}\,(\to\vdash)}{1:A\to B,b+1:C\to A,(b+1)(a+1):C\vdash 1:B}\,(\to\vdash)}{1:A\to B,b+1:C\to A\vdash (b+1)(a+1)(c+1)+1:C\to B}\,(\vdash\to)$$

The entailment multipliers are computed simultaneously with the deduction.
□

It is worth noting that at each deduction step in Example 3.3 the 1-sum holds. This is called *1-sum-invariant propagation*.

Lemma 3.4 (1-sum-invariant propagation). *For every sequent rule in Figures 3 and 4, if the 1-sum holds for the premises it also holds for the conclusion.*

Proof. We first note that the (Axiom) rule has no premiss. In its conclusion we have $1\cdot(B^t)+1\cdot B=1$, so (Axiom) keeps the 1-sum.

We show propagation of one connective and one structural rule. Consider rule $(\vdash \wedge_1)$, and let C correspond to the sum of members of Γ and D to that of Δ. Assuming the 1-sum holds for the rules antecedent, we have:

$$C+D+aA^t=1. \tag{13}$$

But the we have that

$$aA^t(B^t+1)+aA^tB^t=aA^t, \tag{14}$$

such that, by substituting (14) into (13) we obtain

$$C + D + aA^t(B^t + 1) + aA^t B^t = 1 \qquad (15)$$

which corresponds to the conclusion of $(\vdash \wedge_1)$.

Now consider the cut rule. The left and right sequents in the premiss correspond to, respectively,

$$C_1 + D_1 + a_1 A^t = 1 \qquad [\times(A^t + 1)] \qquad (16)$$
$$C_2 + D_2 + a_2(A^t + 1) = 1 \qquad [\times A^t] \qquad (17)$$

such that, by multiplying (16) by $(A^t + 1)$ and (17) by A^t and adding both equations we obtain:

$$(A^t + 1)C_1 + (A^t + 1)D_1 + A^t C_2 + A^t D_2 = (A^t + 1) + A^t = 1 \qquad (18)$$

which corresponds to the conclusion of the cut rule, as desired. The other cases are analogous and are omitted. □

Theorem 3.5. *The labeled sequent rules in Figures 3 and 4 correctly compute a set of entailment multipliers.*

Proof. By induction on the length of the proof. The basic case is one application of (Axiom). The induction cases are dealt by Lemma 3.4. □

The labeled rules of Figures 3 and 4 are not the only possible ones, and many other 1-sum-invariant ways to propagate entailment multipliers are possible.

4 Multipliers for Normal Modal Logics

As modal logics are extensions of classical propositional logic, the result on entailment multipliers extends quite naturally to those logics. We consider here only normal modal logics, that can be dealt with in algebraic terms by *boolean algebras with operators* [3], which in our case becomes a boolean ring with operators.

On the logic side, we extend the propositional language by considering the unary connective $\Box$, and we extend the formula formation rules such that if A is a modal formula $\Box A$ is also a modal formula, which is read "A is necessary". The connective $\Diamond$ is considered a derived connective, $\Diamond A =_{\text{def}} \neg\Box\neg A$, which is read as "$A$ is possible". A axiomatisation of normal modal logics is given by a set of axioms and a set of inference rules. The minimal modal logic **K** is axiomatised by the following axioms:

A0 All propositional classical tautologies
K $\Box(p \to q) \to (\Box p \to \Box q)$

and the inference rules of Modus Ponens (from $\vdash A \to B$ and $\vdash A$ infer $\vdash B$) and of Necessitation (from $\vdash A$ infer $\vdash \Box A$). A *deduction* of a formula A is a sequence of formulas $A_1, \ldots, A_n = A$ such that each A_i is an instance of an axiom or is obtained from previous formulas in the sequence by an application of an inference rule. If A is deducible, we represent it by $\vdash A$ and call it a *modal theorem*. Different modal logics are generated by adding extra axioms, and we represent $\vdash_M A$ to represent theoremhood in modal logic M.

Furthermore, if Γ is a finite set of modal formulas, we represent $\Gamma \vdash_M A$ is $\vdash_M \bigwedge \Gamma \to A$. If Γ is an infinite set of modal formulas, we write $\Gamma \vdash_M A$ if there is a finite set $\Gamma_0 \subset \Gamma$ such that $\Gamma_0 \vdash_M A$.

On the semantic side, we employ the usual Kripke-structures for normal modal logics, which consists of a pair $\langle W, R \rangle$, where W is a set, usually called a set of *possible worlds* and $R \subseteq W \times W$ is a binary relation on W, usually called an *accessibility relation* [7]. A Kripke model for modal logics is a triple $\mathcal{M} = \langle W, R, g \rangle$, where $\langle W, R \rangle$ is a Kripke-structure and $g : \mathcal{P} \to 2^W$ is a modal valuation that associates each (atomic) propositional symbol to a set of possible worlds, namely the worlds in which the symbol is true. If $w \in W$ is a possible world, $\mathcal{M}$ is a Kripke-model and A is a modal formula, we write $\mathcal{M}, w \models A$ if A is true at work w in model $\mathcal{M}$, which is inductively defined as:

- $\mathcal{M}, w \models p$ iff p is atomic and $w \in g(p)$;
- $\mathcal{M}, w \models \neg A$ iff $\mathcal{M}, w \not\models A$;
- $\mathcal{M}, w \models A \wedge B$ iff $\mathcal{M}, w \models A$ and $\mathcal{M}, w \models B$;
- $\mathcal{M}, w \models \Box A$ iff for every w' accessible from w (that is, Rww' holds) then $\mathcal{M}, w' \models A$.

The formula A is modally *valid*, $\models A$ if $\mathcal{M}, w \models A$ for every world $w \in W$ and for every model $\mathcal{M}$. Different normal modal logics are created by imposing restrictions on the accessibility relation R. For modal logic M, we write the *(local) modal entailment expression* $A_1, \ldots, A_n \models_M B_1, \ldots, B_m$ if for every model $\mathcal{M} = \langle W, R, g \rangle$ in the class of models of M, and for every $w \in W$, if $\mathcal{M}, w \models A_i$ for all $1 \leq i \leq n$, then for some B_j, $1 \leq j \leq m$, $\mathcal{M}, w \models B_j$.

On the algebraic side, we consider a *boolean ring with operator* $\blacksquare$, $\mathfrak{B} = \langle \mathcal{B}, \cdot, +, 1, \blacksquare \rangle$. In *normal* modal logics, the operator $\blacksquare$ respects the following restrictions, for every $a, b \in \mathcal{B}$:

(op$_1$) $\blacksquare 1 = 1$;
(op$_2$) $\blacksquare(a \cdot b) = (\blacksquare a) \cdot (\blacksquare b)$.

A modal term a is algebraically *valid* if we can show that $a = 1$. For other normal modal logics, extra equations involving $\blacksquare$ have to be added.

In the translation from formulas to terms and from terms to formulas, we have to add the following:

$$(\Box A)^t = \blacksquare A^t \qquad (\blacksquare a)^\varphi = \Box a^\varphi$$

As modal logics are extensions of classical propositional logics and modal validity is taken care of by $\blacksquare$-equations, it is expected that entailment multipliers generalise to modal logics. We first see a few examples relating to modal logic **K**.

Example 4.1. Consider the statement

$$\Box(p \rightarrow q), \Box p \vdash_{\mathbf{K}} \Box q$$

for which the modal polynomial is

$$x_1 \cdot (\blacksquare(p(q+1)+1)+1) + x_2 \cdot (\blacksquare p + 1) + y \cdot (\blacksquare q)$$

and we see that this polynomial has 1-roots for $x_1 = y = \blacksquare p$ and $x_2 = 1$:

$$\blacksquare p \cdot (\blacksquare(pq + p + 1) + 1) + (\blacksquare p + 1) + \blacksquare p \cdot \blacksquare q$$
$$= \blacksquare p \cdot \blacksquare(pq + p + 1) + \cancel{\blacksquare p} + \cancel{\blacksquare p} + 1 + \blacksquare(pq)$$
$$= \blacksquare(pq + \cancel{p} + \cancel{p}) + 1 + \blacksquare(pq)$$
$$= \cancel{\blacksquare(pq)} + 1 + \cancel{\blacksquare(pq)}$$
$$= 1$$

Normality conditions are applied in the first and second steps; simplifications are indicated. □

Now consider modal logic **T**, which extends modal with an axiom:

(T) $\Box p \rightarrow p$

On the algebraic side, we have to add an equality that corresponds to the validity of that axiom, namely

$$(\Box p \rightarrow p)^t = 1$$
$$\Leftrightarrow p \cdot \blacksquare p + \blacksquare p + 1 = 1$$
$$\Leftrightarrow p \cdot \blacksquare p = \blacksquare p$$

On the semantic side this logic **T** forces the accessibility relation to be reflexive, namely

$$\forall w(Rww)$$

Example 4.2. We take as an example the following statement

$$\Box(p \rightarrow q), p \vdash_{\mathbf{T}} q$$

for which the modal polynomial is

$$x_1 \cdot (\blacksquare(p(q+1)+1)+1) + x_2 \cdot (p+1) + y \cdot q$$

and we see that this polynomial has 1-roots for $x_1 = p(q+1)$, $x_2 = 1$ and $y = p$:

$$p(q+1) \cdot \underbrace{\blacksquare(p(q+1)+1)+1)}_{} + (p+1) + p \cdot q$$

$$= \underline{p(q+1) \cdot (p(q+1)+1)} \cdot \blacksquare(p(q+1)+1) + p(q+1) + p + 1 + pq$$
$$= \cancel{pq} + \cancel{p} + \cancel{p} + 1 + \cancel{pq}$$
$$= 1$$

where the first step uses the property $\blacksquare x = x \blacksquare x$, and then we use $x \cdot (x+1) = 0$ to eliminate the only subterm containing a $\blacksquare$. □

We proceed by considering modal logic **S4**, which extends modal logic **T** with the axiom:

(4) $\Box p \to \Box\Box p$

Again, on the algebraic side, besides the algebraic equation for logic **T**, we have to add an equality that corresponds to the validity of that axiom, namely

$$(\Box p \to \Box\Box p)^t = 1$$
$$\Leftrightarrow \blacksquare\blacksquare p \cdot \blacksquare p + \blacksquare p + 1 = 1$$
$$\Leftrightarrow \blacksquare\blacksquare p \cdot \blacksquare p = \blacksquare p$$

On the semantic side the logic **S4** forces the accessibility relation to be reflexive and transitive, namely

$$\forall w(Rww) \wedge \forall w \forall w' \forall w''(Rww' \wedge Rw'w'' \to Rww'')$$

Example 4.3. We take as a final **S4**-example the following statement

$$\Box(p \to q), \Box\Box p \vdash_{\mathbf{S4}} \Box\Box q$$

for which the modal polynomial is

$$x_1 \cdot (\blacksquare(p(q+1)+1)+1) + x_2 \cdot (\blacksquare\blacksquare p + 1) + y \cdot \blacksquare\blacksquare q$$

and we see that this polynomial has 1-roots for $x_1 = \blacksquare\blacksquare p$, $x_2 = 1$ and $y = \blacksquare\blacksquare p$:

$$\blacksquare\blacksquare p \cdot (\blacksquare(pq+p+1)+1) + (\blacksquare\blacksquare p + 1) + \blacksquare\blacksquare p \cdot \blacksquare\blacksquare q$$
$$= \blacksquare\blacksquare p \cdot \blacksquare(pq+p+1) + \blacksquare\blacksquare p + \blacksquare\blacksquare p + 1 + \blacksquare\blacksquare p \cdot \blacksquare\blacksquare q$$
$$= \blacksquare(\blacksquare p \cdot (pq+p+1)) + 1 + \blacksquare\blacksquare p \cdot \blacksquare\blacksquare q$$
$$= \blacksquare(qp\blacksquare p + p\blacksquare p + \blacksquare p) + 1 + \blacksquare\blacksquare p \cdot \blacksquare\blacksquare q$$
$$= \blacksquare(q\blacksquare p + \blacksquare p + \blacksquare p) + 1 + \blacksquare\blacksquare p \cdot \blacksquare\blacksquare q$$
$$= \blacksquare q \cdot \blacksquare\blacksquare p + 1 + \blacksquare\blacksquare p \cdot \blacksquare\blacksquare q$$
$$= \blacksquare q \cdot \blacksquare\blacksquare q \cdot \blacksquare\blacksquare p + 1 + \blacksquare\blacksquare p \cdot \blacksquare\blacksquare q \cdot \blacksquare q$$
$$= 1$$

where the first step uses the distribution property; the second step uses the normality condition to join $\blacksquare\blacksquare p$ and $\blacksquare(pq+p+1)$; the third step applies distribution laws; the forth step applies $\blacksquare x = x\blacksquare x$; after some further simplification, the sixth step applies both $\blacksquare x\blacksquare\blacksquare x = \blacksquare x$ and $\blacksquare x = x\blacksquare x$, and some final simplification leads to the desired equality to the unit. $\Box$

Theorem 4.4. *Let M be a normal modal logic defined with a finite set of axioms $A_1, \ldots, A_n$. On the algebraic side, suppose the equalities $A_i^t = 1$ hold, $1 \leq i \leq n$. Then a modal statement $\Gamma \vdash_M A$ is derivable iff its associated modal polynomial has 1-roots.*

Proof (Sketch). $\Gamma \vdash_{\mathbf{M}} A$ is provable iff $\vdash_{\mathbf{M}} \bigwedge \Gamma \to A$ is deducible from the axioms. In this deduction, the algebraic translation of every formula must be equal to 1. When the last step is reached, we have that $(\bigwedge \Gamma \to A)^t = 1$, such that by classical manipulations we obtain the multipliers for $\Gamma \vdash_{\mathbf{M}} A$.

On the other hand, if there are multipliers for $\Gamma \vdash_{\mathbf{M}} A$, by classical manipulations we obtain a multiplier a for $\vdash_{\mathbf{M}} \bigwedge \Gamma \to A$. Using the same modal algebraic equalities that were used to show that the multipliers are 1-roots to the statement, we show that $a = 1$. □

5 Conclusion

Entailment multipliers are a characterisation of validity for propositional and modal classical logics. Furthermore, entailment multipliers can be seen as a proof invariants for several inference systems, which allows for the computation of multipliers in parallel with a proof-construction.

Future work on the interactions of algebraic and proof-theoretical methods aims at investigating the use of entailment multipliers to the computation of non-analytic cuts that allow for the computation of short proofs.

We also plan to investigate entailment multipliers for first-order logic, many-valued logics and other non-classical logics.

References

[1] Beame, P., Cook, S., Edmonds, J., Impagliazzo, R., Pitassi, T.: The relative complexity of NP search problems. In: Proceedings of the 27th ACM Symposium on Theory of Computing, pp. 303–314 (1995)

[2] Beame, P., Impagliazzo, R., Kraj'icek, J., Pitassi, T., Pudl'ak, P.: Lower bounds on hilbert's nullstellensatz and propositional proofs. In: Proceedings of the London Mathematical Society, vol. 73, pp. 1–26 (1996)

[3] Blackburn, P., de Rijke, M., de Venema, Y.: Modal Logic. Cambridge Tracts in Theoretical Computer Science, vol. 53. Cambridge University Press, Cambridge (2001)

[4] Buss, S., Impagliazzo, R., Krajicek, J., Pudlak, P., Razborov, A.A., Sgall, J.: Proof complexity in algebraic systems and bounded depth frege systems with modular counting. Computational Complexity 6(3), 256–298 (1997)

[5] Buss, S., Pitassi, T.: Good degree bounds on Nullstellensatz refutations of the induction principle. In: Proceedings from the 11th IEEE Conference on Computational Complexity, pp. 233–242 (1996)

[6] Carnielli, W.: Polynomial ring calculus for many-valued logics. In: Proceedings of 35th International Symposium on Multiple-Valued Logic, Calgary, Canad, pp. 20–25. IEEE Computer Society, Los Alamitos (2005)

[7] Chellas, B.F.: Modal Logic — an Introduction. Cambridge University Press, Cambridge (1980)

[8] D'Agostino, M., Mondadorip, M.: The taming of the cut. Classical refutations with analytic cut. Journal of Logic and Computation 4, 285–319 (1994)

[9] Finger, M., Gabbay, D.: Cut and pay. Journal of Logic, Language and Information 15(3), 195–218 (2006)

[10] Gabbay, D.: Labelled Deductive Systems, vol. 1. Oxford University Press, Oxford (1996)

[11] Garey, M.R., Johnson, D.S.: Computers and Intractability: A Guide to the Theory of NP-Completeness. Freeman, New York (1979)

[12] Lovász, L.: Bounding the independence number of a graph. Annals of Discrete Mathematics 16, 213–223 (1982)

[13] Pitassi, T.: Algebraic propositional proof systems. In: Immerman, N., Kolaitis, P. (eds.) Descriptive Complexity and Finite Models. DIMACS Series in Discrete Mathematics and Theoretical Computer Science, vol. 31, pp. 214–244. DIMACS (1996)

A CTL-Based Logic for Program Abstractions

Martin Lange[1] and Markus Latte[2]

[1] Dept. of Elect. Eng. and Computer Science, University of Kassel, Germany
[2] Dept. of Computer Science, Ludwig-Maximilians-University Munich, Germany

Abstract. We define an action-based extension of the branching-time temporal logic CTL which allows path quantifiers to be restricted by formal languages. The main purpose of this logic is its use in abstract interpretation. A reduction from a concrete system to an abstract one may contain spurious traces which can render the verification of the abstract system useless with respect to the concrete one. We pick up the suggestion to verify a modified property on the abstract system instead of the one that the concrete system is supposed to have. The logic introduced here enables a systematic modification of such properties. We present some ways of such a modification which aim at implicitly excluding spurious traces in the verification of abstracted systems.

1 Introduction

Model checking is one of the most successful automatic verification techniques for all kinds of programs: hardware, protocols, reactive software, etc. In model checking, the program to be verified is given as a transition systems representing the operational semantics of a program with states and transitions between the states, and the property specifying correctness of the program is formalised in a temporal logic.

Various temporal logics have been introduced for model checking. The most prominent ones are the linear-time temporal logic LTL [14] and the branching-time temporal logic CTL [7]. These are not only incomparable in terms of their expressive power but also — and partly thus — incomparable in terms of their pragmatics. CTL model checking is easier than LTL model checking (P- vs. PSPACE-complete [5,15]) whereas LTL satisfiability checking is easier than CTL satisfiability checking (PSPACE- vs. EXPTIME-complete [15,7]).

These results, in particular the model checking complexities, hold w.r.t. finite models. However, many programs, in particular software, occupy an infinite state space. Clearly, model checking infinite-state programs is undecidable in general but it remains decidable for certain classes of infinite-state programs, e.g. pushdown processes, and weak temporal logics like CTL and LTL. It is still just PSPACE-complete for LTL but EXPTIME-complete for CTL [3,19].

This does not immediately enable automatic program verification for infinite-state programs because of several reasons. Programs may not fall into these classes, in particular if the cause for infinity is the use of variables over unbounded domains etc., or the relatively high worst-case complexities may not

A. Dawar and R. de Queiroz (Eds.): WoLLIC 2010, LNAI 6188, pp. 19–33, 2010.

allow efficient implementations in practice. In such cases, it may be necessary to employ a technique that generally reduces the complexity of the underlying verification problem at the expense of total correctness: *abstraction* [6]. It is also applicable in cases of finite systems where state-space explosion renders the verification problem inefficient in practice.

Abstraction is the process of transforming a transition system $\mathcal{T}$ into a (typically) smaller transition system $\mathcal{T}^{\mathsf{abs}}$ which contains at least some of the information that is present in $\mathcal{T}$. Verification of the smaller system is then easier or even possible. However, the abstraction must be chosen such that the verification of the abstract system allows to make assertions about the underlying property and the original system.

Consider, for instance, one of the most well-known abstraction schemes, called $\exists\exists$-abstraction. There, states of the abstract transition system $\mathcal{T}^{\mathsf{abs}}$ result from collapsing sets of states of the original transition system $\mathcal{T}$, and there is a transition between collapsed states S and T iff there are $s \in S$ and $t \in T$ with a transition from s to t in the original system. It is not hard to see that the runs or paths of $\mathcal{T}^{\mathsf{abs}}$ form a superset of the paths of $\mathcal{T}$. Every path in $\mathcal{T}$ can be found in $\mathcal{T}^{\mathsf{abs}}$ but the latter also contains *spurious traces* which are paths that only arise as artefacts of the abstraction but do not exist in the original system $\mathcal{T}$. Now consider a class of simple properties φ to be checked on $\mathcal{T}$, namely temporal properties which quantify over paths in a universal manner only. It is the case that $\mathcal{T}^{\mathsf{abs}} \models \varphi$ implies $\mathcal{T} \models \varphi$ for such φ but not vice-versa because of the relationship between paths in $\mathcal{T}^{\mathsf{abs}}$ and in $\mathcal{T}$. Thus, if the abstracted system is correct w.r.t. φ then so is the original one. If the abstracted system is faulty then nothing is known about the original one because the reason for the error may be a spurious trace. Still, abstraction can thus enable the verification of systems which cannot be model checked under normal circumstances at the expense of completeness for instance.

It turns out that this is all very well in theory but in practice it happens very often that the abstracted system fails the desired property, i.e. spurious traces interfere with the verification task too much. Now note that there is no reason for considering the *original property* on the abstracted system. This observation has led to suggestions regarding the *weakening* of universally path quantified properties, for instance by considering *fair* traces in the abstract system only [2]. This does work in certain cases. However, there is no general relationship between the abstraction scheme and fairness which would guarantee it to work in many cases. A more precise weakening would relativise the path quantification in the property to be checked on the abstract system to paths occurring in the original system. Note that, if this was possible, then it would not only be restricted to $\exists\exists$-abstractions and universally path quantified properties. The same could be done with existentially path quantified properties and all kinds of abstractions.

For this purpose, we suggest a logic which is based on the commonly used branching-time temporal logic CTL and which allows relativised path quantifiers. While there are logics around with very high expressive power, even temporal ones, these typically extend the modal μ-calculus by incorporating all kinds of expressive operators. Such logics are more or less useless in the setting of abstraction. We propose to base such a logic on a commonly used logic $\mathcal{L}$ such that the problem of determining $\mathcal{T} \models \varphi$ for some $\varphi \in \mathcal{L}$ can be transformed into the problem of determining $\mathcal{T}^{\mathsf{abs}} \models \varphi^{\mathsf{abs}}$ for an abstracted system $\mathcal{T}^{\mathsf{abs}}$ and a property φ^{abs} which incorporates information that gets lost between $\mathcal{T}$ and $\mathcal{T}^{\mathsf{abs}}$ into φ. Maybe this could even be automised such that to the outside, only $\mathcal{T}$ and φ would be visible which underpins the need for φ to belong to a commonly used specificaton logic and therefore φ^{abs} to be something based upon that.

In Sect. 2 we introduce *Path Relativised Computation Tree Logic* (CTL^{rel}). It is a simple branching-time temporal logic which is interpreted – like action-based CTL [13] – over transition systems with labeled edges. It extends CTL by allowing path quantifiers to be restricted. The restriction is realised by languages of ω-words aiming at maximal flexibility for the abstraction process. Hence, CTL^{rel} is in fact a family of branching-time temporal logics parametrised by a class of formal languages of ω-words. Sect. 3 then exemplifies the possible use of this logic in the framework of abstraction.

CTL^{rel} is closely related to *Propositional Dynamic Logic with the Delta operator* (ΔPDL) [17,12]. This relationship is, for instance, exploited in Sect. 4 where we first analyse the complexity of model checking and satisfiability problems depending on the class of languages used for quantifier relativisation. From the discussion above it should be clear that model checking is an important problem for such a logic in such a framework. Satisfiability checking is, too. Note that a satisfiable formula CTL formula could easily become unsatisfiable when path quantifiers are arbitrarily relativised. A decidable logic then allows such formulas to be automatically checked before they are being used in verification.

In Sect. 5 we consider the use of CTL^{rel} in the framework of abstract interpretation. We suggest a generic use of the path quantifier relativisation in CTL^{rel} formulas whcih forms the basis for two heuristics that aim at implicitly excluding spurious traces in the verification of abstracted systems. Finally, Sect. 6 contains remarks about future work.

2   CTL with Path Relativisation

Models of CTL with path relativisation are transition systems which — as opposed to ordinary CTL models and like models of action-based CTL — also have labeled edges and need not be total. Let Σ be a finite alphabet and $\mathcal{P}$ be a countably infinite set of atomic propositions. A *transition system* is a tuple $\mathcal{T} = (\mathcal{S}, \rightarrow, \lambda)$ where $\mathcal{S}$ is a set of *states*, $\rightarrow \subseteq \mathcal{S} \times \Sigma \times \mathcal{S}$ is the *transition relation*, and $\lambda : \mathcal{S} \rightarrow 2^{\mathcal{P}}$ labels each state with a finite set of propositions that are true in this state. We write $s \xrightarrow{a} t$ instead of $(s, a, t) \in \rightarrow$.

Let $\mathcal{T} = (\mathcal{S}, \rightarrow, \lambda)$ be a transition system. An $\alpha : \mathcal{S} \rightarrow \mathcal{S}$ is an *abstraction function for* $\mathcal{T}$ if it satisfies the following consistency condition for all $s, t \in \mathcal{S}$: if $\alpha(s) = \alpha(t)$ then $\lambda(s) = \lambda(t)$. The function introduces an equivalence relation $\sim_\alpha$ on $\mathcal{S}$ where $s \sim_\alpha s'$ iff $\alpha(s) = \alpha(s')$. Equivalence classes and the quotient set are written as $[\_]_\alpha$ and $\mathcal{S}/\alpha$, respectively. An equivalence class is called an *abstract state.* We may omit the index α whenever α is clear from the context. The *abstraction of* $\mathcal{T}$ *w.r.t.* α is the transition system $\mathcal{T}^\alpha = (\mathcal{S}/\alpha, \to_\alpha, \lambda_\alpha)$ such that for all $a \in \Sigma$:

- $t \xrightarrow{a}_\alpha t'$ iff there are $s \in t$ and $s' \in t'$ such that $s \xrightarrow{a} s'$, and
- $\lambda_\alpha([t]_\alpha) = \lambda(t)$.

Note that the consistency condition above ensures well-definedness of the labeling function λ_α.

In order to simplify technical details, we assume that Σ always contains a special character d and that each transition system has a distinct state end with $s \xrightarrow{d}$ end for every s including end itself. Furthermore, end has no other incoming or outgoing transitions than these. This means that transition systems are total in the sense that in any state at least a d-action is possible. However, afterwards nothing else is possible any more. Thus, taking a d-transition somehow indicates being in a deadlock state.

A *path* in $\mathcal{T}$ is an infinite sequence $\pi = s_0, a_0, s_1, a_1, \dots$, alternating between states and edge labels, s.t. $s_i \xrightarrow{a_i} s_{i+1}$ for all $i \geq 1$. Note that the assumption above ensures that no maximal paths other than infinite ones exist. We write $\Pi_\mathcal{T}(s)$ for the set of all paths through $\mathcal{T}$ that start in s. An *initial path* is a prefix of a path which ends at a state.

A path $\pi = s_0, a_0, s_1, a_1, \dots$ determines in a unique way the ω-word $a_0 a_1 a_2 \dots$ over Σ. Abusing notation we will identify a path with its determined word of edge labels and sometimes simply write $\pi \in L$ for a path π and a language L. As usual, Σ^ω denotes the set of all infinite words over Σ.

Formulas of CTL *with path relativisation*, CTL^{rel}, are built like CTL formulas with the difference that path quantifiers are syntactically indexed by languages of ω-words. We present the logic in positive normal form which simplifies statements about fragments later on.

$$\varphi ::= q \mid \neg q \mid \varphi \vee \varphi \mid \varphi \wedge \varphi \mid \text{EX}_a\varphi \mid \text{AX}_a\varphi \mid \text{E}_L(\varphi\text{U}\varphi) \mid \text{E}_L(\varphi\text{R}\varphi) \mid$$
$$\text{A}_L(\varphi\text{U}\varphi) \mid \text{A}_L(\varphi\text{R}\varphi)$$

where $q \in \mathcal{P}$, $a \in \Sigma$, and $L \subseteq \Sigma^\omega$.

A formula is *purely existential* if does not contain any subformula of the form $\text{AX}_a\psi$, $\text{A}_L(\psi_1\text{U}\psi_2)$ or $\text{A}_L(\psi_1\text{R}\psi_2)$. Similarly, it is *purely universal* if it does not contain any subformula of the form $\text{EX}_a\psi$, $\text{E}_L(\psi_1\text{U}\psi_2)$ or $\text{E}_L(\psi_1\text{R}\psi_2)$.

Clearly, languages L in the index of a path quantifier are infinite sets of infinite words in general, and the question of syntactic representation of such languages arises. Here we consider automata as such representations, in particular *nondeterministic Büchi automata* (NBA) for ω-regular languages [4], *nondeterministic Büchi visibly-pushdown automata* (NBVPA) [1] for ω-visibly-pushdown languages, and *nondeterministic Büchi pushdown automata* (NBPDA) [16] for ω-context-free languages. By CTL$^{\text{rel}}[\omega\text{REG}]$, CTL$^{\text{rel}}[\omega\text{VPL}]$ and CTL$^{\text{rel}}[\omega\text{CFL}]$ we denote the sets of formulas in which annotated languages are regular, visibly pushdown or context-free, respectively.

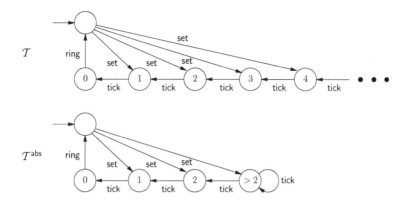

Fig. 1. Transition system of an alarm clock and an abstraction

We allow more propositional and temporal operators as abbreviations: $\mathtt{tt} := q \vee \neg q$ and $\mathtt{ff} := q \wedge \neg q$ for some $q \in \mathcal{P}$, as well as $Q_L \mathrm{F} \varphi := Q_L(\mathtt{tt} \mathrm{U} \varphi)$, $Q_L \mathrm{G} \varphi := Q_L(\mathtt{ff} \mathrm{R} \varphi)$, and $Q(\varphi \circ \psi) := Q_{\Sigma^\omega}(\varphi \circ \psi)$ for $Q \in \{\mathrm{E}, \mathrm{A}\}$ and $\circ \in \{\mathrm{U}, \mathrm{R}\}$.

The semantics of $\mathrm{CTL}^{\mathrm{rel}}$ is given as follows. Let $\mathcal{T} = (\mathcal{S}, \rightarrow, \lambda)$ be a transition system as above. In particular, all paths in it are infinite. For any $s \in \mathcal{S}$ we have:

$$
\begin{aligned}
\mathcal{T}, s \models q \quad &\text{iff} \quad q \in \lambda(s) \\
\mathcal{T}, s \models \neg q \quad &\text{iff} \quad q \notin \lambda(s) \\
\mathcal{T}, s \models \varphi \vee \psi \quad &\text{iff} \quad \mathcal{T}, s \models \varphi \text{ or } \mathcal{T}, s \models \psi \\
\mathcal{T}, s \models \varphi \wedge \psi \quad &\text{iff} \quad \mathcal{T}, s \models \varphi \text{ and } \mathcal{T}, s \models \psi \\
\mathcal{T}, s \models \mathrm{EX}_a \varphi \quad &\text{iff} \quad \text{there is } t \in \mathcal{S} \text{ s.t. } s \xrightarrow{a} t \text{ and } \mathcal{T}, t \models \varphi \\
\mathcal{T}, s \models \mathrm{AX}_a \varphi \quad &\text{iff} \quad \text{for all } t \in \mathcal{S} : \text{ if } s \xrightarrow{a} t \text{ then } \mathcal{T}, t \models \varphi \\
\mathcal{T}, s \models \mathrm{E}_L(\varphi \mathrm{U} \psi) \quad &\text{iff} \quad \exists \pi = s_0, a_0, s_1, a_1, \ldots \in \Pi_{\mathcal{T}}(s) \text{ s.t. } a_0 a_1 a_2 \ldots \in L \text{ and} \\
&\qquad \exists i \in \mathbb{N} \text{ with } \mathcal{T}, s_i \models \psi \text{ and } \forall j < i : \mathcal{T}, s_j \models \varphi \\
\mathcal{T}, s \models \mathrm{E}_L(\varphi \mathrm{R} \psi) \quad &\text{iff} \quad \exists \pi = s_0, a_0, s_1, a_1, \ldots \in \Pi_{\mathcal{T}}(s) \text{ s.t. } a_0 a_1 a_2 \ldots \in L \text{ and} \\
&\qquad \forall i \in \mathbb{N} : \mathcal{T}, s_i \models \psi \text{ or } \exists j < i \text{ s.t. } \mathcal{T}, s_j \models \varphi \\
\mathcal{T}, s \models \mathrm{A}_L(\varphi \mathrm{U} \psi) \quad &\text{iff} \quad \forall \pi = s_0, a_0, s_1, a_1, \ldots \in \Pi_{\mathcal{T}}(s) : \text{ if } a_0 a_1 a_2 \ldots \in L \text{ then} \\
&\qquad \exists i \in \mathbb{N} \text{ with } \mathcal{T}, s_i \models \psi \text{ and } \forall j < i : \mathcal{T}, s_j \models \varphi \\
\mathcal{T}, s \models \mathrm{A}_L(\varphi \mathrm{R} \psi) \quad &\text{iff} \quad \forall \pi = s_0, a_0, s_1, a_1, \ldots \in \Pi_{\mathcal{T}}(s) \text{ if } a_0 a_1 a_2 \ldots \in L \text{ then} \\
&\qquad \forall i \in \mathbb{N} : \mathcal{T}, s_i \models \psi \text{ or } \exists j < i \text{ s.t. } \mathcal{T}, s_j \models \varphi
\end{aligned}
$$

3   Examples

As a first example, consider an alarm clock $\mathcal{T}$ which can be set to count down an arbitrary number of steps and then ring. Its transition system is depicted in the top of Fig. 1. Clearly, an alarm clock should ring eventually once it is set to a certain time, therefore, the alarm clock should not have a state from which an infinite tick-path exists. This property is specifiable in action-based CTL as $\mathsf{AG}\neg\mathsf{EG}_{\mathsf{tick}}\,\mathsf{tt}$.

Now consider an abstraction which identifies all counter values that are greater than 2. This introduces a tick-loop in the state representing all such values. The abstracted system $\mathcal{T}^{\mathsf{abs}}$ is depicted at the bottom of Fig. 1.

It should be clear that $\mathcal{T} \models \mathsf{AG}\neg\mathsf{EG}_{\mathsf{tick}}\,\mathsf{tt}$ since every sequence of tick-actions must eventually lead to the state with counter value 0 and that has no outgoing tick-action. On the other hand, $\mathcal{T}^{\mathsf{abs}} \not\models \mathsf{AG}\neg\mathsf{EG}_{\mathsf{tick}}\,\mathsf{tt}$ since state "> 2" is reachable and has an infinite tick-trace. Note that this trace is spurious. It is possible to mend this fault though by introducing fairness and excluding this spurious trace. Take, for instance the fairness predicate $\Phi := \mathsf{GF}\,\mathsf{tick} \Rightarrow \mathsf{GF}\,\mathsf{ring}$, i.e. if infinitely many ticks are being done then also infinitely many rings are being done. Now it is the case that $\mathcal{T}^{\mathsf{abs}} \models_{fair} \mathsf{AG}\neg\mathsf{EG}_{\mathsf{tick}}\,\mathsf{tt}$ under this fairness predicate, meaning that the CTL path quantifiers in this formula now only range over fair paths, i.e. those that satisfy the fairness predicate Φ. Note that the spurious trace does not, hence, the property holds under this assumption.

While this does work in this particular case, the introduction of a fairness predicate seems rather arbitrary as well as its choice. Furthermore, the chosen fairness predicate almost contradicts the correctness property at hand. Hence, this is almost like only considering that part of the abstracted system which does satisfy the correctness property and then showing that it does indeed. In other words, finding the right fairness predicate may be as hard as showing correctness of the original system.

$\mathsf{CTL}^{\mathsf{rel}}$ offers a more fine-tuned and more systematic way of amending the correctness properties. We will consider another example in which the introduction of fairness is not able to exclude spurious traces that easily. Consider a system containing a buffer into which items can be placed and from which items can be taken. It works such that once something is taken out, it can only be emptied and nothing more can be put into it. The transition system $\mathcal{T}$ is depicted on top in Fig. 2. An abstraction $\mathcal{T}^{\mathsf{abs}}$ which collapses all states containing more than 2 buffer items is depicted below that.

Now consider the correctness property stating that at no point is it possible to execute an out-action followed by an in-action. In action-based CTL it can be written as $\mathsf{AG}\neg\mathsf{EX}_{\mathsf{out}}\mathsf{EX}_{\mathsf{in}}\,\mathsf{tt}$. Clearly, it is satisfied by the original system $\mathcal{T}$ and not satisfied by the abstraction $\mathcal{T}^{\mathsf{abs}}$ because of the spurious trace through the self-loop in the state representing all large buffer contents. The important observation about this is, though, that no fairness predicate can exclude all the spurious traces which cause the violation of the correctness property. This is simply because fairness is concerned with the infinite occurrence of states / actions, etc. or the absence thereof. The characteristics of the spurious traces in this case, however, is the single occurrence of an in-action after a single out-action. It is therefore sensible to restrict the path quantification to traces of the form $\mathsf{in}^{\omega} \cup \mathsf{in}^{*}\mathsf{out}^{*}\mathsf{d}^{\omega}$ where action d indicates, as introduced above, a transition into an imaginary deadlock state.

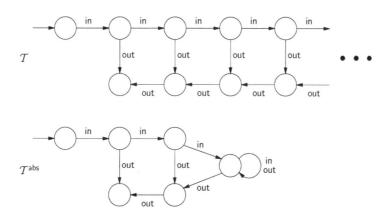

Fig. 2. Transition system of a buffer system and an abstraction

The issue about the right choice of path relativisation still persists, though. As in the first example, the trace predicate $in^\omega \cup in^* out^* d^\omega$ is somehow found miraculously. However, CTL^{rel} allows for a more automatic approach. Note that $\mathcal{T}$ is indeed a visibly pushdown system with push-action in and pop-action out. The language of its traces is a visibly pushdown language (ωVPL), characterised by the property that no out-action occurs after in in-action and on any prefix, the number of out-actions is at most as high as the number of in-actions. Let L be that language. Using CTL^{rel} it is then possible to replace the correctness property above by $AG\neg E_{L \cap \Sigma^* \text{ out in } \Sigma^\omega} Ftt$ for instance and test that on the abstracted system. Note how this restricts path quantification to traces which are present in the original system only. This is of course the essence of excluding spurious traces.

4   Results on CTL^{rel}

We are particularly interested in the complexity of the model checking and satisfiability checking problem for CTL^{rel} relative to the class of formal languages used for the quantifier restrictions. Upper bounds can easily be obtained by relating it to ΔPDL$^?$ — *Propositional Dynamic Logic with Tests and the Delta operator* — over the corresponding class. We therefore first analyse the relationship between CTL^{rel} and well-known logics like that one.

4.1   Expressivity

CTL^{rel} is situated between two cornerstones: CTL [7] and ΔPDL$^?$ [11] i.e. recursive PDL together with delta operators. The former is well-known. The latter is modal logic over a Kleene algebra of accessibility relations with tests. The delta operator then takes a specification formalisms for infinite words and turns it into an existential quantification over paths labeled with a word in this language. This is of course very similar to the mechanism used in purely existential formulas in CTL^{rel}. For a comparison to CTL we simply interpret the usual CTL models as CTL^{rel} models with a single edge label only.

Theorem 1. $\text{CTL} \leq_{\text{lin}} \text{CTL}^{\text{rel}}[\mathfrak{A}]$ *for* $\Sigma^{\omega} \in \mathfrak{A}$, *and* $\text{CTL} \lneqq_{\text{lin}} \text{CTL}^{\text{rel}}[\mathfrak{A}]$ *for* $\mathfrak{A} \supsetneq \omega\text{REG}$.

Proof. The embedding of CTL is trivial using Σ^{ω} as a quantifier restriction, and writing $\text{EX}\psi$ as $\text{EX}_a\psi$ for the unique action a the occurs in the underlying models.

For the strictness, consider $\varphi := \text{E}_L\text{Gtt}$ for a language $L \notin \text{REG}$. If this formula had an equivalent CTL-formula then there would be also a Büchi tree automaton which recognizes exactly the models of φ in a certain representation [18]. Hence, there would also be a Büchi word automaton which accepts precisely the words in L which contradicts $L \notin \omega\text{REG}$. □

We remark that CTL^{rel} does not seem to be an extension of action-based CTL. For instance, the formula $\text{EF}_a q$ in action-based CTL expresses that there is a path of the form $a^*\Sigma^{\omega}$ such that q holds in the *first state after the a^* prefix*. Clearly, CTL^{rel} does not provide a mechanism which can transform information between moments on a path and the inner structure of words in the language restricting those paths.

Theorem 2. $\text{CTL}^{\text{rel}}[\mathfrak{A}] \lneqq_{\text{lin}} \Delta\text{PDL}^?[\mathfrak{A}]$.

Proof. The embedding is proved by induction on the structure of formulas in $\text{CTL}^{\text{rel}}[\mathfrak{A}]$. We detail only the case of $\theta := \text{E}_{\mathcal{A}}\varphi\text{U}\psi$ for an automaton $\mathcal{A}$ with states Q, initial state q_0, and final states F. Let φ' and ψ' be the translations of φ and ψ, respectively. The translation of θ is $\langle\mathcal{B}\rangle\text{tt}$ where $\mathcal{B}$ is an automaton of the same kind as $\mathcal{A}$ with states containing $Q \times \{0,1\}$, initial state $(q_0, 0)$ and final states $F \times \{1\}$. Let $p \xrightarrow[act]{a} q$ denote a transition in $\mathcal{A}$ leading from state p by reading $a \in \Sigma$ to state q while performing operation act on the stack—if applicable. Then $\mathcal{B}$ contains the following three transitions.

$$(q,0) \xrightarrow[nop]{?\varphi'} \xrightarrow[act]{a} (q',0) \qquad (q,0) \xrightarrow[nop]{?\psi'} \xrightarrow[act]{a} (q',1) \qquad (q,1) \xrightarrow[act]{a} (q',1)$$

For the strictness, we consider the property "there is a path on which p holds infinitely often". Obviously, this property is expressible by a delta operator in $\Delta\text{PDL}^?[\omega\text{REG}]$. For the sake of contradiction, assume that there is $\text{CTL}^{\text{rel}}[\mathfrak{A}]$-formula φ expressing this property. Hence, φ also characterizes this property over transition systems over a singleton alphabet Σ. For such systems the quantifiers are relativized either to $\emptyset$ or to Σ^{ω}. Hence, φ can be understood as a CTL-formula. But fairness is not expressible as a CTL-formula [8]. □

4.2   Model Checking

Theorem 3 (Upper and lower bounds). *The model checking problem for* $\text{CTL}^{\text{rel}}[\mathfrak{A}]$ *over a finite transition system is*

- *in PTIME if* $\mathfrak{A}$ *is* ω-*context-free, and*
- *hard for PTIME if* $\Sigma^\omega \in \mathfrak{A}$.

Proof. Given a formula $\varphi \in \text{CTL}^{\text{rel}}[\mathfrak{A}]$ and a transition system $\mathcal{T} = (\mathcal{S}, \rightarrow, \lambda)$, we compute inductively the set of states in $\mathcal{T}$ which satisfy a subformula of φ. Thereto, we extend λ with those formulas. The cases are similar to that of pure CTL. We detail the case of a formula $\mathbf{E}_L(\varphi \mathbf{U} \psi)$ for $L \in \mathfrak{A}$. For presentation assume that L is given as a Büchi automaton $\mathcal{A} = (Q, q_0, \delta, F)$ where Q is the set of states, $q_0 \in Q$, the transition relation $\delta \in Q \times \Sigma \times Q$, and $F \subseteq Q$ are the final states. We construct for every state $s \in \mathcal{S}$ an automaton $\mathcal{B} := (Q \times \mathcal{S} \times \{0, 1\}, (q_0, s, 0), \delta', F')$ recognizing witnessing paths for $\mathbf{E}_L(\varphi \mathbf{U} \psi)$ starting at s. The last component of the state is 1 iff the eventuality is satisfied. So, δ' consists of

$$
\begin{array}{ll}
((q, s, 0), a, (q', s', 0)) & \text{if } \varphi \in \lambda(s) \\
((q, s, i), a, (q', s', 1)) & \text{if } \psi \in \lambda(s) \text{ or } i = 1
\end{array}
$$

where each line requires $q' \in \delta(q, a)$ and $s \xrightarrow{a} s'$ for some $a \in \Sigma$. Finally, $F' := F \times \mathcal{S} \times \{1\}$. A similiar construction is available for PDAs. The emptiness check for this ω-PDA can be done in PTIME [3]. Finally, CTL is hard for PTIME. Hence, so is $\text{CTL}^{\text{rel}}[\mathfrak{A}]$.   □

4.3   Satisfiability

Theorem 4. *The satisfiability problem for* $\text{CTL}^{\text{rel}}[\omega\text{CFL}]$ *is undecidable.*

Proof. Remember that the universality problem (is $L = \Sigma^*$?) for context-free languages (of finite words) is undecidable. Now let $L \in \text{CFL}$ over some Σ and consider the formula $\varphi_L := \mathbf{E}_{\Sigma^* \mathsf{d}^\omega} \mathbf{F} \neg q \ \wedge \ \mathbf{A}_{L\mathsf{d}^\omega} \mathbf{G} q$.

Remember the assumption about paths in CTL^{rel} models being of the form $\Sigma^\omega \cup \Sigma^* \mathsf{d}^\omega$. The first conjunct then says that one of them is of the form $\Sigma^* \mathsf{d}^\omega$ and satisfies $\neg q$ at some point. The second conjunct says that all paths in $L\mathsf{d}^\omega$ satisfy q everywhere. Hence, if $L = \Sigma^*$ then φ_L is clearly unsatisfiable. On the other hand, if there is a $w \in \Sigma^* \setminus L$ then φ_L is for example satisfied in the model which has a single path $w\mathsf{d}^\omega$ such that $\neg q$ holds somewhere on this path.   □

Therefore, we consider smaller classes of languages. Those with particular nice algorithmic and algebraic properties are ωREG and ωVPL for instance.

Theorem 5. *The satisfiability problem for* $\text{CTL}^{\text{rel}}[\omega\text{REG}]$ *is EXPTIME-complete, and for* $\text{CTL}^{\text{rel}}[\omega\text{VPL}]$ *is 2-EXPTIME-complete.*

Proof. The membership follows from Thm. 2 using that $\Delta PDL^?[\omega REG]$ is in EXPTIME [9] and that $\Delta PDL^?[\omega VPL]$ is in 2-EXPTIME [12]. Moreover, the logic CTL$^{rel}[\omega REG]$ is EXPTIME-hard as CTL is [10] so. For the hardness of CTL$^{rel}[\omega VPL]$ one can extend the proof [12] of Löding et al. that PDL plus a certain visibly pushdown language is 2-EXPTIME hard. Besides a standard embedding, one $\Delta PDL^?[\omega VPL]$-expression needs to be rephrased as it uses an alternating between test operators and labels which is not directly expressible in CTL$^{rel}[\omega VPL]$. An another modification takes account of total transition system. $\square$

5   CTL with Path Relativisation in Abstraction

For the subsequent discussion, we fix a transition system $\mathcal{T} = (\mathcal{S}, \rightarrow, \lambda)$ and an abstraction function $\alpha \colon \mathcal{S} \rightarrow \mathcal{S}$. Since the transition relation of the abstraction $\mathcal{T}^\alpha$ is defined by existential quantification, a simple induction yields the following statement.

Proposition 6. *For $s \in \mathcal{S}$ we have*

- *If φ is purely existential then $\mathcal{T}, s \models \varphi$ implies $\mathcal{T}^\alpha, [s]_\alpha \models \varphi$.*
- *If φ is purely universal then $\mathcal{T}^\alpha, [s]_\alpha \models \varphi$ implies $\mathcal{T}, s \models \varphi$.*

Hence, it suffices to verify universally quantified formulas on the abstract system, and a positive answer carries over to the concrete system. In general, completeness, i.e. the converse direction, does not hold since the abstraction might admit spurious traces. A negative model checking result on the abstract system therefore need not reflect an error in the concrete system but it could. In order not to stall the design cycle of a system in the verification phase by having negative model checking results too often, one would like to "get as close to completeness as possible". This clearly requires purely existential formulas to be strengthened and purely universal formulas to be weakened. We therefore propose a general mechanism which uses the path quantifier relativisation in CTL^{rel} and realises this strengthening and weaking at the same time. Hence, it is applicable to arbitrary formulas, not just those that are purely existential or universal.

Definition 7. *Let $L \subseteq \Sigma^\omega$ be a language. The* restriction *of a CTL^{rel}-formula φ w.r.t. L is defined as the homomorphic extension over*

$$\left(Q_{L'}(\psi_1 \circ \psi_2)\right) \upharpoonright L := Q_{L' \cap L}\left((\psi_1 \upharpoonright L) \circ (\psi_2 \upharpoonright L)\right) \quad \text{where } Q \in \{\mathsf{E}, \mathsf{A}\}, \circ \in \{\mathsf{U}, \mathsf{R}\}.$$

Note that ωREG and ωVPL are closed under intersections, hence, CTL$^{rel}[\omega REG]$ and CTL$^{rel}[\omega VPL]$ are closed under restrictions with languages of these respective classes.

A nice property to have would be the following. For all transition systems $\mathcal{T}$, for all abstraction functions α for $\mathcal{T}$ there exists a language $L \neq \emptyset$ such that for all purely existential formulas φ we have: $\mathcal{T}^\alpha, [s]_\alpha \models \varphi \upharpoonright L$ implies $\mathcal{T}, s \models \varphi$. This is not possible however. Assume it was true. Then, it would also apply to transition systems over a singleton alphabet Σ. But then $L = \Sigma^\omega$ and therefore $\varphi \restriction L \equiv \varphi$. Hence, this property would imply the missing converse directions in Prop. 6 which are easy to refute by counterexample.

In the following we therefore present two heuristics which aim at exluding spurious traces through quantifier relativisation. The first one is rather simple and mainly meant to explain the problems involved in this approach. The second one is more sophisticated and aims at closing down on completeness by making certain requirements on the abstraction.

5.1   A Suffix Heuristic

Suppose $\mathcal{T}$ is a transition system with some initial state s, and $\mathcal{T}^\alpha$ is its abstraction w.r.t. some α. Take the CTL formula $\varphi = \mathtt{AGEF}q$ expressing liveness with respect to some proposition q. A natural candidate for the restriction of the path quantifiers in φ would be $L := \Pi_\mathcal{T}(s)$, i.e. the language of all paths in L. Note that not even then does the result of $\mathcal{T}^\alpha, [s]_\alpha \models \varphi \restriction L$ transfer in any way to $\mathcal{T}, s \models \varphi$. The reason for this is the fact that $\Pi_\mathcal{T}(s)$ describes all paths *starting in* s. However, note that the AG-operator intuitively requires the subformula $\mathtt{EF}q$ to be interpreted in *arbitrary* states of $\mathcal{T}$, not just s. Hence, $\mathtt{EF}q$ should be restricted to paths which start in those states that the formula itself is interpreted in. This would require the subformula to "know" which state it is interpreted in. In other words, the existential quantifier should be restricted to certain suffixes of words in $\Pi_\mathcal{T}(s)$.

This could even mean that $\mathtt{E}_L\mathtt{F}q$ is interpreted in the starting state of a path which eventually satisfies q but the restriction to L is too rigid and excludes this path. Hence, while one aims at excluding as many spurious traces as possible, one would also exclude good traces. This calls for an overapproximation in order to fix this problem.

Definition 8. *Let $L \subseteq \Sigma^\omega$. The* suffix-closure *of L is*

$$Suff(L) \ := \ \{w \in \Sigma^\omega \mid \exists v \in \Sigma^* \ s.t. \ vw \in L\}.$$

The heuristics presented here proposes to reduce the verification task of $\mathcal{T}, s \models \varphi$ on the concrete side to $\mathcal{T}^\alpha, [s]_\alpha \models \varphi \restriction Suff(\Pi_\mathcal{T})$ on the abstract side. Note that the existential quantifier in the definition of $Suff(L)$ realises an overapproximation in the sense that – coming back to the example above – the subformula $\mathtt{EF}q$ would of course still be interpreted in an arbitrary but reachable state t of the system, but the quantifier relativisation would restrict the existential path quantifier to suffixes of paths from s. Since some of these pass through t, we have $\Pi_\mathcal{T}(t) \subseteq Suff(\Pi_\mathcal{T}(s))$, and the restricted formula does not exclude good traces. It remains to see how well this does at excluding spurious traces.

Clearly, this heuristic would be worthless if the considered classes of formal languages were not closed under suffixes. However, this is not the case.

Proposition 9. *For all $\mathcal{C} \in \{\omega\mathrm{REG}, \omega\mathrm{VPL}, \omega\mathrm{CFL}\}$ and for all $L \in \mathcal{C}$ we have $Suff(L) \in \mathcal{C}$.*

5.2   A Local Heuristic

Note that the approach suggested in the previous section is global in a sense. Here we propose a local approach which focus on the abstract states, their connections, and the spurious traces that are created within those states.

Definition 10. *For a concrete state s in $\mathcal{T}$ we define its* abstraction language *as a subset of $\Sigma^* \cup \Sigma^\omega$ by*

$$L_s := \{a_0 \ldots a_n \mid \text{there is an initial path } s_0 a_0 \ldots a_{n-1} s_n \text{ in } \mathcal{T} \text{ s. th.}$$
$$s_i \in [s] \text{ for all } 0 \leq i < n \text{ and } s_n \notin [s] \}$$
$$\cup \{a_0 a_1 \ldots \mid \text{there is a path } s_0 a_0 s_1 a_1 \ldots \text{ in } \mathcal{T} \text{ s. th.}$$
$$s_i \in [s] \text{ for all } i \in \mathbb{N} \}$$

The abstract language *of the abstraction $\mathcal{T}^\alpha$ is $L_\alpha := \left(\bigcup_{s \in \mathcal{S}} L_s \right)^\omega$.*

In other words, the abstract language of a state describes all traces within its class. In particular, fragments of spurious traces are excluded. The language L_α is an over-approximation of the transition system. Indeed, it also admits words in $L_s L_t L_\alpha$ when $[s]$ and $[t]$ are not connected. But, therefore, L_α might have a more condensed description than $\mathcal{T}$ itself.

Prop. 6 can be strengthened by a restriction which is compatible with the induced equivalence classes.

Lemma 11 (Soundness). *For any purely existential formula φ we have that $\mathcal{T}, s \models \varphi$ implies $\mathcal{T}^\alpha, [s]_\alpha \models \varphi \restriction L$, for any $L \supseteq L_s L_\alpha$ and $s \in \mathcal{S}$.*

Proof. Induction on φ. We sketch the case $\varphi = \mathbf{E}_{L'}(\psi_0 \mathbf{U} \psi_1)$ only. Consider a witnessing path $\pi := s_0, a_0, s_1, a_1, \ldots$. Then $\pi^\alpha := [s_0]_\alpha, a_0, [s_1]_\alpha, a_1, \ldots$ is a path in $\mathcal{T}^\alpha$. By induction hypothesis we have $\mathcal{T}^\alpha, [s]_\alpha \models \mathbf{E}_{L'}((\psi_0 \restriction L) \mathbf{U} (\psi_1 \restriction L))$. A subsequence of π^α might loop in just one equivalence class. This observation gives rise to a factorization along which $\pi^\alpha \in L_s L_\alpha$ can be shown.   □

For the converse implication we synchronize traces in the abstract system with those in the concrete one.

Definition 12. *The abstraction $\mathcal{T}^\alpha$ is* syntactically traceable *iff $[s] \overset{a}{\longrightarrow}_\alpha [s_0]$ and $[s] \overset{a}{\longrightarrow}_\alpha [s_1]$ imply $s_0 = s_1$ for all $s, s_0, s_1 \in \mathcal{S}$ and $a \in \Sigma$ with $[s_0] \neq [s] \neq [s_1]$.*

Syntactical traceablity is a rather strong and artificial property as it requires that a label determines the targeted state. None of our introductive examples enjoy this property. However in our examples, not the label but the course of the considered trace uniquely specifies the next equivalence class. This observation motivates the following definition.

Definition 13. *The abstraction $\mathcal{T}^\alpha$ is* semantically traceable *iff for all paths $\hat{\pi}$ in $\mathcal{T}^\alpha$ and for all states $s_0, s_1 \in \mathcal{S}$ it holds that $\pi \in L(L_{s_0} L_\alpha \cap L_{s_1} L_\alpha)$ implies $s_0 = s_1$ where $L = \Sigma^* \cap \left(\bigcup_{s \in \mathcal{S}} L_s \right)^*$.*

In the alarm clock example, assume that the sequence set tick leads to the class "> 2". Then the label tick either keeps the trace in this class or brings it to the class "1". Hence, the abstracted system is not syntactically traceable. However, it is semantically traceable as the number of ticks before the clock rings determines the next state.

Proposition 14. *If T^α is syntactically traceable then it is also semantically traceable.*

Theorem 15 (Conditional Completeness). *Let T be semantically traceable. Suppose that for the formulas ψ_0, $\hat{\psi}_0$, ψ_1 and $\hat{\psi}_1$*

$$T^\alpha, [s]_\alpha \models \hat{\psi}_i \text{ implies } T, s \models \psi_i \tag{1}$$

holds for $s \in S$ and $i \in \{0,1\}$. Then for $\circ \in \{U, R\}$, $s \in S$ and $L' \subseteq \Sigma^\omega$ we have

$$T^\alpha, [s]_\alpha \models E_{L \cap L'}(\hat{\psi}_0 \circ \hat{\psi}_1) \text{ implies } T, s \models E_L(\psi_0 \circ \psi_1) \tag{2}$$

where $L' := L_s L_\alpha$.

Proof. Let $\hat{\pi} := \hat{s}_0 a_0 \hat{s}_1 a_1 \ldots$ be a path witnessing the premise of the equation (2). It remains to show that there exists a path π—and not just a sequence of states— in T which follows $\hat{\pi}$. Given that, the property (1) completes the proof. The path $\hat{\pi}$ can be factorized using L' such that the (finite or infinite) word determined by a factor is in L_t for $t \in S$. The first factor is in L_s. Along this factorization we construct π as follows. Assume a factor and a path ending at a concrete state such that its abstraction is the first state in the considered factor. For the first factor this path consists of the state s only. Now, the word of the factor is in L_t for some $t \in S$. Therefore, the definition of this language admits two possibilities. Either, there is an infinite path in $[t]_\alpha$, then we are done. Or there is a finite path π' in $[t]_\alpha$ and a label $a \in \Sigma$ leading π' to a state outside of $[t]_\alpha$. Then we extend π by π' and the said label. By the definition of "semantically traceable", the following node is uniquely determined. $\qquad\square$

Although the restriction on the formulas seems to be rather artificial it avoids the suffix problem. However, the consistency condition for abstraction functions ensures that any formula without E and A meets the property (1). Together with Lem. 11, we have completeness of our method with respect to a certain class of formulas.

Corollary 16 (Conditional Faithfulness). *Let T be semantically traceable and let φ be a formula without EX, AX, and nested quantifiers. We have*

$$T^\alpha, [s]_\alpha \models \varphi \upharpoonright L' \text{ iff } T, s \models \varphi \tag{3}$$

for $L' := L_s L_\alpha$.

The language L' used by the previous theorem and corollary is subsumed by L_α. Hence, modelchecking $\varphi \upharpoonright L_\alpha$ on the abstract system is almost as good as checking $\varphi \upharpoonright L'$.

Note that Cor. 16 is only formulated for formulas without the next-time operators. The fragment for which Cor. 16 states completeness and thus full elimination of spurious traces is therefore in some sense the stutter-invariant part of CTL^{rel} only.

6   Conclusion and Further Work

We have presented a framework for the transformation of correctness properties which should go hand in hand with the transformation of a concrete system into an abstract one. The goal of this transformation is to minimise the significance of spurious traces in the abstract model. We have then suggested two heuristics for certain transformations within this framework.

The work contained herein is obviously not completed. It remains to be seen how these heuristics perform in practice, i.e. how often they can confirm absence of errors in a concrete system (w.r.t. purely universal properties for instance) by confirming that the abstract system is error-free. A dealbreaker may also be the computation of the involved languages which are being factorised into the property. It remains to be seen whether efficient algorithms for these computation problems exist.

On the theoretical side, it is of course possible to consider extensions of CTL^{rel}. It is not too difficult to see that one could introduce test predicates into the formal languages without losing any of the complexity results. Another obvious extension would be CTL^*_{rel}, i.e. CTL^* with path relativisation in the same style. This would have a significantly higher complexity in both model checking and satisfiability checking though.

References

1. Alur, R., Madhusudan, P.: Visibly pushdown languages. In: Proc. 36th Ann. ACM Symp. on Theory of Computing, STOC 2004, pp. 202–211 (2004)
2. Bosnacki, D., Ioustinova, N., Sidorova, N.: Using fairness to make abstractions work. In: Graf, S., Mounier, L. (eds.) SPIN 2004. LNCS, vol. 2989, pp. 198–215. Springer, Heidelberg (2004)
3. Bouajjani, A., Esparza, J., Maler, O.: Reachability analysis of pushdown automata: Application to model-checking. In: Mazurkiewicz, A., Winkowski, J. (eds.) CONCUR 1997. LNCS, vol. 1243, pp. 135–150. Springer, Heidelberg (1997)
4. Büchi, J.R.: On a decision method in restricted second order arithmetic. In: Proc. Congress on Logic, Method, and Philosophy of Science, pp. 1–12. Stanford University Press, Stanford (1962)
5. Clarke, E.M., Emerson, E.A.: Synthesis of synchronization skeletons for branching time temporal logic. In: Kozen, D. (ed.) Logic of Programs 1981. LNCS, vol. 131, pp. 52–71. Springer, Heidelberg (1982)
6. Clarke, E.M., Grumberg, O., Jha, S., Lu, Y., Veith, H.: Counterexample-guided abstraction refinement for symbolic model checking. Journal of the ACM 50(5), 752–794 (2003)

7. Emerson, E.A., Halpern, J.Y.: Decision procedures and expressiveness in the temporal logic of branching time. Journal of Computer and System Sciences 30, 1–24 (1985)
8. Emerson, E.A., Halpern, J.Y.: "sometimes" and "not never" revisited: on branching versus linear time temporal logic. J. ACM 33(1), 151–178 (1986)
9. Emerson, E.A., Jutla, C.S.: The complexity of tree automata and logics of programs. In: Annual IEEE Symposium on Foundations of Computer Science, pp. 328–337 (1988)
10. Fischer, M.J., Ladner, R.E.: Propositional dynamic logic of regular programs. Journal of Computer and System Sciences 18(2), 194–211 (1979)
11. Löding, C., Lutz, C., Serre, O.: Propositional dynamic logic with recursive programs. J. Log. Algebr. Program. 73(1-2), 51–69 (2007)
12. Löding, C., Serre, O.: Propositional dynamic logic with recursive programs. In: Aceto, L., Ingólfsdóttir, A. (eds.) FOSSACS 2006. LNCS, vol. 3921, pp. 292–306. Springer, Heidelberg (2006)
13. De Nicola, R., Vaandrager, F.: Action versus state based logics for transition systems. In: Guessarian, I. (ed.) LITP 1990. LNCS, vol. 469, pp. 407–419. Springer, Heidelberg (1990)
14. Pnueli, A.: The temporal logic of programs. In: Proc. 18th Symp. on Foundations of Computer Science, FOCS 1977, Providence, RI, USA, pp. 46–57. IEEE, Los Alamitos (1977)
15. Sistla, A.P., Clarke, E.M.: The complexity of propositional linear temporal logics. Journal of the Association for Computing Machinery 32(3), 733–749 (1985)
16. Staiger, L.: Handbook of formal languages. In: ω-languages. Beyond words, vol. 3, pp. 339–387. Springer, Heidelberg (1997)
17. Streett, R.S.: Propositional dynamic logic of looping and converse is elementarily decidable. Information and Control 54(1/2), 121–141 (1982)
18. Vardi, M.Y., Wolper, P.: Automata-theoretic techniques for modal logics of programs. J. Comput. Syst. Sci. 32(2), 183–221 (1986)
19. Walukiewicz, I.: Pushdown processes: Games and model-checking. Information and Computation 164(2), 234–263 (2001)

Application of Logic to Integer Sequences: A Survey

Johann A. Makowsky*

Department of Computer Science
Technion–Israel Institute of Technology, Haifa, Israel
janos@cs.technion.ac.il

Abstract. Chomsky and Schützenberger showed in 1963 that the sequence $d_L(n)$, which counts the number of words of a given length n in a regular language L, satisfies a linear recurrence relation with constant coefficients for n, or equivalently, the generating function $g_L(x) = \sum_n d_L(n)x^n$ is a rational function. In this talk we survey results concerning sequences $a(n)$ of natural numbers which

– satisfy linear recurrence relations over $\mathbb{Z}$ or $\mathbb{Z}_m$, and
– have a combinatorial or logical interpretation.

We present the pioneering, but little known, work by C. Blatter and E. Specker from 1981, and its further developments, including results by I. Gessel (1984), E. Fischer (2003), and recent results by T. Kotek and the author.

*For Ernst Specker on the
occasion of his 90th birthday*

1 Sequences of Integers and Their Combinatorial Interpretations

In this talk we discuss sequences $a(n)$ of natural numbers or integers which arise in combinatorics. Many such sequences satisfy linear recurrence relations with constant or polynomial coefficients. The traditional approach to the study of such sequences consists of interpreting $a(n)$ as the coefficients of a generating function $g(x) = \sum_n a(n)x^n$, and of using *analytic methods*, to derive properties of $a(n)$, cf. [FS09]. There is a substantial theory of how to verify and prove identities among the terms of $a(n)$, see [PWZ96].

We are interested in the case where $a(n)$ admits a *combinatorial* or a *logical* interpretation, i.e., $a(n)$ counts the number of some relations or functions on the set $[n] = \{1, \ldots, n\}$ which have a certain property possibly definable in some logical formalism (with or without its natural order). To make this precise, we assume the audience is familiar with the very basics of Logic and Finite

---

* Partially supported by a grant of the Fund for Promotion of Research of the Technion–Israel Institute of Technology and grant ISF 1392/07 of the Israel Science Foundation (2007-2010).

A. Dawar and R. de Queiroz (Eds.): WoLLIC 2010, LNAI 6188, pp. 34–41, 2010.

Model Theory, cf. [EF95, Lib04]. A more general framework for combinatorial interpretations of counting functions is described in [BLL98]. Lack of time does not allow us to use this formalism in this talk. We shall mostly deal with the logics **SOL**, Second Order Logic, and **MSOL**, Monadic Second Order Logic. Occasionally, we formulate statements in the language of automata theory and regular languages and use freely the Büchi-Elgot-Trakhtenbrot Theorem which states that a language is regular iff it is definable in **MSOL** when we view its words of length n as ordered structures on a set of n elements equipped with unary predicates, cf. [EF95].

We define a general notion of *combinatorial interpretations* for finite ordered relational structures.

Definition 1 (Combinatorial interpretation). *A combinatorial interpretation $\mathcal{K}$ of $a(n)$ is given by*

(i) *a class of finite structures $\mathcal{K}$ over a vocabulary*
$\tau = \{R_1, \ldots R_r\} = \{\bar{R}\}$ *or* $\tau_{ord} = \{<_{nat}, \bar{R}\}$
with finite universe $[n] = \{1, \ldots, n\}$ *and a relation symbol* $<_{nat}$ *for the natural order on* $[n]$.
(ii) *The counting function $d_\mathcal{K}(n)$, which counts the number of relations*

$$d_\mathcal{K}(n) = |\{\bar{R} \text{ on } [n] : \langle [n], <_{nat}, \bar{R}\rangle \in \mathcal{K}\}|$$

such that $d_\mathcal{K}(n) = a(n)$.
(iii) *A combinatorial interpretation $\mathcal{K}$ is a* pure combinatorial interpretation *of $a(n)$ if $\mathcal{K}$ is closed under τ-isomorphisms. In particular, if $\mathcal{K}$ does not depend on the natural order $<_{nat}$ on $[n]$, but only on τ.*

Intuitively speaking, a combinatorial interpretation $\mathcal{K}$ of $a(n)$ is a *logical interpretation of $a(n)$* if $\mathcal{K}$ is definable by a formula in some logic formalism, say full Second Order Logic.

Definition 2 (Logical interpretation and Specker sequences)

(i) *A combinatorial interpretation $\mathcal{K}$ of $a(n)$ is an* **SOL**-interpretation (**MSOL**-interpretation) *of $a(n)$, if $\mathcal{K}$ is definable in* **SOL**(τ_{ord}) *(***MSOL**(τ_{ord})*).*
(ii) Pure **SOL**-interpretations (**MSOL**-interpretation) of $a(n)$ *are defined analogously.*
(iii) *We call a sequence $a(n)$ which has a logical interpretation in some fragment $\mathcal{L}$ of* **SOL** *an $\mathcal{L}$-Specker sequence, or just a* Specker sequence *if the fragment is* **SOL**[1].

Remarks 1

(i) *If $a(n)$ has a combinatorial interpretation then for all $n \in \mathbb{N}$ we have $a(n) \geq 0$.*

---

[1] E. Specker was to the best of my knowledge the first to introduce **MSOL**-definability as a tool in analyzing combinatorial interpretations of sequences of non-negative integers.

(ii) *There are only countably many Specker sequences.*
(iii) *Every Specker sequence is computable, and in fact it is in $\sharp \cdot \mathbf{PH}$, [HV95], hence computable in exponential time.*
(iv) *The set of Specker sequences is closed under the point-wise operations of addition and multiplication. The same holds for $\mathbf{MSOL}$-Specker sequences.*

2   Linear Recurrences

We are in particular interested in linear recurrence relations which may hold over $\mathbb{Z}$ or $\mathbb{Z}_m$.

Definition 3 (Recurrence relations). *Given a sequence $a(n)$ of integers we say $a(n)$ is*

(i) C-finite *or* rational *if there is a fixed $q \in \mathbb{N}\setminus\{0\}$ for which $a(n)$ satisfies for all $n > q$*

$$a(n + q) = \sum_{i=0}^{q-1} p_i a(n + i)$$

where each $p_i \in \mathbb{Z}$.

(ii) P-recursive *or* holonomic *if there is a fixed $q \in \mathbb{N}\setminus\{0\}$ for which $a(n)$ satisfies for all $n > q$*

$$p_q(n) \cdot a(n + q) = \sum_{i=0}^{q-1} p_i(n) a(n + i)$$

where each p_i is a polynomial in $\mathbb{Z}[X]$ and $p_q(n) \neq 0$ for any n. We call it simply P-recursive *or* SP-recursive, *if additionally $p_q(n) = 1$ for every $n \in \mathbb{Z}$.*

(iii) MC-finite *(modularly C-finite), if for every $m \in \mathbb{N}, m > 0$ there is $q(m) \in \mathbb{N}\setminus\{0\}$ for which $a(n)$ satisfies for all $n > q(m)$*

$$a(n + q(m)) = \sum_{i=0}^{q(m)-1} p_i(m) a(n + i) \quad \mod m$$

where $q(m)$ and $p_i(m)$ depend only on m, and $p_i(m) \in \mathbb{Z}$. Equivalently, $a(n)$ is MC-finite, if for all $m \in \mathbb{N}$ the sequence $a(n)$ (mod m) is ultimately periodic.

(iv) hypergeometric *if $a(n)$ satisfies for all $n > 2$*

$$p_1(n) \cdot a(n + 1) = p_0(n) a(n)$$

where each p_i is a polynomial in $\mathbb{Z}[X]$ and $p_1(n) \neq 0$ for any n. In other words, $a(n)$ is P-recursive with $q = 1$.

The terminology C-finite and holonomic are due to [Zei90]. P-recursive is due to [Sta80]. P-recursive sequences were already studied in [Bir30, BT33].

The following are well known, see [FS09, EvPSW03].

Lemma 1

(i) *Let $a(n)$ be C-finite. Then there is a constant $c \in \mathbb{Z}$ such that $a(n) \leq 2^{cn}$.*

(ii) *Furthermore, for every holonomic sequence $a(n)$ there is a constant $\gamma \in \mathbb{N}$ such that $\mid a(n) \mid \leq n!^{\gamma}$ for all $n \geq 2$.*

(iii) *The sets of C-finite, MC-finite, SP-recursive and P-recursive sequences are closed under addition, subtraction and point-wise multiplication.*

In general, the bound on the growth rate of holonomic sequences is best possible, since $a(n) = n!^{m}$ is easily seen to be holonomic for integer m, [Ger04].

Proposition 1. *Let $a(n)$ be a function $a : \mathbb{N} \to \mathbb{Z}$.*

(i) *If $a(n)$ is C-finite then $a(n)$ is SP-recursive.*

(ii) *If $a(n)$ is SP-recursive then $a(n)$ is P-recursive.*

(iii) *If $a(n)$ is SP-recursive then $a(n)$ is MC-finite.*

(iv) *If $a(n)$ is hypergeometric then $a(n)$ is P-recursive.*

Moreover, the converses of (i), (ii), (iii) and (iv) do not hold, and no implication holds between MC-finite and P-recursive.

Proposition 2

(i) *There are only countably many P-recursive sequences $a(n)$.*

(ii) *There are continuum many MC-finite sequences.*

3   Logical Interpretations and Linear Recurrences

Modular recurrence relations for sequences with combinatorial interpretation are studied widely, cf. [Fla82, Ges84]. A logical approach to this topic was pioneered in [BS81, BS83] and further pursued in [Spe88, Spe05]. C. Blatter and E. Specker have shown:

Theorem 1 (C. Blatter and E. Specker, [BS81]). *Let $a(n)$ be a Specker sequence which has a pure* **MSOL***-interpretation $\mathcal{K}$ over a finite vocabulary which contains only relation symbols of arity at most two. Then $a(n)$ is MC-finite.*

Remarks 2

(i) *Theorem 1 is not true for* **MSOL***-interpretations with order, i.e. which are not pure, cf. [FM03].*

(ii) *E. Fischer, [Fis03], showed that it is also not true if one allows relation symbols of arity ≥ 4, see also [Spe05].*

(iii) *In the light of Remark 1(ii) and Proposition 2(ii) there cannot be a converse of Theorem 1.*

In 1984 I. Gessel proved the following related result:

Theorem 2 (I. Gessel, [Ges84]). *Let $\mathcal{K}$ be a class of (possibly) directed graphs of bounded degree d which is closed under disjoint unions and components. Then $d_{\mathcal{K}}(n)$ is MC-finite.*

Remark 3. *Theorem 2 does not use logic. However, let $\mathcal{K}$ be a class of connected finite directed graphs, and let $\bar{\mathcal{K}}$ be the closure of $\mathcal{K}$ under disjoint unions. It is easy to see that $\mathcal{K}$ is* **MSOL**-*definable iff $\bar{\mathcal{K}}$ is* **MSOL**-*definable. Let us call a class of directed graphs $\mathcal{K}$ a Gessel class if $\mathcal{K}$ is closed under disjoint unions and components and its members are of bounded degree. Therefore, naturally arising Gessel classes are likely to be definable in* **SOL** *or even* **MSOL***.*

The notion of degree can be extended to arbitrary relational structures $\mathcal{A}$ via the Gaifman graph of $\mathcal{A}$, cf. [EF95]. Inspired by Theorem 1 and Theorem 2, E. Fischer and the author showed:

Theorem 3 (E. Fischer and J.A. Makowsky, [FM03]). *Let $a(n)$ be a Specker sequence which has a pure* **MSOL**-*interpretation $\mathcal{K}$ over any finite relational vocabulary (without restrictions on the arity of the relation symbols), but which is of bounded degree. Then $a(n)$ is MC-finite.*

Let $\mathcal{K}$ be a combinatorial or logical interpretation of $a(n)$. In [Spe88] E. Specker asks whether one can formulate a definability condition on $\mathcal{K}$ which ensures that $a(n)$ is SP-recursive. There are really two questions here:

Question A: Can one formulate a definability condition on combinatorial interpretations $\mathcal{K}$ of $a(n)$ which ensures that $a(n)$ is SP-recursive.

Question B: Can one formulate a definability condition on **pure** combinatorial interpretations $\mathcal{K}$ of $a(n)$ which ensures that $a(n)$ is SP-recursive.

We shall see that the answer to Question A is in the affirmative, but that Question B remains open.

We first note that for C-finite sequences the answer to Question A is affirmative.

Theorem 4 (N. Chomsky and M. Schützenberger, [CS63]). *Let $d_L(n)$ be a counting function of a regular language L. Then $d_L(n)$ is C-finite.*

The converse is not true. However, we proved recently the following:

Theorem 5 ([KM09]). *Let $a(n)$ be a function $a : \mathbb{N} \to \mathbb{Z}$ which is C-finite. Then there are two regular languages L_1, L_2 with counting functions $d_1(n), d_2(n)$ such that $a(n) = d_1(n) - d_2(n)$.*

Remark 4. *We could replace the difference of two sequences in the expression $a(n) = d_1(n) - d_2(n)$ by $a(n) = d_3(n) - c^n$ where $d_3(n)$ also comes from a regular language, and $c \in \mathbb{N}$ is suitably chosen.*

Using the well-known characterization of regular languages in **MSOL**, Theorem 4 and Theorem 5 can be combined, using Lemma 1.

Theorem 6. *Let $a(n)$ be a function $a : \mathbb{N} \to \mathbb{Z}$. $a(n)$ is C-finite iff there are two* **MSOL**-*Specker sequences $d_1(n), d_2(n)$, where the sequences $d_1(n), d_2(n)$ have* **MSOL**-*interpretations over a fixed finite vocabulary which contains $<_{nat}$ and otherwise only unary relation symbols, such that $a(n) = d_1(n) - d_2(n)$.*

4   P-Recursive (Holonomic) Sequences

In the final part of the talk we answer E. Specker's Question A positively by giving two a characterization of P-recursive sequences both inspired by Theorem 6. We also discuss why Question B seems harder to answer.

Both characterizations involve regular languages L over an alphabet Σ, or equivalently, both use **MSOL**-interpretations.

In the first characterization, *regular languages* are augmented by a set of legal *Lattice Paths*, and are called *LP*-interpretations and have no weights. More precisely, we count not only words in L, but the words together with functions which map positions of the word w of length n into $[n]$ subject to certain mild restrictions. The graphs of these functions are reminiscent of lattice paths, [GJ83, GR96].

In the second characterization, *regular languages* are equipped with *weights* which depend both on the letter in the word, and the position of this letter. They are called *PW*-interpretations. More precisely, we count weighted words in a language L where the weight is defined by a position specific scoring matrix, widely used in computational biology to search DNA and protein databases for sequence similarities, cf. [SSGE82, AMS+97]. This approach is also reminiscent to counting weighted homomorphisms, cf. [BCL+06]. Position-independent weights on words were used in [NZ99] for the extension of the powerful (and so far under-utilized) Goulden-Jackson Cluster method for finding the generating function for the number of words avoiding, as factors, the members of a prescribed set. In [Ges84] position-independent weights are used to prove modular congruences.

Acknowledgments

All the new results in this survey are taken from T. Kotek's ongoing work on his Ph.D. thesis [KM10b, KM10a]. I would like to thank T. Kotek for allowing me to use entire passages from our joint manuscripts in this extended abstract of my invited lecture.

References

[AMS+97]   Altschul, S.F., Maddén, T.L., Schaffer, A.A., Zhang, J., Zhang, Z., Miller, W., Lipman, D.J.: Gapped blast and psi-blast: a new generation of protein database search programs. Nucleic Acids Res. 25, 3389–3402 (1997)

[BCL+06]   Borgs, C., Chayes, J., Lovász, L., Sós, V.T., Vesztergombi, K.: Counting graph homomorphisms. In: Klazar, M., Kratochvil, J., Loebl, M., Matousek, J., Thomas, R., Valtr, P. (eds.) Topics in Discret mathematics, pp. 315–371. Springer, Heidelberg (2006)

[Bir30]   Birkhoff, G.D.: General theory of irregular difference equations. Acta Mathematica 54, 205–246 (1930)

[BLL98]   Bergeron, F., Labelle, G., Leroux, P.: Combinatorial Species and Tree-like Structures. Encyclopedia of Mathematics and its Applications, vol. 67. Cambridge University Press, Cambridge (1998)

[BS81]   Blatter, C., Specker, E.: Le nombre de structures finies d'une th'eorie à charactère fin. Sciences Mathématiques, Fonds Nationale de la recherche Scientifique, Bruxelles, 41–44 (1981)

[BS83]   Blatter, C., Specker, E.: Modular periodicity of combinatorial sequences. Abstracts of the AMS 4, 313 (1983)

[BT33]   Birkhoff, G.D., Trjitzinsky, W.J.: Analytic theory of singular difference equations. Acta Mathematica 60, 1–89 (1933)

[CS63]   Chomsky, N., Schützenberger, M.P.: The algebraic theory of context free languages. In: Brafford, P., Hirschberg, D. (eds.) Computer Programming and Formal Systems, pp. 118–161. North Holland, Amsterdam (1963)

[EF95]   Ebbinghaus, H.D., Flum, J.: Finite Model Theory. In: Perspectives in Mathematical Logic, Springer, Heidelberg (1995)

[EvPSW03]   Everest, G., van Porten, A., Shparlinski, I., Ward, T.: Recurrence Sequences. Mathematical Surveys and Monographs, vol. 104. American Mathematical Society, Providence (2003)

[Fis03]   Fischer, E.: The Specker-Blatter theorem does not hold for quaternary relations. Journal of Combinatorial Theory, Series A 103, 121–136 (2003)

[Fla82]   Flajolet, P.: On congruences and continued fractions for some classical combinatorial quantities. Discrete Mathematics 41, 145–153 (1982)

[FM03]   Fischer, E., Makowsky, J.A.: The Specker-Blatter theorem revisited. In: Warnow, T.J., Zhu, B. (eds.) COCOON 2003. LNCS, vol. 2697, pp. 90–101. Springer, Heidelberg (2003)

[FS09]   Flajolet, P., Sedgewick, R.: Analytic Combinatorics. Cambridge University Press, Cambridge (2009)

[Ger04]   Gerhold, S.: On some non-holonomic sequences. Electronic Journal of Combinatorics 11, 1–7 (2004)

[Ges84]   Gessel, I.: Combinatorial proofs of congruences. In: Jackson, D.M., Vanstone, S.A. (eds.) Enumeration and design, pp. 157–197. Academic Press, London (1984)

[GJ83]   Goulden, I.P., Jackson, D.M.: Combinatorial Enumeration. Interscience Series in Discrete Mathematics. Wiley, Chichester (1983)

[GR96]   Gessel, I.M., Ree, S.: Lattice paths and Faber polynomials. In: Balakrishnan, N. (ed.) Advances in combinatorial methods and applications to probability and statistics, pp. 3–14. Birkhäuser, Basel (1996)

[HV95]   Hemaspaandra, V.: The satanic notations: Counting classes beyond $\sharp P$ and other definitional adventures. SIGACTN: SIGACT News (ACM Special Interest Group on Automata and Computability Theory) 26 (1995)

[KM09]   Kotek, T., Makowsky, J.A.: Definability of combinatorial functions and their linear recurrence relations. Electronically available at arXiv:0907.5420 (2009)

[KM10a]   Kotek, T., Makowsky, J.A.: Application of logic to generating functions: Holonomic sequences. Manuscript (2010)

[KM10b]   Kotek, T., Makowsky, J.A.: A representation theorem for holonomic sequences. Manuscript (2010)

[Lib04]   Libkin, L.: Elements of Finite Model Theory. Springer, Heidelberg (2004)

[NZ99]   Noonan, J., Zeilberger, D.: The Goulden-Jackson cluster method: Extensions, applications and implementations. J. Differ. Equations Appl. 5(4-5), 355–377 (1999)

[PWZ96]   Petkovsek, M., Wilf, H., Zeilberger, D.: A=B. AK Peters, Wellesley (1996)

[Spe88]   Specker, E.: Application of logic and combinatorics to enumeration problems. In: Börger, E. (ed.) Trends in Theoretical Computer Science, pp. 141–169. Computer Science Press, Rockville (1988); Reprinted in: Ernst Specker, Selecta, Birkhäuser 1990, pp. 324–350

[Spe05]   Specker, E.: Modular counting and substitution of structures. Combinatorics, Probability and Computing 14, 203–210 (2005)

[SSGE82]   Stormo, G.D., Schneider, T.D., Gold, L., Ehrenfeucht, A.: Use of the 'perceptron' algorithm to distinguish translational initiation sites in e. coli. Nucleic Acid Research 10, 2997–3012 (1982)

[Sta80]   Stanley, R.P.: Differentiably finite power series. European Journal of Combinatorics 1, 175–188 (1980)

[Zei90]   Zeilberger, D.: A holonomic systems approach to special functions identities. J. of Computational and Applied Mathematics 32, 321–368 (1990)

The Two-Variable Fragment with Counting Revisited

Ian Pratt-Hartmann

School of Computer Science
University of Manchester
Manchester M13 9PL
United Kingdom
http://www.cs.man.ac.uk/~ipratt

Abstract. The satisfiability and finite satisfiability problems for the two-variable fragment of first-order logic with counting were shown in [5] to be in NExpTime. This paper presents a simplified proof via a result on integer programming due to Eisenbrand and Shmonina [2].

Keywords: Logic, complexity, counting quantifiers.

1 Introduction

The two-variable fragment with counting quantifiers, here denoted $\mathcal{C}^2$, is the set of function-free, first-order formulas containing at most two variables, but with the counting quantifiers $\exists_{\leq C}$, $\exists_{\geq C}$ and $\exists_{=C}$ (for every $C > 0$) allowed. Thus, for example, the sentences

No professor supervises more than three students
Every student is supervised by at most one professor

may be formalized using the respective $\mathcal{C}^2$-formulas:

$$\neg\exists x(\mathrm{professor}(x) \wedge \exists_{\geq 4} y(\mathrm{student}(y) \wedge \mathrm{supervises}(x, y)))$$
$$\forall x(\mathrm{student}(x) \rightarrow \exists_{\leq 1} y(\mathrm{professor}(y) \wedge \mathrm{supervises}(y, x))).$$

The *satisfiability problem for* $\mathcal{C}^2$, denoted Sat-$\mathcal{C}^2$, is the problem of determining whether a given $\mathcal{C}^2$-formula has a model. The *finite satisfiability problem for* $\mathcal{C}^2$, denoted Fin-Sat-$\mathcal{C}^2$, is the problem of determining whether a given $\mathcal{C}^2$-formula has a finite model. Since $\mathcal{C}^2$ lacks the finite model property, these problems are distinct. Both problems, however, were shown in [5] to be in NExpTime, thus improving earlier results in [3] and [4]. The proof given in that paper features a long, combinatorial argument to show that, if a $\mathcal{C}^2$-formula has a model at all, then it has a model in which only a small number of distinct 'local configurations' arise. The present paper presents a shorter and more perspicuous proof via a result on integer programming due to Eisenbrand and Shmonina [2].

A. Dawar and R. de Queiroz (Eds.): WoLLIC 2010, LNAI 6188, pp. 42–54, 2010.
© Springer-Verlag Berlin Heidelberg 2010

2   Preliminaries

In the sequel, all signatures will be silently assumed to be purely relational. This results in no loss of generality, as function-symbols are not allowed in $\mathcal{C}^2$, and individual constants can easily be simulated by means of unary predicates. We further assume, also without loss of generality, that all predicates have arity 1 or 2. Finally, we assume all structures to be finite or countably infinite. If φ is a $\mathcal{C}^2$-formula, we write $\|\varphi\|$ to denote the total number of symbols in φ. Here, we assume numerical subscripts in counting quantifiers to be coded as *binary* strings. Thus, for example, the number of symbols contributed by a quantifier $\exists_{\leq C}$ is approximately $\lceil \log C \rceil$, where $\lceil r \rceil$ denotes the smallest integer greater than or equal to r. In this paper, all logarithms are base 2.

We begin with the reduction of $\mathcal{C}^2$-formulas to 'Scott-form'.

Lemma 1. *Let ψ be a $\mathcal{C}^2$-formula. We can generate, in time bounded by a polynomial function of $\|\psi\|$, a quantifier-free $\mathcal{C}^2$-formula α, a list of positive integers $C_1, \ldots, C_m$ and a list of binary predicates $f_1, \ldots, f_m$ ($m \geq 1$) such that the formulas ψ and*

$$\varphi = \forall x \forall y (\alpha \vee x \approx y) \wedge \bigwedge_{1 \leq h \leq m} \forall x \exists_{=C_h} y (f_h(x, y) \wedge x \not\approx y) \tag{1}$$

are satisfiable over the same domains containing at least $C + 1$ elements, where $C = \max_h C_h$.

Proof. Routine adaptation of the re-naming technique used in [7]. ∎

Henceforth, then, we may restrict attention to $\mathcal{C}^2$-formulas of the form (1), since the truth of ψ in a model of size C or less can evidently be checked in time bounded by an exponential function of $\|\psi\|$. In the ensuing analysis of such formulas, the binary predicates $f_1, \ldots, f_m$ will play a special role. We adopt the following (non-standard) terminology.

Definition 1. *Let Σ be a signature, and $f_1, \ldots, f_m$ ($m \geq 1$) a tuple of distinct binary predicates in Σ. The pair $\langle \Sigma, (f_1, \ldots, f_m) \rangle$ is called a* classified signature, *and the $f_1, \ldots, f_m$ are referred to as its* featured predicates.

Let Σ be a signature (not necessarily classified). We follow standard terminology, and say that a *1-type* (over Σ) is a maximal consistent set of equality-free literals over Σ involving only the variable x. Likewise, a *2-type* (over Σ) is a maximal consistent set of equality-free literals over Σ involving only the variables x and y. Reference to Σ is suppressed where clear from context. If $\mathfrak{A}$ is any structure interpreting Σ, and $a \in A$, then there exists a unique 1-type $\pi(x)$ over Σ such that $\mathfrak{A} \models \pi[a]$; we denote π by $\mathrm{tp}^{\mathfrak{A}}[a]$. If, in addition, $b \in A$ is distinct from a, then there exists a unique 2-type $\tau(x, y)$ over Σ such that $\mathfrak{A} \models \tau[a, b]$; we denote τ by $\mathrm{tp}^{\mathfrak{A}}[a, b]$. We do not define $\mathrm{tp}^{\mathfrak{A}}[a, b]$ if $a = b$. If π is a 1-type, we say that π is *realized* in $\mathfrak{A}$ if there exists $a \in A$ with $\mathrm{tp}^{\mathfrak{A}}[a] = \pi$. If τ is a 2-type, we say that τ is *realized* in $\mathfrak{A}$ if there exist distinct $a, b \in A$ with $\mathrm{tp}^{\mathfrak{A}}[a, b] = \tau$.

Notation 1. *Let τ be a 2-type over a signature Σ. The result of transposing the variables x and y in τ is also a 2-type, denoted τ^{-1}; and the set of literals in τ not featuring the variable y is a 1-type, denoted $\mathrm{tp}_1(\tau)$. We write $\mathrm{tp}_2(\tau)$ for the 1-type $\mathrm{tp}_1(\tau^{-1})$.*

Note that $\mathrm{tp}_2(\tau)$ is the result of taking the set of literals in τ not featuring the variable x, and then replacing y throughout by x.

Remark 1. If τ is any 2-type over a signature Σ, $\mathfrak{A}$ is a structure interpreting Σ, and a, b are distinct elements of A such that $\mathrm{tp}^{\mathfrak{A}}[a,b] = \tau$, then $\mathrm{tp}^{\mathfrak{A}}[b,a] = \tau^{-1}$, $\mathrm{tp}^{\mathfrak{A}}[a] = \mathrm{tp}_1(\tau)$ and $\mathrm{tp}^{\mathfrak{A}}[b] = \mathrm{tp}_2(\tau)$.

The following terminology, relating to classified signatures, is non-standard:

Definition 2. *Let $\mathfrak{A}$ be a structure interpreting a classified signature $\langle \Sigma, \bar{f} \rangle$ and C a positive integer. We say that $\mathfrak{A}$ is C-bounded if, for all $a \in A$ and all featured predicates f in $\bar{f}$,*

$$1 \leq |\{b \in A \setminus \{a\} \mid \mathfrak{A} \models f[a,b]\}| \leq C.$$

We say that $\mathfrak{A}$ is bounded *if it is C-bounded for some C.*

Thus, $\mathfrak{A}$ is C-bounded just in case, for every featured predicate f, no element of A is non-reflexively related to more than C elements of A by f, and every element of A is non-reflexively related to some element of A by f.

Remark 2. If φ is of the form (1), $C \geq \max_h C_h$ and $\mathfrak{A} \models \varphi$, then $\mathfrak{A}$ is C-bounded.

Definition 3. *Let $\langle \Sigma, \bar{f} \rangle$ be a classified signature, and let τ be a 2-type over Σ. We say that τ is a* message-type *(over Σ) if $f(x,y) \in \tau$ for some featured predicate f. If τ is a message-type such that τ^{-1} is also a message-type, we say that τ is* invertible. *On the other hand, if τ is a 2-type such that neither τ nor τ^{-1} is a message-type, we say that τ is a* silent *2-type.*

Thus, a 2-type τ is an invertible message-type if and only if there are featured predicates f and f' such that $f(x,y) \in \tau$ and $f'(y,x) \in \tau$. The terminology is meant to suggest the following imagery. Let $\mathfrak{A}$ be a structure interpreting the classified signature in question. If $\mathrm{tp}^{\mathfrak{A}}[a,b]$ is a message-type μ, then we may imagine that a sends a message (of type μ) to b. If μ is invertible, then b replies by sending a message (of type μ^{-1}) back to a. If $\mathrm{tp}^{\mathfrak{A}}[a,b]$ is silent, then neither element sends a message to the other.

3   A Result on Solutions to Integer Programming Problems

Our strategy in analysing the problems Sat-$\mathcal{C}^2$ and Fin-Sat-$\mathcal{C}^2$ is to reduce them to integer programming problems. Having done so, we shall employ a variant of a result of Eisenbrand and Shmonina [2] (also used in [6] in connection with the one-variable fragment with counting).

Lemma 2. *Let $\mathcal{E}$ be a set of m linear inequalities of the form*

$$a_0 + a_1 x_1 + \cdots + a_n x_n \le b_0 + b_1 x_1 + \cdots + b_n x_n,$$

in variables $x_1, \ldots, x_n$, where $a_0, b_0 \in \mathbb{N}$ and $a_i, b_i \in \{0,1\}$ for all i $(1 \le i \le n)$. If $\mathcal{E}$ has a solution over $\mathbb{N}$, then it has a solution over $\mathbb{N}$ in which at most $5m(\log m + 1)$ variables take non-zero values.

Proof. Routine adaptation of [6, Theorem 1]. $\square$

Notice that the bound in Lemma 2 depends only on the number of equations, and not on the number of variables, nor indeed on the sizes of the constant terms.

We need to generalize this result slightly to deal with infinite solutions.

Notation 2. *Let $\mathbb{N}^*$ denote the set $\mathbb{N} \cup \{\aleph_0\}$. We extend the ordering $>$ and the arithmetic operations $+$ and $\cdot$ from $\mathbb{N}$ to $\mathbb{N}^*$ in the obvious way. Specifically, we define $\aleph_0 > n$ for all $n \in \mathbb{N}$; we define $\aleph_0 + \aleph_0 = \aleph_0 \cdot \aleph_0 = \aleph_0$ and $0 \cdot \aleph_0 = \aleph_0 \cdot 0 = 0$; we define $n + \aleph_0 = \aleph_0 + n = \aleph_0$ for all $n \in \mathbb{N}$; and we define $n \cdot \aleph_0 = \aleph_0 \cdot n = \aleph_0$ for all $n \in \mathbb{N}$ such that $n > 0$. Under this extension, $>$ remains a total order, and $+$, $\cdot$ remain associative and commutative.*

A system of linear inequalities defining an integer programming problem can of course be re-interpreted so that solutions are sought not over $\mathbb{N}$ but over $\mathbb{N}^*$. (We always assume that the coefficients occurring in such problems are in $\mathbb{N}$.) As an example, the single inequality $x_1 \ge x_1 + 1$ has no solutions over $\mathbb{N}$, but it does have a solution over $\mathbb{N}^*$, namely, $x_1 = \aleph_0$.

Lemma 3. *Let $\mathcal{E}$ be a system of m linear inequalities as in Lemma 2. If $\mathcal{E}$ has a solution over $\mathbb{N}^*$, then $\mathcal{E}$ has a solution over $\mathbb{N}^*$ in which at most $5m(\log m + 1)$ variables take non-zero values.*

Proof. Pick some solution of $\mathcal{E}$ over $\mathbb{N}^*$, and list those inequalities whose right-hand sides are infinite for this solution. For each such inequality, pick one variable x_i with infinite value whose coefficient b_i is 1. By re-ordering the variables if necessary, let $x_1, \ldots, x_k$ be the selected variables, $x_{k+1}, \ldots, x_\ell$ the other variables taking infinite values, and $x_{\ell+1}, \ldots, x_n$ the variables taking finite values. Let $\mathcal{E}'$ be the set of inequalities in $\mathcal{E}$ whose right- (and therefore left-) hand sides are finite for the given solution. Clearly, the coefficients $a_1, \ldots, a_\ell$ and $b_1, \ldots, b_\ell$ are all zero for these inequalities. Assuming $\ell < m$, $\mathcal{E}'$ therefore has a solution $(0, \ldots, 0, x'_{\ell+1}, \ldots, x'_n)$ over $\mathbb{N}$ with at most $5(m-\ell)(\log(m-\ell)+1)$ non-zero values. But then $(\aleph_0, \ldots, \aleph_0, 0, \ldots, 0, x'_{\ell+1}, \ldots, x'_n)$, with k $\aleph_0$s, is a solution for $\mathcal{E}$. $\square$

4   The Main Result

The principal challenge in establishing upper complexity bounds for Sat-$\mathcal{C}^2$ and Fin-Sat-$\mathcal{C}^2$ consists in the very general nature of the structures we must work with. The following two notions help to reduce this generality slightly.

Definition 4. *Let $\mathfrak{A}$ be a structure interpreting a classified signature $\langle \Sigma, \bar{f} \rangle$. We say that $\mathfrak{A}$ is* chromatic *if, for all $a, a', a'' \in A$:*

1. *if $a \neq a'$ and $\mathrm{tp}^{\mathfrak{A}}[a, a']$ is an invertible message-type, then $\mathrm{tp}^{\mathfrak{A}}[a] \neq \mathrm{tp}^{\mathfrak{A}}[a']$; and*
2. *if a, a', a'' are all distinct and both $\mathrm{tp}^{\mathfrak{A}}[a, a']$ and $\mathrm{tp}^{\mathfrak{A}}[a', a'']$ are invertible message-types, then $\mathrm{tp}^{\mathfrak{A}}[a] \neq \mathrm{tp}^{\mathfrak{A}}[a'']$.*

Thus, a structure is chromatic just in case distinct elements connected by a chain of 1 or 2 invertible message-types always have distinct 1-types.

Remark 3. Let $\mathfrak{A}$ be a chromatic structure interpreting a classified signature $\langle \Sigma, \bar{f} \rangle$, and let π' be a 1-type over Σ. Let a be an element of A. Then there is at most one element $a' \in A \setminus \{a\}$ with 1-type π' such that a sends an invertible message to a'. Furthermore, if $\mathrm{tp}^{\mathfrak{A}}[a] = \pi'$, then there is no such element a'.

Definition 5. *Let $\mathfrak{A}$ be a structure interpreting a signature Σ, and Z a positive integer. We say that $\mathfrak{A}$ is Z-differentiated if, for every 1-type π over Σ, the number u of elements in A having 1-type π satisfies either $u \leq 1$ or $u > Z$.*

Thus, in a Z-differentiated structure, every 1-type is realized either at most once or more than Z times (possibly infinitely often).

The following lemmas have straightforward proofs [5, Lemmas 2 and 3].

Lemma 4. *Let $\mathfrak{A}$ be a C-bounded structure interpreting a classified signature $\langle \Sigma, \bar{f} \rangle$, and $m = |\bar{f}|$. Then $\mathfrak{A}$ can be expanded to a chromatic structure $\mathfrak{A}'$ by interpreting $\lceil \log((mC)^2 + 1) \rceil$ new unary predicates.*

Lemma 5. *Let $\mathfrak{A}$ be a chromatic structure interpreting a classified signature $\langle \Sigma, \bar{f} \rangle$, and Z a positive integer. Let Σ' be the signature obtained by adding $\lceil \log Z \rceil$ new unary predicates to Σ. Then $\mathfrak{A}$ can be expanded to a chromatic, Z-differentiated structure interpreting the classified signature $\langle \Sigma', \bar{f} \rangle$.*

Our next task is to acquire the means to talk about 'local configurations' in bounded structures interpreting a classified signature.

Notation 3. *Fix a classified signature $\langle \Sigma, \bar{f} \rangle$ with $\bar{f} = (f_1, \ldots, f_m)$ and $|\Sigma| = s$. We assume a standard enumeration*

$$\pi_1, \ldots, \pi_L$$

of the 1-types over Σ, with arbitrary ordering, where $L = 2^s$. We likewise assume a standard enumeration

$$\mu_1, \ldots, \mu_{M^*}, \mu_{M^*+1}, \ldots, \mu_M,$$

of the message-types over $\langle \Sigma, \bar{f} \rangle$, where $\mu_1, \ldots, \mu_{M^*}$ are the invertible message-types, and $\mu_{M^*+1}, \ldots, \mu_M$ the non-invertible message-types. (Otherwise, the ordering in this enumeration is again arbitrary.)

Table 1. Quick reference guide to symbols used in connection with a classified signature $\langle \Sigma, \bar{f} \rangle$

s	the number of symbols in Σ
$\pi_1, \ldots, \pi_L$	the 1-types over Σ
$\mu_1, \ldots, \mu_{M^*}$	the invertible message-types over $\langle \Sigma, \bar{f} \rangle$
$\mu_{M^*+1}, \ldots, \mu_M$	the non-invertible message-types over $\langle \Sigma, \bar{f} \rangle$
$\sigma_1, \ldots, \sigma_N$	the C-bounded star-types over $\langle \Sigma, \bar{f} \rangle$

The above notation, which will be used throughout this section, is summarized in the first four rows of Table 1. We remark that $M \leq m2^{4s-1}$.

Definition 6. *Let $\mathfrak{A}$ be a bounded structure interpreting a classified signature $\langle \Sigma, \bar{f} \rangle$, and let a be an element of A. The star-type of a in $\mathfrak{A}$, denoted $\mathrm{st}^{\mathfrak{A}}[a]$, is the M-tuple $\sigma = (v_1, \ldots, v_M)$ of natural numbers where, for all j $(1 \leq j \leq M)$,*

$$v_j = |\{b \in A \setminus \{a\} : \mathrm{tp}^{\mathfrak{A}}[a, b] = \mu_j\}|.$$

Evidently, σ satisfies the condition

$$v_j > 0 \text{ implies } \mathrm{tp}_1(\mu_j) = \mathrm{tp}^{\mathfrak{A}}[a],$$

for all j $(1 \leq j \leq M)$. Accordingly, we take a star-type over $\langle \Sigma, \bar{f} \rangle$ to be any M-tuple σ of natural numbers satisfying the condition

$$v_j > 0 \text{ and } v_{j'} > 0 \text{ implies } \mathrm{tp}_1(\mu_j) = \mathrm{tp}_1(\mu_{j'}),$$

for all j, j' $(1 \leq j < j' \leq M)$. We denote the number v_j by $\sigma[j]$, for all j $(1 \leq j \leq M)$. A bounded structure $\mathfrak{A}$ is said to realize a star-type σ if, for some $a \in A$, $\mathrm{st}^{\mathfrak{A}}[a] = \sigma$.

Thus, $\mathrm{st}^{\mathfrak{A}}[a]$ is a description of a's 'local environment' in $\mathfrak{A}$. We remark that, if $\mathfrak{A}$ is not bounded, and $a \in A$, then the cardinalities $|\{b \in A \setminus \{a\} : \mathrm{tp}^{\mathfrak{A}}[a, b] = \mu_j\}|$ may be infinite. For this reason, we restrict attention to bounded structures when talking about star-types of elements.

Certain important characteristics of bounded structures depend only on the star-types they realize.

Definition 7. *Let $\langle \Sigma, \bar{f} \rangle$ be a classified signature, with $\bar{f} = (f_1, \ldots, f_m)$, and let σ be a star-type over $\langle \Sigma, \bar{f} \rangle$. We say that σ is C-bounded, for $C > 0$, if for all h $(1 \leq h \leq m)$,*

$$1 \leq \sum \{v_j \mid 1 \leq j \leq M \text{ and } f_h(x, y) \in \mu_j\} \leq C.$$

Furthermore, we say that σ is chromatic if, for every 1-type π' over Σ, the sum

$$c = \sum \{v_j \mid 1 \leq j \leq M^* \text{ and } \mathrm{tp}_2(\mu_j) = \pi'\}$$

satisfies $c \leq 1$, and satisfies $c = 0$ if $\pi' = \pi$.

Lemma 6. *Let $\mathfrak{A}$ be a bounded structure interpreting a classified signature $\langle \Sigma, \bar{f} \rangle$. Then $\mathfrak{A}$ is C-bounded if and only if every star-type realized in $\mathfrak{A}$ is C-bounded. Furthermore, $\mathfrak{A}$ is chromatic if and only if every star-type realized in $\mathfrak{A}$ is chromatic.*

Proof. Immediate once the definitions are unravelled.

The important point about C-bounded star-types over a finite classified signature $\langle \Sigma, \bar{f} \rangle$ is that there are only finitely many of them. Indeed, for a given $\langle \Sigma, \bar{f} \rangle$, and given C, we may enumerate them in a standard way as

$$\sigma_1, \ldots, \sigma_N, \tag{2}$$

just as we did with the 1-types and message-types (Table 1). Simple calculation shows that $N \leq (C+1)^M$, where M is the number of message-types. It is easy to see that N is in general doubly-exponential in $s = |\Sigma|$; however, the results of Section 3 will ensure that this is no problem. Beware that the listing (2) depends on the bound C of the star-types in question: this parameter is left implicit to reduce notational clutter.

Having obtained characterizations of 'local environments' in structures interpreting classified signatures, we turn our attention to larger-scale aspects of those structures. We begin by considering the special role played by silent 2-types.

Definition 8. *Let $\langle \Sigma, \bar{f} \rangle$ be a classified signature. Define $\Pi^{(2)}$ to be the set of unordered pairs of (not-necessarily distinct) 1-types over Σ:*

$$\Pi^{(2)} = \{\{\pi, \pi'\} \mid \pi, \pi' \text{ 1-types over } \Sigma\}.$$

We call an element of $\Pi^{(2)}$ a quiet pair *(in $\mathfrak{A}$) if there exist distinct $a, a' \in A$ with $\mathrm{tp}^{\mathfrak{A}}[a] = \pi$ and $\mathrm{tp}^{\mathfrak{A}}[a'] = \pi'$, such that the 2-type $\mathrm{tp}^{\mathfrak{A}}[a, a']$ is silent.*

Quiet pairs can always be found in structures with populous 1-types [5, Lemma 4]:

Lemma 7. *Let $\mathfrak{A}$ be a C-bounded structure interpreting a classified signature $\langle \Sigma, \bar{f} \rangle$, and $m = |\bar{f}|$. Suppose that π and π' are 1-types over Σ (not necessarily distinct), both realized in $\mathfrak{A}$ more than $(mC+1)^2$ times. Then $\{\pi, \pi'\}$ is a quiet pair.*

For the purpose of determining satisfiability of $\mathcal{C}^2$-formulas, we can afford to be somewhat relaxed about the silent 2-types any putative model realizes.

Definition 9. *Let $\langle \Sigma, \bar{f} \rangle$ be a classified signature, $\Pi^{(2)}$ the set of unordered pairs of 1-types over Σ, and Ξ the set of silent 2-types over $\langle \Sigma, \bar{f} \rangle$. A* regulator *over $\langle \Sigma, \bar{f} \rangle$ is a partial function $\theta :\subseteq \Pi^{(2)} \to \Xi$ such that*

$$\{\mathrm{tp}_1(\theta(\{\pi, \pi'\})), \mathrm{tp}_2(\theta(\{\pi, \pi'\}))\} = \{\pi, \pi'\},$$

for every $\{\pi, \pi'\} \in \mathrm{dom}(\theta)$. Further, let $\mathfrak{A}$ be a structure interpreting $\langle \Sigma, \bar{f} \rangle$. We say that θ is a regulator for $\mathfrak{A}$, *if $\mathrm{dom}(\theta)$ is the set of quiet pairs in $\mathfrak{A}$, and for every $\{\pi, \pi'\}$ in this set, and any pair of distinct $a, a' \in A$ with $\mathrm{tp}^{\mathfrak{A}}[a] = \pi$, $\mathrm{tp}^{\mathfrak{A}}[a'] = \pi'$ and $\mathrm{tp}^{\mathfrak{A}}[a, a']$ silent, either $\mathrm{tp}^{\mathfrak{A}}[a, a'] = \theta(\{\pi, \pi'\})$ or $\mathrm{tp}^{\mathfrak{A}}[a', a] = \theta(\{\pi, \pi'\})$. Finally, we call $\mathfrak{A}$* regular *if it has a regulator.*

Roughly, a regular structure $\mathfrak{A}$ is one in which, for any quiet pair $\{\pi, \pi'\}$, we can identify a silent 2-type, $\theta(\{\pi, \pi'\})$, that relates—in one direction or the other— *all* the pairs of distinct elements a and a' having respective 1-types π and π' such that $\text{tp}^{\mathfrak{A}}[a, a']$ is silent.

Lemma 8. *Let φ be any formula of the form (1) over a signature Σ, let $\bar{f} = (f_1, \ldots, f_m)$, and suppose $\mathfrak{A}$ is a structure over the classified signature $\langle \Sigma, \bar{f} \rangle$ such that $\mathfrak{A} \models \varphi$. Then there exists a regular structure $\mathfrak{B}$ over $\langle \Sigma, \bar{f} \rangle$ with the same domain, such that $\mathfrak{B} \models \varphi$. Moreover if $\mathfrak{A}$ is chromatic (Z-differentiated, for some $Z > 0$), then so is $\mathfrak{B}$.*

Proof. Consider any quiet pair $\{\pi, \pi'\}$ in $\mathfrak{A}$, and pick distinct b, b' such that $\text{tp}^{\mathfrak{A}}[b] = \pi$ and $\text{tp}^{\mathfrak{A}}[b'] = \pi'$, with $\xi = \text{tp}^{\mathfrak{A}}[b, b']$ silent. Suppose now that there exist distinct $a, a' \in A$ such that $\text{tp}^{\mathfrak{A}}[a] = \pi$ and $\text{tp}^{\mathfrak{A}}[a'] = \pi'$, but $\text{tp}^{\mathfrak{A}}[a, a'] \neq \xi$ and $\text{tp}^{\mathfrak{A}}[a', a] \neq \xi$. Let us alter $\mathfrak{A}$ to obtain a model $\mathfrak{A}'$ (say) by setting $\text{tp}^{\mathfrak{A}'}[a, a'] = \text{tp}^{\mathfrak{A}}[b, b']$; evidently, $\mathfrak{A}' \models \varphi$. Carrying out this transformation uniformly yields the required model $\mathfrak{B}$.

With the above apparatus at our disposal, we are in a position to characterize entire structures in terms of the patterns of local configurations they exhibit.

Definition 10. *Let $\langle \Sigma, \bar{f} \rangle$ be a classified signature, C a positive integer, and $\sigma_1, \ldots, \sigma_N$ the standard enumeration of C-bounded star-types over $\langle \Sigma, \bar{f} \rangle$. A frame is a quintuple $\mathcal{F} = \langle \Sigma, \bar{f}, C, K, \theta \rangle$, where K is a non-empty subset of $\{1, \ldots, N\}$, and θ is a regulator over $\langle \Sigma, \bar{f} \rangle$. We call $\mathcal{F}$ chromatic if every σ_k ($k \in K$) is chromatic. Further, let $\mathfrak{A}$ be a bounded structure interpreting $\langle \Sigma, \bar{f} \rangle$. We say that $\mathcal{F}$ describes $\mathfrak{A}$ just in case $\{\sigma_k \mid k \in K\}$ is exactly the set of star-types realized in $\mathfrak{A}$, and θ is a regulator for $\mathfrak{A}$.*

Lemma 9. *Let $\mathfrak{A}$ be a C-bounded regular structure over a classified signature $\langle \Sigma, \bar{f} \rangle$. Then $\mathfrak{A}$ is described by a frame of the form $\mathcal{F} = \langle \Sigma, \bar{f}, C, K, \theta \rangle$. Further, if $\mathfrak{A}$ is chromatic, then so is $\mathcal{F}$.*

Proof. Lemma 6.

Let φ be a formula of the form (1). If $\mathcal{F}$ describes $\mathfrak{A}$, then $\mathcal{F}$ contains all the information needed to determine whether $\mathfrak{A} \models \varphi$:

Definition 11. *Let φ be any formula of the form (1) over a signature Σ, let $\bar{f} = (f_1, \ldots, f_m)$, and let $\mathcal{F} = \langle \Sigma, \bar{f}, C, K, \theta \rangle$ be a frame, where $C > C_h$ for all h ($1 \leq h \leq m$). We write $\mathcal{F} \models \varphi$ if the following conditions are satisfied:*

1. *for all $k \in K$ and all j ($1 \leq j \leq M$), if $\sigma_k[j] > 0$ then $\models \bigwedge \mu_j \to \alpha(x, y) \wedge \alpha(y, x)$;*
2. *for all $k \in K$ and all h ($1 \leq h \leq m$), the sum of all the $\sigma_k[j]$ ($1 \leq j \leq M$) such that $f_h(x, y) \in \mu_j$ equals C_h.*
3. *for all $\{\pi, \pi'\} \in \text{dom}(\theta)$, $\models \bigwedge \theta(\pi, \pi') \to \alpha(x, y) \wedge \alpha(y, x)$.*

Lemma 10. *Let φ, $\mathcal{F}$ be as in Definition 11, and suppose $\mathfrak{A}$ is a bounded structure over $\langle \Sigma, \bar{f} \rangle$ such that $\mathcal{F}$ describes $\mathfrak{A}$. Then $\mathfrak{A} \models \varphi$ if and only if $\mathcal{F} \models \varphi$.*

Proof. Immediate once the definitions are unravelled.

Lemma 9 tells us that every bounded regular structure is described by some frame. However not every frame describes a structure; and it is important for us to define a class of frames which do. The following notation will prove useful to this end.

Notation 4. *Let $\langle \Sigma, \bar{f} \rangle$ be a classified signature and $C > 0$. With reference to the standard enumerations of Table 1, and, for integers i, k in the ranges $1 \leq i \leq L$, $1 \leq k \leq N$, we write:*

$$o_{ik} = \begin{cases} 1 & \text{if, for some } j \ (1 \leq j \leq M), \ \sigma_k[j] > 0 \ \text{and} \ \mathrm{tp}_1(\mu_j) = \pi_i \\ 0 & \text{otherwise;} \end{cases}$$

$$p_{ik} = \begin{cases} 1 & \text{if, for all } j \ (1 \leq j \leq M), \ \mathrm{tp}_2(\mu_j) = \pi_i \ \text{implies} \ \sigma_k[j] = 0 \\ 0 & \text{otherwise;} \end{cases}$$

$$r_{ik} = \sum_{j \in J} \sigma_k[j], \ \text{where } J = \{j \mid M^* + 1 \leq j \leq M \ \text{and} \ \mathrm{tp}_2(\mu_j) = \pi_i\};$$

$$s_{ik} = \sum_{j \in J} \sigma_k[j], \ \text{where } J = \{j \mid 1 \leq j \leq M \ \text{and} \ \mathrm{tp}_2(\mu_j) = \pi_i\}.$$

In addition, for integers i, j in the ranges $1 \leq i \leq L$, $1 \leq j \leq M^*$, we write:

$$q_{jk} = \sigma_k[j].$$

To understand the meanings of these constants, suppose $\mathfrak{A}$ is a C-bounded structure interpreting $\langle \Sigma, \bar{f} \rangle$. Then, for all i, j and k in the appropriate ranges:

1. $o_{ik} = 1$ just in case every element with star-type σ_k has 1-type π_i;
2. $p_{ik} = 1$ just in case no element with star-type σ_k sends a message to any element having 1-type π_i;
3. q_{jk} counts how many messages of (invertible) type μ_j any element having star-type σ_k sends;
4. r_{ik} is the total number of elements having 1-type π_i to which any element having star-type σ_k sends a non-invertible message; and
5. s_{ik} is the total number of elements having 1-type π_i to which any element having star-type σ_k sends a message.

The following notion now gives us a way of providing a 'statistical summary' of structures. Recall the extended natural numbers introduced in Notation 2.

Definition 12. *Let $\langle \Sigma, \bar{f} \rangle$ be a classified signature, C a positive integer, and $\mathfrak{A}$ a C-bounded structure interpreting $\langle \Sigma, \bar{f} \rangle$. Let $\sigma_1, \ldots, \sigma_N$ be the standard enumeration of the C-bounded star-types. The C-histogram of $\mathfrak{A}$ is the N-tuple $\mathrm{Hist}_C(\mathfrak{A}) = (w_1, \ldots, w_N)$ of elements of $\mathbb{N}^*$, where, for all k $(1 \leq k \leq N)$,*

$$w_k = |\{a \in A : \mathrm{st}^{\mathfrak{A}}[a] = \sigma_k\}|.$$

The following notation will be useful when talking about (putative) histograms of structures.

Notation 5. *Fix some frame $\mathcal{F}$ (and hence the associated constants of Notation 4), and let $w_1, \ldots, w_N$ be variables. We employ the letters u_i ($1 \leq i \leq L$), v_j ($1 \leq j \leq M^*$) and $x_{ii'}$ ($1 \leq i \leq L$, $1 \leq i' \leq L$) as shorthand for the following expressions:*

$$u_i = \sum_{1 \leq k \leq N} o_{ik} w_k \qquad v_j = \sum_{1 \leq k \leq N} q_{jk} w_k \qquad x_{ii'} = \sum_{1 \leq k \leq N} o_{ik} p_{i'k} w_k.$$

To understand the meanings of these expressions, suppose first that $\mathfrak{A}$ is a bounded, regular structure, described by $\mathcal{F} = \langle \Sigma, \bar{f}, C, K, \theta \rangle$, and that $\text{Hist}_C(\mathfrak{A}) = (w_1, \ldots, w_N)$. Then

1. u_i is the number of elements $a \in A$ such that $\text{tp}^{\mathfrak{A}}[a] = \pi_i$;
2. v_j is the number of pairs $\langle a, b \rangle \in A^2$ such that $a \neq b$ and $\text{tp}^{\mathfrak{A}}[a, b] = \mu_j$;
3. $x_{ii'}$ is the number of elements $a \in A$ such that $\text{tp}^{\mathfrak{A}}[a] = \pi_i$ and a does not send a message to any element having 1-type $\pi_{i'}$.

We can now give our long-awaited criterion for a frame to describe a structure.

Definition 13. *Let $\mathcal{F} = \langle \Sigma, \bar{f}, C, K, \theta \rangle$ be a frame, Z a positive integer, $m = |\bar{f}|$, and L, M^*, M, N the constants defined in Table 1. A Z-solution of $\mathcal{F}$ is an N-tuple $\bar{w} = (w_1, \ldots, w_N)$ of elements of $\mathbb{N}^*$ such that, for all k ($1 \leq k \leq N$), $w_k > 0$ if and only if $k \in K$, and such that the following conditions are satisfied for all i ($1 \leq i \leq L$), all i' ($1 \leq i' \leq L$), and all j ($1 \leq j \leq M^*$):*

(C1) $v_j = v_{j'}$, where j' is such that $\mu_j^{-1} = \mu_{j'}$;

(C2) if $u_i = 0$, then $\sum\{w_k \mid s_{ik} > 0\} = 0$; if $u_i = 1$, then $\sum\{w_k \mid s_{ik} > 1\} = 0$;

(C3) $u_i \leq 1$ or $u_i > Z$;

(C4) if $u_i \leq 1$, then for all positive integers $D \leq mC$, we have either $x_{i'i} \geq D$ or $\sum\{w_k \mid o_{ik} = 1 \text{ and } r_{i'k} \geq D\} = 0$;

(C5) if $\{\pi_i, \pi_{i'}\} \notin \text{dom}(\theta)$, then either $u_i \leq 1$ or $u_{i'} \leq 1$;

(C6) if $\{\pi_i, \pi_{i'}\} \notin \text{dom}(\theta)$, then for all positive integers $D \leq mC$, we have either $x_{i'i} \leq D$ or $\sum\{w_k \mid o_{ik} = 1 \text{ and } r_{i'k} \leq D\} = 0$.

We say that $\bar{w}$ is finite if each of its elements is in $\mathbb{N}$. If $\mathcal{F}$ has a (finite) Z-solution, we say that $\mathcal{F}$ is (finitely) Z-solvable.

Remark 4. Noting that the constants $r_{i'k}$ in Definition 13 are bounded by mC, we see that conditions **(C4)** and **(C6)** may be more simply formulated as the collections of conditions

(C4*) if $o_{ik} = 1$ and $u_i \leq 1$, then $r_{i'k} \leq x_{i'i}$;

(C6*) if $\{\pi_i, \pi_{i'}\} \notin \text{dom}(\theta)$ and $o_{ik} = 1$, then $r_{i'k} \geq x_{i'i}$,

respectively, for all i ($1 \leq i \leq L$), i' ($1 \leq i' \leq L$) and k ($1 \leq k \leq N$). The reason for the rather awkward formulation adopted above will emerge presently.

The two main lemmas of this section may now be stated. They tell us that, for sufficiently large Z, we may treat (finitely) Z-solvable, chromatic frames as substitutes for (finite) bounded, Z-differentiated chromatic structures.

Lemma 11. *Let $\mathcal{F} = \langle \Sigma, \bar{f}, C, K, \theta \rangle$ be a frame, $m = |\bar{f}|$, and $Z \geq (mC+1)^2$ be an integer. If $\mathfrak{A}$ is a (finite) bounded, Z-differentiated, structure described by $\mathcal{F}$, then $\mathrm{Hist}_C(\mathfrak{A})$ is a (finite) Z-solution for $\mathcal{F}$.*

Proof (Sketch). See [5, Lemma 13] for full details. It is a routine matter to check the conditions **(C1)**–**(C6)**. Observe that condition **(C3)** is immediate from the assumption that $\mathfrak{A}$ is Z-differentiated. We note in addition that the same assumption may be used in conjunction with Lemma 7 (of this paper) to show that condition **(C5)** obtains. For suppose $\{\pi_i, \pi_{i'}\} \notin \mathrm{dom}(\theta)$. Since $\mathcal{F}$ describes $\mathfrak{A}$, $\{\pi_i, \pi_{i'}\}$ cannot be a quiet pair; hence either $u_i \leq Z$ or $u_{i'} \leq Z$; whence $u_i \leq 1$ or $u_{i'} \leq 1$.

Lemma 12. *Let $\mathcal{F} = \langle \Sigma, \bar{f}, C, K, \theta \rangle$ be a chromatic frame, $m = |\bar{f}|$, and $Z \geq 3mC$ be an integer. If $\mathcal{F}$ has a (finite) Z-solution, then there exists a (finite) bounded structure $\mathfrak{A}$ such that $\mathcal{F}$ describes $\mathfrak{A}$.*

Proof (Sketch). See [5, Lemma 14] for full details. For every $k \in K$, let A_k be a set of cardinality w_k, and let A be the disjoint union of the A_k. We imagine A_k as a set of elements having star-type σ_k, and show that, under the conditions **(C1)**–**(C6)**, these star-type instances can be assembled into a well-defined model $\mathfrak{A}$ with domain A. The construction depends crucially on the assumptions that the frame $\mathcal{F}$ is chromatic, and that condition **(C3)** obtains.

The next lemma tells us that, if Z-solvability is what interests us, we may restrict attention to small frames:

Lemma 13. *Let Z be a positive integer, $\mathcal{F}' = \langle \Sigma, \bar{f}, C, K', \theta \rangle$ a (finitely) Z-solvable frame, $m = |\bar{f}|$ and $s = |\Sigma|$. Then there exists a non-empty $K \subseteq K'$ such that the frame $\mathcal{F} = \langle \Sigma, \bar{f}, C, K, \theta \rangle$ is also (finitely) Z-solvable, and $|K| \leq p(mC)2^{p(s)}$, where p is a fixed polynomial.*

Proof. There are fixed polynomials p', q' such that $p'(mC)2^{q'(s)}$ bounds the number of equations **(C1)**–**(C6)** in Definition 13. (Note that this claim would in general be false if we had replaced **(C4)** and **(C6)** by their simpler variants, **(C4*)** and **(C6*)**.) By Lemmas 2 and 3, there is a polynomial p such that $\mathcal{F}$ has a (finite) solution $w_1, \ldots, w_N$ with at most $p(mC)2^{p(s)}$ non-zero values (but not none). Now let $K = \{k \in K' | w_k \neq 0\}$.

It is well known that the problem of determining whether a system $\mathcal{E}$ of linear inequalities has a solution over $\mathbb{N}$ is NPTIME-complete [1], and similarly for solutions over $\mathbb{N}^*$. Indeed, if $\mathcal{E}$ has a solution over $\mathbb{N}$, then it has a solution whose size (measured in terms of the number of bits required) is bounded by a polynomial function of the total number of bits used to encode $\mathcal{E}$.

Theorem 1. *The problems Sat-$\mathcal{C}^2$ and Fin-Sat-$\mathcal{C}^2$ are in* NEXPTIME.

Proof. Let a $\mathcal{C}^2$-formula ψ be given. By Lemma 1, we may compute a formula φ of the form (1) in polynomial time, such that φ and ψ are satisfiable over the same domains of size greater than $C = \max(\{C_h | 1 \leq h \leq m\})$. Let $Z = (mC + 1)^2$: note that $Z \geq (mC)^2 + 1$, and also $Z \geq 3mC$. Let Σ be the signature of φ together with $2\lceil \log(Z) \rceil$ new unary predicates, and let $\bar{f} = (f_1, \ldots, f_m)$. Thus $\langle \Sigma, \bar{f} \rangle$ is a classified signature. Write $s = |\Sigma|$.

We claim that φ is (finitely) satisfiable if and only if there exists a chromatic (finitely) Z-solvable frame $\mathcal{F} = \langle \Sigma, \bar{f}, C, K, \theta \rangle$ such that $|K| \leq p(mC)2^{p(s)}$ and $\mathcal{F} \models \varphi$, where p is some fixed polynomial, independent of φ. Suppose first that φ has a (finite) model $\mathfrak{A}'$. Evidently, $\mathfrak{A}'$ is C-bounded. By Lemmas 4, 5 and 8, φ has a (finite) C-bounded, chromatic, Z-differentiated, regular model $\mathfrak{A}$ over $\langle \Sigma, \bar{f} \rangle$. By Lemma 9, there exists a chromatic frame $\mathcal{F} = \langle \Sigma, \bar{f}, C, K, \theta \rangle$ describing $\mathfrak{A}$; by Lemma 10, $\mathcal{F} \models \varphi$; and by Lemma 11, $\mathcal{F}$ has a (finite) Z-solution. Taking p to be the fixed polynomial of Lemma 13, we may assume without loss of generality that $|K| \leq p(mC)2^{p(s)}$. Conversely, suppose that $\mathcal{F} = \langle \Sigma, \bar{f}, K, C, \theta \rangle$ is a chromatic frame such that $\mathcal{F} \models \varphi$, and $\mathcal{F}$ has a (finite) Z-solution. By Lemma 12, there exists a (finite) structure $\mathfrak{A}$ such that $\mathcal{F}$ describes $\mathfrak{A}$, and by Lemma 10, $\mathfrak{A} \models \varphi$.

Consider the following non-deterministic procedure, where q_1, q_2 and q_3 are fixed polynomials, and $n = \|\varphi\|$.

1. Guess a chromatic frame $\mathcal{F} = \langle \Sigma, \bar{f}, C, K, \theta \rangle$ with $|K| \leq 2^{q_1(n)}$ and check that $\mathcal{F} \models \varphi$;
2. Guess a system of at most $2^{q_2(n)}$ linear inequalities $\mathcal{E}$ (propositionally) entailing the conditions **(C1)**–**(C6)** for $\mathcal{F}$ to have a Z-solution.
3. Guess a tuple $\bar{w}$ of elements of $\mathbb{N}^*$ whose size (number of bits) is bounded by $2^{q_3(n)}$.
4. If $\bar{w}$ is a solution for $\mathcal{E}$, succeed; else fail.

For all polynomials q_1, q_2 and q_3, this procedure runs in time bounded by an exponential function of $\|\varphi\|$. But the claim of the previous paragraph shows that, for suitable q_1, q_2 and q_3, it has a successfully terminating run if and only φ is satisfiable. This proves that Sat-$\mathcal{C}^2$ is in NEXPTIME. To do the same for Fin-Sat-$\mathcal{C}^2$, we simply modify line 3 to insist that $\bar{w}$ be a tuple of natural numbers.

It is well known that the satisfiability (= finite satisfiability) problem for the two-variable fragment of first-order logic *without* counting quantifiers is already NEXPTIME-hard. Thus, the NEXPTIME bound of Theorem 1 is tight.

Corollary 1. *Let φ be a formula of $\mathcal{C}^2$. If φ is finitely satisfiable, then it is satisfiable in a structure of size bounded by a doubly exponential function of $\|\varphi\|$.*

Proof. In the proof of Theorem 1, if the system $\mathcal{E}$ of equations in line 3 of the procedure has a solution over $\mathbb{N}$, then it has a solution every element of which has size (number of bits) bounded by a polynomial function of $\|\mathcal{E}\|$, and hence by a singly exponential function of $\|\varphi\|$.

It was shown in [3] that there exists a sequence $\{\varphi_n\}$ of finitely satisfiable $\mathcal{C}^2$-formulas where $\|\varphi_n\|$ is bounded above by a polynomial function of n, but the size of the smallest model of φ_n is bounded below by 2^{2^n}. Thus, the doubly-exponential bound of Corollary 1 is tight.

Acknowledgment

The author is indebted to Dr. Yevgeny Kazakov for helpful discussions on the topic of this paper.

References

1. Borosh, I., Treybig, L.: Bounds on the positive integral solutions of linear Diophantine equations. Proceedings of the American Mathematical Society 55(2), 299–304 (1976)
2. Eisenbrand, F., Shmonina, G.: Carathéodory bounds for integer cones. Operations Research Letters 34(5), 564–568 (2006)
3. Grädel, E., Otto, M., Rosen, E.: Two-variable logic with counting is decidable. In: Proceedings of the 12th IEEE Symposium on Logic in Computer Science, pp. 306–317. IEEE Online Publications (1997)
4. Pacholski, L., Szwast, W., Tendera, L.: Complexity results for first-order two-variable logic with counting. SIAM Journal on Computing 29(4), 1083–1117 (1999)
5. Pratt-Hartmann, I.: Complexity of the two-variable fragment with counting quantifiers. Journal of Logic, Language and Information 14, 369–395 (2005)
6. Pratt-Hartmann, I.: On the computational complexity of the numerically definite syllogistic and related logics. Bulletin of Symbolic Logic 14(1), 1–28 (2008)
7. Scott, D.: A decision method for validity of sentences in two variables. Journal of Symbolic Logic 27, 477 (1962)

Intuitionistic Logic and Computability Theory

Sebastiaan A. Terwijn

Radboud University Nijmegen
Department of Mathematics
P.O. Box 9010
6500 GL Nijmegen
The Netherlands
terwijn@math.ru.nl

1 Tutorial 1: Intuitionistic Logic

In this first tutorial we review the basics of intuitionistic logic. We start with L. E. J. Brouwer's philosophy of mathematics, intuitionism, and the subsequent formalization by Heyting [1] of its underlying logic. The Brouwer–Heyting–Kolmogorov interpretation is an informal manner (in fact consisting of various ideas lumped together) of motivating the formal rules of deduction in this logic. Heytings formalization in 1930 was quickly followed by the birth of the theory of computation in the 1930's, and it was immediately suggested that the two should be combined. Kleene's realizability interpretation [3] was one such attempt, that later turned out to be a very useful tool in studying constructive logic in all sorts of ways (cf. [6] for a recent treatment). We discuss the various semantics for intuitionistic logic, and give some necessary lattice-theoretic background on Heyting algebras. We also discuss the principles of intuitionistic provability, that are still not completely understood, in contrast to the classical case. The concept of admissible rule, not very useful classically, is crucial here (cf. [2]).

2 Tutorial 2: Computability Theory

In this second tutorial we briefly review the basic notions of computability theory, viz. the notion of computable function, Turing reducibility and relativization, c.e. sets and the arithmetical hierarchy. We point out some of the basic connections between these and proof-theoretic notions such as arithmetical provability. We discuss continuous functions of the reals and the way these are related to the notion of computable functional. Computable functionals play an important part in relating intuitionistic logic to computability. Finally we discuss Π_1^0-classes, that is, set of reals definable by computable trees. These play a central role in computability theory, and are also connected to the topic of these lectures. Most of this background material can be found in [11].

A. Dawar and R. de Queiroz (Eds.): WoLLIC 2010, LNAI 6188, pp. 55–57, 2010.

3   Computability Theoretic Interpretations of Intuitionistic Logic

In this talk we discuss some of the more recent developments in the area between intuitionistic logic and the theory of computation, in particular the relation with the Medvedev and Muchnik lattices. In a sketchy paper, Kolmogorov [4] suggested to interpret the intuitionistic propositional calculus IPC as a "calculus of problems". Later Medvedev investigated several ways in which this could be made precise, and introduced the lattice that now bears his name [5]. Sorbi [9] is a nice survey paper about the Medvedev lattice. Although initially this approach was unsuccessful in capturing IPC, later work of Skvortsova [7] showed that it could be made to work after all. We explain Skvortsova's result, which is a culmination of ideas from proof theory, lattice theory, and computability, and we discuss recent work with Sorbi [10] about the extent of this approach.

The Medvedev and Muchnik lattices are also of independent interest in the study of computational properties of sets of reals. Both lattices can be seen as generalizations of the Turing degrees, going from singletons to arbitrary sets of reals. In particular the notions of Medvedev and Muchnik reducibility have been applied in recent years to the study of Π_1^0-classes, following work of Simpson (cf. e.g. [8]). We also discuss connections between this topic and intuitionistic logic, and in particular the role played by the set of complete extensions of Peano Arithmetic [12].

References

1. Heyting, A.: Die formalen Regeln der intuitionistischen Logik. Sitzungsberichte der Preussisischen Akademie von Wissenschaften, Physikalisch-mathematische Klasse, 42–56 (1930)
2. Iemhoff, R.: On the rules of intermediate logics. Archive for Mathematical Logic 45(5), 581–599 (2006)
3. Kleene, S.C.: On the interpretation of intuitionistic number theory. Journal of Symbolic Logic 10, 109–124 (1945)
4. Kolmogorov, A.: Zur Deutung der intuitionistischen Logik. Mathematische Zeitschrift 35(1), 58–65 (1932)
5. Medvedev, Y.T.: Degrees of difficulty of the mass problems. Dokl. Akad. Nauk. SSSR 104(4), 501–504 (1955)
6. van Oosten, J.: Realizability: An introduction to its categorical side. Studies in logic and the foundations of mathematics, vol. 152. Elsevier, Amsterdam (2008)
7. Skvortsova, E.Z.: A faithful interpretation of the intuitionistic propositional calculus by means of an initial segment of the Medvedev lattice. Sibirsk. Math. Zh. 29(1), 171–178 (in Russian, 1988)
8. Simpson, S.G.: Π_1^0 sets and models of WKL$_0$. In: Reverse Mathematics 2001. Lecture Notes in Logic, vol. 21. ASL (2005)
9. Sorbi, A.: The Medvedev lattice of degrees of difficulty. In: Cooper, S.B., Slaman, T.A., Wainer, S.S. (eds.) Computability, Enumerability, Unsolvability: Directions in Recursion Theory, London. Mathematical Society Lecture Notes, vol. 224, pp. 289–312. Cambridge University Press, Cambridge (1996)

10. Sorbi, A., Terwijn, S.A.: Intermediate logics and factors of the Medvedev lattice. Annals of Pure and Applied Logic 155, 69–85 (2008)
11. Terwijn, S.A.: Syllabus computabiliy theory, Vienna. Available at the author's web pages (2004)
12. Terwijn, S.A.: The Medvedev lattice of computably closed sets. Archive for Mathematical Logic 45(2), 179–190 (2006)
13. Terwijn, S.A.: Constructive logic and computational lattices, habilitation thesis, Technical University of Vienna (2007)

Foundations of
Satisfiability Modulo Theories

Cesare Tinelli*

Department of Computer Science
The University of Iowa
tinelli@cs.uiowa.edu

Satisfiability Modulo Theories (SMT) studies methods for checking the (un)-satisfiability of first-order formulas with respect to a given logical theory T. Distinguishing features of SMT, as opposed to traditional theorem proving, are that the background theory T need not be finitely or even first-order axiomatizable, and that specialized inference methods are used for each theory of interest. By being theory-specific and restricting their language to certain classes of formulas (such as, typically but not exclusively, quantifier-free formulas), these methods can be implemented into solvers that are more efficient in practice than general-purpose theorem provers.

While originally developed to support deductive software verification, SMT is now also finding applications in several other areas of computer science such as, for instance, hardware verification, model checking, automated test case generation, planning, and optimization.

In addition to devising, studying and implementing efficient *theory solvers* for restricted fragments of a growing number of theories, a considerable research effort in the field has been devoted to the development of generic methods for extending the scope and capabilities of theory solvers and combining them modularly. This effort has benefited from a fruitful interplay between practice, with the development of powerful and efficient architectures for SMT reasoners, and theory, with the development of inference systems aimed at capturing the essence of those architectures, facilitating the study of their logical properties and suggesting ways to extend and improve them.

This talk provides an overview of the theoretical work on the logical foundations of modern SMT systems, highlighting current results as well as present research challenges and future opportunities.

* The author's own research described in this talk was made possible with the partial support of grants #0237422, #0551646 and #0914877 from the US National Science Foundation and grant #FA9550-09-1-0517 from the US Air Force Office of Scientific Research.

A. Dawar and R. de Queiroz (Eds.): WoLLIC 2010, LNAI 6188, p. 58, 2010.

Logical Form as a Determinant of Cognitive Processes

Michiel van Lambalgen

ILLC/Department of Philosophy
University of Amsterdam
Nieuwe Doelenstraat 15
NL1012CP Amsterdam
Fax: +31 20 5254503
M.vanLambalgen@uva.nl

Abstract. We discuss a research program on reasoning patterns in subjects with autism, showing that they fail to engage in certain forms of
non-monotonic reasoning that come naturally to neurotypical subjects.
The striking reasoning patterns of autists occur both in verbal and in
non-verbal tasks. Upon formalising the relevant non-verbal tasks, one
sees that their logical form is the same as that of the verbal tasks. This
suggests that logical form can play a causal role in cognitive processes,
and we suggest that this logical form is actually embodied in the cognitive capacity called 'executive function'.

1 Introduction

The title of this paper may seem provocative, given the current near-consensus
that logic, albeit important in the genesis of cognitive science, has no explanatory
role to play in the study of cognitive processes. This dim view of logic has come
about as a consequence of many different pressures, that will be discussed shortly.
But let us first give the briefest of outlines of why and in what sense logic is
cognitively relevant.

The key notion is that of *logical form*. This is not to be conceived of in the manner of an elementary logic textbook: one takes a sentence in natural language,
translates this *tant bien tant mal* in the language of classical or intensional logic,
and calls the translation the logical form of the sentence. On this conception of
logical form, it pertains only to verbal material, it is a syntactic concept, and
it is based on a fixed choice of syntax, semantics and notion of validity (namely
those embodied in classical or intensional logic).

The conception of logical form advocated here is different in that it eliminates
normative considerations. That is, instead of starting with a logic (e.g. classical
logic) that one deems to be normatively justified and trying to fit that logic to the
data, one uses logic descriptively: one tries to fit *a* logic, i.e. a particular choice of
syntax, semantics and notion of validity, to the data, ideally deriving predictions
about what will be observed in further experiments. As we will see below, most
arguments for the irrelevance of logic to the study of cognitive processes adopt

A. Dawar and R. de Queiroz (Eds.): WoLLIC 2010, LNAI 6188, pp. 59–83, 2010.

a normative stance toward logic; but it may not be immediately obvious that a descriptivist approach can be made relevant to cognitive science, given that most practitioners in the field believe that logic has failed to deliver. The bulk of this paper will try to make the case for logic using reasoning patterns in autistic subjects as an example; but we first consider some *a priori* objections against the use of logic as a modelling tool in cognitive science.

1.1   Why Logic Has Come to Be Seen as Irrelevant for Cognitive Science

1. experiments with reasoning tasks, such as the famous Wason selection task [25], show that logical form is not a determinant of reasoning
2. logic cannot deal with vagueness and graded concepts
3. logic cannot deal with uncertainty and must be replaced by probability theory, which is after all *the* calculus of uncertainty
4. what we know about the neocortex suggests that the computations executed by the brain are very different from logical computations
5. the computational complexity of logic is too high for logic to be a realistic model of cognition

A full discussion would divert us from our main topic, but we will focus on two issues to give a flavour of the arguments and counterarguments. To set the stage, we begin by discussing the selection task and its aftermath. Wason's original task was presented by means of a form as depicted in figure 1. The reader, who has probably seen the task before, should realise that this is all the information provided to the subjects, in order to appreciate the tremendous difficulty posed by this task.

Below is depicted a set of four cards, of which you can see only the exposed face but not the hidden back. On each card, there is a number on one of its sides and a letter on the other.

Also below there is a rule which applies only to the four cards. Your task is to decide which if any of these four cards you *must* turn in order to decide if the rule is true. Don't turn unnecessary cards. Tick the cards you want to turn.

Rule: *If there is a vowel on one side, then there is an even number on the other side.*

Cards:

| A | K | 4 | 7 |

Fig. 1. Wason's selection task

This experiment has been replicated many times, with stable results. If one formulates the rule*If there is a vowel on one side, then there is an even number on the other side.* as an implication $p \rightarrow q$, then the observed pattern of results is typically given as in table 1. Wason believed there to be only one 'logically correct' answer, namely $p, \neg q$, and concluded that according to this standard, the

Table 1. Typical scores in the selection task

p	p, q	$p, \neg q$	$p, q, \neg q$	misc.
35%	45%	5%	7%	8%

vast majority of reasoners are irrational. In addition, the selection task was used to argue that most adults do not reach what Piaget [10] considered the pinnacle of cognitive development, the formal operational stage, which is basically mastery of classical propositional logic. Not only do subjects typically fail to master the *modus tollens* inference supposed to be at work here, they do not even have a workable concept of logical form to guide their reasoning. For if Wason's 'abstract' rule *If there is a vowel on one side, then there is an even number on the other side.*is replaced by the 'concrete' rule *if you want to drink alcohol, you have to be over 18*, performance suddenly jumps to more acceptable levels, around 75%. These two reasoning tasks – 'abstract' and 'concrete' – have the same logical form. If logical form determines performance in a task, performance on these tasks must be comparable. The data show that performance differs considerably, whence logical form is irrelevant to reasoning. A tacit inference followed: if logic plays no role in reasoning, why would it play a role in other domains of cognition? There is much to say against this line of argument (see [16,18]), but here we continue with the argument from uncertainty.

This argument contrasts logic, which is supposed to be dealing in certain truth only, with real life, where

> ...it is, in fact, rational by the highest standards to take proper account of the probability of one's premises in deductive reasoning (Stevenson and Over [21, p. 615]).

> ...performing inferences from statements treated as absolutely certain is uncommon in ordinary reasoning. We are mainly interested in what subjects will infer from statements in ordinary discourse that they may not believe with certainty and may even have serious doubts about [21, p. 621].

It is a moot point whether the implied contrast is at all valid (see Stenning and van Lambalgen [20] for discussion), but for our present purposes it suffices to note that logic is widely perceived to fail on this score. A whole research program, 'Rational Analysis' as practised by Oaksford and Chater [6] is built on this perception. Here is another representative quote:

> [M]uch of our reasoning with conditionals is uncertain, and may be overturned by future information; that is, they are non-monotonic. But logic based approaches to inference are typically monotonic, and hence are unable to deal with this uncertainty. Moreover, to the extent that formal logical approaches embrace non-monotonicity, they appear to be unable to cope with the fact that it is the content of the rules, rather than their logical form, which appears to determine the inferences that people draw. We now argue that perhaps by encoding more of the content of people's knowledge, by probability theory, we may more adequately capture the nature of everyday human inference. This

seems to make intuitive sense, because the problems that we have identified concern how uncertainty is handled in human inference, and probability is the calculus of uncertainty [5, p. 100]; see also [6].

But can all uncertainty be modelled by probability theory? We first give a theoretical argument that casts doubt on this assumption (cf. [19]), and will then consider concrete cases of uncertainty where Bayesian probability goes awry. Consider what is presupposed by the main inference algorithm of probability theory, *Bayesian conditionalisation*. This is an algorithm that gets us from the *a priori* probability $P_0(A)$ of an event A to the *a posteriori* probability $P_1(A)$ given total evidence E:

$$P_1(A) = P_0(A \mid E) = \frac{P_0(E \mid A)P_0(A)}{P_0(E)}.$$

Here, the first equality holds by stipulation; the stipulation is intuitively justified only if E represents *all* the available evidence. The second equality holds in virtue of the definition of conditional probability. But one sees that for this algorithm to work two conditions must be satisfied

1. the *a priori* probability P_0 must be defined on all possible evidence E
2. moreover, for all possible evidence E, $P_0(E) > 0$.

To use Donald Rumsfeld's infamous terminology, probability theory deals with the 'known unknowns' (the space of events is known, but not their truth value), but it is fairly helpless in the face of the 'unknown unknowns' (the case where the space of events is itself not completely known). By the second property just listed, one is barred from assuming that the 'unknown unknowns' all have probability 0, because this implies they can never be used for Bayesian updating. Therefore these events must be known in the sense of being incorporated into the event algebra *and* they must have non-zero probability; but these demands taken together entail totally unrealistic estimation and memory requirements. Therefore it makes sense to look for alternatives to Bayesianism.

We proceed to give two concrete examples that involve these 'unknown unknowns'.

1. Causal reasoning. A causal relationship holds only in a closed system; it is however impossible to specify in advance all the ways in which events may interfere with this closed system. For example, if a stationary billiard ball is hit by a moving billiard ball, it takes over the momentum of the moving ball, but it doesn't if I take it off the billiard table at the instant of collision.
2. Unknown preconditions, also known as the 'frame problem'. If I promise to make my guest a coffee using my espresso machine, I simply assume that all the preconditions for the machine to work properly are satisfied. They may not, in which case I will be brought up short. Nevertheless, I do not check whether these conditions are satisfied, I will in fact be ignorant of most of these preconditions, and hence I cannot have a probability distribution over these conditions from which to compute the chances that I can make my guest happy with an espresso.

In all such cases there is genuine uncertainty in the sense of lack of knowledge, and so probability theory does not apply. But logics can be useful, as long as they are *non-monotonic*. Such logics often operate on the *closed world assumption*: if you have no reason to assume event E occurs, you may assume it does not occur. Here it is not necessary to posit probability theory's fixed event algebra to which the events E must belong. An example can help to illustrate the point. Let us return for a while to my espresso machine. Let p stand for 'I push the button', and q for 'coffee starts flowing into the cup'. Then the proper logical form for the conditional 'if I push the button, then coffee starts flowing into the cup' is *not* the classical material implication $p \to q$. The reason is that if there is an occasion on which I push the button but no coffee is produced, the material implication would have to be declared false, and hence useless to describe the operation of the espresso machine. Instead one should use an 'exception-tolerant' rule informally rendered as 'if I push the button, and nothing abnormal is the case, then coffee is produced', or more formally as (*) $p \wedge \neg ab \to q$. Here the closed world assumption becomes operative. It entails that if we have no concrete information that an abnormality has occurred we may assume it hasn't, i.e. we conclude $\neg ab$. Together with the premise p we then get conclusion q. However, suppose that even though I pushed the button, the machine fails to produce coffee. I then conclude, not that the conditional (*) is wrong, but that something abnormal has occurred. I may for example notice that the machine is not plugged in, which leads to a concrete meaning for the abnormality: if r represents 'the machine is plugged in', then we have $\neg r \to ab$. I don't see any other possible causes for the malfunctioning, however, and again by closed world reasoning I conclude that the machine's not being plugged in is the *only* source of the abnormality, formally $\neg r \leftrightarrow ab$ or equivalently $r \leftrightarrow \neg ab$, whence I obtain a new conditional from (*), namely $p \wedge r \to q$. Since I have now plugged in the machine and pushed the button, I expect the machine to produce coffee. The kind of reasoning just given cannot be represented in Bayesian probability theory; for an extended argument see [20,19].

Notice incidentally that we have analysed a *non-verbal* task in logical terms. Indeed, on the conception of logic advocated here also non-verbal tasks can have a logical form, and in fact a logical form that can be the same as that of a verbal task. This observation will turn out to be important below.

2   Marr's Levels of Explanation and Logic

In the face of such formidable objections as listed in the previous section, it seems a daunting task to defend a continuing role for logic in cognitive science. Still, this is what we shall do. We shall argue, using Marr's model of explanation in cognitive science [4, Chapter 1], that the criticisms directed against logic fall foul of a confusion of levels. More importantly, we show that logic, rightly conceived, can still make a positive contribution to explanation and prediction in cognitive science. The case we focus on is autism. This may seem stony ground indeed: why would there be a role for logic in autism? This disorder, about which more below, has been variously characterised as due to a deficit in 'theory of mind', as defective central processing, as a disorder of affect, and as executive dysfunction, to mention but a few proposed aetiologies. On the face of it, logic has little to do with any of these.

Considering the place of logic in cognitive explanation will clarify these matters. As a starting point we look at David Marr's three levels of cognitive inquiry

1. identification of the information processing task as an input–output function;[1] the competence model is relative to the information processing task considered
2. specification of an algorithm which computes that function
3. neural implementation of the algorithm specified

This tripartite scheme of explanation should be read neither bottom-up nor top-down, but as a set of constraints; for example, the algorithm may be determined both by the competence model and by what is known about neural computation. The competence model is formulated in terms of ideal, mathematical entities and is as such not directly applicable to the real world. It is ideal in two different senses of the term: firstly because it operates with idealised input and output, and secondly because it gives an ideal norm as a mapping from (idealised) input to (idealised) output. There is no reason to expect that actual performance, even when optimal, will always conform to the norm set by the competence model.

In a nutshell, our view of the role of logic in cognitive science is this; logics can act as descriptions of competence models various information processing tasks (Marr's first level). We will illustrate this by considering the cognitive capacity known as executive function.

3   A Common Failure in Psychiatric Disorders: Executive Function

'Executive function' is an umbrella term for processes responsible for higher-level action control that are necessary for maintaining a goal and achieving it in possibly adverse circumstances. There is no unanimity on how to partition executive function into meaningful subcomponents, but we may take executive function to be composed of planning, initiation, inhibition, coordination and control of action sequences, leading toward a goal held in working memory. The reason for our interest in psychiatric disorders is our conviction that there is a strong connection between logic and executive function: at a logical level, the operation of executive function can be described as conditional reasoning and aberrations thereof. This may seem surprising, especially given the prevalent conception of reasoning as a conscious and somewhat laborious activity starting from explicitly given premises. How then can fast and largely automatic executive function be profitably described by a logic? It will turn out, however, that the logics most useful in this context, variants of closed world reasoning, do allow fast and automatic processing.

---

[1] Marr calls this the 'computational level', but this term is infelicitous in view of the next level. We prefer the term 'competence model' instead.

4 Logic and Executive Function

We said above that executive function is composed of planning, initiation, inhibition, coordination and control of action sequences leading toward a goal held in working memory. In the following we abstract from the co-ordination and control component, and concentrate on goal maintenance, planning and (contextually determined) inhibition.

By definition, planning consists in the construction of a *sequence* of actions which will achieve a given goal, taking into account properties of the world and the agent, and also events that might occur in the world. The relevant properties include stable causal relationships obtaining in the world, and also what might be termed 'inertia', in analogy with Newton's first law. If a property has been caused to hold by the occurrence of an event, we expect that the property persists until it is terminated by another event. This is the inertial aspect of causality: a property does not cease to hold (or come to hold) spontaneously, without identifiable cause. Such inertia is a prerequisite for successful action in the world; and we will have to find a formal way to express it. It does however not suffice for successful planning.

The problem is that in the definition of planning, , 'will achieve' definitely cannot mean: '*provably* achieves in classical logic', because of the notorious frame problem: it is impossible to take into account all eventualities whose occurrence might be relevant to the success of the plan, but classical logic forces one to consider all models of the premises, including those that contain farfetched possibilities. Therefore the question arises: how to characterize formally what makes a good plan?

A reasonable informal suggestion is: the plan works to the best of one's present knowledge. More formally, this idea can be reformulated semantically as: the plan achieves the goal in a 'minimal model' of reality; where a minimal model is characterized by the property that, very roughly speaking, every proposition is false which you have no reason to assume to be true. In particular, in the minimal model no events occur which are not forced to occur by the data, and only explicitly mentioned causal influences are represented in the model. This makes planning a form of non-monotonic reasoning.

We thus postulate that the logical form underlying planning is *closed world reasoning*: the principle which (roughly) says that every proposition which is not forced to hold by the data available can be assumed to be false. This applies to propositions about occurrences of events as well as to those expressing causal relationships. One may identify a number of areas in which closed world reasoning is applicable, each time in slightly different form:

1. lists: train schedules, airline databases, ...
2. diagnostic reasoning and abduction
3. unknown preconditions
4. causal and counterfactual reasoning

5. attribution of beliefs and intentions[2]
6. construction of discourse models, in particular event structures from verb tenses

It is of some interest that several psychiatric disorders come with disturbances in one or more forms of reasoning from this list. Children with ADHD ('attention-deficit hyperactivity disorder') tend to have difficulties with ordering events in a narrative. Autists have difficulties with at least 3, 4 and 5. They also have a special relationship with lists, in the sense that they feel lost without lists, such as timetables to organise daily activities; they have great difficulty accommo-dating unexpected changes to the timetable, and try to avoid situations such as holidays in which rigid schedules are not applicable. One may view this as an extreme version of closed world reasoning, sometimes even applied in inappro-priate circumstances. But before one concludes from this that autists are good at closed world reasoning to the point of over-applying it, one must carefully dis-tinguish several components of closed world reasoning. On the one hand, there is the inference from *given* premises to a conclusion. In [18, Chapter 8] it is shown that such inferences can be executed fast by suitable neural networks. In a wider sense, non-monotonic reasoning also involves 'pre-processing' the given situation or discourse, that is, *encoding* the law-like features of a situation in a particular type of premises. Laws and regularities always allow exceptions, and skill at 'exception handling' is required – which involves identifying and encoding the relevant exceptions, and knowing when 'enough is enough'. Autists appear to do worse than normals on this last aspect, although they behave normally with respect to the non-monotonic inferences themselves.

We have thus identified closed world reasoning as a component of executive function. A good formal representation of closed world reasoning as relevant to planning is the event calculus as formulated in logic programming [23]. An informal description suffices for our purposes here. Planning involves a goal, a description of the current situation, a description of causal effects and precon-ditions of actions. The program then derives a sequence of actions which will achieve the goal if no unforeseen events occur, but execution must be stopped and plan recomputed if relevant change of context occurs.

This puts constraints on the neural implementation of the planning algorithm, in the sense that at least the following components are required: working mem-ory needs to hold the goal and the current world model, semantic memory is necessary for the storage of causal properties of actions, and of a general theory of causality; working memory again computes the sequence of actions compris-ing the plan. In the logical model of executive function proposed here inhibition is represented through the special logical form of causal properties of actions, where the link from action to effect is mediated by a slot labelled $\neg ab$:

$$A \wedge \neg ab \rightarrow E \tag{1}$$

---

[2] It may not be obvious that this is a planning problem at all, but section 5.2 will make clear why this is so.

This conditional is read as 'if A and *nothing abnormal is the case*, then E', where the expression '*nothing abnormal is the case*' is governed by closed world reasoning. For instance, if there is nothing known about a possible abnormality, i.e. if the causal system is closed, one concludes $\neg ab$, hence from A it follows that E. If however there is information of the form $C \rightarrow ab$, i.e. if there is a context C which constitutes an abnormality, and C is the case, then the link from A to E is inhibited. In the neural model of closed world reasoning proposed in [18, Chapter 8], ab corresponds to an (artificial) neuron situated between the neurons for A and E, such that C is connected to ab via an inhibitory link; and this is the general way of incorporating contextual influences. Defects in the inhibitory neurons would thus lead to deficient context processing, as we see in autism. In [18, Chapter 9] we present some recent evidence indicating that in the brain of autists inhibition is compromised at the neurological level, among other reasons because inhibitory interneurons are underdeveloped. This theme will not be pursued here. Instead we concentrate on reasoning.

5   Non-monotonicity in Autism: Rules and Exceptions

Autism is a clinical syndrome first described by Leo Kanner in the 1940s, often first diagnosed in children around 2–3 years of age as a deficit in their affective relations and communication. The autistic child typically refuses eye-contact, is indifferent or hostile to demonstrations of affection, and exhibits delayed or abnormal communication, repetitive movements (often self-harming) and is rather indifferent to pain. Autistic children do not engage spontaneously in make-believe play and show little interest in the competitive social hierarchy, and in personal possessions. Autism comes in all severities – from complete lack of language and severe retardation, to mild forms continuous with the 'normal' range of personalities and IQs. Autism is sometimes distinguished from Asperger's syndrome – 'autism without language impairment'? – but Asperger's is probably just the mild end of the autistic spectrum. Autistic children share many symptoms shown by deaf and by blind infants, possibly because of the social isolation imposed by these conditions. There are known biochemical abnormalities associated with autism. There is some evidence of a probably complex genetic basis. Psychological analyses of autistic functioning are not inconsistent with or exclusive of such biochemical or genetic level analyses.

More than any other psychiatric disorder, autism has captured the imagination of the practitioners of cognitive science, because, at least according to some theories, it holds the promise of revealing the essence of what makes us human. This holds especially for the school which views autism as a deficit in 'theory of mind', the ability to represent someone else's feelings and beliefs. Some go so far as to claim that in this respect autists are like our evolutionary ancestors, given that chimpanzees have much less 'theory of mind' than humans. Although we believe such claims need to be qualified, we still agree that autism is important from the point of view of cognitive science.

5.1   Theory of Mind and Reasoning

A famous experiment, the 'false belief' task [9], investigates how autistic subjects reason about other people's belief. The standard design of the experiment is as follows. A child and a doll (Maxi) are in a room together with the experimenter. Maxi and child witness a bar of chocolate being placed in a box. Then Maxi is removed from the room. The child sees the experimenter move the chocolate from the box to a drawer. Maxi is brought back in. The experimenter asks the child: 'Where does Maxi think the chocolate is?' The answers to this question reveal an interesting cut-off point, and a difference between autists and normally developing children. Before the age of about 4 years , the normally developing child responds where the child knows the chocolate to be (i.e. the drawer); after that age, the child responds where Maxi must falsely believe the chocolate to be (i.e. the box). By contrast, autists go on answering 'in the drawer' for a long time.

This experiment has been repeated many times, in many variations, with fairly robust results. Some versions can easily be done at home. There is for instance the 'Smarties' task, which goes as follows. Unbeknownst to the child-subject, a box of Smarties is emptied and refilled with pencils. The child is asked: 'What do you think is in the box?", and it happily answers: 'Smarties!' It is then shown the contents of the box. The pencils are put back into the box, and the child is now asked: 'What do you think your [absent] mother will say is in the box?' We may then observe the same critical age: before age 4, the child answers: 'Pencils!', whereas after age 4 the child will say: 'Smarties!'

The outcomes of these experiments have been argued to support the 'theory of mind deficit' hypothesis on the cause of autism. Proposed by Leslie in 1987 [3], it holds that human beings have evolved a special 'module' devoted specifically to reasoning about other people's minds. As such, this module would provide a cognitive underpinning for empathy. In normals the module would constitute the difference between humans and their ancestors – indeed, chimpanzees seem to be able to do much less in the way of mind-reading. In autists, this module would be delayed or impaired, thus explaining abnormalities in communication and also in the acquisition of language, if it is indeed true that the development of joint attention is crucial to language learning (as claimed for instance by Tomasello [22]).

This seems a very elegant explanation for an intractable phenomenon, and it has justly captured the public imagination. Upon closer examination the question arises whether it is really an explanation, rather than a description of one class of symptoms. For instance, the notion of a 'module' is notoriously hazy. In this context it is obviously meant to be a piece of dedicated neural circuitry. In this way, it can do the double duty of differentiating us from our ancestors and being capable of being damaged in isolation. But it is precisely this isolation, or 'encapsulation' as Fodor called it, that is doubtful. One reason is that evolution does not generally proceed by adding new modules, but instead by tweaking old ones, and another is that much of the problem of functionally characterising human reasoning about minds is about interactions between modules. 'Theory of mind' requires language to formulate beliefs in and it also entails a considerable involvement of working memory. However, as soon as one realises that a 'module' never operates in isolation, then the 'theory of mind deficit' hypothesis begins to lose its hold. We are now invited to look at the (possibly defective) interactions of the 'module' with other cognitive functions (language, working memory, ...), which leads to the possibility that defects in these functions may play a role in autism.

Apart from these theoretical problems, it is experimentally controversial at what stage 'theory of mind' abilities emerge. False-belief tasks were initially proposed as diagnosing a lack of these abilities in normal three-year-olds and their presence in normal four-year-olds [3]. Others have proposed that irrelevant linguistic demands of these tasks deceptively depress three-year-olds' performance. For example, in the 'Maxi' task, the child sees the doll see the chocolate placed in a box, and then the child but not the doll sees the chocolate moved to the drawer. Now if the child is asked 'Where will the doll look for the chocolate *first?*' (instead of 'Where will the doll look for the chocolate?') then children as young as two can sometimes solve the problem [14].[3]

5.2   Reasoning in the False Belief Task

It is tempting to view the false belief task as concerned with reasoning about belief, and hence to attempt a formalisation of the reasoning in some variant of multi-agent epistemic logic. However, a more fine-grained analysis is possible, taking account of the way in which beliefs are formed and maintained. From this analysis it will become clear that the 'theory of mind' capacity is much less *sui generis* than commonly thought, and in fact intimately linked with executive function.

We will now analyse attribution of belief as it occurs in the false belief task as consisting of three components

1. awareness of the causal relation between perception and belief, which can be stated in the form: 'if φ is true in scene S, and agent a sees S, then a comes to believe φ'.
2. awareness of the inertial properties of belief: beliefs do not form spontaneously, but must be generated by limited number of causes, such as perception and inference
3. inhibition of response tendencies when necessary; more generally the involvement of executive function

An agent solving the task correctly first of all needs to have an awareness of the causal relation between perception and belief, component 1. Applied to the situation at hand, this means that Maxi comes to believe that the chocolate is in the box. An application of the principle of inertia (component 2 now yields that

---

[3] Replications of this experiment have not been successful, but there are other quite puzling indications that the standard false belief tasks underestimate children's capacities. It has been observed for example that even when children give the wrong answer, their eyes tend to focus on the correct (i.e. 'false belief') location [7].

Maxi's belief concerning the location of the chocolate persists unless an event occurs which causes him to have a new belief, incompatible with the former. The story does not mention such an event, whence it is reasonable to assume – using closed world reasoning – that Maxi still believes that the chocolate is in the box when he returns to the experimenter's room. An explanation for performance in the false belief also needs to account for the incorrect answers given by children younger than 4 and autists. These subjects almost always answer 'in the drawer', when asked where Maxi believes the chocolate to be.

This is where component 3 comes in. Normal and autistic performance in the false belief task are both analysed as conditional reasoning with instances of the general executive function rule 1. The agent a is supposed to be governed by *response rules* of the type

$$B_a(\varphi) \wedge \neg ab_{a,\varphi} \to R_a(\varphi), \tag{2}$$

in words

If agent a *B*elieves φ and nothing *ab*normal is the case, then he *R*eports φ

The key to understanding performance in the task is the competition between two different instances of 2

1. φ represents the actual location of the chocolate (known to the agent)
2. φ represents Maxi's belief about the location of the chocolate

After substitution, the two resulting response rules can be made to inhibit each other by suitable conditions on the abnormalities. Let p represent the actual location of the chocolate, then we have the following substitution instance of 2

$$B_a(p) \wedge \neg ab_{a,p} \to R_a(p) \tag{3}$$

To model this, we borrow a notion from executive dysfunction theory, and hypothesise that the 'prepotent response' is always for the child to answer where it knows the chocolate to be. In some children, this response can be inhibited, in other children it cannot, for various reasons which we shall explore below.

5.3 Executive Dysfunction and the Box Task

Russell's executive function deficit theory [12] takes as basic the observation that autists often exhibit severe behavioural perseveration. They go on carrying out some routine when the routine is no longer appropriate, and exhibit great difficulty in switching tasks when the context calls for this (that is, when switching is not governed by an explicit rule). This perseveration, also observed in certain kinds of patients with frontal cortex damage, would give rise to many of the symptoms of autism: obsessiveness, insensitivity to context, inappropriateness of behaviour, literalness of carrying out instructions. Task-switching is the brief of executive function.

Indeed, executive function is called upon when a plan has to be redesigned by the occurrence of unexpected events which make the original plan unfeasible.

Autists indeed tend to suffer from rather inflexible planning. This phenomenon is illustrated in a paradigmatic experiment designed by Hughes and Russell [15], the 'box task' (see figure 2).

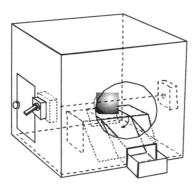

Fig. 2. Russell's box task

The task is to get the marble which is lying on the platform (the truncated pyramid) inside the box. However, when the subject puts her hand through the opening, a trapdoor in the platform opens and the marble drops out of reach. This is because there is an infrared light-beam behind the opening, which, when interrupted, activates the trapdoor-mechanism. The switch on the left side of the box deactivates the whole mechanism, so that to get the marble you have to flip the switch first. In the standard set-up, the subject is shown how manipulating the switch allows one to retrieve the marble after she has first been tricked by the trapdoor mechanism.

Even though this task is non-verbal, the pattern of results is strikingly similar to that exhibited in the false belief task: normally developing children master this task by about age 4, and before this age they keep reaching for the marble, even when the marble drops out of reach all the time. Autistic children go on failing this task for a long time. The performance on this task is conceptualised as follows. The natural, 'prepotent', plan is to reach directly for the marble, but this plan fails. The child then has to re-plan, taking into account the information about the switch. After age 4 the normally developing child can indeed integrate this information, that is, inhibit the pre-potent response, and come up with a new plan. It is hypothesised that autists cannot inhibit this prepotent response because of a failure in executive function. But to add precision to this diagnosis we have to dig deeper.

It is important to note here, that the ability to plan and re-plan when the need arises due to changed context, is fundamental to human cognition, no less fundamental than 'theory of mind' abilities. Human beings (and other animals too) act, not on the basis of stimulus-response chains, but on the basis of (possibly distant) goals which they have set themselves. That goal, together with a world-model lead to a plan which suffices to reach the goal in the assumed circumstances. But it is impossible to enumerate *a priori* all events which might possibly form an obstacle in reaching the goal. It is therefore generally wise to keep open the possibility that one has overlooked a precondition, while at the same time not allowing this uncertainty to inhibit one's actions. It is perhaps this flexibility that autists are lacking. This point can be reformulated in logical terms. The autist's concept of a rule is one in which the consequent invariably follows the antecedent. By contrast, a normal subject's rule is more likely to be of the exception-tolerant variety. Indeed, Russell writes

> [T]aking what one might call a 'defeasibility stance' towards rules is an innate human endowment – and thus one that might be innately lacking ... [H]umans appear to possess a capacity – whatever that is – for abandoning one relatively entrenched rule for some novel ad hoc procedure. The claim can be made, therefore, that this capacity is lacking in autism, and it is this that gives rise to failures on 'frontal' tasks – not to mention the behavioural rigidity that individuals with the disorder show outside the laboratory [13, p. 318].

Russell goes on to say that one way this theory might be tested is through the implication that "children with autism will fail to perform on tasks which require an appreciation of the defeasibility of rules such as 'sparrows can fly'." This is what we shall do; but to get started we first need a logical description of what goes on in the box task.

5.3.1   Closed World Reasoning in the Box Task

For the formalisation we borrow some self-explanatory notation from the situation calculus. Let c be a variable over contexts, then the primitives are

– the predicate $do(a, c)$, meaning 'perform action a in context c'
– the function $result(a, c)$, which gives the new context after a has been performed in c.

The actions we need are g ('grab'), u ('switch up'), d ('switch down'). We furthermore need the following context-dependent properties:

– $possess(c)$: the child possesses the marble in c
– $up(c)$: the switch is up in c (= correct position)
– $down(c)$: the switch is down in c (= wrong position).

The following equations give the rules appropriate for the box task

$$down(c) \wedge do(u, c)\neg ab'(c) \rightarrow up(result(u, c)) \tag{4}$$
$$do(g, c) \wedge \neg ab(c) \rightarrow possess(result(g, c)) \tag{5}$$

We first model the reasoning of the normal child > 4 yrs. Initially, closed world reasoning for $ab(c)$ gives $\neg ab(c)$, reducing the rule 5 to

$$do(g, c) \rightarrow possess(result(g, c)) \tag{6}$$

which prompts the child to reach for the marble without further ado. After repeated failure, she reverts to the initial rule 5, and concludes that after all $ab(c)$. After the demonstration of the role of the switch, she forms the condition

$$down(c) \rightarrow ab(c) \tag{7}$$

She then applies closed world reasoning for ab to 7, to get

$$down(c) \leftrightarrow ab(c) \tag{8}$$

which transforms rule 5 to

$$do(g, c) \wedge up(c) \rightarrow possess(result(g, c)) \tag{9}$$

Define context c_0 by putting $c = result(u, c_0)$ and apply closed world reasoning to rule 4, in the sense that $ab'(c)$ is set to $\bot$ due to lack of further information, and $\rightarrow$ is replaced by $\leftrightarrow$. Finally, we obtain the updated rule, which constitutes a new plan for action

$$down(c_0) \wedge do(u, c_0) \wedge c = result(u, c_0) \wedge do(g, c) \rightarrow possess(result(g, c)) \tag{10}$$

As in the previous tasks, both the normal child younger than 4, and the autistic child are assumed to operate in effect with a rule of the form

$$do(g, c) \rightarrow possess(result(g, c)) \tag{11}$$

which cannot be updated, only replaced *in toto* by a new rule such as 10.

It is tempting to speculate on the computational complexities of both these procedures. Russell wrote that 'humans appear to possess a capacity – whatever that is – for abandoning one relatively entrenched rule for some novel ad hoc procedure [13, p. 318]'. The preceding considerations suggest that 'abandoning one relatively entrenched rule' may indeed be costly, but that normal humans get around this by representing the rule in such a way that it can be easily updated. It is instructive to look at the computation that the normal child older than 4 is hypothesised to be performing. The only costly step appears to be the synthesis of the rule 7; the rest is straightforward logic programming which is very efficient. The rule 5 is never abandoned; a new rule is derived without having to ditch 5 first.

To close this discussion, we compare the false belief task to the box task from the point of view of the formal analysis. The tasks are similar in that for successful solution one must start from rules of the form $A \wedge \neg ab \rightarrow E$, identify conditions which constitute an abnormality, and apply closed world reasoning; and also that in both cases a failure of ab to exercise its inhibitory function leads to the inability to inhibit the prepotent response. A difference is that in the false belief task, one needs a 'theory' relating ab to sensory, or inferred, information, whereas it suffices to operate with rules for actions in the box task.

5.4   The Suppression Task as a Formal Analogue of the Box Task

When considered formally, all tasks mentioned have a logical structure in common, besides showing undeniable differences. The common logical structure is closed world reasoning applied to possible exceptions. The question is whether the formal analogies between the tasks are indicative of a single cognitive function exercised in these tasks. We claim there is: it is executive function, conceptualised as reasoning with exception-tolerant, mutually inhibiting conditionals.[4]

It is therefore an interesting challenge to try to devise a task which captures precisely this common core. Surprisingly, a task with the required properties has been around for a long time, although it was not treated as such: Byrne's 'suppression task' [1].

If one presents a subject with the following premisses:

(1)   a.   *If she has an essay to write she will study late in the library.*
        b.   *She has an essay to write.*

roughly 90% of subjects[5] draw the conclusion 'She will study late in the library' (we will later discuss what the remaining 10% may be thinking). Next suppose one adds the premiss

(2)   *If the library is open, she will study late in the library.*

and one asks again: what follows? In this case, only 60% concludes 'She will study late in the library'. This known as the 'suppression' of *modus ponens*.

However, if instead of the above, the premiss

(3)   *If she has a textbook to read, she will study late in the library*

is added, then the percentage of 'She will study late in the library'–conclusions is around 95%.

In this type of experiment one investigates not only *modus ponens* (MP), but also *modus tollens* (MT), and the 'fallacies' *affirmation of the consequent* (AC), and *denial of the antecedent* (DA), with respect to both types of added premisses, (2) and (3). The results are that MT is suppressed in the presence of a premiss of the form (2) (but not (3)), and that both AC and DA are suppressed in the presence of a premiss of the form (3) (but not (2)).

Byrne interpreted her data in terms of the 'mental rules' – 'mental models' debate, viewing the results as support for the latter. In [17], we gave a very different interpretation of the suppression phenomenon as an instance of closed world reasoning, of whch the following is a brief synopsis.

5.5   A Formal Analysis

Byrne viewed the suppression effect mainly as showing that subjects are not guided by the rules of classical logic, but instead let their inferences be

---

[4] Here one shouldn't think of reasoning as a conscious activity, but as a largely automatic process describable in logical terms.

[5] The figures we use come from the experiment reported in [2], since the experiments reported in this study have more statistical power than those of [1].

determined by semantic content. We believe a more informative account of the suppression effect can be given, also establishing its relevance outside the reasoning domain, namely as showing that (normal) subjects are capable of flexible management of rules in context. For instance, normal subjects generally allow rules to have exceptions (and actions to have unknown preconditions), and they are quite good at exception-handling. This capacity involves some form of closed world reasoning, which counsels to take an exception into account if and only if one is forced to do so. To take our paradigmatic example, in

'If Marian has an essay to write she will study late in the library.
Marian has an essay to write.'

no exception is made salient, therefore the subject can draw the *modus ponens* inference: 'She will study late in the library'. The addition of premiss (2)

'If the library is open, Marian will study late in the library'

makes salient a possibly disabling condition in first rule, namely the library's being shut. But since no other disabling conditions are mentioned, it is assumed that there aren't any. The task at hand is to turn this intuition into a formal model.

Here we sketch how a formal analysis could go; the full technical treatment can be found in Stenning and van Lambalgen [17]. Speaking informally, we represent conditionals such as

If Marian has an essay to write she will study late in the library.

as *defaults* of the form

If Marian has an essay to write, *and nothing abnormal is the case*, she will study late in the library.

As in our attempted formalization of the box task, the italicized phrase introduces an overt marker for a possible abnormality or unknown precondition, which can be given concrete semantic content by other material given by the discourse. The claim is that this is a natural thing for a subject to do, because most rules indeed have exceptions, or unstated preconditions.

Formally, we write a conditional as

$$p \wedge \neg ab \to q,$$

where ab is a proposition letter representing an unspecified abnormality. The logic governing ab is *closed world reasoning*. We will forego the general definition of this type of non-monotonic reasoning (including the properties of the implication symbol $\to$ used in the formalization), but will illustrate the idea by means of examples related to the suppression task.

In general, one may give ab concrete content by adding implications of the form

$$s \to ab,$$

which express that the eventuality denoted by s constitutes an abnormality. Now suppose that there are n such implications in all, i.e., we have the implications

$$s_1 \to ab, \ldots, s_n \to ab.$$

In the absence of further implications beyond the n mentioned, we want to conclude that we have listed *all* abnormalities. This can be done by *defining ab* as

$$ab \leftrightarrow \bigvee_{i \leq n} s_i.$$

Two special cases are of particular interest. If $n = 1$, i.e. if we only have the implication $s \to ab$, the definition yields $ab \leftrightarrow s$. Furthermore, for the case $n = 0$, the definition entails that ab is false, i.e. $\neg mathitab$. That is, if there is no information about the abnormality ab, we assume it does not occur.

These formal stipulations will help us explain the logic behind the suppression task. We do two illustrative cases; for the full treatment we refer to [17].

Modus ponens. Consider again

> If Marian has an essay to write she will study late in the library.
> Marian has an essay to write.

Formally, this becomes

$$p \wedge \neg ab \to q; \; p.$$

Closed world reasoning yields $\neg ab$, which suffices to draw the conclusion q. Therefore modus ponens also follows in this nonclassical context, once closed world reasoning is applied. Failure to apply modus ponens may then be evidence of a resistance to apply closed world reasoning to the abnormality.[6]

The situation becomes slightly more complicated in the case of a further type (3) premiss:

> If Marian has an essay to write she will study late in the library.
> If Marian has an exam she studies late in the library.
> Marian has an essay to write.

There are now two conditional premisses, each with its own disabling abnormality. The formalization thus becomes

$$p \wedge \neg ab \to q; \; r \wedge \neg ab' \to q; \; p.$$

Since the discourse does not provide information either about ab or about ab', they are both set to false, that is, we have $\neg ab$ and $\neg ab'$. The discourse thus becomes equivalent to

$$p \vee r \to q; \; p,$$

which again justifies the conclusion q.

Real complications arise in the case of a premiss of type (2):

> If Marian has an essay to write she will study late in the library.
> If the library is open Marian studies late in the library.
> Marian has an essay to write.

Again there are two conditional premisses, each with its own disabling abnormality, but in this case there is interaction, because the antecedent of the second conditional highlights a possible precondition. The formalization is therefore not

$$p \wedge \neg ab \to q; \ r \wedge \neg ab' \to q; \ p,$$

as it was in the previous case, but rather

$$p \wedge \neg ab \to q; \ r \wedge \neg ab' \to q; \underline{\neg r \to ab}; \ p,$$

where the added underlined implication reflects the assumption that the second conditional has made an abnormality for the first conditional salient. Closed world reasoning applied to this implication yields $ab \leftrightarrow \neg r$, and if we then substitute r for $\neg ab$ in the first conditional we get

$$p \wedge r \to q,$$

to which modus ponens can no longer be applied. The conclusion from this formal exercise is that suppression of modus ponens can be explained as an instance of closed world reasoning. This is definitely *not* to say that subjects *should* choose this underlying formal representation. It is very well possible to stick to the classical interpretation of the conditional, not containing a marker for a possible exception, in which case modus ponens should not be suppressed – indeed this is a plausible hypothesis to explain what autists appear to be doing.

Denial of the antecedent. Fallacies and their suppression can be explained similarly. As an example we treat denial of the antecedent, in the case of the premisses

> If Marian has an essay to write she will study late in the library.
> Marian does not have an essay to write.

The premisses can be formalized as

$$p \wedge \neg ab \to q; \ \neg p,$$

and since there is no information about ab, by closed world reasoning one may assume $\neg ab$. This particular fallacy involves more closed world reasoning however: one also has to assume that, in the absence of further information, $p \wedge \neg ab$ is the *only* reason to conclude q, so that we have in effect

$$q \leftrightarrow p \wedge \neg ab.$$

Given $\neg p$, it indeed follows from this that $\neg q$.

Suppose we now add a further conditional premiss of type (3), to get

If Marian has an essay to write she will study late in the library.
If Marian has an exam she studies late in the library.
Marian does not have an essay to write.

The formalization is

$$p \wedge \neg ab \rightarrow q; \ r \wedge \neg ab' \rightarrow q; \ \neg p.$$

Closed world reasoning yields $\neg ab$ and $\neg ab'$, which reduces the formalized premisses to

$$p \rightarrow q; \ r \rightarrow q; \ \neg p.$$

Closed world reasoning applied to the two implications $p \rightarrow q$ and $r \rightarrow q$ yields

$$q \leftrightarrow p \vee r,$$

from which given only $\neg p$ nothing follows. The addition of the second conditional premiss may thus lead to a suppression of DA inferences.

It is of some importance for our discussion of the autism data to distinguish the two forms of closed world reasoning that play a role here. On the one hand there is the closed world reasoning applied to abnormalities or exceptions, which takes the form: 'assume only those exceptions occur which are explicitly listed'. On the other hand there is the closed world reasoning applied to rules, which takes the form of diagnostic reasoning: 'if B has occurred and the only known rules with B as consequent are $A_1 \rightarrow B, \ldots, A_n \rightarrow B$, then assume one of $A_1, \ldots, A_n$ has occurred'. These forms of closed world reasoning are in principle independent, and in our autist population we indeed see a dissociation between the two.

6   Autists and the Suppression Task

Given the formal analogy between the box task and the suppression task, we are led to expect that autists have a very specific difficulty with closed world reasoning about exceptions:

(4)   Autists can apply closed world reasoning, but have a decreased ability in handling exceptions to rules.

We thus expect a refusal to suppress the inferences MP and MT in case the second conditional premise is of the additional type. To show that the problem is really specific to exceptions, and not a problem about integrating new information, or with closed world reasoning generally, one may look at autists' reasoning with AC and DA, in which case suppression is independent of exception-handling. Here one would expect behaviour which is comparable to normals. One must thus distinguish two forms of closed world reasoning that play a role here. On the one hand there is closed world reasoning applied to abnormalities or exceptions, which takes the form: 'assume only those exceptions occur which are explicitly listed'. On the other hand there is closed world reasoning applied to rules, which takes the form of diagnostic reasoning: 'if B has occurred and the only known rules with B as consequent are $A_1 \rightarrow B, \ldots, A_n \rightarrow B$, then assume one of $A_1, \ldots, A_n$ has occurred'. These forms of closed world reasoning are in principle independent, and in our autist population we indeed observed a dissociation between the two.

Table 2 presents the data as relevant to the suppression task (data taken from Pijnacker et al [11]).

Table 2. Results on suppression task in autists (n=28) and matched controls (n=28). Taken from [11].

% responses	ASD			Control		
	yes	no	maybe	yes	no	maybe
MP	89.6	0.0	10.4	96.1	2.5	1.4
MP add	71.0	1.1	28.0	51.1	0.7	48.2
MP alt	92.9	0.4	6.8	97.5	0.7	1.8
MT	1.4	79.6	19.0	2.5	92.8	4.7
MT add	0.7	62.1	37.1	0.7	45.0	54.3
MT alt	0.4	90.3	9.3	1.1	95.0	3.9
AC	45.0	1.1	53.9	67.1	2.1	30.7
AC add	28.1	1.1	70.9	35.7	0.0	64.3
AC alt	12.2	2.2	85.7	9.6	0.0	90.4
DA	1.1	48.0	50.9	0.4	69.1	30.6
DA add	2.9	28.9	68.2	2.5	33.6	63.9
DA alt	3.2	15.7	81.1	1.1	10.4	88.5

As predicted, suppression of fallacies (DA and AC) with an alternative premiss does occur and the percentages we find are roughly the same as those found in research with normal subjects (cf. table 2). Suppression of MP, by contrast, is much rarer in our subjects than in normals. In the dialogues subjects often ignored the additional premiss completely in their overt reasoning. With regard to suppression of MT the results are less dramatic, and harder to interpret, in particular because the rate of endorsement for MT with an alternative premiss is somewhat higher than that for the base case. Nevertheless, the percentage of MT conclusions drawn to problems with an additional premiss is higher than for the normal subjects – autists are not suppressing.

These observations lend some support to the hypothesis (4), that it is specifically processing exceptions that creates difficulties for autistic subjects. DA and AC showed the pattern familiar from neurotypical subjects, suggesting that this type of closed world reasoning, where exceptions do not figure, presents no difficulties. The behaviour in MP and MT conditions (especially the former), where implicit exceptions need to be acknowledged to achieve suppression, was different from neurotypical subjects, showing much less suppression. Perhaps (4) is not the ultimate formulation of the hypothesis, but that there is something very distinct about autists' handling of defeasible rules seems certain.

7   An Apparent Counterexample: The 'Tubes Task'

Here we discuss some potential problems with the 'logical' account of executive dysfunction raised by other pieces of data. The box task is superficially similar to another task devised by Russell, the 'tubes task'.

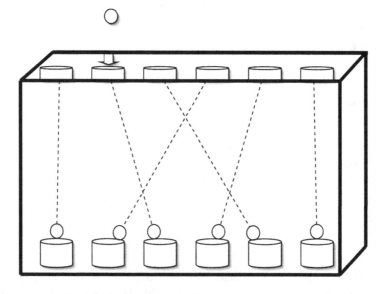

Fig. 3. Russell's tubes task

What one sees in this schematic drawing is a series of four holes into which a ball can be dropped, to land in a small container below. A ball dropped through the leftmost opening will end up in the catch-tray directly underneath, but a ball dropped through the rightmost opening travels through an opaque tube to end up in the catch-tray which is second from left. The child sees the ball being dropped through an opening, and has to retrieve it from one of the catch-trays below. When the ball is dropped in the rightmost opening, children of age 3 or younger tend to look in the catch-tray directly underneath the opening, probably applying the (defeasible) rule that things fall vertically. Older children, *including also autistic children*, manage to inhibit the 'prepotent' response and search in the correct catch-tray, adequately representing the trajectory of the ball as guided by the tube.

The apparent puzzle posed by performance on this task is that in this case autistic children *are* able to switch rules effortlessly. Russell explains this by a distinction between 'arbitrary' rules imposed by the experimenter (as in the box task), and rules based on fairly transparent physical principles (as in the tubes task). Autists would be impaired on the former but not the latter, incidentally showing that autism, viewed as executive dysfunction, must be a rather specific executive deficit. If both kinds of defeasible rules require the same kind of closed world reasoning about abnormalities, the hypothesis that it is this form of reasoning that is difficult for autists, is defeated.

The first thing to observe here is that the rules involved in the two tasks have different logical forms, and so require different reasoning. In the box task, correct performance hinges on the ability to amend the *antecedent* of the rule, whereas in the case of the tubes task it is the consequent (i.e. the catch-tray) that has to be changed. In the box task, the original plan has to be changed by incorporating another action,, whereas in the case of the tubes task one action has to be replaced by another. This suggests that what happens in the tubes task need not be viewed as rule-switching, but can also been seen as the application of a *single* IF-THEN-ELSE rule, where the action to be taken depends on the satisfaction or non-satisfaction of an explicit precondition: unimpeded fall of the ball. On this analysis, the difference between box task and tubes task would be that in the former case a new rule has to be synthesized on the spot by exception-handling, whereas in the latter case the switch is between components of a given single rule.

It seems that autistic subjects have less difficulty with synthesizing an IF-THEN-ELSE rule from instructions shown to them, then with rule-construction by exception-handling. Indeed, a standard 'Go/No Go' task is of the IF-THEN-ELSE form. For instance, in one such task, subjects were shown different letters of the alphabet that flashed one at a time on a computer screen. They were asked to respond by pressing a key in every case except when they saw the letter X. The first task was a Go task, in which the letter X never appeared and in this way subjects were allowed to build up a tendency to respond. Immediately afterward, subjects performed a Go/No Go task in which the letter X did appear in the lineup, at which point the subject had to control the previously built impulse to respond. Autists are not particularly impaired at such a task, although they do become confused when they have to shift rapidly between one target stimulus and another (Ozonoff et al. [8]).

At a more abstract level, what the analysis of the empirical difference between the box and tubes tasks just given highlights is that, before one can discuss whether autists have difficulties with rule-switching, the proper definition of 'rule' in this context has to be clarified. If the preceding considerations are correct, than a rule can be more general than the 'condition – action' format.

8 Conclusion: The Role of Logic in Cognitive Processes

The hidden message of the preceding discussion is that logic plays a role in the description of cognitive processes if these processes involve planning. In the analysis presented here there is a continuity between rigidity in motor behaviour, lack of flexibility in planning, and insensitivity to possible exceptions to rules, whether verbal or non-verbal. Elsewhere, we have argued that the same planning mechanism appears to be operating from motor planning all the way to discourse integration (see van Lambalgen and Hamm [23]), and that there is an explanation in logical terms for difficulties with discourse comprehension and production observed in some psychiatric disorders, notably ADHD ([24]).

Planning has a distinctive logical form, which is different from classical logic, but has considerable cognitive advantages, such as the existence of an implementation in artificial neural nets [18, Chapter 8]. However, what is characteristic of the approach outlined above is that explanations of cognitive phenomena are not sought at Marr's algorithmic and neural levels, as theories in cognitive science tend to do, but rather at Marr's computational level, by means of logical descriptions of planning and its failures. One consequence of such a strategy is that theories that are perceived to be very different and whose relative merits are hotly debated (such as theory of mind deficit and executive dysfunction in the case of autism), upon analysis turn out to be two sides of the same coin, and not at all in opposition. Likewise, such a logical analysis has the potential to tighten the relationship between theory and experimental predictions.

References

1. Byrne, R.M.J.: Suppressing valid inferences with conditionals. Cognition 31, 61–83 (1989)
2. Dieussaert, K., Schaeken, W., Schroyen, W., d'Ydewalle, G.: Strategies during complex conditional inferences. Thinking and Reasoning 6(2), 125–161 (2000)
3. Leslie, A.: Pretence and representation: the origins of a 'theory of mind'. Psychological Review 94, 412–426 (1987)
4. Marr, D.: Vision: A Computational investigation into the human representation and processing of visual information. W.H. Freeman, San Fransisco (1982)
5. Oaksford, M., Chater, N.: Probabilities and pragmatics in conditional inference: suppression and order effects. In: Hardman, D., Macchi, L. (eds.) Thinking: psychological perspectives on reasoning, judgment and decision making, vol. 6, pp. 95–122. John Wiley & Sons, Chichester (2003)
6. Oaksford, M., Chater, N.: Bayesian rationality. Oxford University Press, Oxford (2007)
7. Onishi, K.H., Baillargeon, R.: Do 15-month-old infants understand false beliefs? Science 308, 255–258 (2005)
8. Ozonoff, S., Strayer, D.L., McMahon, W.M., Filloux, F.: Executive function abilities in children with autism and tourette syndrom: an information-processing approach. Journal of Child Psychology and Psychiatry 35, 1015–1032 (1994)
9. Perner, J., Leekham, S., Wimmer, H.: Three-year olds' difficulty with false belief: the case for a conceptual deficit. British Journal of Developmental Psychology 5, 125–137 (1987)

10. Piaget, J.: Logic and psychology. Manchester University Press, Manchester (1953)
11. Pijnacker, J., Geurts, B., van Lambalgen, M., Buitelaar, J., Kan, C., Hagoort, P.: Conditional reasoning in high-functioning adults with autism. Neuropsychologia 47(3), 644–651 (2009)
12. Russell, J.: Autism as an executive disorder. Oxford University Press, Oxford (1997)
13. Russell, J.: Cognitive theories of autism. In: Harrison, J.E., Owen, A.M. (eds.) Cognitive deficits in brain disorders, pp. 295–323. Dunitz, London (2002)
14. Siegal, M., Beattie, K.: Where to look first for children's knowledge of false beliefs. Cognition 38, 1–12 (1991)
15. Smid, H.: Reasoning with rules and exceptions in autism. Msc thesis, ILLC, Amsterdam (2005), http://staff.science.uva.nl/~michiell
16. Stenning, K., van Lambalgen, M.: A little logic goes a long way: basing experiment on semantic theory in the cognitive science of conditional reasoning. Cognitive Science 28(4), 481–530 (2004)
17. Stenning, K., van Lambalgen, M.: Semantic interpretation as reasoning in non-monotonic logic: the real meaning of the suppression task. Cognitive Science 29(6), 919–960 (2005)
18. Stenning, K., van Lambalgen, M.: Human reasoning and cognitive science. MIT Press, Cambridge (2008)
19. Stenning, K., van Lambalgen, M.: 'Non-monotonic' does not mean 'probabilistic' (Commentary on Oaksford and Chater's 'Précis of Bayesian Rationality)'. Behavioral and Brain Sciences 32(1), 102–103 (2009)
20. Stenning, K., van Lambalgen, M.: Logic in a noisy world. In: Oaksford, M. (ed.) The psychology of conditionals. Oxford University Press, Oxford (2010)
21. Stevenson, R., Over, D.: Deduction from uncertain premisses. Quarterly Journal of Experimental Psychology A 48(3), 613–643 (1995)
22. Tomasello, M.: Constructing a language. A usage-based theory of language acquisition. Harvard University Press, Boston (2003)
23. van Lambalgen, M., Hamm, F.: The proper treatment of events. Blackwell, Oxford (2004)
24. van Lambalgen, M., van Kruistum, C., Parigger, E.M.: Discourse processing in attention-deficit hyperactivity disorder (ADHD). Journal of Logic, Language and Information 17, 467–487 (2008)
25. Wason, P.C.: Reasoning about a rule. Quarterly Journal of Experimental Psychology 20, 273–281 (1968)

Formal Lifetime Reliability Analysis Using Continuous Random Variables

Naeem Abbasi, Osman Hasan, and Sofiène Tahar

Dept. of Electrical & Computer Engineering, Concordia University
1455 de Maisonneuve W., Montreal, Quebec, H3G 1M8, Canada
{n_ab,o_hasan,tahar}@ece.concordia.ca

Abstract. Reliability has always been an important concern in the design of engineering systems. Recently proposed formal reliability analysis techniques have been able to overcome the accuracy limitations of traditional simulation based techniques but can only handle problems involving discrete random variables. In this paper, we extend the capabilities of existing theorem proving based reliability analysis by formalizing several important statistical properties of continuous random variables, for example, the second moment and the variance. We also formalize commonly used reliability theory concepts of survival function and hazard rate. With these extensions, it is now possible to formally reason about important reliability measures associated with the life of a system, for example, the probability of failure and the mean-time-to-failure of the system operating in an uncertain and harsh environment, which is usually continuous in nature. We illustrate the modeling and verification process with the help of an example involving the reliability analysis of electronic system components.

1 Introduction

Tragedies such as the industrial accident in the union carbide pesticide plant in Bhopal India [2], space shuttles Columbia and Challenger accidents [18], and the high-speed train accident near the village of Eschede in Lower Saxony in Germany [13] all highlight the importance of design reliability in various disciplines of engineering. The reliability of a system is defined as the probability that it will adequately perform its specified purpose for a specified period of time under the specified environmental conditions [14]. The two most popular representations of the distribution of the lifetime of a system are the survival function and the hazard function [14]. The survival function describes the probability that a system is functioning at any time t, and the hazard function describes the failure risk at a time t.

Traditionally, reliability analysis has been done using paper and pencil and simulation based approaches. In engineering applications, the paper and pencil approach very quickly becomes impractical because of the amount of detail involved. Simulation based reliability analysis is popular because of the availability of a number of automated tools. Unfortunately, the simulation based analysis

A. Dawar and R. de Queiroz (Eds.): WoLLIC 2010, LNAI 6188, pp. 84–97, 2010.
© Springer-Verlag Berlin Heidelberg 2010

is neither accurate not can it truly model random behavior. Computer simulations rely on floating-point numbers representation of system parameters which can lead to errors in reliability analysis and thus can have costly consequences. Moreover, simulation based techniques use pseudo random number generators for simulating the random behavior and require a large amount of computing resources. Formal methods based techniques are 100% accurate and allow the modeling and analysis of true random behavior and thus provide an alternative approach for reliability analysis of the critical parts of a system.

In this paper, we build on the work of [10] and [11] and formalize important definitions of the statistical properties of continuous random variables that play an important role in reliability engineering. The work in [11] deals with discrete random variables whereas the work in [10] only presents the formal verification of expectation properties for continuous random variables. In this paper, we verify a general expression for the second moment of positive continuous random variables, that range over a positive unbounded interval $[0, \infty)$, hence suitable for modeling lifetime behavior of engineering system components.

$$E[X^2] = \lim_{n \to \infty} \left[\sum_{i=0}^{n2^n - 1} (\frac{i}{2^n})^2 P \left\{ \frac{i}{2^n} \leq X < \frac{i+1}{2^n} \right\} + nP(X \geq n) \right] \quad (1)$$

where X is the random variable and P represents the probability measure. We utilize this general expression to verify several important reliability analysis related statistical properties such as the second moment and variance of the exponential random variable.

The rest of the paper is organized as follows: Section 2 reviews related work. Section 3 presents the formalization and verification of statistical properties of continuous random variables. Section 4 describes the formalization of reliability theory concepts of survival and hazard functions. For illustration purposes, Section 5 presents the reliability analysis of a capacitor. Finally, Section 6 concludes the paper.

2   Related Work

One of the earliest example of detailed reliability studies in engineering systems dates back to 1938 [4]. In this study, factors for the improvement of service reliability for electrical power systems were considered. In the field of electronics the concepts of reliability were initially introduced after second world war to improve the performance of communication and navigational systems [16].

In order to predict the reliability one must model the system and its constituent components in such a way that captures the failure mechanisms. For example in case of electronic systems a method called the part failure method has been shown to be very accurate [5]. This method has been extensively used by military engineers to predict useful life times of systems and to develop highly reliable systems and equipments. This method is based on calculation of failure rates of individual components that make up the system and then by using appropriate formulas transform it into the reliability of the whole system. Standards such as [6,7,17] are some of the examples which specify adequate performance requirements and environmental conditions for reliability modeling, analysis, and risk assessment.

In order to analyze systems formally in a theorem proving environment it is important to have an infrastructure for reasoning about the underlying mathematical concepts of probability and statistics. Until recently it was only possible to reason about reliability problems that involved discrete random variable in a theorem proving environment. Hurd [12] formalized a probability theory and discrete random variables in the HOL theorem prover [8]. Building upon [12], Hasan [9] formalized statistical properties of single and multiple discrete random variables. Hasan [9] also formalized a class of continuous random variables for which the inverse CDF functions can be expressed in a closed form. Hasan *et. al* [11] presented higher-order-logic formalizations of some core reliability theory concepts and successfully formalized and verified the conditions for almost always repairability for reconfigurable memory arrays in the presence of stuck-at and coupling faults. In this paper, we build upon the higher-order-logic formalization of [11], and formalize new representations of the lifetime distributions, namely the survival and hazard functions, and statistical properties such as the moments and variance of continuous random variables which was not possible in the framework presented in [11]. In [10], Hasan *et. al* formalized expectation for both bounded and unbounded continuous random variables in the HOL theorem prover. Their work utilized the Lebesgue integration theory developed in [3] and [15]. In this paper, we utilize the formalization of Borel sigma algebra of [15] and several key Lebesgue integral properties of [3].

Other formal methods based techniques, such as probabilistic model checking, can be used to analyze reliability, however, they do not have support for the verification of statistical properties (moments and variance) of the commonly used lifetime distributions [1,19]. The proposed reliability analysis approach on the other hand is capable of handling both probabilistic and statistical reliability properties.

3   Statistical Properties of Lifetime Distributions

In this section, we present the formalization of the definitions of several important statistical properties of random variables in HOL. These statistical properties summarize some of the most important aspects of the probability distribution of a random variable. For example, the coefficients of skewness is a measure of symmetry of the probability distribution of a random variable. Other formalized definitions include the expectation of a function of a random variable, first, second and n-th moments, variance, standard deviation, mean absolute deviation, and coefficients of variation and kurtosis of a random variable, as summarized in Table 1. In these formalized definitions, rv is a random variable. m represents a probability space defined as: $m = (\mathcal{U}, \mathcal{E}, \mathbb{P})$, where $\mathcal{U}$ is a sample space, $\mathcal{E}$ is a set of events, and $\mathcal{P}$ is the probability measure. The function *expec* represents the expectation or the first moment of the random variable.

Table 1. Statistical Properties and their HOL Formalizations

Property	Definition	HOL Formalization
expec. h(X)	$E[h(X)]$	⊢ ∀m rv h. fun_rv m rv h = expec m (λx. h (rv x))
first moment	$E[X]=\mu$	⊢ ∀m rv. first_moment m rv = expec m (λx. rv x)
second moment	$E[X^2]=\mu_2$	⊢ ∀m rv. second_moment m rv = expec m (λx. (rv x) pow 2)
Nth moment	$E[X^N]=\mu_N$	⊢ ∀m rv N. nth_moment m rv N = expec m (λx. (rv x) pow N)
variance	σ^2	⊢ ∀m rv. variance m rv = expec m (λx. ((rv x) - expec m rv) pow 2)
standard deviation	σ	⊢ ∀m rv. std_dev m rv = sqrt(variance m rv)
coef. of variation	$\frac{\sigma}{\mu}$	⊢ ∀m rv. coef_of_var m rv = (std_dev m rv)/(expec m rv)
mean abs. deviation	$E[\|X-\mu\|]$	⊢ ∀m rv. m_abs_dev m rv = expec m (λx. abs((rv x) - expec m rv))

coef. of skewness	$E[(\frac{X-\mu}{\sigma})^3]$
	$=\alpha_3$
		⊢ ∀m rv. skew m rv = expec m
		    (λx. ((rv x) - expec m rv) pow 3)
		    /((std_dev m rv) pow 3)

coef. of kurtosis	$E[(\frac{X-\mu}{\sigma})^4]$
	$=\alpha_4$
		⊢ ∀m rv. kurt m rv = expec m
		    (λx. ((rv x) - expec m rv) pow 4)
		    /((std_dev m rv) pow 4)

3.1 Verification of Statistical Properties

The verification of the second moment relation for an unbounded continuous random variable, given in Equation (1), is described in this section.

Definition 1: *Second Moment of a Random Variable*
⊢ ∀ rv. second_moment $(\mathcal{U}, \mathcal{E}, \mathbb{P})$ rv = $\int_{\mathcal{U}}$ rv^2 d$\mathbb{P}$

The function second_moment accepts a probability space, $(\mathcal{U}, \mathcal{E}, \mathbb{P})$, and a random variable rv that maps infinite Boolean sequences to real numbers [9]. In Hurd's [12] formalization of the probability space $(\mathcal{U}, \mathcal{E}, \mathbb{P})$, $\mathcal{U}$ represents the universal set of all Boolean sequences.

Theorem 1 formally states the second moment relation for a positive valued unbounded continuous random variable.

Theorem 1: *Second Moment of an Unbounded Random Variable*
⊢ ∀ rv. (∀ s. 0 ≤ rv s) ∧ (∀ x. {s | rv s ≥ x} ∈ $\mathcal{E}$)
    (∀ x y. x < y ⇒ {s | x ≤ rv s < y} ∈ $\mathcal{E}$) ⇒
    $\Big($second_moment $(\mathcal{U}, \mathcal{E}, \mathbb{P})$ rv =

$\lim_{n \to \infty} \Big[\sum_{i=0}^{n2^n-1} (\frac{i}{2^n})^2 \mathbb{P}\{s \mid \frac{i}{2^n} \le rv\ s < \frac{i+1}{2^n}\} + n\mathbb{P}\{s \mid rv\ s \ge n\} \Big] \Big)$

The first assumption in Theorem 1 states that the random variable rv is positive. The second and third assumptions guarantee that the sets that arise in this verification are measurable events. The entire range of the unbounded random variable is divided into two main intervals, namely $[0, n)$ and $[n, \infty)$. The first interval corresponds to $[0, n2^n - 1]$ summation term, while the second term covers the rest of the positive unbounded interval. It is assumed that the sequence (rv_n) is defined as:

$$rv_n(x) = \sum_{i=0}^{n2^n-1} (\tfrac{i}{2^n}) \mathbb{I}_{\left\{ s \mid \frac{i}{2^n} \leq rv\ s < \frac{i+1}{2^n} \right\}}(x) + n\mathbb{I}_{\left\{ s \mid rv\ s \geq n \right\}}(x)$$

where $\mathbb{I}_A(x)$ is a real-valued function of a set A, such that: $\mathbb{I}_A(x) = 1$ if $x \in A$, and $\mathbb{I}_A(x) = 0$ if $x \notin A$.

In order to utilize any definition or property of Lebesgue integration theory with the above theorem, we first needed to show that the triplet $(\mathcal{U}, \mathcal{E}, \mathbb{P})$ is a measure space with a positive measure. We verified these conditions based on the corresponding theorems available in Hurd's [12] formalization of the probability space $(\mathcal{E}, \mathbb{P})$ along with the definition of measure in [3] under the given assumptions.

The convergence of a positive measurable function to the Lebesgue integral property [3] and the Modus Ponens (MP) rule are then used to split the proof goal of Theorem 1 into the following five subgoals. They correspond to the monotonicity (equation 2) and positive simple-function requirement on rv_n (equations 3, 4, and 5) and the three other assumptions (equation 6) described below [3]:

$$\texttt{mono\_increasing} \left[\sum_{i=0}^{n2^n-1} (\frac{i}{2^n})^2 \mathbb{I}_{\left\{ s \mid \frac{i}{2^n} \leq rv\ s < \frac{i+1}{2^n} \right\}}(x) + n\mathbb{I}_{\left\{ s \mid rv\ s \geq n \right\}} \right] \quad (2)$$

$$\left[\sum_{i=0}^{n2^n-1} (\frac{i}{2^n})^2 \mathbb{I}_{\left\{ s \mid \frac{i}{2^n} \leq rv\ s < \frac{i+1}{2^n} \right\}}(x) + n\mathbb{I}_{\left\{ s \mid rv\ s \geq n \right\}} \right] \leq rv(x)^2 \quad (3)$$

$$\lim_{n \to \infty} \left[\sum_{i=0}^{n2^n-1} (\frac{i}{2^n})^2 \mathbb{I}_{\left\{ s \mid \frac{i}{2^n} \leq rv\ s < \frac{i+1}{2^n} \right\}}(x) + n\mathbb{I}_{\left\{ s \mid rv\ s \geq n \right\}} \right] = rv(x)^2 \quad (4)$$

$$\exists y. \lim_{n \to \infty} \left[\sum_{i=0}^{n2^n-1} (\frac{i}{2^n})^2 \mathbb{P}\left\{ s \mid \frac{i}{2^n} \leq rv\ s < \frac{i+1}{2^n} \right\} + n\mathbb{P}\left\{ s \mid rv\ s \geq n \right\} \right] = y \quad (5)$$

$$\left(\forall i. (i < 2^n) \Rightarrow \left\{ s \mid \frac{i}{2^n} \leq rv\ s < \frac{i+1}{2^n} \right\} \in \mathcal{E}\right) \wedge \left(\forall i. 0 \leq \frac{i}{2^n}\right) \wedge (\texttt{FINITE}\{i \mid i < 2^n\}) \quad (6)$$

We verified the monotonically increasing property in the first subgoal based on the following two facts. First, the indicator function in the subgoal only becomes 1 for only one interval or one particular value of i. Second, as the argument of the sequence, i.e., n, increases the intervals become finer and the resulting value of the sequence becomes larger and from the way rv_n is defined, it is then possible to show that $rv_n^2(x) \leq rv_{n+1}^2(x)$.

The second subgoal, which corresponds to the pre-conditions for the function rv_n to be a positive simple-function, consists of three subgoals. These three subgoals can be discharged based on the third assumption of Theorem 1, arithmetic reasoning and set theory principles, respectively.

We consider two cases for the third subgoal. For the case when $i < n2^n$, the third subgoal is true as there is only one i, say i', for which the real value of $(rv\ x)$ would fall in the interval $[\frac{i}{2^n}, \frac{i+1}{2^n})$ out of all $n2^n$ possible values for i. Thus the indicator function would be 1 for this particular i only and 0 otherwise, which means that the summation would be equal to $(\frac{i'}{2^n})^2$. Now, substituting this value for the summation in the third subgoal along with the fact that $rv\ x$ lies in the interval $[\frac{i'}{2^n}, \frac{i'+1}{2^n})$ leads to its verification. Similar reasoning and properties of rv_n are used to discharge the case when $i \geq n2^n$.

The fourth subgoal is proved using the definition of limit of a real sequence, the monotonicity of the given sequence and reasoning regarding the indicator function similar to the previous subgoal. Finally, the real sequence in the fifth subgoal can be verified to be pointwise convergent by verifying that it is monotonic, just like the sequence in the first subgoal since the probability term will only be non-zero for one particular value of i, either between 0 and $n2^n$ interval or when i is greater than or equal to $n2^n$. In both cases, it is shown that $rv_n(x) \leq rv(x)$ thus concluding the verification of Theorem 1.

3.2   Moments and Variance of Lifetime Distributions

In this section, we utilize Theorem 1 for the verification of the second moment and variance properties of the exponential random variable. The second moment for the continuous exponential random variable, is formalized as follows:

Theorem 2: *Second Moment of the Exponential(m) Random Variable*
$\vdash \forall\ \mathtt{m}.\ (0 < \mathtt{m}) \Rightarrow \big(\mathtt{second\_moment}\ (\mathcal{U}, \mathcal{E}, \mathbb{P})\ (\mathtt{exp\_rv\ m}) = \frac{2}{\mathtt{m}^2}\big)$

We start the proof process by rewriting the left hand side using the general second moment theorem for the unbounded random variables (Theorem 1).

$$\lim_{n \to \infty} \sum_{i=0}^{n2^n-1} (\tfrac{i}{2^n})^2 \mathbb{P}\left\{ \mathtt{s}\ \middle|\ \tfrac{i}{2^n} \leq (\mathtt{exp\_rv\ m})\ \mathtt{s} < \tfrac{i+1}{2^n} \right\}$$
$$+ \mathbb{P}\left\{ \mathtt{s}\ \middle|\ \mathtt{n} \leq (\mathtt{exp\_rv\ m})\ \mathtt{s} \right\} = \tfrac{2}{\mathtt{m}^2}$$

Then using set theory properties and the definition of *CDF* of the exponential random variable, we show that

$$\mathbb{P}\left\{s \mid \frac{i}{2^n} \le (\exp\_rv\ m)\ s < \frac{i+1}{2^n}\right\} + n\mathbb{P}\left\{s \mid n \le (\exp\_rv\ m)\ s\right\}$$
$$= \left[(e^{-m\frac{i}{2^n}})(1 - e^{-\frac{m}{2^n}}) + ne^{-mn}\right]$$

We then rewrite the left hand side of the subgoal with the above result and arrive at the following subgoal.

$$\lim_{n\to\infty}\left[\sum_{i=0}^{n2^n-1}(\tfrac{i}{2^n})^2(e^{-m\frac{i}{2^n}})(1 - e^{-\frac{m}{2^n}}) + ne^{-mn}\right] = \tfrac{2}{m^2}$$

In order to evaluate the limit terms, we first prove the following sum of a sequence containing terms of type (i^2P^i).

$$\sum_{i=0}^{M-1}(i^2P^i) = \frac{P^M(M^2P^2 - 2M^2P + M^2 - 2MP^2 + 2MP + P^2 + P)}{(P-1)^3} - \frac{P(P+1)}{(P-1)^3}$$

We then specialize this result for the case when $M = n2^n$ and $P = e^{\frac{-m}{2^n}}$ as follows:

$$\sum_{i=0}^{n2^n-1} i^2(e^{-\frac{m}{2^n}})^i = \frac{n^22^n e^{\frac{-m}{2^n}(n2^n)}}{(e^{-\frac{m}{2^n}}-1)} - \frac{2(n2^n)(e^{\frac{-m}{2^n}(n2^n+1)})}{(e^{-\frac{m}{2^n}}-1)^2} + \frac{(e^{\frac{-m}{2^n}(n2^n)}-1)(e^{\frac{-m}{2^n}})(e^{\frac{-m}{2^n}}+1)}{(e^{-\frac{m}{2^n}}-1)^3}$$

Using the above results and with a fair amount of rewriting effort together with product and sum limit theorems, we arrive at the following subgoal.

$$\lim_{n\to\infty}\left[-n^2e^{-mn}\right] + \lim_{n\to\infty}\left[-\frac{2ne^{-mn}e^{\frac{-m}{2^n}}}{2^n(1-e^{\frac{-m}{2^n}})}\right] + \lim_{n\to\infty}\left[-\frac{(e^{-mn}-1)(e^{\frac{-m}{2^n}})(e^{\frac{-m}{2^n}}+1)}{2^{2n}(1-e^{\frac{-m}{2^n}})^2}\right]$$
$$+ \lim_{n\to\infty}\left[ne^{-mn}\right] = \tfrac{2}{m^2}$$

We then show that the first and fourth terms on the left hand side of the above subgoal approach zero as n tends to ∞, that is, $\lim_{n\to\infty}\left[-n^2e^{-mn}\right] = 0$ and $\lim_{n\to\infty}\left[ne^{-mn}\right] = 0$.

The evaluation of the second and third limit terms required a lot of rewriting effort in HOL, and the proof steps are explained in the following. First we prove the following two limit expressions in HOL using L'hopital's rule.

$$\lim_{x\to0}\left[\frac{xe^{mx}}{1-e^{-mx}}\right] = \lim_{x\to0}\left[\frac{x(-me^{mx})+e^{mx}}{0-(-me^{-mx})}\right] = \tfrac{1}{m}, \text{ and}$$

$$\lim_{x\to0}\left[\frac{x}{1-e^{-mx}}\right] = \lim_{x\to0}\left[\frac{1}{0-(-me^{-mx})}\right] = \tfrac{1}{m}$$

Then we specialize the above two results for the case when $x = \frac{1}{2^n}$ and show

that $\lim_{n\to\infty}\left[\frac{e^{\frac{-m}{2^n}}}{2^n(1-e^{\frac{-m}{2^n}})}\right] = \tfrac{1}{m}$ and $\lim_{n\to\infty}\left[\frac{1}{2^n(1-e^{\frac{-m}{2^n}})}\right] = \tfrac{1}{m}$

Then using the sum and product limit theorem we rewrite the second and third limit terms as follows:

$$\lim_{n\to\infty}\left[2ne^{-mn}\frac{e^{\frac{-m}{2^n}}}{2^n(1-e^{\frac{-m}{2^n}})}\right] = (2)\left(\lim_{n\to\infty}[ne^{-mn}]\right)\left(\lim_{n\to\infty}\left[\frac{e^{\frac{-m}{2^n}}}{2^n(1-e^{\frac{-m}{2^n}})}\right]\right)$$
$$= (2)(0)(\tfrac{1}{m}) = 0$$

$$\lim_{n\to\infty}\left[-\frac{(e^{-mn}-1)(e^{\frac{-m}{2^n}})(e^{\frac{-m}{2^n}}+1)}{2^{2n}(1-e^{\frac{-m}{2^n}})^2}\right] =$$
$$\lim_{n\to\infty}[-(e^{-mn}-1)]\lim_{n\to\infty}\left[\frac{e^{-mn}}{2^n(1-e^{\frac{-m}{2^n}})}\right]\left(\lim_{n\to\infty}\left[\frac{e^{-mn}}{2^n(1-e^{\frac{-m}{2^n}})}\right]+\lim_{n\to\infty}\left[\frac{1}{2^n(1-e^{\frac{-m}{2^n}})}\right]\right) =$$
$$(1)(\tfrac{1}{m})(\tfrac{1}{m}+\tfrac{1}{m}) = \tfrac{2}{m^2}$$

Finally, we substitute these limits in the above subgoal and show that the left hand side is equal to the right hand side thus completing the proof of the second moment of the exponential random variable.

Theorem 3: *Variance of the Exponential(m) Random Variable*
$\vdash \forall$ m. $(0 < m) \Rightarrow (\texttt{variance } (\mathcal{U}, \mathcal{E}, \mathbb{P}) \texttt{ (exp\_rv m)} = \tfrac{1}{m^2})$

The verification steps for the variance of the exponential random variable involve some rewriting using the definition of the variance and the expectation and the second moment theorems. The resulting subgoal $(\frac{2}{m^2}) - (\frac{1}{m})^2 = \frac{1}{m^2}$ is easily shown to be true, based on arithmetic reasoning, thus completing the proof of the variance of the exponential random variable.

4   Reliability Theory Formalization

In this section, we present the formalization of the concepts of survival and hazard functions.

4.1   Survival Function

The survival function represents the probability that a component is functioning at one particular time t and is formalized in HOL as follows:

Definition 2: *Survival Function*
$\vdash \forall$rv. $\texttt{survival\_function} = (\lambda\texttt{t. 1 - CDF rv t})$

where CDF is the cumulative distribution function of random variable *rv*. Both survival function and CDF in HOL are of type $(((\text{num} \to \text{bool}) \to \text{real}) \to \text{real} \to \text{real})$.

Theorem 4: *Survival Function, Exponential(m) Random Variable*
$\vdash \forall$ m t. $(0 < m) \wedge (0 \leq t) \Rightarrow$
$\qquad\qquad (\texttt{survival\_function } (\lambda\texttt{s. exp\_rv m s) t} = (\lambda\texttt{s. } e^{-ms})\texttt{ t})$

Theorem 4 was verified using the definitions of survival function and CDF of exponential random variable together with set theory properties. If T represents the Time-to-Failure of an electronic system component, for example, then using

Theorem 4, we can now formally reason about probabilities of failure events at any time t i.e., $P\{T \le t\}$, or between any two times t_1 and t_2, i.e., $P\{t_1 \le T \le t_2\}$.

Besides Theorem 4, we also formally verified three important existence properties of the survival function in HOL:

Property 1: *Survival function at time 0 is equal to 1*
⊢ ∀rv. (∀x. CDF_in_events_bern rv x) ⇒
$$\text{(survival\_function rv 0 = 1)}$$

where the assumption of Property 1 ensures that events of the type $\{s|fs \le x\}$, which define the CDF, are in the sample space.

Property 2: *Survival function approaches 0 for very large values of times*
⊢ ∀rv. (∀x. CDF_in_events_bern rv x) ⇒
$$\text{(λn. survival\_function rv ((λn. \&n) n)) → 0}$$

and

Property 3: *Survival function is a non increasing function*
⊢ ∀rv a b. (a<b) ∧ (∀x. CDF_in_events_bern rv x) ⇒
$$\text{(survival\_function rv b} \le \text{survival\_function rv a)}$$

4.2   Hazard Function

The hazard function or instantaneous failure rate is used to model the amount of risk associated with a component at a given time t and is formalized in HOL as follows:

Definition 3: *Hazard Function*
⊢ ∀rv t. hazard_function rv t = @l.
    ((λa. (survival_function rv t - survival_function rv (t + a))
                        / ((a) (survival_function rv t))) → 1) 0

The HOL function hazard_function takes as input a random variable rv and a real value t and returns a real value l such that the incremental parameter a in the above definition approaches zero.

Using the definitions of hazard function, survival function, and CDF of exponential random variable we formally verify that the hazard function of an exponential random variable is a constant and is given by its parameter m.

Theorem 5: *Hazard Function, Exponential(m) Random Variable*
⊢ ∀ m t. (0 < m) ∧ (0 ≤ t) ⇒
$$\text{(hazard\_function (λs. exp\_rv m s) t} = m)$$

The hazard function gives an indication of how a component ages. Its units are usually given as the number of failures per unit time. A larger hazard function suggests that the component is under greater risk of failure. Using Theorem 5, we can now formally reason about the amount of failure risks associated with a component when operating under certain stress conditions. The results presented in this section are 100% accurate, completely general and exhaustive as opposed to simulation based techniques where approximate numerical results are available for a very restricted set of parameters.

5   Reliability Analysis of a Capacitor

Capacitors are an essential component of many electrical systems ranging from basic electronics used in medical devices to avionics used in aircrafts, artificial satellites and space shuttles. Uninterruptable power supplies and inverters commonly used in renewable energy power systems contain capacitors for filtering and smoothing of rectified power line voltages. Moreover, they are used in electrical power transmission and distributions networks for power factor correction. Their reliability is absolutely essential for correct behavior of electronics used in safety critical systems and in efficient operation of electrical power systems.

Exponential distribution is the most appropriate distribution for modeling the reliability behavior of a capacitor. The exponential probability distribution parameter in reliability theory is sometimes also called the failure rate. Definition 4 gives the base failure rate for a capacitor [5].

Definition 4: *Base Failure Rate, Capacitor*
⊢ ∀ A B VRop Ns Top NT G H.
    res_failure_rate_base A B VRop Ns Top NT G H =
    (A) (real_pow (real_pow (VRop / Ns) H + 1) B)
    (exp (real_pow ((Top + 273) / NT) G))

where A is the adjustment and B is the shaping factor (specified in [5]), VRop is the electrical stress ratio and is defined as the ratio of the operating to rated power. Ns is a stress constant, Top is the operating temperature, NT is the temperature constant, and G and H are called the acceleration constants (specified in [5]). The HOL function real_pow takes two real numbers as input and returns a real number. The returned number is equal to the first argument raised to the power of second argument of the function (i.e., real_pow A b = A^b). exp represents the exponential function. In the part failure method, the quality and environment stress factors are used to adjust the base failure rate of a component according to the operating environment and expected stress levels. The definitions of these two factors are given in [5] and are formalized in HOL as follows.

Definition 5: *Quality Stress Factor*
⊢ ∀ quality.
    cap_stress_factor_quality quality =
    (if quality = 0 then 15 / 10 else
    (if quality = 1 then 1 else
    (if quality = 2 then 3 / 10 else
    (if quality = 3 then 1 / 10 else 3 / 100))))

Definition 6: *Environment Stress Factor*
⊢ ∀ environment.
    cap_stress_factor_environment environment =
    (if environment = 0 then 1 else
    (if environmeht = 1 then 1 else
    (if environment = 2 then 2 else

```
(if environment = 3 then 4 else
(if environment = 4 then 5 else
(if environment = 5 then 7 else
(if environment = 6 then 15 / 2 else
(if environment = 7 then 8 else 15)))))))))
```

The HOL formalization of these stress factors accepts a natural number as input and returns the corresponding stress value. The formalization of the capacitor part failure rate, operating in a certain environment under certain electrical stress levels, is given in Definition 7.

Definition 7: *Part Failure Rate, Capacitor*
⊢ ∀ A B VRop Ns Top NT G H n m.
  cap_failure_rate_part A B VRop Ns Top NT G H n m =
  (cap_failure_rate_base A B VRop Ns Top NT G H)
  (cap_stress_factor_environment n) (cap_stress_factor_quality m)

5.1   Capacitor Lifetime Model

The capacitor life time in HOL is modeled using a function that takes as input the capacitor failure rate and returns a function of exponential random variable of type ((num→bool)→real).

Definition 8: *Capacitor Lifetime Model*
⊢ ∀ A B VRop Ns Top NT G H n m. cap_lifetime_model
cap_failure_rate_part A B VRop Ns Top NT G H n m = (λs. exp_rv
(cap_failure_rate_part A B VRop Ns Top NT G H n m) s)

5.2   Verification of Reliability Properties

The survival and hazard functions and three important statistical properties of capacitor life time are presented in this section.

Survival and Hazard Functions. Theorems 6 and 7 formally prove the survival and hazard function properties of the capacitor.

Theorem 6: *Survival Function, Exponential Random Variable*
⊢ ∀ A B VRop Ns Top NT G H n m t.
  $(0 < t) \wedge (0 < A) \wedge (0 \leq B) \wedge (0 \leq G) \wedge (0 \leq H) \wedge$
  $(0 < Ns) \wedge (0 < NT) \wedge (0 \leq VRop) \wedge (VRop \leq 1) \wedge$
  $(0 \leq n) \wedge (0 \leq m) \Rightarrow$ (survival_function (λs.
  exp_rv (cap_failure_rate_part A B VRop Ns Top NT G H n m) s) t
  = exp(-(cap_failure_rate_part A B VRop Ns Top NT G H n m) t))

All assumptions except for $(0 < t)$ ensure that the capacitor part failure rate (cap_failure_rate_part A B VRop Ns Top NT G H n m) is a positive real number.

Theorem 7: *Hazard Rate, Exponential Random Variable*
⊢ ∀ A B VRop Ns Top NT G H n m t.
  (0 < t) ∧ (0 < A) ∧ (0 ≤ B) ∧ (0 ≤ G) ∧ (0 ≤ H) ∧
  (0 < Ns) ∧ (0 < NT) ∧ (0 ≤ VRop) ∧ (VRop ≤ 1) ∧
  (0 ≤ n) ∧ (0 ≤ m) ⇒ (hazard_function (λs.
  exp_rv (cap_failure_rate_part A B VRop Ns Top NT G H n m) s) t
  = cap_failure_rate_part A B VRop Ns Top NT G H n m)

The proof of Theorem 7 involved rewriting with the definitions of survival and hazard functions, part failure rate and the CDF of the exponential random variable. The limit term is simplified using L'hopital's rule.

Statistical Properties. We formally verified several statistical properties of the capacitor lifetime using the proposed reliability analysis method in the HOL theorem prover. Three of which are presented below, namely, the mean, the second moment, and the variance of Time-to-Failure of the capacitor.

Theorem 8: *Mean Time-to-Failure (MTTF), Exponential(m)*
⊢ ∀ A B VRop Ns Top NT G H n m t.
  (0 < t) ∧ (0 < A) ∧ (0 ≤ B) ∧ (0 ≤ G) ∧ (0 ≤ H) ∧
  (0 < Ns) ∧ (0 < NT) ∧ (0 ≤ VRop) ∧ (VRop ≤ 1) ∧
  (0 ≤ n) ∧ (0 ≤ m) ⇒ mttf $(\mathcal{U}, \mathcal{E}, \mathbb{P})$ (λs.
  exp_rv (cap_failure_rate_part A B VRop Ns Top NT G H n m) s) =
  $\dfrac{1}{(cap\_failure\_rate\_part ABV RopN sTopNTGHnm)}$

Theorem 9: *Second Moment of Time-to-Failure, Exponential(m)*
⊢ ∀ A B VRop Ns Top NT G H n m t.
  (0 < t) ∧ (0 < A) ∧ (0 ≤ B) ∧ (0 ≤ G) ∧ (0 ≤ H) ∧
  (0 < Ns) ∧ (0 < NT) ∧ (0 ≤ VRop) ∧ (VRop ≤ 1) ∧
  (0 ≤ n) ∧ (0 ≤ m) ⇒ second_moment $(\mathcal{U}, \mathcal{E}, \mathbb{P})$ (λs.
  exp_rv (cap_failure_rate_part A B VRop Ns Top NT G H n m) s) =
  $\dfrac{2}{(cap\_failure\_rate\_part ABV RopN sTopNTGHnm)^2}$

Theorem 10: *Variance of Time-to-Failure, Exponential(m)*
⊢ ∀ A B VRop Ns Top NT G H n m t.
  (0 < t) ∧ (0 < A) ∧ (0 ≤ B) ∧ (0 ≤ G) ∧ (0 ≤ H) ∧
  (0 < Ns) ∧ (0 < NT) ∧ (0 ≤ VRop) ∧ (VRop ≤ 1) ∧
  (0 ≤ n) ∧ (0 ≤ m) ⇒ variance $(\mathcal{U}, \mathcal{E}, \mathbb{P})$ (λs.
  exp_rv (cap_failure_rate_part A B VRop Ns Top NT G H n m) s) =
  $\dfrac{1}{(cap\_failure\_rate\_part ABV RopN sTopNTGHnm)^2}$

The proofs of the above statistical properties were greatly facilitated by corresponding exponential random variable statistical properties, described in Section 3. It is important to note that the reliability analysis results proved in this section are completely generic expressions rather than numerical values as is the case in simulation based techniques. Moreover these results are 100% accurate as we are dealing with real numbers rather than floating point numbers as is the case in simulation based techniques. Such analysis was not previously possible in a theorem proving environment and we believe it to be a major step forward in the direction of the formal reliability analysis of engineering systems.

6   Conclusions

In this paper, we presented an approach for the reliability analysis of engineering systems in the sound environment of the HOL theorem prover. The approach builds upon existing formalizations of continuous random variables. We presented the formalization of two commonly used lifetime distribution representations, namely the survival and hazard functions. We also presented the formalizations of several important statistical properties of random variables and the formal proof of a general expression for the second moment of a continuous random variable using probability, measure and Lebesgue integration theories. We then used this expression to prove the second moment and variance relations for the exponential random variable. The usefulness of the proposed reliability analysis method was demonstrated with the help of reliability analysis of a capacitor, an essential building block in electrical and electronic systems. The HOL formalization and proof effort described in this paper took approximately 110 man-hours and consists of around 4000 lines of HOL code.

We are currently working on the formalization of other lifetime probability distributions such as Weibull and Gamma distributions to further enhance the proposed reliability analysis approach. The proposed method at this time allows one to define arbitrary lifetime distributions as long as a closed form expression for its CDF inverse exists, which makes it suitable for a large set of reliability analysis problems in engineering. We also plan to conduct the reliability analysis of multi component systems with and without redundancy.

References

1. Baier, C., Haverkort, B., Hermanns, H., Katoen, J.P.: Model Checking Algorithms for Continuous time Markov Chains. IEEE Transactions on Software Engineering 29(4), 524–541 (2003)
2. Broughton, E.: The Bhopal Disaster and its Aftermath: A Review. Environmental Health 4(6), 1–6 (2005)
3. Coble, A.: Anonymity, Information and Machine-assisted Proof. PhD Thesis, University of Cambridge, Cambridge, UK (2009)
4. Dean, S.M.: Considerations involved in making system investments for improved service reliability. EEI Bulletin (6), 491–496 (1938)
5. U. S. Department of Defence. Reliability Prediction of Electronic Equipment, Military handbook, MIL-HDBK-217B (1974)
6. U. S. Department of Defense. Reliability-Centered Maintenance (RCM) Requirements for Naval Aircraft, Weapon Systems, and Support Equipment, MIL-HDBK-2173 (1998)
7. FIDES. Reliability Methodology for Electronic Systems (2009)

8. Gordon, M.J.C., Melham, T.F.: Introduction to HOL: A Theorem Proving Environment for Higher-Order Logic. Cambridge University Press, Cambridge (1993)
9. Hasan, O.: Formal Probabilistic Analysis using Theorem Proving. PhD Thesis, Concordia University, Montreal, QC, Canada (2008)
10. Hasan, O., Abbasi, N., Akbarpour, B., Tahar, S., Akbarpour, R.: Formal Reasoning about Expectation Properties for Continuous Random Variables. In: Cavalcanti, A., Dams, D.R. (eds.) FM 2009. LNCS, vol. 5850, pp. 435–450. Springer, Heidelberg (2009)
11. Hasan, O., Tahar, S., Abbasi, N.: Formal Reliability Analysis using Theorem Proving. IEEE Transactions on Computers 59(5), 579–592 (2010)
12. Hurd, J.: Formal Verification of Probabilistic Algorithms. PhD Thesis, University of Cambridge, Cambridge, UK (2002)
13. Investigative Documentary on National Geographic Channel. Derailment at Eschede (High Speed Train Wreck), Seconds From Disaster (2007)
14. Leemis, L.M.: Reliability, Probabilistic Models and Statistical Methods (2009)
15. Mhamdi, T., Hasan, O., Tahar, S.: On the Formalization of the Lebesgue Integration Theory in HOL. In: Interactive Theorem Proving. LNCS, vol. 6172, pp. 387–402. Springer, Heidelberg (2010)
16. Myers, R.H., Ball, L.W.: Reliability Engineering for Electronic Systems. Wiley, Chichester (1964)
17. Institute of Electrical and Electronics Engineers. IEEE Standard Reliability Program for the Development and Production of Electronic Systems and Equipment, IEEE 1332 (1998)
18. Rogers Commission report, Report of the Presidential Commission on the Space Shuttle Challenger Accident, vol. 1, ch.4. p. 72 (1986),
    http://history.nasa.gov/rogersrep/v1ch4.htm
19. Rutten, J., Kwaiatkowska, M., Normal, G., Parker, D.: Mathematical Techniques for Analyzing Concurrent and Probabilisitc Systems. CRM Monograph Series, vol. 23. American Mathematical Society, Providence (2004)

Modal Logics with Counting

Carlos Areces, Guillaume Hoffmann, and Alexandre Denis

INRIA Nancy Grand Est, France
{firstname.lastname}@loria.fr

Abstract. We present a modal language that includes explicit operators to count the number of elements that a model might include in the extension of a formula, and we discuss how this logic has been previously investigated under different guises. We show that the language is related to graded modalities and to hybrid logics. We illustrate a possible application of the language to the treatment of plural objects and queries in natural language. We investigate the expressive power of this logic via bisimulations, discuss the complexity of its satisfiability problem, define a new reasoning task that retrieves the cardinality bound of the extension of a given input formula, and provide an algorithm to solve it.

1   Counting, Modally

Suppose there are at least two apples (say, on the table, but we don't care at the moment where the apples are). First-order logic ($\mathcal{FOL}$) with equality has no problem expressing this fact[1]:

$$\exists x.\exists y.(x \neq y \land Apple(x) \land Apple(y)).$$

We can actually dispense with equality, if we introduce counting quantifiers [1]

$$\exists^{\geq 2} x. Apple(x).$$

But suppose that we want to dispense with *quantifiers* instead, and count in terms of a propositional (or a modal) language. The following representation seems quite natural (arguably, even more natural than the first-order counterparts with or without counting quantifiers)

$$Apple \geq 2.$$

In this paper we will investigate propositional and modal languages extended with such counting operators. Let us be bold and introduce, already, the formal syntax and semantics of the basic modal logic with counting $\mathcal{MLC}$, the main language we want to explore:

---

[1] It is well known that $\mathcal{FOL}$ can express any finite counting quantifier.

A. Dawar and R. de Queiroz (Eds.): WoLLIC 2010, LNAI 6188, pp. 98–109, 2010.

Definition 1 (Syntax). *Let* Prop $= \{p_1, p_2, \ldots\}$ *(the* propositional symbols*) and* Rel $= \{r_1, r_2, \ldots\}$ *(the* relational symbols*) be disjoint, countable infinite sets. The set* Forms *of formulas of* $\mathcal{MLC}$ *over signature* $\langle$Prop, Rel$\rangle$ *is defined as:*

$$\text{Forms} ::= \bot \mid p \mid \neg\varphi \mid (\varphi_1 \wedge \varphi_2) \mid \langle r \rangle \varphi \mid (\varphi \geq n) \mid (\varphi \leq n),$$

for $p \in$ Prop, $r \in$ Rel, $\varphi, \varphi_1, \varphi_2 \in$ Forms *and* n *a natural number. Other Boolean and modal operators are defined as usual, and we define* $(\varphi = n)$ *as* $(\varphi \geq n) \wedge (\varphi \leq n)$, $(\varphi > n)$ *as* $(\varphi \geq (n+1))$ *and* $(\varphi < n)$ *as* $(\varphi \leq (n-1))$ *if* $n > 0$ *or* $\bot$ *otherwise.*

We will call $\mathcal{PLC}$ the "propositional fragment," i.e., the fragment obtained by dropping $\langle r \rangle \varphi$. Let us now introduce the semantics.

Definition 2 (Semantics). *Given a signature* $\mathcal{S} = \langle$Prop, Rel$\rangle$, *a model for* $\mathcal{S}$ *is a tuple* $\langle W, (R_r)_{r \in \text{Rel}}, V \rangle$, *satisfying the following conditions: (i)* $W \neq \emptyset$ *(elements in* W *are called states); (ii) each* R_r *is a binary relation on* W *(usually called accessibility relations); (iii)* $V :$ Prop $\rightarrow 2^W$ *is a labeling function.*
Given the model $\mathcal{M} = \langle W, (R_r)_{r \in \text{Rel}}, V \rangle$ *and* $w \in W$, *the semantics for the different operators is defined as follows:*

$$
\begin{array}{lll}
\mathcal{M}, w \models p & \Longleftrightarrow & w \in V(p), \quad p \in \text{Prop} \\
\mathcal{M}, w \models \neg\varphi & \Longleftrightarrow & \mathcal{M}, w \not\models \varphi \\
\mathcal{M}, w \models \varphi \wedge \psi & \Longleftrightarrow & \mathcal{M}, w \models \varphi \text{ and } \mathcal{M}, w \models \psi \\
\mathcal{M}, w \models \langle r \rangle \varphi & \Longleftrightarrow & \text{there is } w' \text{ such that } R_r(w, w') \text{ and } \mathcal{M}, w' \models \varphi \\
\mathcal{M}, w \models (\varphi \geq n) & \Longleftrightarrow & |\{w \mid \mathcal{M}, w \models \varphi\}| \geq n \\
\mathcal{M}, w \models (\varphi \leq n) & \Longleftrightarrow & |\{w \mid \mathcal{M}, w \models \varphi\}| \leq n.
\end{array}
$$

We will say that a formula φ *is* satisfiable, *if there is a model* $\mathcal{M}$ *and a state* w *in its domain such that* $\mathcal{M}, w \models \varphi$. *For a set of formulas* $\Gamma \cup \{\varphi\}$ *we say that* $\Gamma \models \varphi$ *if and only if for any model* $\mathcal{M}$ *and any* w *in its domain* $\mathcal{M}, w \models \Gamma$ *implies* $\mathcal{M}, w \models \varphi$ *(this relation is sometimes called* local entailment*). The* extension $\|\varphi\|^{\mathcal{M}}$ *of a formula* φ *in a model* $\mathcal{M}$ *is the set* $\{w \mid \mathcal{M}, w \models \varphi\}$, *and the* theory *of* w *in* $\mathcal{M}$, *notation* $\text{Th}^{\mathcal{M}}(w)$, *is the set* $\{\varphi \mid \mathcal{M}, w \models \varphi\}$. *When the model* $\mathcal{M}$ *is clear from context we will drop the super-indexes. We will write* $\mathcal{M}, w \equiv_{\mathcal{MLC}} \mathcal{M}', w'$ *if* $\text{Th}^{\mathcal{M}}(w) = \text{Th}^{\mathcal{M}'}(w')$.

It should be clear from Definitions 1 and 2 that $\mathcal{MLC}$ is indeed the basic modal logic $\mathcal{ML}$ [2] extended with the counting operators. We will be mainly discussing extensions of $\mathcal{ML}$ for simplicity. We could have naturally added the counting operators to any modal logic, e.g., temporal logic with counting.
    The $\mathcal{MLC}$ language and, in particular, its sublanguage $\mathcal{PLC}$ have been investigated under different guises. $\mathcal{PLC}$ is introduced as the logic $S5_n$ by Fine in [3] where the, by now well studied, notion of *graded modalities* was introduced. The semantic definition of the graded modality $\langle r \rangle_n \varphi$ is given by the condition

$$\mathcal{M}, w \models \langle r \rangle_n \varphi \iff |\{w' \mid R_r(w, w') \text{ and } \mathcal{M}, w' \models \varphi\}| \geq n.$$

$S5_n$ is the logic obtained when the $\langle r \rangle_n$ operator is restricted to models where R_r is interpreted as an equivalence relation. Now, if R_r is the universal relation, then $\langle r \rangle_n \varphi$ is trivially equivalent to $(\varphi \geq n)$. But a well known result (see, e.g. [2]) establishes that the modal logic of the universal relation coincides with the modal logic obtained when we only require the accessibility relation to be an equivalence relation. The main contribution of [3] is to provide sound and complete axiomatizations for these languages. The original results of Fine were extended by van der Hoek and de Rijke in [4,5]. In addition to providing further axiomatizations, investigating normal forms, and establishing the complexity of the satisfiability problem for different logics with graded modalities, the authors propose these languages as a modal framework where some ideas from the Theory of Generalized Quantifiers [6] could be investigated by means of modal tools.

The relation between $\mathcal{MLC}$ and graded modalities was also discovered in the field of description logics. In this area, graded modalities are called *cardinality restrictions* and Baader *et al.* investigate in [7] *concept cardinality restrictions* which coincide exactly with the counting operators we defined. Interestingly, they decide to add concept cardinality restrictions not as operators of the concept language, but as a more expressive kind of terminological axioms, and they remark that they can express classical terminological axioms of the form $\varphi \sqsubseteq \psi$. $\varphi \sqsubseteq \psi$ is satisfied in the model if the interpretation of φ is a subset of the interpretation of ψ, and indeed this is the case exactly when $((\varphi \wedge \neg\psi) \leq 0)$. The main contribution of [7] is the definition of sound, complete and terminating tableaux calculus for these languages. A detailed complexity analysis of their satisfiability problem and optimal tableau calculi are given in [8].

Another way of explaining why counting operators can express terminological axioms is realizing that they can express the universal modality $A\varphi$ [9]:

$$\mathcal{M}, w \models A\varphi \iff \text{for all } w', \mathcal{M}, w' \models \varphi.$$

$A\varphi$ is equivalent to $((\neg\varphi) \leq 0)$, and $\varphi \sqsubseteq \psi$ is equivalent to $A(\varphi \to \psi)$. Actually, counting modalities can also express *nominals* (i.e., special propositional symbol whose interpretations are restricted to singleton subsets of the domain) by just stating $(p = 1)$ for p a propositional symbol, and hence they can be considered also as hybrid logics [10].

In this article, we provide new results about the $\mathcal{MLC}$ language. Our first contribution is conceptual, rather than technical, and it can be simple put as follows. The counting operators $(\varphi \geq n)$ and $(\varphi \leq n)$ are interesting on their own, independently of their relation with graded modalities. They are *global* operators (with a behavior similar to the universal modality or satisfiability operators), and they can be naturally combined with local operators (as is commonly done in hybrid languages). They are also modular, and they can naturally be added to any modal language. In a slogan: counting operators are the modal counterpart of first-order counting quantifiers.

In Section 2 we show how $\mathcal{MLC}$ can be used as representation language in a natural language application modeling queries including plurals. In Section 3 we will investigate the expressive power of $\mathcal{MLC}$ using a suitable notion of bisimulation. In Section 4 we first discuss the complexity of the satisfiability problem, drawing from previously known results, we then introduce a new reasoning task and devise an algorithm to solve it.

2   Representing Plurals in Natural Language

We discuss here a possible representation of plurals and references in $\mathcal{MLC}$, intended to be used in natural language processing tasks such as reference resolution or generation as is done in, e.g., [11]. The idea is to represent the information introduced in a discourse as a set of $\mathcal{MLC}$ formulas Γ, and to be able to express and answer queries of the form "how many of a certain kind of objects are there?" in this context. This representation does not aim to solve all the issues concerning the use of plurals in natural language (e.g., the distributive versus collective readings of certain adjectives when applied to sets of objects), which are known to be difficult to model [12]. For further details see, for example, [13].

As we saw in the previous section, $\mathcal{MLC}$ enables us to assert the cardinality of a proposition in the model. For example, $\Gamma = \{(Apple \wedge Red) = 2\}$ represents the sentence "there are two red apples", and the query "how many $(Apple \wedge Red)$?" should return "2". But suppose that we want to *refer* to "two red apples" (i.e., we don't know how many red apples are there in total, but we want to refer to two of them). For the representation of this kind of reference we need to be able to *name* the referred group of object by, for example, introducing a new propositional symbol a_1 and adding to Γ the formula[2]:

"two red apples": $(a_1 = 2) \wedge (a_1 \sqsubseteq (Apple \wedge Red))$

In this case, a query "how many $(Apple \wedge Red)$?" cannot be answered (i.e., is undefined) since the total number of apples in the model is not known. But the query "how many a_1?" should return "2".

If now we add that there are also two green apples and want to refer to that group, we need to introduce another propositional symbol a_2 and add to Γ:

"two green apples": $(a_2 = 2) \wedge (a_2 \sqsubseteq (Apple \wedge Green))$

Now, the number of apples that are in the group formed by a_1 and a_2 (i.e., $a_1 \vee a_2$) is also undefined because nothing prevents those two sets from overlapping. If we explicitly say that the group are disjoint ($a_1 \sqsubseteq \neg a_2$) or that the colors are mutually exclusive ($Green \sqsubseteq \neg Red$) for that we should be able to answer "4".

Suppose that now we learn that "three of the apples are rotten." This reference creates a new group containing all the apples mentioned up to now:

$$(a_3 \sqsubseteq (a_1 \vee a_2)) \ \wedge \ ((a_1 \vee a_2) \sqsubseteq a_3)$$

And then assert that three of them are rotten by adding to Γ $(a_3 \wedge Rotten) = 3$). If we further discover that all the red apples are rotten ($a_1 \sqsubseteq Rotten$), querying for "how many green apples are rotten," i.e., "how many $(a_2 \wedge Rotten)$" will returns "1".

In Section 4 we introduce the inference task of counting that corresponds to the finite cardinality queries we just discussed. But first, in the next section, we investigate in detail the expressive power of $\mathcal{MLC}$.

---

[2] Remember that $\varphi \sqsubseteq \psi$ is a short hand for $\mathsf{A}(\varphi \to \psi)$ or, equivalently, $(\varphi \wedge \neg \psi) \leq 0$.

3   The Expressive Power of $\mathcal{MLC}$

To get more familiar with the language, let us start with some examples of what can be expressed in $\mathcal{MLC}$. We can, for example, fix the size of the model to any finite cardinality by setting

$$(\top = n)$$

for n a natural number. The formula also shows that, if numbers are coded in binary, then neither $\mathcal{MLC}$ nor $\mathcal{PLC}$ has the polysize model property.

Proposition 1. *If numbers are coded in binary, then there are formulas in $\mathcal{PLC}$ (and hence also in $\mathcal{MLC}$) whose only models are exponentially larger.*

Notice that counting operators can be nested. For example $((p \geq 1) \geq 1)$ is a well formed formula, which it is actually equivalent to $(p \geq 1)$. But, as it is discussed in [4], every formula in $\mathcal{MLC}$ is equivalent to a formula where each counting operator appears under the scope of neither modal nor counting operators. The proof uses the fact that for any counting subformula σ appearing in a formula φ we have that the following is valid

$$\varphi[\sigma] \leftrightarrow (\sigma \rightarrow \varphi[\sigma/\top]) \wedge (\neg\sigma \rightarrow \varphi[\sigma/\bot])$$

Other operators with a global semantics, like the universal modality A or satisfiability operators i:, have the same property. Notice though, that the formula we obtain after extracting all counting operators can be exponentially larger. If we only require equi-satisfiability (and not equivalence), we can use the method of [14] to obtain a formula which is only polynomially larger. We will return to this issue in Section 4.

As we mentioned in the introduction, the hybrid logic $\mathcal{H}(A)$ (the basic modal logic extended with nominals and the universal modality [10]) is a sublogic of $\mathcal{MLC}$, as the language can express nominals and the universal modality. It can even express the difference modality $D\varphi$ [15] with semantics

$$\mathcal{M}, w \models D\varphi \iff \text{there is } w' \neq w \text{ and } \mathcal{M}, w' \models \varphi$$

as $D\varphi$ is equivalent to $(\varphi \rightarrow (\varphi \geq 2)) \wedge (\neg\varphi \rightarrow (\varphi \geq 1))$. On the other hand, the expressive power of counting and graded modalities is incomparable. We will establish this in Theorem 3 using a suitable notion of bisimulation for $\mathcal{MLC}$ that we now introduce

Definition 3 (Bisimulation). *A bisimulation between two models $\mathcal{M} = \langle W, (R_r)_{r \in \mathsf{Rel}}, V \rangle$ and $\mathcal{M}' = \langle W', (R'_r)_{r \in \mathsf{Rel}}, V' \rangle$ is a non-empty binary relation E between their domains (that is, $E \subseteq W \times W'$) such that whenever wEw' we have:*

Atomic harmony: *w and w' satisfy the same propositional symbols.*
Zig: *if $R_r wv$ then there exists a point $v' \in W'$ such that vEv' and $R'_r w'v'$.*
Zag: *if $R'_r w'v'$ then there exists a point $v \in W$ such that vEv' and $R_r wv$.*
Bijectivity: *E contains a bijection between W and W'.*

For two models $\mathcal{M}$ and $\mathcal{M}'$ and two elements w and w' in their respective do-mains, we write $\mathcal{M}, w \leftrightarrow \mathcal{M}', w'$ if there exists a bisimulation between $\mathcal{M}, w$ and $\mathcal{M}', w'$ linking w and w'.

Theorem 1. *If $\mathcal{M}, w \leftrightarrow \mathcal{M}', w'$ then $\mathcal{M}, w$ and $\mathcal{M}', w'$ satisfy the same formulas of $\mathcal{MLC}$.*

Proof. Assume there is a bisimulation E between $\mathcal{M}$ and $\mathcal{M}'$. Because of Atomic harmony, Zig and Zag, we know that E preserves all formulas of the basic modal language [2]. We only need to consider the counting operators.

Suppose then that $\varphi = (\psi \geq n)$ and let f be one bijection that by defini-tion is contained in the bisimulation linking $\mathcal{M}$ and $\mathcal{M}'$. Assume that $\mathcal{M}, w \models (\psi \geq n)$. By inductive hypothesis $f(\|\psi\|^{\mathcal{M}}) \subseteq \|\psi^{\mathcal{M}'}\|$ and because f is a injec-tive $|f(\|\psi\|^{\mathcal{M}})| \geq n$, hence $\mathcal{M}', w' \models (\psi \geq n)$. For the other direction, assume $\mathcal{M}', w' \models (\psi \geq n)$. Because f is a bijection we can consider $f^{-1}(\|\psi\|^{\mathcal{M}'})$ which has size greater than n , and by inductive hypothesis we know that it is a subset of $\|\psi\|^{\mathcal{M}}$. Hence $\mathcal{M}, w \models (\psi \geq n)$. The case for $\varphi = (\psi \leq n)$ is similar.

As usual, the converse is not necessarily true but it holds on finite models.

Theorem 2. *Let $\mathcal{M} = \langle W, R, V \rangle$ and $\mathcal{M}' = \langle W', R', V' \rangle$ be two finite models and $(w, w') \in W \times W'$, $\mathcal{M}, w \leftrightarrow \mathcal{M}', w'$ if and only if $\mathcal{M}, w \equiv_{\mathcal{MLC}} \mathcal{M}', w'$.*

Proof. The implication from left to right is given by Theorem 1. For the other implication, we have to prove that $\equiv_{\mathcal{MLC}}$ is a bisimulation between $\mathcal{M}$ and $\mathcal{M}'$ that links w and w'. Atomic harmony, Zig and Zag are proved in the standard way (see [2]). To prove that $\equiv_{\mathcal{MLC}}$ contains a bijection reason as follows.

Consider every pair of subsets (C, C'), $C \subseteq W$, $C' \subseteq W'$ such that for all $(a, b) \in C \times C'$, $\mathcal{M}, a \equiv_{\mathcal{MLC}} \mathcal{M}', b$. There is at least one such pair by hypothesis. Enumerate these pairs as $(C_1, C_1'), \ldots, (C_n, C_n')$ (as the model is finite there is only a finite number of them), and let $\Sigma_1, \ldots, \Sigma_n$ be such that $\Sigma_i = \mathsf{Th}(a)$ for some $a \in C_i \cup C_i'$ (by construction all elements in $C_i \cup C_i'$ satisfy the same formulas of $\mathcal{MLC}$). Now choose for each i, $\varphi_i \in \Sigma_i$ such that for all $j \neq i$, $\varphi_i \notin \Sigma_j$. Notice that $|C_i| = \|\varphi_i\|^{\mathcal{M}}|$ and that $|C_i'| = \|\varphi_i\|^{\mathcal{M}'}|$, we want to prove that $|C_i| = |C_i'|$. But by hypothesis $\mathcal{M}, w \equiv_{\mathcal{MLC}} \mathcal{M}', w'$, and then $\mathcal{M}, w \models \varphi_i = n$ if and only if $\mathcal{M}', w' \models \varphi_i = n$.

As C_i and C_i' have the same cardinality we can define an injective function $f : \bigcup C_i \to \bigcup C_i'$, such that for $a \in C_i, f(a) \in C_i'$. It only rests to prove that f is total and surjective.

Suppose there is $a \in W$ such that $a \notin \bigcup C_i$, then there is no element a' in W' such that $\mathcal{M}, a \equiv_{\mathcal{MLC}} \mathcal{M}', a'$. For each $a_i' \in W'$, let φ_i be a formula such that $\varphi_i \in \mathsf{Th}(a)$ but $\varphi_i \notin \mathsf{Th}(a')$. But then $\mathcal{M}, w \models (\bigwedge \varphi_i \geq 1)$ while $\mathcal{M}, w' \not\models (\bigwedge \varphi_i \geq 1)$ contradicting hypothesis. In a similar way we can prove that f is surjective.

Notice that $\mathcal{MLC}$-bisimulations are not isomorphisms. The following two models, for example, are $\mathcal{MLC}$-bisimilar but not isomorphic.

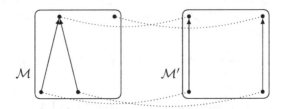

$\mathcal{M}$ and $\mathcal{M}'$ can be differentiated by the first order sentences $\exists x. \forall y. (\neg R(x, y) \wedge \neg R(y, x))$. But there is no $\mathcal{MLC}$ formula which is globally true in one model but false in the other. On the other hand, [6] proves that every sentence of first-order logic with equality and only monadic propositional symbols is equivalent to the translation of a formula in $\mathcal{PLC}$.

We now return to the comparison of $\mathcal{MLC}$ and graded modalities.

Theorem 3. *The expressive power of counting modalities and graded modalities is incomparable (when interpreted on the set of all possible models).*

Proof. Consider the following two models $\mathcal{M}$ and $\mathcal{M}'$. It is not difficult to verify that the dotted arrows defines a $\mathcal{MLC}$-bisimulation.

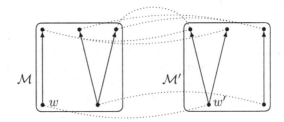

$\mathcal{M}, w \not\models \langle r \rangle_2 \top$ while $\mathcal{M}', w' \models \langle r \rangle_2 \top$ while no formula of $\mathcal{MLC}$ can differentiate w and w'[3]. For the other direction, just consider a model with one state and another model with two states. Clearly, the models cannot be distinguished using graded modalities (as they can only count the number of successors) but the counting forma formula ($\top \leq 1$) differentiates them.

4   Inference in $\mathcal{MLC}$

The complexity of the satisfiability problem for $\mathcal{MLC}$ and $\mathcal{PLC}$ have been studied in the literature. As we mention in Section 3, when dealing with complexity we should take care of whether numbers are coded in unary or binary. Let us call $\mathcal{L}^u$ and $\mathcal{L}^b$ the unary and binary coding, respectively, for either $\mathcal{MLC}$ or $\mathcal{PLC}$. Then, the previously established results are as follows.

---

[3] The proof goes through using the same models even if we add past operators to the language, as the bisimulation shown also satisfies the standard conditions Zig^{-1} and Zag^{-1} which preserve past operators [2].

Theorem 4. *1. $\mathcal{PLC}^u$-SAT is NP-complete [5].*
2. $\mathcal{MLC}^u$-SAT is ExpTime-complete [16,8].
3. $\mathcal{PLC}^b$-SAT is NP-hard and in PSpace [4].
4. $\mathcal{MLC}^b$-SAT is ExpTime-hard and in 2-NExpTime [8].

Proof. Hardness in all cases is clear, we only comment on the upper bounds. The proof of 1) is via the polysize model property. The proof of 2) is by a linear satisfiability preserving translation into $\mathcal{H}(\mathsf{A})$ as we will show below. The proof of 3) is by a direct algorithm that solves satisfiability. The proof of 4) is by a linear satisfiability preserving translation into C^2, first order logic with only two variables and counting quantifiers.

The satisfiability problem is not our main focus here, although it is going to be an essential part of the following inference task "exactly how many φ states are implied by the theory Γ?" Formally

Definition 4. *Let $\Gamma \cup \{\varphi\}$ be a finite set of formulas in $\mathcal{MLC}$, we define the function $|\varphi|$ in Γ as follows[4]*

$$|\varphi| \text{ in } \Gamma = \begin{cases} n & \text{if } \Gamma \models (\varphi = n) \text{ and } \Gamma \text{ consistent} \\ \text{undefined} & \text{otherwise} \end{cases}$$

For instance, given $\Gamma = \{(p = 2), (q = 3), (\neg(p \leftrightarrow \neg q) \leq 0)\}$, we have that $|p \vee q|$ in Γ will be defined as 5.

We will show an algorithm that solves this task using any model building procedure. In particular we will show how model building algorithms for $\mathcal{H}(\mathsf{A})$ like those proposed in [17,18] can be used. We introduce first the notion of *negation normal form* for $\mathcal{MLC}$.

Definition 5. *Given $\varphi \in$ Forms the negation normal form of φ is obtained applying the following rules*

$$\neg\neg\varphi \rightsquigarrow \varphi$$
$$\neg(\varphi_1 \wedge \varphi_2) \rightsquigarrow (\neg\varphi_1) \vee (\neg\varphi_2)$$
$$\neg(\varphi_1 \vee \varphi_2) \rightsquigarrow (\neg\varphi_1) \wedge (\neg\varphi_2)$$
$$\neg\langle r \rangle \varphi \rightsquigarrow [r]\neg\varphi$$
$$\neg[r]\varphi \rightsquigarrow \langle r \rangle\neg\varphi$$
$$\neg(\varphi \geq 0) \rightsquigarrow \bot$$
$$\neg(\varphi \geq n) \rightsquigarrow \varphi \leq (n-1) \text{ for } n > 0$$
$$\neg(\varphi \leq n) \rightsquigarrow \varphi \geq (n+1)$$

As we mentioned in Section 3, every formula in $\mathcal{MLC}$ is equivalent to a formula where each counting operators has been *extracted* and it appears under the scope of neither modal nor counting operators. Each $\mathcal{MLC}$ formula is equivalent to its extracted, negation normal form. Let $\mathcal{MLC}^{en}$ be set of extracted formulas of $\mathcal{MLC}$ in negation normal form. We now present a translation from $\mathcal{MLC}^{en}$ to

---

[4] We recall that the implication $\models$ is to be taken as local, see Definition 2.

$\mathcal{H}(A)$ formulas, which follows a very similar procedure to the one presented by Tobies for Description Logics in [8]. Tr_π works by traversing formulas and adding new nominals so that counting claims are preserved (π is used to ensure that we always introduce new nominals, initially π is set to the empty string; $i{:}\varphi$ is a satisfiability statement defined in $\mathcal{H}(A)$ as $\mathsf{A}(\neg i \vee \varphi)$).

$$\mathsf{Tr}_\pi(p) = p$$
$$\mathsf{Tr}_\pi(\neg\varphi) = \neg\mathsf{Tr}_\pi(\varphi)$$
$$\mathsf{Tr}_\pi(\varphi \wedge \psi) = \mathsf{Tr}_{\pi 0}(\varphi) \wedge \mathsf{Tr}_{\pi 1}(\psi)$$
$$\mathsf{Tr}_\pi(\varphi \vee \psi) = \mathsf{Tr}_{\pi 0}(\varphi) \vee \mathsf{Tr}_{\pi 1}(\psi)$$
$$\mathsf{Tr}_\pi(\langle r\rangle\varphi) = \langle r\rangle\mathsf{Tr}_\pi(\varphi)$$
$$\mathsf{Tr}_\pi([r]\varphi) = [r]\mathsf{Tr}_\pi(\varphi)$$
$$\mathsf{Tr}_\pi(\varphi \geq n) = (\textstyle\bigwedge_{1\leq i<j\leq n} x_i^\pi{:}\neg x_j^\pi) \wedge (\textstyle\bigwedge_{1\leq i\leq n} x_i^\pi{:}\varphi)$$
$$\mathsf{Tr}_\pi(\varphi \leq n) = \mathsf{A}(\neg\varphi \vee \textstyle\bigvee_{1\leq i\leq n} x_i^\pi)$$

in particular $Tr_\pi(\varphi \geq 0) = \top$ and $Tr_\pi(\varphi \leq 0) = \mathsf{A}(\neg\varphi)$.

Let us call $\varphi^{\mathcal{H}_\pi}$ the formula obtained from the $\mathcal{MLC}$ formula φ by first extracting counting operators, transforming into negation normal form, and applying Tr_π; we write $\varphi^{\mathcal{H}}$ when π is the empty prefix.

Suppose now that $\mathcal{M}$ is a model satisfying $\varphi^{\mathcal{H}}$ returned by the model builder. We will show that counting has not been affected by the translation.

Definition 6. *We call a model $\mathcal{M}'$ a naming extension of $\mathcal{M}$ if it is a conservative extension of $\mathcal{M}$ for an extended language that only adds nominals.*

Theorem 5. *Let $\varphi \in \mathcal{MLC}$, and π an arbitrary prefix. Then $\mathcal{M}, w \models \varphi$ if and only if $\mathcal{M}', w \models \varphi^{\mathcal{H}_\pi}$ for $\mathcal{M}'$ a naming extension of $\mathcal{M}$.*

Proof. We can disregard the extraction and negation normal form steps of the transformation since they are equivalence preserving.

[$\Rightarrow$] The atomic, negation and modal connectors cases are immediate. For any model $\mathcal{M}$ let us represent as $\mathcal{M}+N$ any naming extension of $\mathcal{M}$ where N is the function that assigns nominals to elements of the domain of $\mathcal{M}$. Assume $\mathcal{M}, w \models \varphi_1 \wedge \varphi_2$, i.e., $\mathcal{M}, w \models \varphi_1$ and $\mathcal{M}, w \models \varphi_2$. By induction hypothesis $\mathcal{M}+N_1, w \models \varphi_1^{\mathcal{H}_{\pi 0}}$ and $\mathcal{M}+N_2, w \models \varphi_2^{\mathcal{H}_{\pi 1}}$. As N_1 and N_2 are defined on different nominals we can obtain $N = N_1 \cup N_2$ and we have $\mathcal{M}+N, w \models \varphi_1^{\mathcal{H}_{\pi 0}} \wedge \varphi_2^{\mathcal{H}_{\pi 1}}$, and hence $\mathcal{M}+N, w \models (\varphi_1 \wedge \varphi_2)^{\mathcal{H}_\pi}$. The case for $\varphi_1 \vee \varphi_2$ is handled similarly.

Assume $\mathcal{M}, w \models \varphi \geq n$, i.e., there exist n different states v_1 to v_n such that for all $1 \leq i \leq n$, $\mathcal{M}, v_i \models \varphi$. For any π, choose $N = \bigcup_{1\leq i\leq n}(x_i^\pi, v_i)$ to obtain $\mathcal{M}+N, w \models (\bigwedge_{1\leq i<j\leq n} x_i^\pi{:}\neg x_j^\pi) \wedge (\bigwedge_{1\leq i\leq n} x_i^\pi{:}\varphi)$ as needed.

Now, assume $\mathcal{M}, w \models \varphi \leq n$. Let v_1 to v_m ($m \leq n$) be all the states of $\mathcal{M}$ satisfying φ. For any π, introduce n nominals x_1^π to x_n^π and a mapping N such that for $1 \leq i \leq n$ there exists j, $1 \leq j \leq m$ such that $(x_i^\pi, v_j) \in N$ (two nominals can be true in the same state). Then $\mathcal{M}+N, u \models \neg\varphi \vee \bigvee_{1\leq i\leq n} x_i$ for u an arbitrary state, and $\mathcal{M}+N, w \models \varphi^{\mathcal{H}}$.

[$\Leftarrow$] Let $\varphi \in \mathcal{MLC}$ and π an arbitrary prefix, and $\mathcal{M}'$ a naming extension of $\mathcal{M}$ such that $\mathcal{M}', w \models \varphi^{\mathcal{H}_\pi}$. If φ is a modal formula the implication is trivial.

Assume $\mathcal{M}', w \models (\varphi \geq n)^{\mathcal{H}_\pi}$. By definition $\mathcal{M}', w \models (\bigwedge_{1 \leq i < j \leq n} x_i^\pi : \neg x_j^\pi) \wedge (\bigwedge_{1 \leq i \leq n} x_i^\pi : \varphi)$. Since x_1^π to x_n^π are all true at different states $\mathcal{M}, w \models \varphi \geq n$.

Assume $\mathcal{M}', w \models (\varphi \leq n)^{\mathcal{H}(\pi)}$, i.e., $\mathcal{M}', w \models \mathsf{A}(\neg\varphi \vee \bigvee_{1 \leq i \leq n} x_i^\pi)$. Then an arbitrary u of $\mathcal{M}'$, $\mathcal{M}', u \models \neg\varphi \vee \bigvee_{1 \leq i < n} x_i^\pi$. Hence, either $\mathcal{M}', u \models \neg\varphi$ or $\mathcal{M}', u \models x_i^\pi$ for a given $i \in [[1..m]]$, ie $\{u\} = V(x_i^\pi)$ for $i \in [[1..m]]$. So there can not be more than n distinct states satisfying φ in $\mathcal{M}$ and $\mathcal{M}, w \models \varphi \leq n$.   □

Thus we can say that for a given $\mathcal{MLC}$ formula φ, a model of $\varphi^{\mathcal{H}}$ is a model of φ. We can now present the algorithm that carries out the reasoning task of counting. Given P a decision procedure for $\mathcal{H}(\mathsf{A})$, Γ a finite set of $\mathcal{MLC}$ formulas and φ a $\mathcal{MLC}$ formula:

1: **if** $P(\Gamma^{\mathcal{H}})$ returns UNSAT **then**
2:　　**return** 'undefined'
3: **else**
4:　　let n $= |\|\varphi\|^{\mathcal{M}}|$ for $\mathcal{M}$ a model returned by P
5:　　**if** $P((\Gamma \wedge \neg(\varphi = n))^{\mathcal{H}})$ returns UNSAT **then**
6:　　　　**return** n
7:　　**else**
8:　　　　**return** 'undefined'
9:　　**end if**
10: **end if**

Intuitively, our counting algorithm uses a model of the theory Γ to have a candidate answer n to the question "how many φ are implied by Γ?". We then test satisfiability of $(\Gamma \wedge \neg(\varphi = n))^{\mathcal{H}}$ to get the answer.

Theorem 6. *The algorithm above computes $|\varphi|$ in Γ.*

Our solving of the counting task relies essentially on the satisfiability problem and on the model building task carried out by the previously mentioned decision procedures. Another way of carrying this out would be to go the proof-theoretic way and directly try to derive the cardinality of φ given a theory Γ. However, this involves using an axiomatization of $\mathcal{MLC}$ which we currently lack, so given the tools we have, the satisfiability-based approach seems more adequate.

A more feasible alternative would be to solve the satisfiability problem in $\mathcal{MLC}$ directly. As some tableaux systems for Decription Logics with global counting already exist [7], a dedicated calculus for $\mathcal{MLC}$ seems easy to obtain. For a practical implementation, combining tableaux with arithmetic reasoning, as it has been done in [19,20,21], seems a good direction to take. The idea is to separate the counting constraints of the tableau and solve them with a constraint programming or a linear integer programming system. Thus unsatisfiable tableaux can be found efficiently even for large cardinality constraints.

5   Conclusions

In this paper we investigated various aspects of modal logics containing the counting quantifiers $(\varphi \geq n)$ and $(\varphi \leq n)$, motivated by the natural language application of representing and querying plural objects in a discourse.

These quantifiers have been introduced before in different areas (generalized quantifiers, modal logics, and description logics), and some of their previously known properties have been outlined (existence of extracted normal forms, complexity of the satisfiability problem, etc.). In this article we investigate expressive power and inference.

With respect to the former, we introduce the notion of $\mathcal{MLC}$ bisimulations, prove that it preserves $\mathcal{MLC}$ formulas and that it characterizes $\mathcal{MLC}$-equivalent finite models. A natural next step would be to investigate "van Benthem characterization" results [22]. I.e., to verify whether any formula of the first-order language with equality (in the appropriate signature) invariant under $\mathcal{MLC}$ bisimulations is equivalent to the translation of an $\mathcal{MLC}$ formula. We strongly conjecture that this is the case.

With respect to inference, we defined a new task that given a theory Γ and a formula φ returns the cardinality of the extension of φ in any model of Γ if such cardinality is fixed to be a finite natural number. We show that this task can be solved in terms of a calculus for the hybrid logic $\mathcal{H}(\mathsf{A})$ that can return a model for any satisfiable formula (e.g., tableaux based calculi as those defined by [17,18]). The proposed algorithm involves a translation into $\mathcal{H}(\mathsf{A})$ that might return an exponentially larger formula even when numbers are coded in unary. We conjecture that the polynomial satisfiability preserving translation of [14] could be used instead (but assuming, again, that numbers are coded in unary). The complexity of the problem when numbers are coded in binary is open. As we mentioned in Section 4, the complexity of satisfiability for $\mathcal{MLC}$ and $\mathcal{PLC}$ when numbers are coded in unary has been established [5,16,8]. On the other hand, to our knowledge the problem is still open when numbers are given in binary.

References

1. Mostowski, A.: On a generalization of quantifiers. Fundamenta Mathematicae 44, 12–36 (1957)
2. Blackburn, P., de Rijke, M., Venema, Y.: Modal Logic. Cambridge University Press, Cambridge (2001)
3. Fine, K.: In so many possible worlds. Notre Dame Journal of Formal Logics 13(4), 516–520 (1972)
4. van der Hoek, W., de Rijke, M.: Generalized quantifiers and modal logic. Journal of Logic, Language and Information 2(1), 19–58 (1993)
5. van der Hoek, W., de Rijke, M.: Counting objects. Journal of Logic and Computation 5(3), 325–345 (1995)
6. Westerståhl, D.: Quantifiers in formal and natural languages. In: Gabbay, D., Guenthner, F. (eds.) Handbook of Philosophical Logic, vol. IV, pp. 1–1331. Reidel, Dordrecht (1989)
7. Baader, F., Buchheit, M., Hollunder, B.: Cardinality restrictions on concepts. Artificial Intelligence 88(1-2), 195–213 (1996)
8. Tobies, S.: Complexity results and practical algorithms for logics in Knowledge Representation. PhD thesis, LuFG Theoretical Computer Science, RWTH-Aachen (2001)
9. Goranko, V., Passy, S.: Using the universal modality: Gains and questions. Journal of Logic and Computation 2(1), 5–30 (1992)

10. Areces, C., ten Cate, B.: Hybrid logics. In: Blackburn, P., Wolter, F., van Benthem, J. (eds.) Handbook of Modal Logics, pp. 821–868. Elsevier, Amsterdam (2006)
11. Varges, S., Deemter, K.V.: Generating referring expressions containing quantifiers. In: Proc. of IWCS 2006 (2005)
12. Asher, N., Wang, L.: Ambiguity and anaphora with plurals in discourse. In: Proc. of Semantics and Linguistic Theory 13 (SALT 13), University of Washington, Seattle, Washington (2003)
13. Franconi, E.: A treatment of plurals and plural quantifications based on a theory of collections. In: Minds and Machines, pp. 453–474 (1993)
14. Areces, C., Gorín, D.: Coinductive models and normal forms for modal logics. Logic Journal of the IGPL (to appear, 2010)
15. de Rijke, M.: The modal logic of inequality. The Journal of Symbolic Logic 57(2), 566–584 (1992)
16. Areces, C., Blackburn, P., Marx, M.: The computational complexity of hybrid temporal logics. Logic Journal of the IGPL 8(5), 653–679 (2000)
17. Bolander, T., Blackburn, P.: Termination for hybrid tableaus. Journal of Logic and Computation 17(3), 517–554 (2007)
18. Kaminski, M., Schneider, S., Smolka, G.: Terminating tableaux for graded hybrid logic with global modalities and role hierarchies. In: Giese, M., Waaler, A. (eds.) TABLEAUX 2009. LNCS (LNAI), vol. 5607, pp. 235–249. Springer, Heidelberg (2009)
19. Ohlbach, H.J., Koehler, J.: Modal logics, description logics and arithmetic reasoning. Artif. Intell. 109(1-2), 1–31 (1999)
20. Haarslev, V., Timmann, M., Möller, R.: Combining tableaux and algebraic methods for reasoning with qualified number restrictions. In: Proc. of Description Logics 2001, pp. 152–161 (2001)
21. Faddoul, J., Farsinia, N., Haarslev, V., Möller, R.: A hybrid tableau algorithm for ALCQ. In: Proc. of ECAI 2008, pp. 725–726. IOS Press, Amsterdam (2008)
22. van Benthem, J.: Modal correspondence theory. In: Gabbay, D., Guenthner, F. (eds.) Handbook of Philosophical Logic, vol. 2, pp. 167–247. Springer, Heidelberg (1984)

Verification of the Completeness of Unification Algorithms à la Robinson[*]

Andréia B. Avelar[1],[**], Flávio L. C. de Moura[2], André Luiz Galdino[3],
and Mauricio Ayala-Rincón[1],[2],[***]

Departamentos de [1]Matemática e [2]Ciência da Computação
Universidade de Brasília, Brasília, Brazil
[3]Departamento de Matemática, Universidade Federal de Goiás, Catalão, Brazil
andreia@mat.unb.br, {ayala,flaviomoura,galdino}@unb.br

Abstract. This work presents a general methodology for verification of the completeness of first-order unification algorithms à la Robinson developed in the higher-order proof assistant PVS. The methodology is based on a previously developed formalization of the theorem of existence of most general unifiers for unifiable terms over first-order signatures. Termination and soundness proofs of any unification algorithm are proved by reusing the formalization of this theorem and completeness should be proved according to the specific way in that non unifiable inputs are treated by the algorithm.

1 Introduction

In a previous development, done in the PVS proof assistant [15], a formalization of the theorem of existence of most general unifiers (mgu's) for unifiable terms over first-order theories was presented. That development was given as the PVS *theory* unification [1]. The formalization was based on three constructive operators: given a pair of unifiable terms as input, the first one generates the first position of conflict whenever the terms are different; the second one builds a resolution for the conflict and; the third one builds an mgu. These operators use the powerful machinery of types available in PVS in order to build a dependent type of pairs of unifiable terms as input. Thus, these operators correspond to a sound and complete unification algorithm restricted to unifiable terms in the style of Robinson's original unification algorithm [17]. This theorem of existence is enough for several applications, as for instance, for a formalization of the well-know Knuth-Bendix Critical Pair Theorem [12] presented in [10]. The failure cases that appear for non unifiable terms are not treated in that formalization. But all the proof techniques applied are reusable as a general methodology useful to verify termination and soundness of unification algorithms in this style

---

[*] Work supported by the District Federal Research Foundation - FAP-DF 8-004/2007.

[**] Author supported by the Brazilian Research Council CNPq.

[***] Corresponding author partially supported by the Brazilian Research Council CNPq.

A. Dawar and R. de Queiroz (Eds.): WoLLIC 2010, LNAI 6188, pp. 110–124, 2010.

of unification. The verification of completeness of any unification algorithm depends upon proving that the specific treatment of the failure cases given by the unification algorithm is adequate.

In [17], a constructive proof of correctness of the unification algorithm was introduced in order to prove, by contradiction, the completeness of the resolution method for the propositional calculus. The introduced unification algorithm either gives as output an mgu for each unifiable pair of terms, or fails whenever the terms are not unifiable. The proof of correctness of this algorithm consists in proving that the algorithm always terminates, and that, when it terminates an mgu is provided if and only if the terms are unifiable. Several variants of this first-order unification algorithm appear in well-known textbooks on computational and mathematical logic, semantics of programming languages, rewriting theory, etc (e.g., [14,7,4,3,2]). Since the formalization follows the classical proof schema, which is one of the main positive aspects of the current work, no analytic presentation of this proof will be given here.

The general proof methodology is illustrated by a specification of a unification algorithm provided in the PVS *theory* `robinsonunification` that imports the *theory* `unification`. Both *theories* are available in the NASA Langley PVS Libraries and at `http://ayala.mat.unb.br/publications.html` inside the PVS library `trs` for term rewriting systems, that was introduced in [9]. Among the rewriting results formalized in `trs` can be mentioned the critical pair theorem [10] and Newman's lemma [8].

Sections 2 and 3 present basic notions on first-order unification and explain how these notions were specified, respectively. Section 4 presents a specification of a unification algorithm à la Robinson; Section 5 explains how the verification methodology works in order to prove termination and soundness for the case of unifiable terms. Section 6 illustrates the solution to prove completeness, that is, it shows how to deal with failure in unification. Related work and conclusions are then presented.

2   Basic Notions on First-Order Unification

Consider a signature Σ in which function symbols and their associated arities are given (that is, the arity n ($n \in \mathbb{N}$) for each function symbol f in Σ is known) and a enumerable set V of variables is given. The set of well-defined terms, denoted by $T(\Sigma, V)$, over the signature Σ and the set V is recursively defined as:

- $x \in V$ is a well-defined term;
- for each n-ary function symbol $f \in \Sigma$ and well-defined terms $t_1, \ldots, t_n$, $f(t_1, \ldots, t_n)$ is a well-defined term.

Note that constants are 0-ary function symbols, and hence are well-defined terms.

In the sequel, for brevity "terms" instead of "well-defined terms" will be used.

A substitution in $T(\Sigma, V)$, by convention denoted by lowercase Greek letters, is a function from a finite set of variables to $T(\Sigma, V)$.

Definition 1 (Substitution). *A substitution σ is defined as a function from V to $T(\Sigma, V)$, such that the domain of σ, defined as the set of variables $\{x \mid x \in V, \sigma(x) \neq x\}$ and denoted by $Dom(\sigma)$, is finite.*

The homomorphic extension of a substitution from the set V to $T(\Sigma, V)$ is given as usual and denoted as $\hat{\sigma}$.

Definition 2 (Homomorphic extension of a substitution). *The homomorphic extension of a substitution σ, denoted as $\hat{\sigma}$, is inductively defined over the set $T(\Sigma, V)$ as*
- *$x\hat{\sigma} := x\sigma$;*
- *$f(t_1, \ldots, t_n)\hat{\sigma} := f(t_1\hat{\sigma}, \ldots, t_n\hat{\sigma})$.*

Given the notion of homomorphic extension, it is possible to define substitution composition.

Definition 3 (Composition of substitutions). *Consider two substitutions σ and τ, its composition is defined as the substitution $\sigma \circ \tau$ such that $Dom(\sigma \circ \tau) = Dom(\sigma) \cup Dom(\tau)$ and for each variable x in this domain, $x(\sigma \circ \tau) := (x\tau)\hat{\sigma}$.*

Two terms s and t are said to be unifiable whenever there exists a substitution σ such that $s\sigma = t\sigma$.

Definition 4 (Unifiers). *The set of unifiers of two terms s and t is defined as*

$$U(s,t) := \{\sigma \mid s\sigma = t\sigma\}$$

Definition 5 (Most generality of substitutions). *Given two substitutions σ and τ, σ is said to be most general than τ whenever, there exists a substitution γ such that $\gamma \circ \sigma = \tau$. This is denoted as $\sigma \leq \tau$.*

Definition 6 (Most General Unifier). *Given two terms s and t such that $U(s,t) \neq \emptyset$. A substitution σ such that for each $\tau \in U(s,t)$, $\sigma \leq \tau$, is said to be a most general unifier of s and t. For short it is said that σ is an mgu of s and t.*

Now, it is possible to state the theorem of existence of mgu's.

Theorem 1 (Existence of mgu's). *Let s and t be terms built over a signature $T(\Sigma, V)$. Then, $U(s,t) \neq \emptyset$ implies that there exists an mgu of s and t.*

The analytic proof of this theorem is constructive and the first introduced proof was by Robinson itself in [17]. In this paper, a unification algorithm was introduced, which either gives as output a most general unifier for each unifiable pair of terms or fails when there are no unifiers. The proof of correctness of this algorithm, which consists in proving that the algorithm always terminates and that when terminates gives an mgu implies the existence theorem. Several variants of this first-order unification algorithm appear in well-known textbooks on computational and mathematical logic, semantics of programming languages, rewriting theory, etc. (e.g., [14,7,4,3,2]). Since the formalization follows the classical proof schema, no analytic presentation of this proof will be given here.

3   Specification of Basic Notions

The *subtheory* robinsonunification, inside the *theory* trs, imports *subtheories* for substitution, terms and positions, among others. The most relevant notions related with unification are inside the *sub-theories* positions, subterm and substitution. The PVS notions used for specifying these basic concepts are taken from the prelude *theories* for finite_sequences and finite_sets. Namely, finite sequences are used to specify well-formed terms which are built from variables and function symbols with their associated arities. For doing this the PVS DATATYPE mechanism is applied to define recursive types.

```
term[variable: TYPE+, symbol: TYPE+, arity: [symbol -> nat]] :
                                                        DATATYPE
BEGIN
 vars(v:variable): vars?
 app(f:symbol,
     args:{args:finite_sequence[term] |
                                 args'length=arity(f)}): app?
END term
```

Notice that the fact that a term is well-formed, that is, that function symbols are applied to the right number of arguments is guaranteed by typing the arguments of each function symbol f as a finite sequence of length arity(f).

Finite sets and sequences are also used to specify sets of subterms and sets of term positions, as is shown below.

The (finite) set of positions of a term t is recursively defined on the structure of the term as follows, where only_empty_seq is a set containing only an empty finite sequence, that is the set containing the root position only.

```
positionsOF(t: term): RECURSIVE positions =
   (CASES t OF
      vars(t): only_empty_seq,
      app(f, st): IF length(st) = 0
                  THEN only_empty_seq ELSE
                    union(only_empty_seq,
                      IUnion((LAMBDA (i: upto?(length(st))):
                               catenate(i, positionsOF(st(i-1)) ))))
                  ENDIF
      ENDCASES)
MEASURE t BY <<
```

In the *subtheory* subterm, the subterm of t at position p also is specified in a recursive way (now on the length of p), as follows:

```
subtermOF(t: term, (p: positions?(t))): RECURSIVE term =
  (IF length(p) = 0 THEN  t  ELSE
     LET st = args(t),  i = first(p),  q = rest(p)  IN
          subtermOF(st(i-1), q)                         ENDIF)
MEASURE length(p)
```

where **first** and **rest** are constructors that return, respectively, the first element and the rest of a finite sequence, and **positions?(t)** is the (dependent) type of all positions in **t**, which is specified as follows:

```
positions?(t: term): TYPE = {p: position | positionsOF(t)(p)}
```

Several necessary results on terms, subterms and positions are formalized by induction on the structure of terms following the lines of these definitions. For instance, properties such as the one that states that the set of positions of a term is finite (lemma **positions_of_terms_finite** in the *subtheory* positions) and the one that states that the set of variables occurring in a term is finite (lemma **vars_of_term_finite** in the *subtheory* subterm) are proved by structural induction on terms. Also, several useful rules for computing with positions and subterms are specified. For example,

```
pos_subterm: LEMMA
  FORALL (p, q: position, t: term):
    positionsOF(t)(p o q)
      => subtermOF(t, p o q) = subtermOF(subtermOF(t, p), q)
```

is formalized in the *subtheory* subterm, where p o q means the concatenation of the sequences p and q denoted by *pq* in standard rewriting notation, and its proof is given by induction on the length of p according to the formal definitions given above.

The *subtheory* substitution specifies the algebra of substitutions in which the type of substitutions is built as functions from variables to terms sig : [V -> term] with finite domain: Sub?(sig): bool = is_finite(Dom(sig)) and Sub: TYPE = (Sub?). Also, the notions of domain, range, and the variable range are specified, closer to the usual theory of substitution as presented in well-known textbooks (e.g., [2]). These notions are specified as follows:

```
Dom(sig): set[(V)] = {x: (V) | sig(x) /= x}
Ran(sig): set[term] =
   {y: term | EXISTS (x: (V)): member(x, Dom(sig))  &  y = sig(x)}
VRan(sig): set[(V)] =
                 IUnion(LAMBDA (x | Dom(sig)(x)): Vars(sig(x)))
```

where the operator **IUnion** can be found in the PVS prelude *theory*, (V) denote the type of all terms that are variables and **Vars(t)** denotes the set of all variables occurring in a term **t**.

Also, in the *subtheory* substitution the homomorphic extension ext(sig) of a substitution sig is specified inductively over the structure of terms, and the composition of two substitutions, denoted by comp, is specified as

```
comp(sigma, tau)(x: (V)): term = ext(sigma)(tau(x))
```

In standard rewriting notation, the homomorphic extension of a substitution σ from its domain of variables to the domain of terms is denoted by $\hat{\sigma}$, but to simplify notation, usually textbooks do not distinguish between a substitution σ and its extension $\hat{\sigma}$. In the formalization this distinction should be maintained carefully.

Several important results, that are useful for the development of *subtheory* unification were formalized in the *subtheory* substitution, as for instance, the property that states that the application of an homomorphic extension of a substitution preserves of the original set of positions of the term. This property is specified as,

```
ext_preserv_pos: LEMMA
    FORALL (p: position, s: term, sigma: Sub):
          positionsOF(s)(p) => positionsOF(ext(sigma)(s))(p)
```

4 Specification of Unification Algorithms

The methodology of verification of first-order unification algorithms is based on the formalization of the existence of first-order mgu's as presented in the *theory* unification which consists of 57 lemmas from which 30 are *type proof obligations* or *type correctness conditions* (TCCs) that are lemmas automatically generated by the type-checker of the prover. The specification file has 272 lines and its size is 9.5 KB and the proof file has 11.424 lines and 638.4 KB. The verification of the completeness of a unification algorithm is given in the *theory* robinsonunification and consists of 49 lemmas from which 25 are TCCs in a specification file of 252 lines of code (9.0 KB) and a file of proofs of 12.397 lines of proofs (747.8 KB).

The notion of most general substitution is given as

```
<=(theta, sigma): bool = EXISTS tau: sigma = comp(tau, theta)
```

From this definition, one proves that the relation <= is a pre-order, that is, it is reflexive and transitive. The notions of unifier, unifiable, the set of unifiers of two terms and a mgu of two terms are defined as

```
unifier(sigma)(s,t): bool = ext(sigma)(s) = ext(sigma)(t)

unifiable(s,t): bool = EXISTS sigma: unifier(sigma)(s,t)

U(s,t): set[Sub] = {sigma: Sub | unifier(sigma)(s,t)}

mgu(theta)(s,t): bool =          member(theta, U(s,t)) &
        FORALL sigma: member(sigma, U(s,t)) => theta <= sigma
```

Several auxiliary lemmas related with the previous notions were also formalized; for instance, unifier_o formalizes the fact that, whenever $\sigma \in U(s\theta, t\theta)$, $\sigma \circ \theta \in U(s,t)$.

```
unifier_o: LEMMA    member(sig, U(ext(theta)(s),ext(theta)(t)))
                    => member(comp(sig,theta), U(s,t))
```

The key point of the proposed general methodology of proof is to reuse the proof techniques inside the theory unification. In this *theory*, a unification algorithm, called unification_algorithm, restricted to unifiable terms, is given for which the main two properties formalized are:

- the restricted algorithm **terminates** and
- it is **sound**, that is, it gives as output an mgu of the (unifiable) inputs.

Thus, reusing the proof techniques for formalizing these two properties, it is possible to complete the verification of any unification algorithm that has as input two terms that may not be unifiable. What remains in order to verify a unification algorithm is to prove the **completeness** of the specific treatment of the exception cases; i.e., to prove the completeness of the treatment of non unifiable terms according to the specific algorithmic methodology.

The unification algorithm inside unification receives two unifiable terms as arguments, gives a substitution as output and is specified as follows:

```
unification_algorithm(s: term, (t: term | unifiable(s,t))):
 RECURSIVE Sub =
  IF s = t THEN identity
  ELSE LET sig = sub_of_frst_diff(s, t) IN
   comp(unification_algorithm((ext(sig))(s),(ext(sig)(t))) , sig)
  ENDIF
MEASURE Card(union(Vars(s), Vars(t)))
```

In this specification, the function sub_of_frst_diff provides the *linkage substitution*, that is the one that resolves the first conflict appearing from left to right between the two terms s and t. The proof of the existence of this linkage substitution, that is a link from a variable to a term without occurrences of this variable is formalized inside the *theory* unification and the methodology of proof is reusable for any unification algorithm in the Robinson style. In the *theory* robinsonunification, the type dependence on the parameters t and s is eliminated in order to obtain a constructive unification algorithm for unrestricted terms. In general, completeness of any algorithm should be proved guaranteeing that it detects all possible fail cases, that is, conflicts without resolution, whenever the terms are not unifiable. Inside robinsonunification is specified a unification algorithm as the operator robinson_unif_algorithm.

```
robinson_unif_algorithm(s, t: term): RECURSIVE Sub =
 IF s = t THEN identity
 ELSE LET sig = link_of_frst_diff(s,t) IN
   IF sig = fail THEN fail
   ELSE LET sigma = robinson_unif_algorithm(ext(sig)(s),
                                      ext(sig)(t)) IN
```

```
        IF sigma = fail THEN fail ELSE comp(sigma, sig) ENDIF
    ENDIF
ENDIF
MEASURE Card(union(Vars(s), Vars(t)))
```

This operator calls the function `link_of_frst_diff`, that in contrast to the function `sub_of_frst_diff`, used by the `unification_algorithm` operator, allows as parameters different unrestricted terms and gives as output either "fail" or a linkage substitution, whenever the first found conflict between the terms is solvable. The key point of any unification algorithm à la Robinson is exactly the way which unresolved conflicts are reported.

The operator `link_of_frst_diff` has as parameters two different terms and invokes the operator `first_diff` that returns the position of the first conflict between these terms.

```
link_of_frst_diff(s: term , (t: term | s /= t )): Sub =
 LET k: position = first_diff(s,t) IN
 LET sp = subtermOF(s,k) , tp = subtermOF(t,k) IN
  IF vars?(sp)
   THEN IF NOT member(sp, Vars(tp))
        THEN (LAMBDA (x: (V)): IF x = sp THEN tp ELSE x ENDIF)
        ELSE fail ENDIF
   ELSE
    IF vars?(tp)THEN
      IF NOT member(tp, Vars(sp)
      THEN (LAMBDA (x: (V)): IF x = tp THEN sp ELSE x ENDIF)
      ELSE fail ENDIF
    ELSE fail ENDIF
  ENDIF
```

The specification of the operator `first_diff` is presented below. The parameters of this operator are two unrestricted, but different terms.

```
first_diff(s: term, (t: term | s /= t ) ): RECURSIVE position =
    (CASES s OF
       vars(s): empty_seq,
       app(f, st):
        IF length(st) = 0 THEN empty_seq ELSE
         (CASES t OF
            vars(t): empty_seq,
            app(fp, stp):
            IF f = fp THEN LET k: below[length(stp)] =
              min({kk: below[length(stp)] |
                   subtermOF(s,#(kk+1)) /= subtermOF(t,#(kk+1))}) IN
                add_first(k+1,first_diff(subtermOF(s,#(k+1)),
                                          subtermOF(t,#(k+1))))
            ELSE empty_seq ENDIF
```

```
    ENDCASES) ENDIF
  ENDCASES)
MEASURE s BY <<
```

Inside `unification` the functions `resolving_diff` and `sub_of_frst_diff` play the same role as the functions `first_diff` and `link_of_frst_diff`, respectively, but the latter can receive as argument non unifiable terms.

5   Reusing the Proof Technology: Termination and Soundness

Exactly the same inductive proof technology applied in the *theory* `unification` is possible for formalizing the properties of the corresponding operators in the *theory* `robinsonunification` for unifiable inputs. Here, it is explained how the properties of termination and soundness are formalized for unifiable inputs inside `unification`.

Termination. The formalization of this property follows the usual proof methodology: to prove that after each recursive input the measure, that is given by the number of variables occurring in the terms, decrease. The measure of the operator `unification_algorithm` is the cardinality of the union of the sets of variables occurring in its parameters s and t. The PVS type-checker automatically generates the type proof obligation below that guarantees termination.

```
unification_algorithm_TCC6: OBLIGATION
  FORALL (s, (t | unifiable(s, t))):
    NOT s = t =>
      (FORALL (sig: Sub):
        sig = sub_of_frst_diff(s, t) =>
          Card(union(Vars(ext(sig)(s)), Vars(ext(sig)(t))))
          <
          Card(union(Vars(s), Vars(t))))
```

This TCC is not automatically proved and it requires the proof of the auxiliary lemma:

```
vars_ext_sub_of_frst_diff_decrease: LEMMA
  FORALL (s: term, t: term | unifiable(s, t) & s /= t):
    LET sig = sub_of_frst_diff(s, t) IN
      Card(union( Vars(ext(sig)(s)), Vars(ext(sig)(t))))
      < Card(union( Vars(s), Vars(t)))
```

The proof of this lemma requires the existence of a linkage substitution σ for the first conflicting position, which maps a variable into a term without occurrences of this variable. This guarantees that the mapped variable disappears from the instantiated terms $\hat{\sigma}(s)$ and $\hat{\sigma}(t)$, and hence the decreasingness property holds.

Soundness. Inside the *theory* unification the correctness of the restricted unification algorithm is given by the lemma:

```
unification:LEMMA  unifiable(s,t) => EXISTS theta: mgu(theta)(s,t)
```

The proof of this lemma is obtained from two auxiliary lemmas: the first one, states that the substitution given by the operator unification_algorithm is, in fact, a unifier and the second one that it is an mgu.

```
unification_algorithm_gives_unifier: LEMMA
    unifiable(s,t) => member(unification_algorithm(s, t), U(s, t))

unification_algorithm_gives_mg_subs: LEMMA
    member(rho, U(s, t)) => unification_algorithm(s, t) <= rho
```

The former lemma is proved by induction on the cardinality of the set of variables occurring in s and t, for which, three auxiliary lemmas are necessary:

- the lemma vars_ext_sub_of_frst_diff_decrease described in the previous subsection, which guarantees that the cardinality of the set of variables decreases;
- the lemma

```
ext_sub_of_frst_diff_unifiable: LEMMA
    FORALL (s: term, t: term | unifiable(s, t) & s /= t):
        LET sig = sub_of_frst_diff(s, t) IN
            unifiable(ext(sig)(s), (ext(sig)(t)))
```

  which states that the instantiations of two different and unifiable terms $s\hat{\sigma}$ and $t\hat{\sigma}$ with the substitution σ that resolves the first conflict between these terms, are still unifiable; and
- the lemma unifier_o presented in Section 4, which states that for any unifier θ of $s\hat{\sigma}$ and $t\hat{\sigma}$, $\theta \circ \sigma$ is a unifier of s and t.

The formalization of the lemma unification_algorithm_gives_mg_subs is done by induction on the same measure. For proving this lemma two auxiliary lemmas are applied: the lemma vars_ext_sub_of_frst_diff_decrease and the lemma presented below, which states that for each unifier ρ of s and t, two different and unifiable terms, and given σ the substitution that resolves the first difference between these terms, there exists θ such that $\theta \circ \sigma = \rho$.

```
sub_of_frst_diff_unifier_o: LEMMA
    FORALL (s: term, t: term | unifiable(s, t) & s /= t):
        member(rho, U(s, t)) =>
            LET sig = sub_of_frst_diff(s, t) IN
                EXISTS theta: rho = comp(theta, sig)
```

6   Treatment of Exceptions: Proof of Completeness

The *theory* robinsonunification illustrates the application of the methodology of proof. The main operators inside this *theory* give a treatment of failing cases in such a way that whenever unsolvable conflicts between non unifiable terms are detected (by the operator first_diff) the substitution "fail" is returned. This substitution is built explicitly as the substitution with the singleton domain {xx} and image ff(xx), where xx and ff are, respectively, a specific variable and a unary function symbol. In this way, the substitution fail is discriminated from any other possible unifier which is built by the function robinson_unif_algorithm, for all pair of terms. The formalization of the property of termination follows the same indcutive techniques of the ones used in the proof of the lemma vars_ext_sub_of_frst_diff_decrease in the *theory* unification.

In the *theory* robinsonunification termination is formalized, as it is usually done in the literature on unification, as the lemma termination_lemma presented below. This states that for two terms s and t whose first difference is solvable by the linkage substitution σ (sig) the cardinality of the set of variables occurring in s and t is bigger than the cardinality of the set of variables occurring in $s\hat{\sigma}$ and $t\hat{\sigma}$.

```
termination_lemma : LEMMA
FORALL (s : term, t : term | s /= t):
      LET sig = link_of_frst_diff(s, t) IN
         NOT sig = fail =>
            Card(union( Vars(ext(sig)(s)), Vars(ext(sig)(t))))
            < Card(union( Vars(s), Vars(t)))
```

The formalization of the previous lemma is obtained by applying the two main lemmas presented below. The former, states that whenever the first difference is solvable the linkage substitution has as domain a singleton and the latter that the set of variables occurring in $s\hat{\sigma}$ and $t\hat{\sigma}$ is exaclty the set of variables occurring in the terms s and t minus the unique variable in the domain of σ.

```
dom_link_of_frst_diff_is : LEMMA
    FORALL (s : term, t : term | s /= t):
      LET sig = link_of_frst_diff(s, t) IN
        NOT sig = fail AND p = first_diff(s, t) =>
            IF vars?(subtermOF(s, p))
               THEN Dom(sig) = singleton(subtermOF(s, p))
               ELSE Dom(sig) = singleton(subtermOF(t, p))
            ENDIF

union_vars_ext_link : LEMMA
    FORALL (s : term, t : term | s /= t) :
        LET sig = link_of_frst_diff(s, t) IN
            NOT sig = fail =>
```

```
union(Vars(ext(sig)(s)), Vars(ext(sig)(t)))
  = difference(union( Vars(s), Vars(t)), Dom(sig))
```

Similarly, the approach of formalization of the property of soundness is followed in the *theory* robinsonunification in order to verify the lemmas below.

```
robinson_unif_algorithm_gives_unifier : LEMMA
  unifiable(s,t) IFF
  member(robinson_unif_algorithm(s, t), U(s, t))

robinson_unif_algorithm_gives_mg_subs : LEMMA
    member(rho, U(s, t)) =>
        robinson_unif_algorithm(s, t) <= rho
```

The former lemma states that the algorithm gives as output a unifier, whenever the input terms are unifiable, and the latter lemma that the output is in fact an mgu of the input unifiable terms. It is important to remark that completeness of the unification_algorithm holds, but for unifiable terms. The formalization approach is extended for unifiable terms for the robinson_unif_algorithm operator obtaining what it called here soundness. Both lemmas are proved by induction on the measure of the operator robinson_unif_algorithm, that is the cardinality of the set of variables occurring in the input terms.

In order to obtain completeness, two additional lemmas that distinguish the selected fail substitution from any possible unifier are necessary. These lemmas respectively state that, for unifiable inputs, the substitution built by the operator robinson_unif_algorithm has as domain a subset of variables occurring in the input terms, and as range terms whose variables also range in this set and that conform a set of variables disjoint from the domain. This distinguish the substitution fail from any resolving substitutions.

```
rob_uni_alg_dom_subset_union_vars: LEMMA
 unifiable(s, t) =>
    LET sigma = robinson_unif_algorithm(s, t) IN
       subset?( Dom(sigma), union(Vars(s), Vars(t)) )

rob_uni_alg_dom_ran_disjoint: LEMMA
 unifiable(s,t) =>
    LET sigma = robinson_unif_algorithm(s, t) IN
       subset?(VRan(sigma) ,
                difference( union(Vars(s), Vars(t)), Dom(sigma)))
```

Also, it is necessary to formalize an auxiliary lemma that states that the algorithm gives as output fail exactly when the input terms are not unifiable.

```
robinson_unif_algorithm_fails_iff_non_unifiable : LEMMA
 NOT unifiable(s,t) IFF robinson_unif_algorithm(s,t) = fail
```

All previous lemmas were proved by induction on the cardinality of variables occurring in the terms s and t.

The completeness theorem states that, for given terms s and t, the operator robinson_unif_algorithm either returns fail or the mgu of these terms correctly. Its formalization follows easily from the previous lemmas on soundness and failure.

```
completeness_robinson_unif_algorithm : THEOREM
    IF unifiable(s,t) THEN  mgu(robinson_unif_algorithm(s,t))(s,t)
                      ELSE  robinson_unif_algorithm(s,t) = fail
    ENDIF
```

Notice that in the specific approach to deal with failing cases given in the *theory* robinsonunification, the property of idempotence is a simple corollary proved as consequence of the selection of fail.

7   Related Work

To the best of our knowledge, the first formalization of the unification algorithm was given by Paulson [16]. Paulson's formalization of Manna and Waldinger's theory of unification was done in the theorem prover LCF and subsequently this approach was followed by Konrad Slind in the theory Unify in the proof assistant Isabelle/HOL from which an improved version called unification is available now. Similarly to our approach, idempotence of the computed unifiers is unnecessary to prove neither termination nor correctness of the specified unification algorithm.

In contrast with our termination proof, which is based on the fact that the number of different variables occurring in the terms being unified decreases after each step of the unification algorithm (Section 5), the termination proof of the theory Unify is based on separated proofs of *non-nested* and *nested* termination conditions and the unification algorithm is specified based on a specification of terms built by a binary combinator operator.

Additional facts that make our formalization closer to the usual theory of unification (algorithms) as presented in well-known textbooks (e.g., [14,2]), is the decision to present terms as a data type built from variables and the operator app that builds terms as an application of a function symbol (of a given arity) to a sequence of terms with the right size. In this way, the substitution was specified as a function from variables to terms and its homomorphic extension is straightforward.

An algorithm similar to Robinson's one was extracted from a formalization done in the Coq proof assistant [18]. That formalization uses a generalized notion of terms, that uses binary constructors in the style of Manna and Waldinger, whose translation to the usual notation is not straightforward.

In [19], Ruiz-Reina *et al* presented a formalization in ACL2 of the correctness of an implementation of an $O(n^2)$ run-time unification algorithm. The specification is based on Corbin and Bidot's development [6] as presented in [2] in which terms are represented as directed acyclic graphs (DAGs). The merit of this formalization is that by taking care of an specific data structure such as DAGs for representing terms, the correctness proof results much more elaborated than the current one. But here, the focus is to have a natural mechanical proof of the completeness of any unification algorithm in the Robinson style, reusing the general methodology for the verification of termination and soundness, which come from the proof of existence of mgu's for unifiable terms. Although the representation of terms is sophisticated (via DAGs), the refereed formalization diverges from textbooks proofs of correctness of the unification algorithm in which it is first-order restricted. In fact, instead of representing second-order objects such as substitutions as functions from the domain of variables to the range of terms, they are specified as first-order association lists. In our approach, taking the decision to specify substitutions as functions allows us to apply all the theory of functions available in the higher-order proof assistant PVS, which makes our formalization very close to the ones available in textbooks.

Programming and proving are closely related in what concerns the construction of correct software. In fact, declarative programming style is much closer to formal specification than imperative programming, and this permits one to think about the extraction of executable code from a PVS specification. In [11], a unification algorithm à la Robinson is specified, and functional code is generated via a translator that is in its prototype stage. This specification of the unification algorithm is proved sound and complete but it just claims that whenever the given terms are unifiable, the output substitution is the most general one. This property can be proved using the technology provided by our specification.

8   Conclusions and Future Work

The formalization of the theorem of existence of mgu's for unifiable terms, previously developed in PVS, provides general proving techniques for the treatment of the properties of termination and soundness of unification algorithms. For the treatment of non necessarily unifiable terms, this methodology can be reused taking into account how the exceptions or failing cases are specifically treated by any algorithm. The application of the general methodology of verification of completeness was illustrated by showing how verification is given for a specification of the unification algorithm in which the failing cases were (correctly) detected and distinguished by giving as output a non-idempotent substitution.

Recently, in [5], a certified resolution algorithm for the propositional calculus is extracted from a Coq specification. This specification uses the built in pattern matching of the Coq proof assistant that is enough to deal with resolution in the propositional calculus. An extension to first-order logic will requires first-order unification and hence an explicit treatment of unification as presented here. As future work, it is of great interest the extraction of certified unification algorithms alone, or in several contexts of its possible applications such as the ones of first-order resolution and of type inference. Notice that for doing this it is essential to give constructive specifications such as the current one. Several contributions on the extraction of executable code from PVS specifications were given in [13], among others.

References

1. Avelar, A.B., de Moura, F.L.C., Ayala-Rincón, M., Galdino, A.: A Formalization of The Existence of Most General Unifiers. Universidade de Brasília (2010), http://ayala.mat.unb.br/publications.html
2. Baader, F., Nipkow, T.: Term Rewriting and *All That*. CUP (1998)
3. Bezem, M., Klop, J.W., de Vrijer, R. (eds.): Term Rewriting Systems by TeReSe. Cambridge Tracts in Theor. Comput. Sci., CUP, vol. 55 (2003)
4. Burris, S.N.: Logic for Mathematics and Computer Science. Prentice Hall, Englewood Cliffs (1998)
5. Constable, R., Moczydlowski, W.: Extracting the resolution algorithm from a completeness proof for the propositional calculus. Annals of Pure and Applied Logic 161(3), 337–348 (2009)
6. Corbin, J., Bidoit, M.: A Rehabilitation of Robinson's Unification Algorithm. In: IFIP Congress, pp. 909–914 (1983)
7. Ebbinghaus, H.D., Flum, J., Thomas, W.: Mathematical Logic. Springer, Heidelberg (1984)
8. Galdino, A.L., Ayala-Rincón, M.: A Formalization of Newman's and Yokouchi Lemmas in a Higher-Order Language. J. of Form. Reasoning 1(1), 39–50 (2008)
9. Galdino, A.L., Ayala-Rincón, M.: A PVS *Theory* for Term Rewriting Systems. In: Proceedings of the 3rd Workshop on Logical and Semantic Frameworks, with Applications (LSFA). Electr. Notes Theor. Comput. Sci., vol. 247, pp. 67–83. Elsevier, Amsterdam (2009)
10. Galdino, A.L., Ayala-Rincón, M.: A Formalization of the Knuth-Bendix(-Huet) Critical Pair Theorem. J. of Automated Reasoning, doi: 10.1007/s10817-010-9165-2 (2010)
11. Jacobs, B., Smetsers, S., Schreur, R.W.: Code-carrying theories. Formal Asp. Comput. 19(2), 191–203 (2007)
12. Knuth, D.E., Bendix, P.B.: Simple Words Problems in Universal Algebras. In: Leech, J. (ed.) Computational Problems in Abstract Algebra, pp. 263–297. Pergamon Press, Oxford (1970)
13. Lensink, L., Muñoz, C., Goodloe, A.: From verified models to verifiable code. Technical Memorandum NASA/TM-2009-215943, NASA, Langley Research Center, Hampton VA 23681-2199, USA (June 2009)
14. Lloyd, J.W.: Foundations of Logic Programming. In: Symbolic Computation – Artificial Intelligence, 2nd edn., Springer, Heidelberg (1987)
15. Owre, S., Rushby, J.M., Shankar, N.: PVS: A Prototype Verification System. In: Kapur, D. (ed.) CADE 1992. LNCS (LNAI), vol. 607, pp. 748–752. Springer, Heidelberg (1992)
16. Paulson, L.C.: Verifying the Unification Algorithm in LCF. Science of Computer Programming 5(2), 143–169 (1985)
17. Robinson, J.A.: A Machine-oriented Logic Based on the Resolution Principle. Journal of the ACM 12(1), 23–41 (1965)
18. Rouyer, J.: Développement de l'algorithme d'unification dans le calcul des constructions. Technical Report 1795, INRIA (1992)
19. Ruiz-Reina, J.-L., Martín-Mateos, F.-J., Alonso, J.-A., Hidalgo, M.-J.: Formal Correctness of a Quadratic Unification Algorithm. J. of Automated Reasoning 37(1-2), 67–92 (2006)

Mechanisation of PDA and Grammar Equivalence for Context-Free Languages

Aditi Barthwal[1] and Michael Norrish[2,1]

[1] Australian National University
Aditi.Barthwal@anu.edu.au
[2] Canberra Research Lab., NICTA
Michael.Norrish@nicta.com.au

Abstract. We provide a formalisation of the theory of pushdown automata (PDAs) using the HOL4 theorem prover. It illustrates how provers such as HOL can be used for mechanising complicated proofs, but also how intensive such a process can turn out to be. The proofs blow up in size in way difficult to predict from examining original textbook presentations. Even a meticulous text proof has "intuitive" leaps that need to be identified and formalised.

1 Introduction

A context-free grammar provides a simple and precise mechanism for describing the methods by which phrases in languages are built from smaller blocks, capturing the "block structure" of sentences in a natural way. The simplicity of the formalism makes it amenable to rigorous mathematical study. Context-free grammars are also simple enough to allow the construction of efficient parsing algorithms using pushdown automata (PDAs). These "predicting machines" use knowledge about their stack contents to determine whether and how a given string can be generated by the grammar. For example, PDAs can be used to to build efficient parsers for LR grammars, some of which theory we have already mechanised [1].

This paper describes the formalisation of CFGs (Section 2) and PDAs (Section 3) using HOL4 [4], following Hopcroft & Ullman [2]. The formalisation of this theory is not only interesting in its own right, but also gives insight into the kind of manipulations required to port a pen-and-paper proof to a theorem prover. The mechanisation proves to be an ideal case study of how intuitive textbook proofs can blow up in size, and how details can change during formalisation. The crux of the paper is in Sections 4 and 5, describing the mechanisation of the result that the two formalisms are equivalent in power.

The theory outlined in this paper is part of the crucial groundwork for bigger results such as the SLR parser generation cited above. The theorems, even though well-established in the field, become novel for the way they have to be "reproven" in a theorem prover. Proofs must be recast to be concrete enough for the prover: patching deductive gaps which are easily grasped in a text proof, but beyond the automatic capabilities of the tool. The library of proofs, techniques and notations developed here provides the basis from which further work on verified language theory can proceed at a quickened pace.

A. Dawar and R. de Queiroz (Eds.): WoLLIC 2010, LNAI 6188, pp. 125–135, 2010.
© Springer-Verlag Berlin Heidelberg 2010

2   Context-Free Grammars

A context-free grammar (CFG) is represented in HOL using the following type definitions:

```
symbol = NTS of 'nts | TS of 'ts
rule = rule of 'nts => ('nts, 'ts) symbol list
grammar = G of ('nts, 'ts) rule list => 'nts
```

(The => arrow indicates curried arguments to an algebraic type's constructor. Thus, the rule constructor is a curried function taking a value of type 'nts (the symbol at the head of the rule), a list of symbols (giving the rule's right-hand side), and returning an ('nts,'ts) rule.)

Thus, a rule pairs a value of type 'nts with a symbol list. Similarly, a grammar consists of a list of rules and a value giving the start symbol. Traditional presentations of grammars often include separate sets corresponding to the grammar's terminals and non-terminals. It's easy to derive these sets from the grammar's rules and start symbol, so we shall occasionally write a grammar G as a tuple (V, T, P, S) in the proofs to come. Here, V is the list of non-terminals, T is the list of terminals, P is the list of productions and S is the start symbol.

Definition 1. *A list of symbols (or* sentential form*) s derives t in a single step if s is of the form* $\alpha A \gamma$*, t is of the form* $\alpha \beta \gamma$*, and if* $A \rightarrow \beta$ *is one of the rules in the grammar. In HOL:*

HOL Definition 1
derives g *lsl rsl* $\Longleftrightarrow$
    $\exists s_1 \ s_2 \ rhs \ lhs.$
        s_1 ++ [NTS *lhs*] ++ s_2 = *lsl* $\wedge$ s_1 ++ *rhs* ++ s_2 = *rsl* $\wedge$
        rule *lhs rhs* $\in$ rules g
(The infix ++ denotes list concatenation. The ϵ denotes membership.)

We write (derives g)* sf_1 sf_2 to indicate that sf_2 is derived from sf_1 in zero or more steps, also written $sf_1 \Rightarrow^* sf_2$ (where the grammar g is assumed). This is concretely represented using what we call derivation lists. If an arbitrary binary relation R holds on adjacent elements of ℓ which has x as its first element and y as its last element, then this is written $R \vdash \ell \lhd x \rightarrow y$. In the context of grammars, R relates sentential forms. Later we will use the same notation to relate derivations in a PDA. Using the concrete notation has simplified automating the proofs of many theorems. We will also use the rightmost derivation relation, rderives, and its closure.

Definition 2. *The* language *of a grammar consists of all the words (lists of only terminal symbols) that can be derived from the start symbol.*

HOL Definition 2
language g =
    $\{\, tsl \mid$ (derives g)* [NTS (startSym g)] *tsl* $\wedge$ isWord *tsl* $\}$

3   Pushdown Automata

The PDA is modelled as a record containing the start state (start or q_0), the starting stack symbol (ssSym or Z_0), list of final states (final or F) and the next state transitions (final or δ).

pda =
   <| $start$: 'state;
        $ssSym$: 'ssym;
        $next$: ('isym, 'ssym, 'state) trans list;
        $final$: 'state list |>

The input alphabets (Σ), stack alphabets (Γ) and the states for the PDA (Q) can be easily extracted from the above information. In the proofs, we will refer to a PDA M as the tuple $(Q, \Sigma, \Gamma, \delta, q_0, Z_0, F)$ for easy access to the components. We have used lists instead of sets to avoid unncessary finiteness constraints in our proofs.

The trans type implements a single transition. A transition is a tuple of an 'optional' input symbol, a stack symbol and a state, and the next state along with the stack symbols (possibly none) to be added onto the current stack. The trans type describes a transition in the PDA's state machine. The $next$ field of the record is a list of such transitions.

   trans = ('isym option # 'ssym # 'state) # ('state # 'ssym list)

In HOL, a PDA transition in machine M is expressed using a binary relation on "instantaneous descriptions" of the tape, the machine's stack, and its internal state. We write $M \vdash (q, i :: \alpha, s) \rightarrow (q', i', s')$ to mean that in state q, looking at input i with stack s, M can transition to state q', with the input becoming i' and the stack becoming s'. The input i' is either the same as $i :: \alpha$ (referred to as an ϵ move) or is equal to α. Here, consuming the input symbol i corresponds to SOME i and ignoring the input symbol is NONE in the trans type.

Using the concrete derivation list notation, we write ID $M \vdash \ell \lhd x \rightarrow y$ to mean that the list ℓ is a sequence of valid instantaneous descriptions for machine M, starting with description x and ending with y. Transitions are not possible in the state where the stack is empty and only ϵ moves are possible in the state where the input is empty. In this paper, we will consider the language "accepted by empty stack" (laes):[1]

Definition 3   (Language accepted "by empty stack")

$$laes\,(M) \;=\; \{\, w \mid M \vdash (q_0, w, Z_0) \rightarrow^* (p, \epsilon, \epsilon) \;\; for\;some\;p\;in\;Q\}$$

To be consistent with the notation in Hopcroft and Ullman, predicate laes is referred to as $N(M)$ in the proofs to follow. When the acceptance is by empty stack, the set of final states is irrelevant, so we usually let the list of final states be empty.

---

[1] In the background mechanisation we have proved that this language is equivalent to the other standard notion: "accepted by final state".

In the remainder of the paper we focus on the equivalence of PDAs and CFGs. Constructing a PDA for a CFG is a straightforward process so instead we devote much of the space to explaining the construction of a CFG from PDA and its equivalence proof. In order to illustrate the huge gap between a textbook *vs.* theorem prover formalisation, we try to follow Hopcroft and Ullman as closely as possible. As in the book, for the construction of a PDA from a CFG, we assume the grammar is in Greibach normal form.

4   Constructing a PDA for a CFG

Let $G = (V, T, P, S)$ be a context-free grammar in Greibach normal form generating L. We construct machine M such that $M = (q, T, V, \delta, q, S, \phi)$, where $\delta(q, a, A)$ contains (q, γ) whenever $A \rightarrow a\gamma$ is in P. Every production in a grammar that is in GNF has to be of the form $A \rightarrow a\alpha$, where a is a terminal symbol and α is a string (possibly empty) of non-terminal symbols (isGnf). The automaton for the grammar is constructed by creating transitions from the grammar productions, $A \rightarrow a\alpha$ that read the head symbol of the RHS (a) and push the remaining RHS (α) on to the stack. The terminals are interpreted as the input symbols and the non-terminals are the stack symbols for the PDA.

```
trans q (rule ℓ r) = ((SOME (HD r),NTS ℓ,q),q,TL r)
grammar2pda g q =
  (let ts = MAP (trans q) (rules g) in
    ⟨start := q; ssSym := NTS (startSym g); next := ts;
     final := []⟩)
```

(Here HD returns the first element in the list and TL returns the remaining list. Function MAP applies a given function to each element of a list.)

The PDA M simulates leftmost derivations of G. Since G is in Greibach normal form, each sentential form in a leftmost derivation consists of a string of terminals x followed by a string of variables α. M stores the suffix α of the left sentential form on its stack after processing the prefix x. Formally we show that

$$S \overset{l}{\Rightarrow}{}^* x\alpha \text{ by a leftmost derivation if and only if } (q, x, A) \rightarrow_M^* (q, \epsilon, \alpha) \qquad (1)$$

This turns out to be straightforward process in HOL and is done by representing the grammar and the machine derivations using derivation lists. Let dl represent the grammar derivation from S to $x\alpha$ and dl' represent the derivation from (q, x, A) to (q, ϵ, α) in the machine. Then an induction on dl gives us the "if" portion of (1) and induction on dl' gives us the "only if" portion of (1). Thus, we can conclude the following,

HOL Theorem 1
$$\forall g. \text{ isGnf } g \Rightarrow \exists m. \ x \in \text{ language } g \iff x \in \text{ laes } m$$

5   Constructing a CFG from a PDA

The CFG for a PDA is constructed by encoding every possible transition step in the PDA as a rule in the grammar. The LHS of each production encodes the starting and final state of the transition while the RHS encodes the contents of the stack in the final state.

Let M be the PDA $(Q, \delta, q_0, Z_0, \phi)$ and Σ and Γ the derived input and stack alphabets, respectively. We construct $G = (V, \Sigma, P, S)$ such that V is a set containing the new symbol S and objects of the form $[q, A, p]$; for q and p in Q, and A in Γ.

The productions P are of the following form: (**Rule 1**) $S \rightarrow [q_0, Z_0, q]$ for each q in Q; and (**Rule 2**) $[q, A, q_{m+1}] \rightarrow a[q_1, B_1, q_2][q_2, B_2, q_3]...[q_m, B_m, q_{m+1}]$ for each $q, q_1, q_2, ..., q_{m+1}$ in Q, each a in $\Sigma \cup \{\epsilon\}$, and $A, B_1, B_2, ..., B_m$ in Γ, such that $\delta(q, a, A)$ contains $(q_1, B_1 B_2...B_m)$ (if $m = 0$, then the production is $[q, A, q_1] \rightarrow a$). The variables and productions of G have been defined so that a leftmost derivation in G of a sentence x is a simulation of the PDA M when fed the input x. In particular, the variables that appear in any step of a leftmost derivation in G correspond to the symbols on the stack of M at a time when M has seen as much of the input as the grammar has already generated.

From text to automated text: For **Rule 1** we only have to ensure that the state q is in Q. On the other hand, there are multiple constraints underlying the statement of **Rule 2** which will need to be isolated for mechanisation and are summarised below.

C2.1 The states q, q_1 and p belong in Q (a similar statement for terminals and non-terminals can be ignored since they are derived);

C2.3 the corresponding machine transition is based on the values of a and m and steps from state q to some state q_1 replacing A with $B_1...B_m$;

C2.3 the possibilties of generating the different grammar rules based on whether $a = \epsilon$, $m = 0$ or a is a terminal symbol;

C2.4 if $m > 1$ *i.e.* more than one nonterminal exists on the RHS of the rule then

    C2.4.1 α is composed of only nonterminals;

    C2.4.2 a nonterminal is an object of the form $[q, A, p]$ for PDA from-state q and to-state p, and stack symbol A;

    C2.4.3 the from-state of the first object is q_1 and the to-state of the last object is q_{m+1};

    C2.4.4 the to-state and from-state of adjacent nonterminals must be the same;

    C2.4.5 the states encoded in the nonterminals must belong to Q.

Whether we use a functional approach or a relational one, the succinctness of the above definition is hard to capture in HOL. Using relations we can avoid concretely computing every possible rule in the grammar and thus work at a higher level of abstraction. The extent of details to follow are characteristic of mechanising such a proof. The relation `pda2grammar` captures the restrictions on the rules for the grammar corresponding to a PDA.

HOL Definition 3
```
pda2grammar M g ⟺
    pdastate (startSym g) ∉ statesList M ∧
    set (rules g) = p2gStartRules M (startSym g) ∪ p2gRules M
```

The nonterminals are a tuple of a from-state, a stack symbol and a to-state, the states and the stack symbols belonging to the PDA. As long as one of the components is not in the PDA, our start symbol will be new and will not overlap with the symbols constructed from the PDA. The first conjunct of pda2grammar ensures this. The function p2gStartRules corresponds to **Rule 1** and the function (p2gRules) ensures that each rule conforms with **Rule 2**. As already mentioned, **Rule 2** turns out to be more complicated to mechanise due to the amount of detail hidden behind the concise notation.

The p2gRules predicate (see Figure 1) enforces the conditions **C2.1**, **C2.2**, **C2.3** (capturing the four possibilities for a rule, $A \rightarrow \epsilon$; $A \rightarrow a$, $A \rightarrow a\alpha$, where a is a terminal symbol and $A \rightarrow \alpha$ for nonterminals α).

HOL Definition 4

```
p2gRules M =
  {rule (q,A,q₁) [] | ((NONE,A,q),q₁,[]) ∈ M.next} ∪
  {rule (q,A,q₁) [TS ts] |
    ((SOME (TS ts),A,q),q₁,[]) ∈ M.next} ∪
  {rule (q,A,p) ([TS ts] ++ L) |
    L ≠ [] ∧
    ∃ mrhs q₁.
      ((SOME (TS ts),A,q),q₁,mrhs) ∈ M.next ∧
      ntslCond M (q₁,p) L ∧ MAP transSym L = mrhs ∧
      p ∈ statesList M} ∪
  {rule (q,A,p) L |
    L ≠ [] ∧
    ∃ mrhs q₁.
      ((NONE,A,q),q₁,mrhs) ∈ M.next ∧ ntslCond M (q₁,p) L ∧
      MAP transSym L = mrhs ∧ p ∈ statesList M}
```

Fig. 1. Definition of p2gRules

Condition ntslCond captures **C2.4** by describing the structure of the components making up the RHS of the rules when α is nonempty (*i.e.* has one or more nonterminals). The component $[q, A, p]$ is interpreted as a non-terminal symbol and q (frmState) and p (toState) belong in the states of the PDA (**C2.4.2**), the conditions on q' and q_l that reflects **C2.4.3** condition on q_1 and q_{m+1} respectively, **C2.4.4** using relation adj and **C2.4.5** using the last conjunct.

HOL Definition 5

```
ntslCond M (q',ql) ntsl ⟺
  EVERY isNonTmnlSym ntsl ∧
  (∀ e₁ e₂ p s. ntsl = p ++ [e₁; e₂] ++ s ⇒ adj e₁ e₂) ∧
  frmState (HD ntsl) = q' ∧ toState (LAST ntsl) = ql ∧
  (∀ e. e ∈ ntsl ⇒ toState e ∈ statesList M) ∧
  ∀ e. e ∈ ntsl ⇒ frmState e ∈ statesList M
```
(The ; is used to separate elements in a list and LAST returns the last element in a list.)

The constraints described above reflect exactly the information corresponding to the two criteria for the grammar rules. On the other hand, it is clear that the automated definition looks and is far more complex to digest. Concrete information that is easily gleaned by a human reader from abstract concepts has to be explicitly stated in a theorem prover.

Now that we have a CFG for our machine we can plunge ahead to prove the following.

Theorem 1. *If L is $N(M)$ for some PDA M, then L is a context-free language.*

To show that $L(G) = N(M)$, we prove by induction on the number of steps in a derivation of G or the number of moves of M that

$$(q, x, A) \to_M^* (p, \epsilon, \epsilon) \text{ iff } [q, A, p] \overset{l}{\underset{G}{\Rightarrow}}{}^* x . \tag{2}$$

5.1 Proof of the "if" portion of (2)

First we show by induction on i that if $(q, x, A) \to^i (p, \epsilon, \epsilon)$, then $[q, A, p] \Rightarrow^* x$.

HOL Theorem 2
```
ID M ⊢ dl ◁ (q,x,[A]) → (p,[],[]) ∧ isWord x ∧
pda2grammar M g ⇒
(derives g)* [NTS (q,A,p)] x
```

Proof. The proof is based on induction on the length of dl. The crux of the proof is breaking down the derivation such that a single stack symbol gets popped off after reading some (possibly empty) input.

Let $x = a\gamma$ and $(q, a\gamma, A) \to (q_1, \gamma, B_1 B_2 ... B_n) \to^{i-1} (p, \epsilon, \epsilon)$. The single step is easily derived based on how the rules are constructed. For the $i - 1$ steps, the induction hypothesis can be applied as long as the derivations involve a single symbol on the stack. The string γ can be written $\gamma = \gamma_1 \gamma_2 ... \gamma_n$ where γ_i has the effect of popping B_j from the stack, possibly after a long sequence of moves. Note that B_1 need not be the nth stack symbol from the bottom during the entire time γ_1 is being read by M. In general, B_j remains on the stack unchanged while $\gamma_1, \gamma_2 ... \gamma_{j-1}$ is read. There exist states $q_2, q_3, ..., q_{n+1}$, where $q_{n+1} = p$, such that $(q_j, \gamma_j, B_j) \to^* (q_j, \epsilon, \epsilon)$ by fewer than i moves (q_j is the state entered when the stack first becomes as short as $n - j + 1$). These observations are easily assumed by Hopcroft and Ullman or for that matter any human reader. The more concrete construction for mechanisation is as follows.

Filling in the gaps: For a derivation of the form, $(q_1, \gamma, B_1 B_2 ... B_n) \to^i (p, \epsilon, \epsilon)$, this is asserted in HOL by constructing a list of objects $(q0, \gamma_j, B_j, q_n)$ (combination of the object's from-state, input, stack symbols and to-state), such that $(q0, \gamma_j, B_j) \to^i (q_n, \epsilon)$, where $i > 0$, γ_j is input symbols reading which stack symbol B_j gets popped off from the stack resulting in the transition from state q_0 to q_n. The from-state of the first object in the list is q_1 and the to-state of the last object is p. Also, for each adjacent pair e_1 and e_2, the to-state of e_1 is the same as the from-state of e_2. This process of popping off the B_j stack symbol turns out to be a lengthy one and is reflected in the proof statement of HOL Theorem 3.

To be able to prove this, it is neccessary to provide the assertion that each derivation in the PDA can be divided into two parts, such that the first part (list dl_0) corresponds to reading n input symbols to pop off the top stack symbol. This is our HOL Theorem 4.

The proof of above is based on another HOL theorem that if $(q, \gamma\eta, \alpha\beta) \to^i (q', \eta, \beta)$ then we can conclude $(q, \gamma, \alpha) \to^i (q', \epsilon, \epsilon)$ (proved in HOL). This is a good example of a proof where most of the reasoning is "obvious" to the reader. This when translated

HOL Theorem 3

    ID M ⊢ dl ◁ (q, inp, stk) → $(qf, [], [])$ ⇒
    ∃ℓ.
      inp = FLAT (MAP tupinp ℓ) ∧ stk = MAP tupstk ℓ ∧
      (∀e. e ∈ MAP tuptost ℓ ⇒ e ∈ statesList M) ∧
      (∀e. e ∈ MAP tupfrmst ℓ ⇒ e ∈ statesList M) ∧
      (∀h t.
        ℓ = h::t ⇒
        tupfrmst h = q ∧ tupstk h = HD stk ∧
        tuptost (LAST ℓ) = qf) ∧
      ∀e_1 e_2 pfx sfx.
        ℓ = pfx ++ [e_1; e_2] ++ sfx ⇒
        tupfrmst e_2 = tuptost e_1 ∧
        ∀e.
          e ∈ ℓ ⇒
          ∃m.
            m < |dl| ∧
            NRC (ID M) m (tupfrmst e, tupinp e, [tupstk e])
              (tuptost e, [], [])

(Relation NRC R m x y is the RTC closure of R from x to y in m steps.)

HOL Theorem 4

    ID p ⊢ dl ◁ (q, inp, stk) → $(qf, [], [])$ ⇒
    ∃dl_0 q_0 i_0 s_0 $spfx$.
      ID p ⊢ dl_0 ◁ (q, inp, stk) → (q_0, i_0, s_0) ∧ |s_0| = |stk| − 1 ∧
      (∀q' i' s'. (q', i', s') ∈ FRONT dl_0 ⇒ |stk| ≤ |s'|) ∧
      ((∃dl_1.
          ID p ⊢ dl_1 ◁ (q_0, i_0, s_0) → $(qf, [], [])$ ∧ |dl_1| < |dl| ∧
          |dl_0| < |dl|) ∨
        (q_0, i_0, s_0) = $(qf, [], [])$))

(Predicate FRONT ℓ returns the list ℓ minus the last element.)

into a theorem prover results in a cascading structure where one has to provide the proofs for steps that are considered "trivial". The gaps outlined here are just the start of the bridging process between the text proofs and the mechanised proofs.

Proof resumed: Once these gaps have been taken care of, we can apply the inductive hypothesis to get

$$[q_j, B_j, q_{j+1}] \overset{l}{\Rightarrow}{}^* \gamma_j \text{ for } 1 \le j \le n. \tag{3}$$

This leads to, $a[q_1, B, q_2][q_2, B_2, q_3]...[q_n, B_n, q_{n+1}] \overset{l}{\Rightarrow}{}^* x$.

Since $(q, a\gamma, A) \to (q_1, \gamma, B_1 B_2...B_n)$, we know that

$[q, A, p] \overset{l}{\Rightarrow} a[q_1, B, q_2][q_2, B_2, q_3]...[q_n, B_n, q_{n+1}]$, so finally we can conclude that $[q, A, p] \overset{l}{\Rightarrow}{}^* a\gamma_1\gamma_2...\gamma_n = x$.

The overall structure of the proof follows Hopcroft and Ullman but for each assertion made in the book, we have to provide concrete proofs before we can proceed any further. These proofs were quite involved, only a small subset of which has been shown above due to space restrictions.

5.2   Proof of the "only if" portion of (2)

Now suppose $[q, A, p] \Rightarrow^i x$. We show by induction on i that $(q, x, A) \rightarrow^* (p, \epsilon, \epsilon)$.

HOL Theorem 5
```
derives g ⊢ dl ◁ [NTS (q,A,p)] → x ∧ q ∈ statesList M ⇒
isWord x ⇒
pda2grammar M g ⇒
M ⊢ (q,x,[A]) →* (p,[],[])
```

Proof. The basis, $i = 1$, is immediate, since $[q, A, p] \rightarrow x$ must be a production of G and therefore $\delta(q, x, A)$ must contain (p, ϵ). Note x is ϵ or in Σ here. In the inductive step, there are three cases to be considered. The first is the trivial case, $[q, A, p] \Rightarrow a$, where a is a terminal. Thus, $x = a$ and $\delta(q, a, A)$ must contain (p, ϵ). The other two possibilities are, $[q, A, p] \Rightarrow a[q_1, B_1, q_2]...[q_n, B_n, q_{n+1}] \Rightarrow^{i-1} x$, where $q_{n+1} = p$ or $[q, A, p] \Rightarrow [q_1, B_1, q_2]...[q_n, B_n, q_{n+1}] \Rightarrow^{i-1} x$, where $q_{n+1} = p$. The latter case can be considered a specialisation of the first one such that $a = \epsilon$. Then x can be written as $x = a x_1 x_2 ... x_n$, where $[q_j, B_j, q_{j+1}] \Rightarrow^* x_j$ for $1 \leq j \leq n$ and possibly $a = \epsilon$. This has to be formally asserted in HOL. Let α be of length n. If $\alpha \Rightarrow^m \beta$, then α can be divided into n parts, $\alpha = \alpha_1 \alpha_2 ... \alpha_n$ and $\beta = \beta_1 \beta_2 ... \beta_n$, such that $\alpha_i \Rightarrow^i \beta_i$ in $i \leq m$ steps.

HOL Theorem 6
```
derives g ⊢ dl ◁ x → y ⇒
∃ℓ.
    x = MAP FST ℓ ∧ y = FLAT (MAP SND ℓ) ∧
    ∀ a b.
        (a,b) ∈ ℓ ⇒
        ∃ dl'. |dl'| ≤ |dl| ∧ derives g ⊢ dl' ◁ [a] → b
```
(The FLAT *function returns the elements of (nested) lists,* SND *returns the second element of a pair.)*

Inserting $B_{j+1}...B_n$ at the bottom of each stack in the above sequence of ID's gives us,

$$(q_j, x_j, B_j B_{j+1}...B_n) \rightarrow^* (q_{j+1}, \epsilon, B_{j+1}...B_n). \tag{4}$$

The first step in the derivation of x from $[q, A, p]$ gives us,

$$(q, x, A) \rightarrow (q_1, x_1 x_2 ... x_n, B_1 B_2 ... B_n) \tag{5}$$

is a legal move of M. From this move and (4) for $j = 1, 2, ..., n$, $(q, x, A) \rightarrow^* (p, \epsilon, \epsilon)$ follows. In Hopcroft and Ullman, the above two equations suffice to deduce the result we are interested in.

Unfortunately, the sequence of reasoning here is too coarse-grained for HOL4 to handle. The intermediate steps need to be explicitly stated for the proof to work out using a theorem prover. These steps can be further elaborated as follows.[2] By our induction hypothesis,

$$(q_j, x_j, B_j) \rightarrow^* (q_{j+1}, \epsilon, \epsilon). \tag{6}$$

Now consider the first step, if we insert $x_2...x_n$ after input x_1 and $B_2...B_n$ at the bottom of each stack, we see that

$$(q_1, x_1...x_n, B_1...B_n) \rightarrow^* (p, \epsilon, \epsilon). \tag{7}$$

Another fact that needs to be asserted explicitly is reasoning for (7).

This is done by proving the affect of inserting input/stack symbols on the PDA transitions. Now from the first step, (5) and (7), $(q, x, A) \rightarrow^* (p, \epsilon, \epsilon)$ follows.

Equation (2) with $q = q_0$ and $A = Z_0$ says $[q_0, Z_0, p] \Rightarrow^* x$ iff $(q_0, x, Z_0) \rightarrow^* (p, \epsilon, \epsilon)$. This observation, together with **Rule 1** of the construction of G, says that $S \Rightarrow^* x$ if and only if $(q_0, x, Z_0) \rightarrow^* (p, \epsilon, \epsilon)$ for some state p. That is, x is in $L(G)$ if and only if x is in $N(M)$ and we have

HOL Theorem 7
```
pda2grammar M g ∧ isWord x ⇒
((derives g)* [NTS (startSym g)] x ⟺
    ∃p. M ⊢ (M.start,x,[M.ssSym]) →* (p,[],[]))
```

To avoid the above being vacuous, we additionally prove the following:

HOL Theorem 8
```
INFINITE U(:δ) ⇒ ∀m. ∃g. pda2grammar m g
```

The `INFINITE` condition is on the type of state in the PDA. This is necessary to be a able to choose a fresh state (not in the PDA) to create the start symbol of the grammar as mentioned before.

6   Related Work and Conclusions

In the field of language theory, Nipkow [3] provided a verified and executable lexical analyzer generator. This work is the closest in nature to the mechanisation we have done.

A human reader is not concerned with issues such as finiteness of sets which have to be dealt with explicitly in a theorem prover. The form of definitions (relations *vs.* functions) has a huge impact on the size of the proof as well as the ease of automation. These do not necessarily overlap. A number of what we call "gap" proofs have been omitted due to space restrictions. These "gaps" cover the deductive steps that get omitted in a textbook proof and the intermediate results needed because of the particular mechanisation technique. Formalisation of a theory results in tools, techniques and an infrastructure that forms the basis of verifying tools based on the theory for example

---

[2] Their HOL versions can be found as part of the source code.

parsers, compilers, etc. Working in a well understood domain is useful in understanding the immense deviations that automation usually results in. More often than not the techniques for dealing with a particular problem in a domain are hard to generalise. The only solution in such cases is to have an extensive library at one's call.

The mechanised theory of PDAs is ~9000 lines and includes various closure properties of CFGs such as union, substitution and inverse homomorphism. It took 6 months to complete the work which includes over 600 lemmas/theorems. HOL sources for the work are available at `http://users.rsise.anu.edu.au/~aditi/`.

Acknowledgements. NICTA is funded by the Australian Government as represented by the Department of Broadband, Communications and the Digital Economy and the Australian Research Council through the ICT Centre of Excellence program.

References

1. Barthwal, A., Norrish, M.: Verified, executable parsing. In: Castagna, G. (ed.) ESOP 2009. LNCS, vol. 5502, pp. 160–174. Springer, Heidelberg (2009)
2. Hopcroft, J.E., Ullman, J.D.: Introduction to Automata Theory, Languages and Computation. Addison-Wesley, Reading (1979)
3. Nipkow, T.: Verified lexical analysis. In: Grundy, J., Newey, M. (eds.) TPHOLs 1998. LNCS, vol. 1479, pp. 1–15. Springer, Heidelberg (1998)
4. Slind, K., Norrish, M.: A brief overview of HOL4. In: Mohamed, O.A., Muñoz, C., Tahar, S. (eds.) TPHOLs 2008. LNCS, vol. 5170, pp. 28–32. Springer, Heidelberg (2008); See also the HOL website at `http://hol.sourceforge.net`

On the Role of the Complementation Rule for Data Dependencies over Incomplete Relations

Flavio Ferrarotti[1], Sven Hartmann[2], and Sebastian Link[1]

[1] School of Information Management, Victoria University of Wellington, New Zealand
[2] Institut für Informatik, Technische Universität Clausthal, Germany

Abstract. Recently, an axiomatization for functional dependencies (FDs) and multivalued dependencies (MVDs) has been established where arbitrary attributes can be specified as NOT NULL. That is, the information stored over such attributes must not be incomplete. The axiomatization subsumes previous axiomatizations of FDs and MVDs where every attribute is declared to be NOT NULL, and where no attribute is declared to be NOT NULL. We establish axiomatizations which underpin formally the intuition that the complementation rule is a mere means of database normalization. The results unburden the existing theory of the strong assumption that all attributes are known at the time when the dependencies are specified. The findings extend and unify previous results for the special cases above.

1 Introduction

A database system manages a collection of persistent information in a shared, reliable, effective and efficient way. Most commercial database systems are still founded on *the relational model of data* [10]. Data administrators utilize various classes of data dependencies to restrict the relations in the database to those considered meaningful to the application at hand. According to [12] functional dependencies (FDs) capture around two-thirds, and multivalued dependencies (MVDs) around one-quarter of all uni-relational dependencies (those defined over a single relation schema) that arise in practice. In particular, MVDs are frequently exhibited in database applications [37], e.g. after denormalization or in views [1]. While research on this topic has been extensive, only very recently a theory has been established that can reason about FDs and MVDs exhibited by relations that satisfy arbitrary NOT NULL constraints [21].

Example 1. Consider a table SUPPLIES with column headers *A(rticle)*, *S(upplier)*, *L(ocation)* and *C(ost)*. The table collects information about suppliers that deliver articles from a location at a certain cost.

> *CREATE TABLE* SUPPLIES
> *(Article CHAR[20],*
> *Supplier VARCHAR NOT NULL,*
> *Location VARCHAR NOT NULL,*
> *Cost CHAR[8]);*

A. Dawar and R. de Queiroz (Eds.): WoLLIC 2010, LNAI 6188, pp. 136–147, 2010.

Suppose the database management system enforces the following constraints: The FD $A \to S$ says that for every article there is a most one supplier, the FD $AL \to C$ says that the costs are determined by the article and the location, and the MVD $S \twoheadrightarrow AC$ says that the supplier determines the article and cost pairs independently of the location. Do the following meaningful constraints also need to be enforced explicitly, or are they already enforced implicitly: i) the MVD $A \twoheadrightarrow L$ and ii) the FD $A \to C$?   □

Indeed, the declaration of *Supplier* and *Location* as NOT NULL guarantees that both $A \twoheadrightarrow L$ and $A \to C$ are implied by $A \to S$; $AL \to C$ and $S \twoheadrightarrow AC$. However, reasoning about FDs and MVDs in the presence of an arbitrary null-free subschema (NFS), i.e. the set of attributes declared NOT NULL, is subtle. For example, if S is not declared NOT NULL, then neither the FD nor the MVD is implied. Consequently, the opportunity to specify an arbitrary NFS provides the data administrator with a flexible mechanism to control the expressiveness of the consequence relation. Dedicated tools for reasoning about FDs and MVDs in the presence of arbitrary NFSs have been established [21]. The set

$$\mathfrak{D} = \{\mathcal{R}_\mathrm{F}, \mathcal{D}_\mathrm{F}, \mathcal{U}_\mathrm{F}, \mathcal{U}_\mathrm{M}, \mathcal{T}_\mathrm{M}, \mathcal{C}_\mathrm{M}^R, \mathcal{I}_\mathrm{FM}, \mathcal{T}_\mathrm{FM}\}$$

of inference rules from Table 1 is a finite axiomatization [21].

Example 2. Let $R = ASLC$, $R_s = SL$, $\Sigma = \{A \to S; AL \to C; S \twoheadrightarrow AC\}$ as in Example 1. The inference

$$
\begin{array}{c}
\dfrac{A \to S}{\mathcal{I}_\mathrm{FM} : A \twoheadrightarrow S} \quad \dfrac{S \twoheadrightarrow AC}{\mathcal{C}_\mathrm{M}^R : S \twoheadrightarrow L} \quad \dfrac{}{\mathcal{R}_\mathrm{F} : A \to A} \\[2ex]
\dfrac{\mathcal{T}_\mathrm{M} : \qquad A \twoheadrightarrow L}{\mathcal{U}_\mathrm{M} : \qquad A \twoheadrightarrow AL} \quad \dfrac{}{\mathcal{I}_\mathrm{FM} : A \twoheadrightarrow A} \quad AL \to C \\[2ex]
\dfrac{\mathcal{T}_\mathrm{FM} : \qquad\qquad A \to C}{}
\end{array}
$$

shows that $A \twoheadrightarrow L$ and $A \to C$ can be inferred from Σ by $\mathfrak{D}$. Since $\mathfrak{D}$ is sound, in particular, it follows that both dependencies are implied by Σ.   □

The inference in Example 2 can be criticized in two different aspects. When inferring MVDs, then applications of the R-complementation rule $\mathcal{C}_\mathrm{M}^R$ should be restricted to the very last step of the inference (if necessary at all). The ability to have inferences with this property for all implied MVDs would establish an axiomatization that appropriately reflects the database normalization process. Moreover, for every implied FD there should be an inference with no applications of the R-complementation rule $\mathcal{C}_M^R$ at all. The desirability of these two features has already been motivated and axiomatizations with these features have been established for the special cases where every attributes is NOT NULL [8,9,29] and where every attribute is NULL [30]. In this paper, we will show that the axiomatization $\mathfrak{D}$ has neither of these features. Subsequently, we will establish a finite axiomatization with both features. The results provide a unifying framework for all previous findings on these issues.

Example 3. Suppose the four attributes Article, Supplier, Location and Cost only constitute the fragment of a view that we are currently aware of. That is, the underlying schema information is undetermined. Therefore, applications of the MVD complementation rule are not sound in this setting since the underlying universe is no longer known. For example, while the MVD $S \twoheadrightarrow AC$ implies the MVD $S \twoheadrightarrow L$ over the schema SUPPLIES, $S \twoheadrightarrow AC$ does not imply $S \twoheadrightarrow L$ when the schema is undetermined. Consequently, if $S \twoheadrightarrow L$ is perceived as a meaningful semantic constraint that must be enforced by the DBMS, then we need to specify this MVD explicitly as well.   □

As a second contribution of this paper we establish a finite axiomatization for the combined class of FDs, MVDs and arbitrary null-free subschema over undetermined universes. Again, this result subsumes all previous findings on this subject, in particular the special case where every attribute is NOT NULL [8,9,29] and the special case where every attribute is NULL [30].

Organization. We summarize previous work in Section 2. The basic definitions are given in Section 3. In Section 4 we establish an axiomatization of FDs and MVDs in the presence of an arbitrary NFS that enjoys both of the features. We establish an axiomatization over undetermined universes in Section 5. We conclude in Section 6.

2   Related Work

Data dependencies have been studied thoroughly in the relational model of data, cf. [1]. Applications comprise almost the full range of database topics, e.g. normalization, requirements engineering and schema validation, data mining, database security, view maintenance and query optimization. They have received considerable attention in other data models as well . New application areas involve data cleaning, data transformations, consistent query answering, data exchange and data integration.

FDs capture around two-thirds and MVDs around one-quarter of all uni-relational dependencies that arise in applications [12,37]. For total relations, Armstrong [3] established the first axiomatization for FDs. Beeri, Fagin, and Howard extended this axiomatization to the combined class of FDs and MVDs [6]. Biskup [8], Link [29] and Biskup/Link [9] studied notions of FD and MVD implication where the underlying set of attributes is not fixed. In the same papers, axiomatizations were presented that clarify the role of the R-complementation rule as a mere means of database normalization [8,9,29]. In general, axiomatizations can be applied by designers and administrators to validate the specification of explicit knowledge, to design and fine-tune databases or to optimize queries. An axiomatization ensures that all opportunities of utilizing implicit knowledge have been exploited. An analysis of the completeness argument can provide invaluable hints for finding algorithms that efficiently decide the implication problem.

One of the most important extensions of Codd's basic relational model [10] is incomplete information [11,23,26]. This is mainly due to the high demand for the correct handling of such information in real-world applications. Approaches to deal with incomplete information comprise incomplete relations, or-relations or fuzzy relations. In this paper we focus on incomplete relations. In the literature many kinds of null values have been proposed; for example, "missing" or "value unknown at present" [15], "non-existence" [31], "inapplicable" [15], "no information" [38] and "open" [14]. Most of the previous work on data dependencies is based on Zaniolo's no-information interpretation. This interpretation is valid for most database instances that occur in practice, since SQL allows only one unmarked null value. Consequently, the no information interpretation can model missing as well as incomplete information. Only recently, the set $\mathfrak{D} = \{\mathcal{R}_F, \mathcal{D}_F, \mathcal{U}_F, \mathcal{U}_M, \mathcal{T}_M, \mathcal{C}_M^R, \mathcal{I}_{FM}, \mathcal{T}_{FM}\}$ was shown to form an axiomatization for the combined class of FDs and MVDs in the presence of an arbitrary null-free subschema R_s [21], cf. Table 1. Moreover, it was shown [21] that the implication of FDs and MVDs in the presence of an arbitrary NFS R_s is equivalent to that of a fragment in Cadoli and Schaerf's R_s-3 logics [32]. The theory has unified previously orthogonal frameworks. For example, Beeri, Fagin and Howard's axiomatization [6] is covered when every attribute is NOT NULL, i.e. when $R_s = R$. Lien's axiomatization [27] is subsumed as the special case where every attribute is NULL, i.e., when $R_s = \emptyset$. Finally, Atzeni and Morfuni's axiomatization [4] $\mathfrak{AM} = \{\mathcal{R}_F, \mathcal{D}_F, \mathcal{U}_F, \mathcal{T}_F\}$ for FDs in the presence of an arbitrary NFS R_s is also subsumed. Link [30] presented an axiomatization for the class of MVDs that clarifies the role of the R-complementation rule, but only for the special case where every attribute is NOT NULL.

3   Preliminaries

We summarize the basic notions of data dependencies over partial relations.

Let $\mathfrak{A} = \{A_1, A_2, \ldots\}$ be a (countably) infinite set of distinct symbols, called attributes (column names). A *relation schema* is a finite non-empty subset R of $\mathfrak{A}$. Each attribute A of a relation schema R is associated with an infinite domain $dom(A)$ which represents the possible values that can occur in column A. To encompass incomplete information every column may have a null value, denoted by $\mathtt{ni} \in dom(A)$. The intention of $\mathtt{ni}$ is to mean "no information". This interpretation can model missing as well as incomplete information [4,38].

For attribute sets X and Y we may write XY for $X \cup Y$. If $X = \{A_1, \ldots, A_m\}$, then we may write $A_1 \cdots A_m$ for X. In particular, we may write simply A to represent the singleton $\{A\}$. A *tuple* over R (R-tuple or simply tuple, if R is understood) is a function $t : R \rightarrow \bigcup_{A \in R} dom(A)$ with $t(A) \in dom(A)$ for all $A \in R$. The null value occurrence $t(A) = \mathtt{ni}$ associated with an attribute A in a tuple t means that no information is available about the attribute A for the tuple t. For $X \subseteq R$ let $t[X]$ denote the restriction of the tuple t over R to X. A (partial) *relation* r over R is a finite set of tuples over R. Let t_1 and t_2 be two tuples over R. It is said that t_1 *subsumes* t_2 if for every attribute $A \in R$, $t_1[A] = t_2[A]$ or $t_2[A] = \mathtt{ni}$ holds. In consistency with previous work [4,27,38], the following restriction will be imposed, unless stated otherwise: No relation shall contain two tuples t_1 and t_2 such that t_1 subsumes t_2. With no null values present this means that no duplicate tuples occur.

For a tuple t over R and a set $X \subseteq R$, t is said to be X-total if for all $A \in X$, $t[A] \neq \text{ni}$. Similar, a relation r over R is said to be X-total, if every tuple t of r is X-total. A relation r over R is said to be a *total relation* if it is R-total.

We recall projection and join operations [4,27]. Let r be some relation over R. Let X be some subset of R. The *projection* $r[X]$ of r on X is the set of tuples t for which (i) there is some $t_1 \in r$ such that $t = t_1[X]$ and (ii) there is no $t_2 \in r$ such that $t_2[X]$ subsumes t and $t_2[X] \neq t$. For $Y \subseteq X$, the *Y-total projection* $r_Y[X]$ of r on X is $r_Y[X] = \{t \in r[X] \mid t \text{ is } Y\text{-total}\}$. Given an X-total relation r over R and an X-total relation s over S such that $X = R \cap S$ the *natural join* $r \bowtie s$ of r and s is the relation over $R \cup S$ which contains those tuples t for which there are tuples $t_1 \in r$ and $t_2 \in s$ with $t_1 = t[R]$ and $t_2 = t[S]$ [4,27].

Functional dependencies are important for the relational [5,7,10] and other data models [2,16,17,18,19,20,22,24,25,28,33,34,35,36]. According to Lien [27], a *functional dependency with nulls* (FD) over R is a statement $X \to Y$ where $X, Y \subseteq R$. The FD $X \to Y$ over R is satisfied by a relation r over R ($\models_r X \to Y$) if and only if for all $t_1, t_2 \in r$ the following holds: if t_1 and t_2 are X-total and $t_1[X] = t_2[X]$, then $t_1[Y] = t_2[Y]$. For total relations the FD definition reduces to the standard definition of a functional dependency [1], and so is a sound generalization. It is also consistent with the no-information interpretation [4,27].

In fact, tuples with nulls in attributes in X cannot cause a violation of the FD $X \to Y$: the nulls mean that no information is available about those attributes. Two X-total tuples t_1, t_2 where $t_1[X] = t_2[X]$ and t_2 is A-total while t_1 is not, violate any FD $X \to Y$ with $A \in Y$: t_1 indicates that no information is available about the value for A associated with $t_1[X]$, while t_2 indicates that the value for A associated with $t_2[X] = t_1[X]$ does exist. Hence, it violates the natural requirement of an FD that if the values for X are the same for two tuples, both tuples must contain the same information for the attributes in Y.

According to Lien [27], a *multivalued dependency with nulls* (MVD) over R is a statement $X \twoheadrightarrow Y$ where $X, Y \subseteq R$. The MVD $X \twoheadrightarrow Y$ over R is satisfied by a relation r over R ($\models_r X \twoheadrightarrow Y$) if and only if for all $t_1, t_2 \in r$ the following holds: if t_1 and t_2 are X-total and $t_1[X] = t_2[X]$, then there is some $t \in r$ such that $t[XY] = t_1[XY]$ and $t[X(R - Y)] = t_2[X(R - Y)]$. Informally, the relation r satisfies $X \twoheadrightarrow Y$ when every X-total value determines the set of values on Y independently of the set of values on $R - Y$. It has been shown that $\models_r X \twoheadrightarrow Y$ if and only if $r_X[R] = r_X[XY] \bowtie r_X[X(R - Y)]$ [27]. Again, the MVD definition is a sound generalization of the standard definition over total relations [13].

Following Atzeni and Morfuni [4], a *null-free subschema* (NFS) over the relation schema R is a an expression R_s where $R_s \subseteq R$. The NFS R_s over R is satisfied by a relation r over R ($\models_r R_s$) if and only if r is R_s-total. SQL allows the specification of attributes as NOT NULL, cf. Example 1. Hence, the set of attributes declared NOT NULL forms the single NFS over the underlying relation schema.

For a set Σ of constraints over some relation schema R, we say that a relation r over R *satisfies* Σ ($\models_r \Sigma$) if r satisfies every $\sigma \in \Sigma$. If for some $\sigma \in \Sigma$ the relation r does not satisfy σ we say that r violates σ (and violates Σ) and write $\not\models_r \sigma$ ($\not\models_r \Sigma$). We will consider different classes $\mathcal{C}$ of constraints over a single relation schema, e.g. FDs and MVDs.

In schema design data dependencies are normally specified as semantic constraints on the relations intended to be instances of the schema.

During the design process or the lifetime of a database one usually needs to determine further dependencies which are implied by the given ones. Let R be a relation schema, let $R_s \subseteq R$ denote an NFS over R, and let $\Sigma \cup \{\varphi\}$ be a set of data dependencies over R in the class $\mathcal{C}$. We say that Σ R-*implies* φ in the presence of R_s ($\Sigma \models_{R_s}^R \varphi$) if every relation r over R that satisfies Σ and R_s also satisfies φ. If Σ does not R-imply φ in the presence of R_s we may also write $\Sigma \not\models_{R_s}^R \varphi$.

For a set Σ of data dependencies in $\mathcal{C}$ over a relation schema R and an NFS R_s over R, let $\Sigma^*_{(R,R_s)} = \{\varphi \in \mathcal{C} \mid \Sigma \models_{R_s}^R \varphi\}$ be its *semantic closure*. In order to determine the logical consequences of a set of FDs and MVDs with respect to R-implication one can utilise a syntactic approach by applying inference rules, e.g. those in Table 1. These inference rules have the form

$$\frac{\text{premise}}{\text{conclusion}}\ \text{condition},$$

and inference rules without any premises are called axioms. An inference rule is called sound for the R-implication of dependencies in the presence of an NFS, if whenever the set of dependencies in the premise of the rule and the NFS are satisfied by some relation over R and the dependencies and NFS satisfy the conditions of the rule, then the relation also satisfies the dependency in the conclusion of the rule. For a finite set $\Sigma \cup \{\varphi\}$ of dependencies and a set $\mathfrak{R}$ of inference rules let $\Sigma \vdash_{\mathfrak{R}} \varphi$ denote the *inference* of φ from Σ by $\mathfrak{R}$. That is, there is some sequence $\gamma = [\sigma_1, \ldots, \sigma_n]$ of dependencies such that $\sigma_n = \varphi$ and for every σ_i is an element of Σ or results from an application of an inference rule in $\mathfrak{R}$ to some dependencies in $\{\sigma_1, \ldots, \sigma_{i-1}\}$. For a finite set Σ of dependencies in $\mathcal{C}$, let $\Sigma^+_{\mathfrak{R}} = \{\varphi \mid \Sigma \vdash_{\mathfrak{R}} \varphi\}$ be its *syntactic closure* under inferences by $\mathfrak{R}$. A set $\mathfrak{R}$ of inference rules is said to be *sound* (*complete*) for the R-implication of dependencies in $\mathcal{C}$ in the presence of an NFS if for every relation schema R, for every NFS R_s over R and for every set Σ of dependencies in $\mathcal{C}$ over R we have $\Sigma^+_{\mathfrak{R}} \subseteq \Sigma^*_{(R,R_s)}$ ($\Sigma^*_{(R,R_s)} \subseteq \Sigma^+_{\mathfrak{R}}$). The (finite) set $\mathfrak{R}$ is said to be a (finite) *axiomatization* for the R-implication of dependencies in $\mathcal{C}$ in the presence of an NFS if $\mathfrak{R}$ is both sound and complete for the R-implication of dependencies in $\mathcal{C}$ in the presence of an NFS.

4   Appropriate Reasoning

The goal of this section is to establish an axiomatization for the R-implication of FDs and MVDs in the presence of an NFS that enjoys the features described in the introduction. For this purpose we assume that sets $\mathfrak{R}$ of inference rules do not contain rules that are dependent on the underlying relation schema R with the exception of the R-complementation rule $\mathcal{C}_M^R$. First we extend the notion of an *appropriate inference system* [9] to the presence of an arbitrary NFS.

Definition 1. *Let $\mathfrak{R}$ denote a set of inference rules that is complete for the R-implication of FDs and MVDs in the presence of an NFS.*

$\mathfrak{R}$ is said to be complementary *for the R-implication of FDs and MVDs if for every relation schema R, for every NFS R_s over R, for every set Σ of FDs and MVDs over R, and for every MVD φ over R such that φ is R-implied by Σ in the presence of R_s there is an inference of φ from Σ by $\mathfrak{R}$ in which the R-complementation rule $\mathcal{C}_M^R$ is applied at most once and if it is applied, then it is applied only in the very last step of the inference.*

$\mathfrak{R}$ is said to be adequate *for the R-implication of FDs and MVDs if for every relation schema R, for every NFS R_s over R, for every set Σ of FDs and MVDs over R, and for every FD φ over R such that φ is R-implied by Σ in the presence of R_s there is an inference of φ from Σ by $\mathfrak{R}$ in which the R-complementation rule $\mathcal{C}_M^R$ is not applied at all.*

$\mathfrak{R}$ is said to be appropriate *for the R-implication of FDs and MVDs in the presence of an NFS if $\mathfrak{R}$ is complementary and adequate.* □

The next result illustrates that the properties of complementarity and adequacy cannot be taken for granted.

Theorem 1. *$\mathfrak{D}$ is neither complementary nor adequate for the R-implication of FDs and MVDs in the presence of an NFS.* □

An immediate question is whether there exist any axiomatizations that are complementary and/or adequate. Before we can give an affirmative answer to this question, we introduce additional inference rules that we will require to identify such axiomatizations.

Lemma 1. *The additive null transitivity rule $\mathcal{T}_M^*$, null subset rule $\mathcal{S}_M$ and mixed null subset rule $\mathcal{S}_{FM}$ are sound for the R-implication of FDs and MVDs in the presence of an NFS.* □

We are now ready to present our first main result. For this purpose let

$$\mathfrak{U} = \{\mathcal{R}_F, \mathcal{D}_F, \mathcal{U}_F, \mathcal{U}_M, \mathcal{T}_M^*, \mathcal{T}_M, \mathcal{S}_M, \mathcal{I}_{FM}, \mathcal{T}_{FM}, \mathcal{S}_{FM}\}$$

and let $\mathfrak{F} = \mathfrak{U} \cup \{\mathcal{C}_M^R\}$. The completeness of $\mathfrak{D}$ implies the completeness of $\mathfrak{F}$, and Lemma 1 shows that $\mathfrak{F}$ is an axiomatization for the R-implication of FDs and MVDs in the presence of an NFS. We will now show that $\mathfrak{F}$ is appropriate. The proof is constructive in the sense that it can be utilized to transform any inference that does not enjoy the features into an inference that does.

Theorem 2. *Let Σ be a set of FDs and MVDs over relation schema R, and $R_s \subseteq R$. For every inference γ from Σ by the system $\mathfrak{D}$ there is an inference ξ from Σ by the system $\mathfrak{F}$ with the following properties:*

Table 1. Inference rules for FDs and MVDs in the presence of an NFS R_s

$$\frac{}{XY \rightarrow Y}$$
(reflexivity, $\mathcal{R}_F$)

$$\frac{X \rightarrow YZ}{X \rightarrow Y}$$
(decomposition, $\mathcal{D}_F$)

$$\frac{X \rightarrow Y; X \rightarrow Z}{X \rightarrow YZ}$$
(FD union, $\mathcal{U}_F$)

$$\frac{X \rightarrow Y; Y \rightarrow Z}{X \rightarrow Z} Y \subseteq XR_s$$
(null transitivity, $\mathcal{T}_F$)

$$\frac{X \twoheadrightarrow Y; X \twoheadrightarrow Z}{X \twoheadrightarrow YZ}$$
(MVD union, $\mathcal{U}_M$)

$$\frac{X \twoheadrightarrow W; Y \twoheadrightarrow Z}{X \twoheadrightarrow ZW} Y \subseteq X(W \cap R_s)$$
(additive null transitivity, $\mathcal{T}_M^*$)

$$\frac{X \twoheadrightarrow W; Y \twoheadrightarrow Z}{X \twoheadrightarrow Z - W} Y \subseteq X(W \cap R_s)$$
(null pseudo-transitivity, $\mathcal{T}_M$)

$$\frac{X \twoheadrightarrow W; Y \twoheadrightarrow Z}{X \twoheadrightarrow Z \cap W} Y \subseteq XR_s; (Y - X) \cap W = \emptyset$$
(null subset, $\mathcal{S}_M$)

$$\frac{X \twoheadrightarrow Y}{X \twoheadrightarrow R - Y}$$
(R-complementation, $\mathcal{C}_M^R$)

$$\frac{X \rightarrow Y}{X \twoheadrightarrow Y}$$
(implication, $\mathcal{I}_{FM}$)

$$\frac{X \twoheadrightarrow W; Y \rightarrow Z}{X \rightarrow Z \cap W} Y \subseteq XR_s; (Y - X) \cap W = \emptyset$$
(null mixed subset, $\mathcal{S}_{FM}$)

$$\frac{X \twoheadrightarrow W; Y \rightarrow Z}{X \rightarrow Z - W} Y \subseteq X(W \cap R_s)$$
(null mixed pseudo-transitivity, $\mathcal{T}_{FM}$)

1. *if γ infers an MVD, then*
   - *γ and ξ infer the same MVD,*
   - *in ξ the R-complementation rule is applied at most once, and*
   - *if the R-complementation rule is applied in ξ, then it is applied as the last rule.*
2. *if γ infers an FD, then*
   - *γ and ξ infer the same FD, and*
   - *in ξ the R-complementation rule is not applied at all.*   □

As an example of Theorem 2 we illustrate how the inappropriate inferences by the system $\mathfrak{D}$ from Example 2 can be replaced by appropriate inferences by the system $\mathfrak{F}$.

Example 4. Let $R = ASLC$, $R_s = SL$, $\Sigma = \{A \rightarrow S; AL \rightarrow C; S \twoheadrightarrow AC\}$ as in Example 2. First we show an inference of the MVD $A \twoheadrightarrow L$ from Σ and R_s that utilizes the R-complementation rule $\mathcal{C}_M^R$ only in the last step.

$$
\begin{array}{l}
\quad\quad\quad\quad A \to S \\
\hline
\mathcal{I}_{\mathrm{FM}} : \ A \twoheadrightarrow S \quad\quad S \twoheadrightarrow AC \\
\hline
\mathcal{T}_{\mathrm{M}}^* : \quad\quad\quad A \twoheadrightarrow ACS \\
\hline
\mathcal{C}_{\mathrm{M}}^R : \quad\quad\quad A \twoheadrightarrow L
\end{array}
$$

Next we show an inference of the FD $A \to C$ from Σ and R_s that does not require any application of the R-complementation rule $\mathcal{C}_{\mathrm{M}}^R$.

$$
\begin{array}{l}
\quad\quad\quad A \to S \\
\hline
\mathcal{I}_{\mathrm{FM}} : \ A \twoheadrightarrow S \quad S \twoheadrightarrow AC \\
\hline
\mathcal{T}_{\mathrm{M}}^* : \quad\quad A \twoheadrightarrow ACS \quad\quad AL \to C \\
\hline
\mathcal{S}_{\mathrm{FM}} : \quad\quad\quad\quad A \to C
\end{array}
$$

For the application of the null mixed subset rule $\mathcal{S}_{\mathrm{FM}}$ note that $AL \subseteq ALS$ and $(AL - A) \cap ACS = \emptyset$ hold. In particular, the example showcases applications of the additive null transitivity rule $\mathcal{T}_{\mathrm{M}}^*$ and the null mixed subset rule $\mathcal{S}_{\mathrm{FM}}$.   □

Corollary 1. $\mathfrak{F}$ *is an appropriate finite axiomatization for the R-implication of FDs and MVDs in the presence of an NFS.*   □

Among others Theorem 2 shows that $\mathfrak{U}$ is nearly complete for the R-implication of FDs and MVDs in the presence of an NFS. Indeed, $\mathfrak{U}$ enables us to infer every R-implied FD. Moreover, for every R-implied MVD $X \twoheadrightarrow Y$ the system $\mathfrak{U}$ enables us to infer $X \twoheadrightarrow Y$ itself or $X \twoheadrightarrow R - Y$.

Corollary 2. *Let $\Sigma \cup \{\varphi\}$ be a finite set of FDs and MVDs over the relation schema R. Then*

- *If φ denotes an FD, then: $\varphi \in \Sigma_{\mathfrak{F}}^+$ if and only if $\varphi \in \Sigma_{\mathfrak{U}}^+$.*
- *If φ denotes the MVD $X \twoheadrightarrow Y$, then: $X \twoheadrightarrow Y \in \Sigma_{\mathfrak{F}}^+$ if and only if $X \twoheadrightarrow Y \in \Sigma_{\mathfrak{U}}^+$ or $X \twoheadrightarrow (R - Y) \in \Sigma_{\mathfrak{U}}^+$.*   □

Another interpretation of Corollary 2 is the following: if $\mathfrak{U}$ is utilized to infer FDs, then the underlying universe does not need to be fixed at all; and if $\mathfrak{U}$ is utilized to infer MVDs, then the fixing of a universe can be deferred until the very last step of the inference.

5   Undetermined Universes

The system $\mathfrak{U}$ is almost complete for the R-implication of FDs and MVDs in the presence of an NFS. We show now that if we do not fix a relation schema R, then $\mathfrak{U}$ is actually complete for the corresponding notion of implication.

FDs, MVDs and NFSs are syntactical expressions as before, but their attribute sets are finite subsets of our countably infinite set $\mathfrak{A}$. Let $Dom(r)$ denote the domain of a relation r, i.e., the set of attributes over which the relation is defined. For an FD or MVD σ let $lhs(\sigma)$ and $rhs(\sigma)$ denote the attribute sets on the left-hand side and right-hand side, respectively. That is, $lhs(\sigma) = X$ and $rhs(\sigma) = Y$

if σ denotes the MVD $X \twoheadrightarrow Y$ or the FD $X \rightarrow Y$. Let $Attr(\sigma)$ denote the set of attributes that occur in σ, i.e., $Attr(\sigma) = lhs(\sigma) \cup rhs(\sigma)$. A relation r is said to satisfy the FD $X \rightarrow Y$ if $XY \subseteq Dom(r)$ and for all tuples $t_1, t_2 \in r$ the following holds: if $t_1[X] = t_2[X]$ and t_1 is X-total, then $t_1[Y] = t_2[Y]$. A relation r is said to satisfy the MVD $X \twoheadrightarrow Y$ if $Attr(\sigma) \subseteq Dom(r)$ and for all tuples $t_1, t_2 \in r$ the following holds: if $t_1[X] = t_2[X]$ and t_1 is X-total, then there is some $t \in r$ such that $t[XY] = t_1[XY]$ and $t[X(Dom(r) - Y)] = t_2[X(Dom(r) - Y)]$. Finally, a relation r satisfies the NFS R_s if $R_s \subseteq Dom(r)$ and r is R_s-total.

Definition 2. *Let $\Sigma \cup \{\varphi\}$ be a set of FDs and MVDs and R_s an NFS. We say that Σ implies φ in the presence of R_s if and only if every relation r satisfies the following condition: if $\bigcup_{\sigma \in \Sigma} Attr(\sigma) \cup Attr(\varphi) \cup R_s \subseteq Dom(r)$ and r satisfies all $\sigma \in \Sigma$ and R_s, then r also satisfies φ.* □

The notions of *soundness* and *completeness* are simply adapted to the context of undetermined universes by dropping the reference to the underlying relation schema R from the corresponding notions in the context of fixed universes.

Let $\Sigma \cup \{\varphi\}$ be a set of FDs and MVDs, R_s an NFS, and let R be some relation schema such that $\bigcup_{\sigma \in \Sigma} Attr(\sigma) \cup Attr(\varphi) \cup R_s \subseteq R$ holds. Based on the definition of an MVD and FD, respectively, the following hold:

1. If φ denotes an MVD, then Σ R-implies φ in the presence of R_s whenever Σ implies φ in the presence of R_s, but not necessarily vice versa.
2. If φ denotes an FD, then Σ R-implies φ in the presence of R_s if and only if Σ implies φ in the presence of R_s.

Next we illustrate that R-implication of an MVD does not necessarily entail the implication of the MVD.

Example 5. The MVD $S \twoheadrightarrow A, C$ SUPPLIES-implies the MVD $S \twoheadrightarrow L$ in the presence of $R_s = \emptyset$, but $S \twoheadrightarrow A, C$ does not imply $S \twoheadrightarrow L$ in the presence of R_s:

Supplier	Article	Cost	Location	Quantity
Taratua&Co	Kea	ni	Gisborne	2
Taratua&Co	Kea	ni	Wellington	3

□

We are now able to state our second main result of this paper.

Theorem 3. *The set $\mathfrak{U}$ is a finite axiomatization for the implication of FDs and MVDs in the presence of an NFS over undetermined universes.* □

6 Conclusion

We have established two finite axiomatizations of functional and multivalued dependencies over attribute sets in which arbitrarily many attributes can be declared NOT NULL. The axiomatizations capture the notion of semantic implication over fixed and undetermined universes, respectively. Together, they provide strong formal evidence for the intuition that the complementation rule is a mere means of database normalization. The results generalize several previous findings on the subject.

Acknowledgement

This research is supported by the Marsden fund council from Government funding, administered by the Royal Society of New Zealand. The second author is supported by a research grant of the Alfried Krupp von Bohlen and Halbach foundation, administered by the German Scholars organization.

References

1. Abiteboul, S., Hull, R., Vianu, V.: Foundations of Databases. Addison-Wesley, Reading (1995)
2. Arenas, M., Libkin, L.: A normal form for XML documents. ACM Trans. Database Syst. 29(1), 195–232 (2004)
3. Armstrong, W.W.: Dependency structures of database relationships. Information Processing 74, 580–583 (1974)
4. Atzeni, P., Morfuni, N.: Functional dependencies and constraints on null values in database relations. Information and Control 70(1), 1–31 (1986)
5. Beeri, C., Bernstein, P.: Computational problems related to the design of normal form relational schemas. ACM Trans. Database Syst. 4(1), 30–59 (1979)
6. Beeri, C., Fagin, R., Howard, J.H.: A complete axiomatization for functional and multivalued dependencies in database relations. In: SIGMOD Conference, pp. 47–61. ACM, New York (1977)
7. Bernstein, P.: Synthesizing third normal form relations from functional dependencies. ACM Trans. Database Syst. 1(4), 277–298 (1976)
8. Biskup, J.: Inferences of multivalued dependencies in fixed and undetermined universes. Theor. Comput. Sci. 10(1), 93–106 (1980)
9. Biskup, J., Link, S.: Appropriate reasoning about data dependencies in fixed and undetermined universes. In: FoIKS Conference, pp. 58–77 (2006)
10. Codd, E.F.: A relational model of data for large shared data banks. ACM Commun. 13(6), 377–387 (1970)
11. Codd, E.F.: Extending the database relational model to capture more meaning. ACM Trans. Database Syst. 4(4), 397–434 (1979)
12. Delobel, C., Adiba, M.: Relational database systems. North Holland, Amsterdam (1985)
13. Fagin, R.: Multivalued dependencies and a new normal form for relational databases. ACM Trans. Database Syst. 2(3), 262–278 (1977)
14. Gottlob, G., Zicari, R.: Closed world databases opened through null values. In: VLDB Conference, pp. 50–61. IEEE Computer Society, Los Alamitos (1988)
15. Grant, J.: Null values in a relational data base. Inf. Process. Lett. 6(5), 156–157 (1977)
16. Hartmann, S., Kirchberg, M., Link, S.: A subgraph-based approach towards functional dependencies for XML. In: SCI Conference, pp. 200–205 (2003)
17. Hartmann, S., Koehler, H., Link, S., Trinh, T., Wang, J.: On the notion of an XML key. In: Schewe, K.-D., Thalheim, B. (eds.) SDKB 2008. LNCS, vol. 4925, pp. 114–123. Springer, Heidelberg (2008)
18. Hartmann, S., Link, S.: Characterising nested database dependencies by fragments of propositional logic. Ann. Pure Appl. Logic 152(1-3), 84–106 (2008)
19. Hartmann, S., Link, S.: Efficient reasoning about a robust XML key fragment. ACM Trans. Database Syst. 34(2) (2009)

20. Hartmann, S., Link, S.: Numerical constraints on XML data. Inf. Comput. 208(5), 521–544 (2010)
21. Hartmann, S., Link, S.: When data dependencies over SQL tables meet the Logics of Paradox and S-3. In: PODS Conference (2010)
22. Hartmann, S., Link, S., Schewe, K.-D.: Weak functional dependencies in higher-order data models. In: Seipel, D., Turull-Torres, J.M.a. (eds.) FoIKS 2004. LNCS, vol. 2942, pp. 134–154. Springer, Heidelberg (2004)
23. Imielinski, T., Lipski Jr, W.: Incomplete information in relational databases. J. ACM 31(4), 761–791 (1984)
24. Langeveldt, W., Link, S.: Empirical evidence for the usefulness of Armstrong relations in the acquisition of meaningful functional dependencies. Inf. Syst. 35(3), 352–374 (2010)
25. Levene, M., Loizou, G.: Axiomatisation of functional dependencies in incomplete relations. Theor. Comput. Sci. 206(1-2), 283–300 (1998)
26. Levene, M., Loizou, G.: Database design for incomplete relations. ACM Trans. Database Syst. 24(1), 80–125 (1999)
27. Lien, E.: On the equivalence of database models. J. ACM 29(2), 333–362 (1982)
28. Link, S.: Consistency enforcement in databases. In: Bertossi, L., Katona, G.O.H., Schewe, K.-D., Thalheim, B. (eds.) Semantics in Databases 2001. LNCS, vol. 2582, pp. 122–143. Springer, Heidelberg (2003)
29. Link, S.: Charting the completeness frontier of inference systems for multivalued dependencies. Acta Inf. 45(7-8), 565–591 (2008)
30. Link, S.: On the implication of multivalued dependencies in partial database relations. Int. J. Found. Comput. Sci. 19(3), 691–715 (2008)
31. Mikinouchi, A.: A consideration on normal form of not-necessarily-normalised relation in the relational data model. In: VLDB Conference, pp. 447–453 (1977)
32. Schaerf, M., Cadoli, M.: Tractable reasoning via approximation. Artif. Intell. 74, 249–310 (1995)
33. Toman, D., Weddell, G.: On keys and functional dependencies as first-class citizens in description logics. J. Autom. Reasoning 40(2-3), 117–132 (2008)
34. Vincent, M., Liu, J., Liu, C.: Strong functional dependencies and their application to normal forms in XML. ACM Trans. Database Syst. 29(3), 445–462 (2004)
35. Weddell, G.: Reasoning about functional dependencies generalized for semantic data models. ACM Trans. Database Syst. 17(1), 32–64 (1992)
36. Wijsen, J.: Temporal FDs on complex objects. ACM Trans. Database Syst. 24(1), 127–176 (1999)
37. Wu, M.: The practical need for fourth normal form. In: ACM SIGCSE Conference, pp. 19–23 (1992)
38. Zaniolo, C.: Database relations with null values. J. Comput. Syst. Sci. 28(1), 142–166 (1984)

Decidability and Undecidability Results on the Modal μ-Calculus with a Natural Number-Valued Semantics

Alexis Goyet[1], Masami Hagiya[2], and Yoshinori Tanabe[3]

[1] Ecole Normale Supérieure
[2] University of Tokyo
[3] National Institute of Informatics, Japan

Abstract. In our previous study, we defined a semantics of modal μ-calculus based on min-plus algebra $\mathbf{N}_\infty$ and developed a model-checking algorithm. $\mathbf{N}_\infty$ is the set of all natural numbers and infinity (∞), and has two operations min and plus. In our semantics, disjunctions are interpreted by min and conjunctions by plus. This semantics allows interesting properties of a Kripke structure to be expressed using simple formulae. In this study, we investigate the satisfiability problem in the $\mathbf{N}_\infty$ semantics and show decidability and undecidability results: the problem is decidable if the logic does not contain the implication operator, while it becomes undecidable if we allow the implication operator.

1 Introduction

The modal μ-calculus, which uses fixed-point operators, can express various properties of Kripke structures, such as reachability and the existence of infinite paths, both accurately and simply [1].

To enhance the expressiveness of the modal μ-calculus, attempts have been made to define semantics that interpret formulae through algebra using richer structures than those used in the standard semantics (i.e., interpreting formulae as true or false). For example, De Morgan algebras are used to express the logics that allows uncertainty or inconsistency, and model checking techniques have been explored [2,3]. Heyting-valued Kripke structures are also investigated in connection with the intuitionistic logic [4]. In the researches of weighted automata [5,6], weights are taken from semirings.

We have proposed a semantics of modal μ-calculus in which the truth values of formulae are members of $\mathbf{N}_\infty = \mathbf{N} \cup \{\infty\}$ [7]. $\mathbf{N}_\infty$ is an algebra called *min-plus algebra* with two binary operations, one is taking the minimum and the other the sum. The algebraic properties of min-plus algebras have been extensively studied and they have been applied to solve problems in formal language theory, such as the finite power property problem [8]. They are also widely used to analyze discrete event systems, optimization, etc. [9]. What is important in our

A. Dawar and R. de Queiroz (Eds.): WoLLIC 2010, LNAI 6188, pp. 148–160, 2010.

context is that a min-plus algebra is a commutative dioid, which can be regarded as a generalization of Boolean algebra. Thus, we have naturally decided that in our $\mathbf{N}_\infty$ semantics, the disjunction is interpreted by the *min* operator, which corresponds to the join operator of the Boolean algebra, and the conjunction is interpreted by the plus operator, which corresponds to the meet operator. The truth and the falsehood are also naturally interpreted by 0 and ∞, respectively. Using this semantics, various quantitative values of Kripke structure can be represented by formulae of the modal μ-calculus, such as the shortest path between two states or the number of states that satisfies a property.

Let $\mathcal{L}$ be the modal μ-calculus with our $\mathbf{N}_\infty$ semantics and $\mathcal{L}^-$ the sublogic of $\mathcal{L}$ in that the implication operator does not appear. The model checking problem and the satisfiability problem are two fundamental problems of the modal μ-calculus. We have established a solution to the former for $\mathcal{L}^-$ [7] and for $\mathcal{L}$ [10]. In this paper, we investigate the latter. In the $\mathbf{N}_\infty$ semantics, the truth value $[\![\varphi]\!]^\mathcal{K}(s)$ of a formula φ at a state s of a Kripke structure $\mathcal{K}$ is an element of $\mathbf{N}_\infty$. The satisfiability problem in this semantics can be stated as to decide whether there is a Kripke structure $\mathcal{K}$ and its state s such that $[\![\varphi]\!]^\mathcal{K}(s) = 0$.

We have two main results. One is that the satisfiability problem of $\mathcal{L}$ is undecidable. We prove this by reducing Post's correspondence problem [11]. The main reason of this undecidability is that one can compare truth values of two formulae. In fact, we show that the following extension of the satisfiability problem for $\mathcal{L}^-$ is undecidable: for given closed formulae φ and ψ of $\mathcal{L}^-$, determine whether there is a Kripke structure $\mathcal{K}$ and its state s such that $[\![\varphi]\!]^\mathcal{K}(s) = [\![\psi]\!]^\mathcal{K}(s)$. The undecidability result for $\mathcal{L}$ directly follows from this fact.

The other is that the satisfiability problem of $\mathcal{L}^-$ is decidable. We show this by reducing the problem to the satisfiability problem of the modal μ-calculus with the standard semantics. To achieve this, for closed formula φ of $\mathcal{L}^-$, we define its translation, namely, formulae $\mathrm{tr}(\varphi, 0)$ and $\mathrm{tr}(\varphi, \infty)$ of the standard modal μ-calculus such that $[\![\mathrm{tr}(\varphi, 0)]\!]^\mathcal{K}(t) = 0$ is realized (i.e., φ is satisfiable) if and only if $\mathrm{tr}(\varphi, 0)$ is satisfiable and $[\![\mathrm{tr}(\varphi, \infty)]\!]^\mathcal{K}(t) = \infty$ is realized if and only if $\mathrm{tr}(\varphi, \infty)$ is satisfiable. The difficulty lies in the case of $\mathrm{tr}(\nu X\varphi, \infty)$. In the standard semantics, refuting $\nu X\varphi$ amounts to finding a witness that φ is false with finitely many repetitions. This no longer holds for the $\mathbf{N}_\infty$ semantics, because an infinite sum of finite values (truth) can be infinite (falsehood). The key fact to overcome the difficulty is that the value of $\nu X\varphi$ is infinite if and only if the following conditions are satisfied: (1) the claim that the value *may* be infinite cannot be refuted through *infinitely* many repetitions and (2) a witness that shows the value *must* be *positive* can be obtained after *finitely* many repetitions.

The remainder of this paper is organized as follows. In Section 2, the variants of the modal μ-calculus considered in this paper are introduced and the $\mathbf{N}_\infty$-semantics is defined. In Section 3, the undecidability result is presented. In Section 4, we define the translation and describe an outline of the decidability result. Section 5 concludes the paper.

$$[\![\textbf{false}]\!]^{\rho}(t) = \infty \quad [\![\textbf{1}]\!]^{\rho}(t) = 1 \quad [\![p]\!]^{\rho}(t) = L(p,t) \quad [\![X]\!]^{\rho}(t) = \rho(X,t)$$

$$[\![\psi_1 \vee \psi_2]\!]^{\rho}(t) = \min([\![\psi_1]\!]^{\rho}(t), [\![\psi_2]\!]^{\rho}(t)) \qquad [\![\psi_1 \wedge \psi_2]\!]^{\rho}(t) = [\![\psi_1]\!]^{\rho}(t) + [\![\psi_2]\!]^{\rho}(t)$$

$$[\![\psi_1 \to \psi_2]\!]^{\rho}(t) = [\![\psi_2]\!]^{\rho}(t) \,\dot{-}\, [\![\psi_1]\!]^{\rho}(t) \qquad [\![\neg\psi]\!]^{\rho}(t) = [\![\psi \to \textbf{false}]\!]^{\rho}(t)$$

$$[\![\Diamond\psi]\!]^{\rho}(t) = \min([\![\psi]\!]^{\rho}(t') \mid (t,t') \in R) \qquad [\![\Box\psi]\!]^{\rho}(t) = \sum([\![\psi]\!]^{\rho}(t') \mid (t,t') \in R)$$

$$[\![\mu X\psi]\!]^{\rho}(t) = \inf\{F_\alpha(t) \mid \alpha \in \text{On}\}, \text{ where } F_\alpha(t') = \inf\{[\![\psi]\!]^{\rho[X \mapsto F_\beta]}(t') \mid \beta < \alpha\}$$

$$[\![\nu X\psi]\!]^{\rho}(t) = \sup\{G_\alpha(t) \mid \alpha \in \text{On}\}, \text{ where } G_\alpha(t') = \sup\{[\![\psi]\!]^{\rho[X \mapsto G_\beta]}(t') \mid \beta < \alpha\}$$

Fig. 1. Value of formulae

2 Preliminaries

2.1 Syntax and Semantics

Let PS be the set of propositional symbols and PV be the set of propositional variables. The formulae of language $\mathcal{L}$ is defined as follows:

$$\varphi ::= \textbf{false} \mid 1 \mid p \mid X \mid \varphi \vee \varphi \mid \varphi \wedge \varphi \mid \varphi \to \varphi \mid \neg\varphi \mid \Diamond\varphi \mid \Box\varphi \mid \mu X\varphi \mid \nu X\varphi$$

where $p \in$ PS and $X \in$ PV. All occurrences of X in $\mu X\varphi$ and $\nu X\varphi$ must be positive in φ. The sublogic $\mathcal{L}^-$ of $\mathcal{L}$ consists of all the formulae in which the operator "$\to$" does not appear. (Note that the negation operator still exists in $\mathcal{L}^-$ although it could be defined in terms of the implication operator.)

$\mathcal{K} = (T, R, L)$ is a *Kripke structure* for $\mathcal{L}$ if T is a set, $R \subseteq T \times T$, and $L :$ PS $\times T \to \mathbf{N}_\infty$. The set of Kripke structures for $\mathcal{L}$ is denoted by KS$_\mathcal{L}$. T, R, and L are written as $|\mathcal{K}|$, $\mathcal{K}.R$, and $\mathcal{K}.L$, respectively. A function $\rho :$ PV $\times T \to \mathbf{N}_\infty$ is called a *valuation*.

For formula φ of $\mathcal{L}$ and $t \in T$, the value $[\![\varphi]\!]^{\mathcal{K},\rho}(t) \in \mathbf{N}_\infty$ of φ at t is given in Figure 1. $\mathcal{K}$ and/or ρ are omitted if they are clear from the context. In the figure, On is the class of ordinal numbers. For any function f, $f[a \mapsto b]$ is the function g whose domain is $\text{dom}(f) \cup \{a\}$, and whose values are defined by $g(a) = b$ and $g(x) = f(x)$ for any $x \in \text{dom}(f) \setminus \{a\}$.

Because $\mathbf{N}_\infty$ is only a commutative dioid and not a Boolean algebra, one of the distributive laws $[\![\varphi \vee (\psi_1 \wedge \psi_2)]\!](t) = [\![(\varphi \vee \psi_1) \wedge (\varphi \vee \psi_2)]\!](t)$ does not hold, although the other, $[\![\varphi \wedge (\psi_1 \vee \psi_2)]\!](t) = [\![(\varphi \wedge \psi_1) \vee (\varphi \wedge \psi_2)]\!](t)$, does hold. Also, $[\![\neg\Box\varphi]\!](t) = [\![\Diamond\neg\varphi]\!](t)$ does not necessarily hold if a state has infinite successors. The definition for the implication is similar to the definition in Heyting-valued models for the intuitionistic logic. (Note that $a \,\dot{-}\, b$ for $a, b \in \mathbf{N}_\infty$ is the smallest $x \in \mathbf{N}_\infty$ that satisfies $b + x \geq a$.) The definition for the negation is defined naturally using the implication.

We introduce a set AV that consists of the four "abstract" values of $\mathbf{N}_\infty$: Zer, Fin, Pos, and Inf. Their meanings are given by a function $\gamma : \text{AV} \to \mathcal{P}(\mathbf{N}_\infty)$ defined by $\gamma(\text{Zer}) = \{0\}$, $\gamma(\text{Inf}) = \{\infty\}$, $\gamma(\text{Pos}) = \mathbf{N}_\infty \setminus \{0\}$, and $\gamma(\text{Fin}) = \mathbf{N}_\infty \setminus \{\infty\}$.

Let $a \in AV$. A closed formula φ of $\mathcal{L}$ is *a-satisfiable* if there is $\mathcal{K} \in KS_{\mathcal{L}}$ and $t \in |\mathcal{K}|$ such that $[\![\varphi]\!]^{\mathcal{K}}(t) \in \gamma(a)$. Formula φ is *satisfiable* if it is Zer-satisfiable.

For each $p \in PS$, we consider new propositional symbols p_0 and p_∞, and denote the set of all such symbols by PS': $PS' = \{p_0 \mid p \in PS\} \cup \{p_\infty \mid p \in PS\}$. Let Mod' be the set of two new modality symbols "1" and "∞:" $Mod' = \{1, \infty\}$. We denote the standard modal μ-calculus with propositional symbols PS' and modality symbols Mod' by $\mathcal{L}'$: its formulae are defined by:

$$\varphi ::= p' \mid X \mid \neg\varphi \mid \varphi \vee \varphi \mid \varphi \wedge \varphi \mid \langle m \rangle \varphi \mid [m]\varphi \mid \mu X\varphi \mid \nu X\varphi$$

where $p' \in PS'$, $m \in Mod'$, and X is a propositional variable. Again, X must be positive in $\mu X\varphi$ and $\nu X\varphi$. The semantics of $\mathcal{L}'$ is defined through Kripke structures $\mathcal{K}' = (S, R', L')$ where S is a set, $R' : Mod' \to \mathcal{P}(S \times S)$, and $L' : PS' \to \mathcal{P}(S)$, in the standard manner [1,12]. (For each $m \in Mod'$, $R'(m)$ is the transition relation for m.) The set of Kripke structure for $\mathcal{L}'$ is denoted by $KS_{\mathcal{L}'}$. The satisfaction relation is denoted by $\mathcal{K}', s \models \varphi'$ for $s \in S$ and formula φ' of $\mathcal{L}'$. We then have all classical relations such as $s \models \neg(\varphi' \vee \psi') \iff s \models \neg\varphi' \wedge \neg\psi'$.

We need to introduce a few notations. Let φ be a formula of $\mathcal{L}$ or $\mathcal{L}'$. The symbol σ is used to stand for either fixed-point operator, μ or ν. If the binding formula of propositional variable X in a given formula φ is $\sigma X\psi$, we denote $\sigma X\psi$ by $BF(X)$, ψ by $BFS(X)$, and σ by σ_X. Variable X is called a *μ-variable* (resp. *ν-variable*) if $\sigma_X = \mu$ (resp. $\sigma_X = \nu$). The set of μ-variables (resp. ν-variables) is denoted by PV_μ (resp. PV_ν). When ψ_1 is a subformula of ψ_2, we write $\psi_1 \leq \psi_2$. For $X, Y \in PV$, we write $X \preceq Y$ if $BF(X) \leq BF(Y)$, and $X \prec Y$ if $X \preceq Y$ and $X \neq Y$.

2.2 Application of the Semantics

Using this semantics, any natural number-valued function defined on the state space of Kripke structures by using fixed-point operations with addition and taking the minimum as basic operations can be represented by a formula of the modal μ-calculus. Examples of values calculated using such a function contain the shortest path, the proof number in a game tree, or the number of states that satisfies a particular property. Examples are also found in data flow analysis.

For example, the shortest path from a state s to a state that satisfies p is $[\![\mu X(p \vee \Diamond(\mathbf{1} \wedge X))]\!](s)$. For more discussion, refer to Section 4 of [13].

3 Undecidability

In this section, we prove that the problem of whether two formulae of $\mathcal{L}^-$ can be of equal value is undecidable. From this fact, it directly follows that the satisfiability problem of logic $\mathcal{L}$ is undecidable.

Let us give names to related problems. FORMEQ is the following problem: for two given formulae φ and ψ of $\mathcal{L}^-$, decide whether there is a Kripke structure $\mathcal{K} = (S, R, L)$ and $s \in S$ such that $[\![\varphi]\!]^{\mathcal{K}}(s) = [\![\psi]\!]^{\mathcal{K}}(s)$. FORMLEQ is the problem obtained from FORMEQ by replacing $[\![\varphi]\!]^{\mathcal{K}}(s) = [\![\psi]\!]^{\mathcal{K}}(s)$ with $[\![\varphi]\!]^{\mathcal{K}}(s) \leq [\![\psi]\!]^{\mathcal{K}}(s)$.

We will show that both FORMEQ and FORMLEQ are undecidable by reducing Post's correspondence problem PCP [11] of alphabet $\{0,1\}$ to these problems. As an intermediate problem, we introduce EQFIN, which is to decide, for given formulae $\varphi_1, \ldots, \varphi_k$ and $\psi_1, \ldots, \psi_k$ of $\mathcal{L}^-$, whether there is a Kripke structure $\mathcal{K} = (S, R, L)$ and $s \in S$ such that $[\![\varphi_i]\!]^{\mathcal{K}}(s) = [\![\psi_i]\!]^{\mathcal{K}}(s) < \infty$ for every $i = 1, \ldots, k$.

Let m be a natural number and φ be a formula in $\mathcal{L}$. We define formula $\overline{m}$ by $\overline{0} = \mathbf{true}$ and $\overline{m+1} = \overline{m} \wedge \mathbf{1}$. Here, $\mathbf{true}$ is an abbreviation for $\neg\mathbf{false}$. Formula $m * \varphi$ is defined by $0 * \varphi = \mathbf{true}$ and $m * \varphi = ((m-1) * \varphi) \wedge \varphi$. We have $[\![\overline{m}]\!](t) = m$ and $[\![m * \varphi]\!](t) = m \cdot ([\![\varphi]\!](t))$.

Lemma 1. EQFIN *can be reduced to* FORMEQ *and* FORMLEQ.

Proof. Assume that formulae φ_i and ψ_i are given for $i = 1, \ldots, k$.

Let $\varphi_i' = (\overline{2} \wedge \varphi_i) \vee (\neg\varphi_i)$ and $\psi_i' = (\overline{2} \wedge \psi_i) \vee (\mathbf{1} \wedge \neg\psi_i)$. We then have $[\![\varphi_i']\!](t) = [\![\psi_i']\!](t)$ if and only if $[\![\varphi_i]\!](t) = [\![\psi_i]\!](t) < \infty$.

Let φ' be $(\varphi_1' \wedge \psi_1') \wedge \cdots \wedge (\varphi_k' \wedge \psi_k')$ and ψ' be $2 * (\varphi_1' \vee \psi_1') \wedge \cdots \wedge 2 * (\varphi_k' \vee \psi_k')$. Clearly $[\![\varphi']\!](t) \leq [\![\psi']\!](t)$ if and only if $[\![\varphi']\!](t) = [\![\psi']\!](t)$ if and only if for all $i = 1, \ldots, k$, $[\![\varphi_i']\!](t) = [\![\psi_i']\!](t)$, which is equivalent to $[\![\varphi_i]\!](t) = [\![\psi_i]\!](t) < \infty$. ∎

Our remaining task is to reduce PCP to EQFIN. Assume that finite number of pairs $(\alpha_1, \beta_1), \ldots, (\alpha_n, \beta_n)$ of words from alphabet $\{0,1\}$ are given. We need to decide whether there exists a non-empty sequence $i_1, \ldots, i_m$ of indices such that $\alpha_{i_1} \cdots \alpha_{i_m} = \beta_{i_1} \cdots \beta_{i_m}$. Without loss of generality, we can assume that $(\alpha_i, \beta_i) \neq (\alpha_j, \beta_j)$ if $i \neq j$.

We will introduce a few definitions and notations. A formula φ is a *condition* if for any Kripke structure $\mathcal{K} = (S, R, L)$ and $s \in S$, $[\![\varphi]\!]^{\mathcal{K}}(s)$ is either 0 or ∞. A sequence of states $(s_i)_i$ is a *path* if $(s_i, s_{i+1}) \in R$ for all i such that s_i and s_{i+1} are defined.

For any word α, its reversed word is denoted by $\overleftarrow{\alpha}$. We define $c(\alpha)$ as the value of $\overleftarrow{\alpha}$ regarded as a binary number, and $d(\alpha)$ as $2^{|\alpha|}$, where $|\alpha|$ is the length of α. For example, $c(10110) = 01101_2 = 13$ and $d(10110) = 2^5 = 32$. Note that α is uniquely determined from $c(\alpha)$ and $d(\alpha)$.

We will now introduce several formulae to describe properties of sequences of the pairs. Their definitions are given in Figure 2, where $p \in \mathrm{PS}$, $x \in \mathbf{N}$, and p_T, p_E, p_A^C, p_A^D, p_B^C, and p_B^D are different fixed propositional symbols.

Their intended meanings are as follows: $\mathrm{Geq}(p, x)$ has the value 0 if there is a path that starts from an adjacent state to the current state, that is of length x, and that reaches to a node where the value of p is finite. $\mathrm{Eq}(p, x)$ has the value 0 if x is the maximum length of such paths. These are conditions.

In a Kripke structure, some nodes represents a pair (α_i, β_i). The propositional symbol p_T is used to mark states. They form a sequence, and p_E is used to mark the end of the sequence. We need to express that these states actually form a sequence, i.e., they do not branch or form a cycle. For this purpose, we use Formulae NumTiles and LenTiles. Consider an unwound tree of the states

$$\text{Geq}(p, 0) = \textbf{true} \qquad \qquad \text{Geq}(p, x+1) = \Diamond(\neg\neg p \land \text{Geq}(p, x))$$

$$\text{Eq}(p, x) = \text{Geq}(p, x) \land \neg\text{Geq}(p, x+1)$$

$$\text{NumTiles} = \nu X(\neg p_\text{T} \lor (\neg\neg p_\text{T} \land \textbf{1} \land \Box X))$$

$$\text{LenTiles} = \nu X(\neg p_\text{T} \lor (\neg\neg p_\text{T} \land \textbf{1} \land \Diamond X))$$

$$\text{Tile}(\alpha, \beta) = \neg\neg p_\text{T} \land \neg p_\text{E} \land \text{Eq}(p_\text{A}^\text{C}, c(\alpha)) \land \text{Eq}(p_\text{A}^\text{D}, d(\alpha)) \land \text{Eq}(p_\text{B}^\text{C}, c(\beta)) \land \text{Eq}(p_\text{B}^\text{D}, d(\beta))$$

$$\text{StrA} = \mu X((\textbf{1} \land \neg\neg p_\text{E}) \lor \bigvee_{i=1}^{n} (\text{Tile}(\alpha_i, \beta_i) \land \overline{c(\alpha_i)} \land (d(\alpha_i) * \Diamond X)))$$

$$\text{StrB} = \mu X((\textbf{1} \land \neg\neg p_\text{E}) \lor \bigvee_{i=1}^{n} (\text{Tile}(\alpha_i, \beta_i) \land \overline{c(\beta_i)} \land (d(\beta_i) * \Diamond X)))$$

Fig. 2. Formulae used in EQFIN

that hereditarily satisfy p_T beginning at state s. Then, $\llbracket\text{NumTiles}\rrbracket(s)$ equals the number of the nodes of the tree and $\llbracket\text{LenTiles}\rrbracket(s)$ is the depth of the tree. Therefore, the states with p_T form a finite list if and only if $\llbracket\text{NumTiles}\rrbracket(s) = \llbracket\text{LenTiles}\rrbracket(s) < \infty$.

When $\llbracket\text{Tile}(\alpha, \beta)\rrbracket(s) = 0$ for a state s, we consider that s represents a pair (α, β). Note that for any state s, there is at most one such pair (α, β).

If $\llbracket p_\text{E}\rrbracket(s) < \infty$, then $\llbracket\text{StrA}\rrbracket(s) = 1$. On the other hand, if $\llbracket p_\text{E}\rrbracket(s) = \infty$ and $\llbracket\text{Tile}(\alpha_i, \beta_i)\rrbracket(s) = 0$, then $\llbracket\text{StrA}\rrbracket(s) = c(\alpha_i) + d(\alpha_i) \cdot \min\{\llbracket\text{StrA}\rrbracket(s') \mid (s, s') \in R\}$. Therefore, the $|\alpha_i|$ least significant bits of the binary expression of number $\llbracket\text{StrA}\rrbracket(s)$ is $\overleftarrow{\alpha_i}$. Suppose that states $s_1, \ldots, s_m, s_\text{END}$ forms a list, $1 \leq i_1, \ldots, i_m \leq n$, $\llbracket\text{Tile}(\alpha_{i_j}, \beta_{i_j})\rrbracket(s_j) = 0$ for $j = 1, \ldots, m$, $\llbracket p_\text{E}\rrbracket(s_\text{END}) = 0$, $\llbracket p_\text{T}\rrbracket(s) = \infty$ if $s \notin \{s_1, \ldots, s_m\}$, and $\llbracket p_\text{E}\rrbracket(s) = \infty$ if $s \neq s_\text{END}$. Then, the binary expression of $\llbracket\text{StrA}\rrbracket(s_1)$ is $1\overleftarrow{\alpha_{i_m}} \cdots \overleftarrow{\alpha_{i_1}}$ and that of $\llbracket\text{StrB}\rrbracket(s_1)$ is $1\overleftarrow{\beta_{i_m}} \cdots \overleftarrow{\beta_{i_1}}$.

Lemma 2. *PCP can be reduced to* EQFIN.

Proof. We only give a proof sketch here based on the intended meanings of the formulae mentioned above.

As an instance of EQFIN, we take the following pairs of formulae: $(\varphi_1, \psi_1) = (\text{NumTiles}, \text{LenTiles})$, $(\varphi_2, \psi_2) = (\text{StrA}, \text{StrB})$, and $(\varphi_3, \psi_3) = (\neg p_\text{E}, \textbf{true})$.

Suppose that there is a Kripke structure $\mathcal{K} = (S, R, L)$ and $s \in S$ such that $\llbracket\varphi_l\rrbracket^\mathcal{K}(s) = \llbracket\psi_l\rrbracket^\mathcal{K}(s) < \infty$ for $l = 1, 2, 3$. By the equation for $l = 1$, there exists a sequence of states $s_1, \ldots, s_m$ that satisfy p_T and that forms a list. By the equation for $l = 2$, for each $j = 1, \ldots, m$, there is a unique index i_j such that $\llbracket\text{Tile}(\alpha_{i_j}, \beta_{i_j})\rrbracket(s_j) = 0$, and we have $1\overleftarrow{\alpha_{i_m}} \cdots \overleftarrow{\alpha_{i_1}} = 1\overleftarrow{\beta_{i_m}} \cdots \overleftarrow{\beta_{i_1}}$. Therefore, $\alpha_{i_1} \cdots \alpha_{i_m} = \beta_{i_1} \cdots \beta_{i_m}$. Finally, the equation for $l = 3$ guarantees $m \geq 1$.

If there is a sequence of indices $i_1, \ldots, i_m$ such that $\alpha_{i_1} \cdots \alpha_{i_m} = \beta_{i_1} \cdots \beta_{i_m}$, we construct a Kripke structure $\mathcal{K} = (S, R, L)$ and $s \in S$ such that $\llbracket\varphi_i\rrbracket^\mathcal{K}(s) = \llbracket\psi_i\rrbracket^\mathcal{K}(s) < \infty$, as illustrated in Figure 3, where L is defined as follows: for $p = p_\text{T}$ and $p = p_\text{E}$, $L(p, s) = 0$ if p is marked in the circle for that s in the figure; otherwise, $L(p, s) = \infty$. For $y \in \{\text{C}, \text{D}\}$, $\xi \in \{\text{A}, \text{B}\}$, $j \in \{1, \ldots, m\}$, and

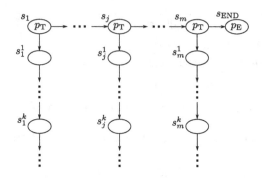

Fig. 3. Kripke structure for EQFIN

$k \in \mathbf{N}$, $L(p_\xi^y, s_j^k) = 0$ if $k \le y(\xi_{i_j})$; otherwise, $L(p_\xi^y, s_j^k) = \infty$. Using the intended meanings of the formulae, one can see that $[\![\varphi_l]\!](s_1) = [\![\psi_l]\!](s_1) < 0$ holds for $l = 1, 2, 3$.   ∎

By combining Lemmas 1 and 2, we have:

Theorem 1. *Problems* FORMEQ *and* FORMLEQ *are undecidable.*

Corollary 1. *The satisfiability problem of* $\mathcal{L}$ *is undecidable.*

Proof. FORMLEQ can be reduced to the satisfiability problem of $\mathcal{L}$: for given formulae φ and ψ of $\mathcal{L}^-$, $\varphi \to \psi$ is a formula in $\mathcal{L}$ and $[\![\varphi]\!](t) \le [\![\psi]\!](t)$ is equivalent to $[\![\varphi \to \psi]\!](t) = 0$.   ∎

4   Decidability

It can be shown that the satisfiability problem of $\mathcal{L}^-$ is decidable. In this paper, however, due to the page limitation, we will not give its proof for which an interested reader can refer to [14]. Instead, the intuition is presented in this section.

4.1   Outline of the Decidability Proof

Let φ be a closed formula in $\mathcal{L}^-$ and $a \in \mathrm{AV}$. We want to decide whether there is $\mathcal{K} \in \mathrm{KS}_\mathcal{L}$ and $t \in |\mathcal{K}|$ such that $[\![\varphi]\!]^\mathcal{K}(t) \in \gamma(a)$. For this purpose, we introduce a translation (Section 4.2): for a closed formula φ of $\mathcal{L}^-$ and $a \in \mathrm{AV}$, a closed formula $\mathrm{tr}(\varphi, a)$ is defined so that the following theorem holds:

Theorem 2. φ *is a-satisfiable if and only if* $\mathrm{tr}(\varphi, a)$ *is satisfiable.*

This theorem gives a decision procedure for $\mathcal{L}^-$, because $\mathcal{L}'$ is decidable.

We introduce a concept called (φ, a)-*simulation between* $(\mathcal{K}, t)$ *and* $(\mathcal{K}', s)$, where $\mathcal{K} \in \mathrm{KS}_\mathcal{L}$, $\mathcal{K}' \in \mathrm{KS}_{\mathcal{L}'}$, $t \in |\mathcal{K}|$, and $s \in |\mathcal{K}'|$. With regard to the simulation, we can prove the following lemma (Lemmas 8–10 of [14]).

Lemma 3

(1) If the simulation exists, we have $[\![\varphi]\!]^{\mathcal{K}}(t) \in \gamma(a) \iff \mathcal{K}', s \models \mathrm{tr}(\varphi, a)$.

(2) If formula φ of $\mathcal{L}^-$ is a-satisfiable, then there exist $\mathcal{K}$, $\mathcal{K}'$, t, s, and (φ, a)-simulation between $(\mathcal{K}, t)$ and $(\mathcal{K}', s)$ such that $[\![\varphi]\!]^{\mathcal{K}}(t) \in \gamma(a)$.

(3) If formula ψ of $\mathcal{L}'$ is satisfiable, then there exist $\mathcal{K}$, $\mathcal{K}'$, t, s, and (φ, a)-simulation between $(\mathcal{K}, t)$ and $(\mathcal{K}', s)$ such that $\mathcal{K}', s \models \psi$.

Theorem 2 immediately follows from Lemma 3: if φ is a-satisfiable, we find, by (2), $\mathcal{K}$, $\mathcal{K}'$, t, s and a simulation such that $[\![\varphi]\!]^{\mathcal{K}}(t) \in \gamma(a)$, and we have $\mathcal{K}', s \models \mathrm{tr}(\varphi, a)$ by (1). The other direction is shown using (3).

We will not give the definition of the simulation, which is rather complex. Instead, we just mention here that the simulation guarantees the correspondence between the number of the successors in $\mathcal{K}$ and the modality of the successor in $\mathcal{K}'$; if the former is finite, the latter should be 1 ($\in \mathrm{Mod}'$), and if the former is infinite, the latter should be ∞ ($\in \mathrm{Mod}'$). For example, suppose a ($\Box\varphi, \mathrm{Inf}$)-simulation exists between $(\mathcal{K}, t)$ and $(\mathcal{K}', s)$, and $t \in |\mathcal{K}|$ has successors t_i for all $i \in \mathbf{N}$. If $[\![\varphi]\!](t_i) = 1$ for all $i \in \mathbf{N}$, then, $[\![\Box\varphi]\!](t) = \infty$. In this case, s has an ∞-successor s' (i.e., $(s, s') \in R(\infty)$) such that $s' \models \mathrm{tr}(\varphi, \mathrm{Pos})$. On the other hand, if $[\![\varphi]\!](t_0) = \infty$ and $[\![\varphi]\!](t_i) = 0$ for all $i \in \mathbf{N} \setminus \{0\}$, then s has an 1-successor s' such that $s' \models \mathrm{tr}(\varphi, \mathrm{Inf})$. By referring to Figure 4 in the next section, you can see that $s \models \mathrm{tr}(\Box\varphi, \mathrm{Inf})$ holds in both cases.

4.2 Translation

Let us denote the set of functions from $\mathrm{PV} \times \mathrm{AV}$ to $\{0, 1, 2, 3\}$ by $\mathcal{V}$. In order to define $\mathrm{tr}(\varphi, a)$, we first define $\mathrm{tr}(\varphi, a, V)$ for $V \in \mathcal{V}$ as in Figure 4. Then, the translation $\mathrm{tr}(\varphi, a)$ is defined as $\mathrm{tr}(\varphi, a, V_I)$, where V_I is defined by $V_I(X, a) = 0$ for all X and a. For translation examples, refer to the appendix. In the rest of this section, we explain the intuition of the translation.

For a given closed formula ψ, we define two translations $\mathrm{tr}(\psi, \mathrm{Zer}, V)$ and $\mathrm{tr}(\psi, \mathrm{Inf}, V)$, where ψ is a subformula of φ. These are formulae of $\mathcal{L}^-$; the former means $[\![\varphi]\!](t) = 0$, the latter $[\![\varphi]\!](t) = \infty$. The other two formulae $\mathrm{tr}(\varphi, \mathrm{Pos}, V)$ and $\mathrm{tr}(\varphi, \mathrm{Fin}, V)$ appearing in Figure 4 are their negations. Let us temporarily ignore the third parameter V.

We consider the propositional symbols p_0 and p_∞ as expressions of $[\![p]\!](t) = 0$ and $[\![p]\!](t) = \infty$, respectively. With this in mind, the first line of Figure 4 can be read naturally. The translations of **1** are also natural.

Let us skip the propositional variable X. The translations of negation, disjunction, and conjunction are natural from the definitions in Figure 1.

For the diamond and box operations, the two modalities introduced in $\mathcal{L}'$ distinguish situations with finite successors from those with infinite successors. For example, consider $\mathrm{tr}(\Box\psi, \mathrm{Inf})$, which means $[\![\Box\psi]\!](t) = \infty$. There are two cases. In one case, there is a successor t' of t that satisfies $[\![\psi]\!](t') = \infty$. In the other case, there are infinitely many successors t' of t such that $[\![\psi]\!](t') > 0$. This observation leads to the definition in Figure 4.

$$\begin{array}{ll}
\mathrm{tr}(p, \mathrm{Zer}, V) = p_0 \wedge \neg p_\infty. & \mathrm{tr}(p, \mathrm{Pos}, V) = \neg p_0 \vee p_\infty. \\
\mathrm{tr}(p, \mathrm{Inf}, V) = \neg p_0 \wedge p_\infty. & \mathrm{tr}(p, \mathrm{Fin}, V) = p_0 \vee \neg p_\infty. \\
\mathrm{tr}(\mathbf{1}, \mathrm{Zer}, V) = \mathrm{tr}(\mathbf{1}, \mathrm{Inf}, V) = \mathbf{false}. & \mathrm{tr}(\mathbf{1}, \mathrm{Fin}, V) = \mathrm{tr}(\mathbf{1}, \mathrm{Pos}, V) = \mathbf{true}. \\
\mathrm{tr}(X, a, V) = \mathrm{tr}(\mathrm{BF}(X), a, V). &
\end{array}$$

$$\mathrm{tr}(\neg\psi, \mathrm{Zer}, V) = \mathrm{tr}(\neg\psi, \mathrm{Fin}, V) = \mathrm{tr}(\psi, \mathrm{Inf}, V[(X, a) \mapsto 3 \mid V(X, a) = 2]).$$
$$\mathrm{tr}(\neg\psi, \mathrm{Pos}, V) = \mathrm{tr}(\neg\psi, \mathrm{Inf}, V) = \mathrm{tr}(\psi, \mathrm{Fin}, V[(X, a) \mapsto 3 \mid V(X, a) = 2]).$$

$$\mathrm{tr}(\psi_1 \vee \psi_2, a, V) = \begin{cases} \mathrm{tr}(\psi_1, a, V) \vee \mathrm{tr}(\psi_2, a, V) & \text{if } a \in \{\mathrm{Zer}, \mathrm{Fin}\}. \\ \mathrm{tr}(\psi_1, a, V) \wedge \mathrm{tr}(\psi_2, a, V) & \text{if } a \in \{\mathrm{Inf}, \mathrm{Pos}\}. \end{cases}$$

$$\mathrm{tr}(\psi_1 \wedge \psi_2, a, V) = \begin{cases} \mathrm{tr}(\psi_1, a, V) \wedge \mathrm{tr}(\psi_2, a, V) & \text{if } a \in \{\mathrm{Zer}, \mathrm{Fin}\}. \\ \mathrm{tr}(\psi_1, a, V) \vee \mathrm{tr}(\psi_2, a, V) & \text{if } a \in \{\mathrm{Inf}, \mathrm{Pos}\}. \end{cases}$$

$$\mathrm{tr}(\Diamond\psi, a, V) = \begin{cases} \langle 1 \rangle \mathrm{tr}(\psi, a, V) \vee \langle \infty \rangle \mathrm{tr}(\psi, a, V) & \text{if } a \in \{\mathrm{Zer}, \mathrm{Fin}\}. \\ [1]\mathrm{tr}(\psi, a, V) \wedge [\infty]\mathrm{tr}(\psi, a, V) & \text{if } a \in \{\mathrm{Inf}, \mathrm{Pos}\}. \end{cases}$$

$$\mathrm{tr}(\Box\psi, a, V) = \begin{cases} [1]\mathrm{tr}(\psi, a, V) \wedge [\infty]\mathrm{tr}(\psi, \mathrm{Zer}, V) & \text{if } a \in \{\mathrm{Zer}, \mathrm{Fin}\}. \\ \langle 1 \rangle \mathrm{tr}(\psi, a, V) \vee \langle \infty \rangle \mathrm{tr}(\psi, \mathrm{Pos}, V) & \text{if } a \in \{\mathrm{Inf}, \mathrm{Pos}\}. \end{cases}$$

If $V(X, a) = 1$ or $V(X, a) = 2$, $\quad \mathrm{tr}(\mu X\psi, a, V) = \mathrm{tr}(\nu X\psi, a, V) = X_a.$
If $V(X, a) = 3$, $\qquad\qquad\qquad \mathrm{tr}(\mu X\psi, a, V) = \mathrm{tr}(\nu X\psi, a, V) = X_{\mathrm{neg}}.$
If $V(X, a) = 0$,

$$\mathrm{tr}(\mu X\psi, a, V) = \begin{cases} \mu X_a \ \mathrm{tr}(\psi, a, V'[(X, a) \mapsto 1]) & \text{if } a \in \{\mathrm{Zer}, \mathrm{Fin}\}. \\ \nu X_a \ \mathrm{tr}(\psi, a, V'[(X, a) \mapsto 1]) & \text{if } a \in \{\mathrm{Inf}, \mathrm{Pos}\}. \end{cases}$$

$$\mathrm{tr}(\nu X\psi, \mathrm{Zer}, V) = \nu X_{\mathrm{Zer}} \ \mathrm{tr}(\psi, \mathrm{Zer}, V'[(X, \mathrm{Zer}) \mapsto 1]).$$
$$\mathrm{tr}(\nu X\psi, \mathrm{Pos}, V) = \mu X_{\mathrm{Pos}} \ \mathrm{tr}(\psi, \mathrm{Pos}, V'[(X, \mathrm{Pos}) \mapsto 1]).$$
$$\mathrm{tr}(\nu X\psi, \mathrm{Fin}, V) =$$
$$\nu X_{\mathrm{neg}}\mu X_{\mathrm{Fin}} \ (\mathrm{tr}(\psi, \mathrm{Fin}, V'[(X, \mathrm{Fin}) \mapsto 2]) \vee \mathrm{tr}(\nu X\psi, \mathrm{Zer}, V'[(X, \mathrm{Fin}) \mapsto 2])).$$
$$\mathrm{tr}(\nu X\psi, \mathrm{Inf}, V) =$$
$$\mu X_{\mathrm{neg}}\nu X_{\mathrm{Inf}} \ (\mathrm{tr}(\psi, \mathrm{Inf}, V'[(X, \mathrm{Inf}) \mapsto 2]) \wedge \mathrm{tr}(\nu X\psi, \mathrm{Pos}, V'[(X, \mathrm{Inf}) \mapsto 2])).$$

$$(V' = V[(Y, a) \mapsto 0 \mid Y \prec X, a \in \mathrm{AV}])$$

Fig. 4. Translation

In some cases of the fixed-point operator, the following simple definitions work: $\mathrm{tr}(\sigma X\psi, a) = \sigma X \mathrm{tr}(\psi, a)$ for $a \in \{\mathrm{Zer}, \mathrm{Fin}\}$ and $\mathrm{tr}(\sigma X\psi, a) = \overline{\sigma} X \mathrm{tr}(\psi, a)$ for $a \in \{\mathrm{Inf}, \mathrm{Pos}\}$, where $\overline{\sigma}$ is the other operator, namely, $\overline{\mu} = \nu$ and $\overline{\nu} = \mu$. Now, we go back to the propositional variable. We want a simple definition, namely, $\mathrm{tr}(X, a) = X$. However, for this definition to work, at least the value of a should be the same as that of when the binding fixed-point operator σX was processed. Otherwise, X must be "expanded" again, namely, $\mathrm{tr}(X, a) = \mathrm{tr}(\mathrm{BF}(X), a)$. The third parameter V is introduced for this purpose: $V(X, a) = 1$ means that the value was a when σX was processed.

However, $\mathrm{tr}(\nu X\psi, \mathrm{Fin}, V)$ has its own problem. The combination of ν and Fin (or its complement Inf) is different from the other combinations (and from the standard semantics) in that the calculation of the fixed-point may not terminate because there is an infinite, strictly increasing sequence in $\mathbf{N}_\infty$. We found a key fact (Lemma 12 (5) of [14]), which can be expressed using a game between the prover and the refuter: If $\llbracket \varphi \rrbracket(s) < \infty$ holds, then the prover can reach a node of the game that claims the value is zero. This discussion leads us to an improved (but still incorrect) definition: $\mathrm{tr}_1(\nu X \psi, \mathrm{Fin}) = \mu X_{\mathrm{Fin}}(\mathrm{tr}(\psi, \mathrm{Fin}) \vee \mathrm{tr}(\nu X \psi, \mathrm{Zer}))$.

The remaining issue corresponds to the negation. A double negation resets any finite value of a formula to 0. Therefore, if a computing path passes negation symbols infinitely many times, the value remains finite regardless other conditions. To reflect the fact, we introduce another propositional variable X_{neg}. The two values 2 and 3 of $V(\varphi, a)$ are used to remember whether the path has encountered the negation symbol.

5   Conclusions

We presented decidability and undecidability results on the modal μ-calculus with the $\mathbf{N}_\infty$-semantics. The logic is decidable if it does not contain the implication operator. On the other hand, the satisfiability problem becomes undecidable if the logic contains the implication operator.

In the future, we plan to strengthen our decidability result to the problem in the form of $\llbracket \varphi \rrbracket^{\mathcal{K}}(t) = n$ for a given formula φ and $n \in \mathbf{N}_\infty$. It might be difficult to extend our translation to this problem, because we need to handle complex conditions. Instead, we plan to utilize a game expression of the $\mathbf{N}_\infty$ semantics that we have recently established [15], combined with the standard technique of alternating automata [16].

Acknowledgements

This work was partially supported by Kakenhi, Grant-in-Aid for Scientific Research (C-21500006), from the Japan Society for the Promotion of Science.

References

1. Kozen, D.: Results on the propositional μ-calculus. Theoret. Comput. Sci. 27(3), 333–354 (1983)
2. Gurfinkel, A., Chechik, M.: Multi-valued model checking via classical model checking. In: Amadio, R.M., Lugiez, D. (eds.) CONCUR 2003. LNCS, vol. 2761, pp. 263–277. Springer, Heidelberg (2003)
3. Bruns, G., Godefroid, P.: Model checking with multi-valued logics. In: Díaz, J., Karhumäki, J., Lepistö, A., Sannella, D. (eds.) ICALP 2004. LNCS, vol. 3142, pp. 281–293. Springer, Heidelberg (2004)
4. Kameyama, Y., Kinoshita, Y., Nishizawa, K.: Weighted Kripke structures and refinement of models. In: 23rd Conference of Japan Society for Software Science and Technology (2006)
5. Droste, M., Gastin, P.: Weighted automata and weighted logics. Theor. Comput. Sci. 380(1-2), 69–86 (2007)

6. Meinecke, I.: A weighted μ-calculus on words. In: Developments in Language Theory, 13th International Conference, DLT 2009, pp. 384–395 (2009)
7. Ikarashi, D., Tanabe, Y., Nishizawa, K., Hagiya, M.: Modal μ-calculus on min-plus algebra N_∞. In: 10th Workshop on Programming and Programming Languages (PPL 2008), Japanese Society on Software Science and Technology, pp. 216–230 (2008)
8. Simon, I.: Limited subsets of a free monoid. In: 19th Annual Symposium on Foundations of Computer Science, pp. 143–150 (1978)
9. Baccelli, F., Cohen, G., Olsder, G.J., Quadrat, J.P.: Synchronization and Linearity: An Algebra for Discrete Event Systems. John Wiley & Sons, Chichester (1992)
10. Ikarashi, D., Tanabe, Y., Nishizawa, K., Hagiya, M.: Modal μ-calculus on min-plus algebra N-infinity. In: Computer Software, Japan Society for Software Science and Technology (to appear)
11. Post, E.L.: A variant of a recursively unsolvable problem. Bull. Amer. Math. Soc. 52(4), 264–268 (1946)
12. Zappe, J.: Modal μ-calculus and alternating tree automata. In: Grädel, E., Thomas, W., Wilke, T. (eds.) Automata, Logics, and Infinite Games. LNCS, vol. 2500, pp. 171–184. Springer, Heidelberg (2002)
13. Tanabe, Y., Hagiya, M.: Fixed-point computations over functions on integers with operations min, max and plus. In: 6th Workshop on Fixed Points in Computer Science (FICS 2009), pp. 108–115 (2009)
14. Goyet, A., Hagiya, M., Tanabe, Y.: Decidability and undecidability results of modal μ-calculi with N_∞ semantics. In: PRO Workshop, Information Processing Society of Japan (June 2009),
http://cent.xii.jp/tanabe.yoshinori/09/06/ninfmu.pdf
15. Tanabe, Y., Hagiya, M.: Games and natural number-valued semantics of the modal μ-calculus. In: 26th Conference of Japan Society for Software Science and Technology (2009), http://cent.xii.jp/tanabe.yoshinori/09/09/72.pdf
16. Kupferman, O., Vardi, M.Y.: Weak alternating automata and tree automata emptiness. In: 30th Annual ACM Symposium on the Theory of Computing, pp. 224–233 (1998)
17. Wilke, T.: Alternating tree automata, parity games, and modal μ-calculus. Bull. Soc. Math. Belg. 8(2) (2001)

Appendix: Translation Examples

Let us compute $\psi'_{1p} = \text{tr}(\varphi_1, \text{Pos})$, where $\varphi_1 = \nu X(p \wedge \Box X)$.

$$
\begin{aligned}
\psi'_{1p} &= \text{tr}(\varphi_1, \text{Pos}, V_I) \\
&= \mu X_{\text{Pos}} \, \text{tr}(p \wedge \Box X, \text{Pos}, V_2) \\
&= \mu X_{\text{Pos}} \, (\text{tr}(p, \text{Pos}, V_2) \vee \text{tr}(\Box X, \text{Pos}, V_2)) \\
&= \mu X_{\text{Pos}} \, ((\neg p_0 \vee p_\infty) \vee \langle 1 \rangle \text{tr}(X, \text{Pos}, V_2) \vee \langle \infty \rangle \text{tr}(X, \text{Pos}, V_2)) \\
&= \mu X_{\text{Pos}} \, ((\neg p_0 \vee p_\infty) \vee \langle 1 \rangle \text{tr}(\varphi_1, \text{Pos}, V_2) \vee \langle \infty \rangle \text{tr}(\varphi_1, \text{Pos}, V_2)) \\
&= \mu X_{\text{Pos}} \, ((\neg p_0 \vee p_\infty) \vee \langle 1 \rangle X_{\text{Pos}} \vee \langle \infty \rangle X_{\text{Pos}})
\end{aligned}
$$

where $V_2 = V_I[(X, \text{Pos}) \mapsto 1]$. This formula means that a state that satisfies $\neg p_0$ or p_∞ is reachable through transitions labeled by 1 or ∞ (i.e., any transition).

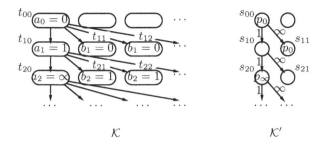

Fig. 5. Kripke structures $\mathcal{K}$ and $\mathcal{K}'$

Next, we try $\psi'_{1i} = \mathrm{tr}(\varphi_1, \mathrm{Inf})$.

$$\psi'_{1i} = \mathrm{tr}(\varphi_1, \mathrm{Pos}, V_I)$$

$$= \mu X_{\mathrm{neg}} \nu X_{\mathrm{Inf}}(\mathrm{tr}(p \wedge \Box X, \mathrm{Inf}, V_3) \wedge \mathrm{tr}(\varphi_1, \mathrm{Pos}, V_3))$$

$$= \mu X_{\mathrm{neg}} \nu X_{\mathrm{Inf}}((\mathrm{tr}(p, \mathrm{Inf}, V_3) \vee \mathrm{tr}(\Box X, \mathrm{Inf}, V_3)) \wedge \psi'_{1p}) \tag{1}$$

$$= \mu X_{\mathrm{neg}} \nu X_{\mathrm{Inf}}(((\neg p_0 \wedge p_\infty) \vee \langle 1 \rangle \mathrm{tr}(X, \mathrm{Inf}, V_3) \vee \langle \infty \rangle \mathrm{tr}(X, \mathrm{Pos}, V_3)) \wedge \psi'_{1p})$$

$$= \mu X_{\mathrm{neg}} \nu X_{\mathrm{Inf}}(((\neg p_0 \wedge p_\infty) \vee \langle 1 \rangle X_{\mathrm{Inf}} \vee \langle \infty \rangle \mathrm{tr}(\varphi_1, \mathrm{Pos}, V_3)) \wedge \psi'_{1p})$$

$$= \mu X_{\mathrm{neg}} \nu X_{\mathrm{Inf}}(((\neg p_0 \wedge p_\infty) \vee \langle 1 \rangle X_{\mathrm{Inf}} \vee \langle \infty \rangle \psi'_{1p}) \wedge \psi'_{1p}) \tag{2}$$

$$\equiv \nu X_{\mathrm{Inf}}(((\neg p_0 \wedge p_\infty) \vee \langle 1 \rangle X_{\mathrm{Inf}} \vee \langle \infty \rangle \psi'_{1p}) \wedge \psi'_{1p}) \tag{3}$$

where $V_3 = V_I[(X, \mathrm{Inf}) \mapsto 2]$. In (1) and (2), the same computation as in $\mathrm{tr}(\varphi_1, \mathrm{Pos}, V_I)$ was applied. For (3), note that X_{neg} appears only in the binding fixed-point operator. Here, $\psi_1 \equiv \psi_2$ means that ψ_1 and ψ_2 are equivalent, i.e., for any Kripke structure $\mathcal{K}'$ and its state s', $\mathcal{K}', s' \models \psi_1$ if and only if $\mathcal{K}', s' \models \psi_2$.

Let us consider the following Kripke structures $\mathcal{K} = (T, R, L) \in \mathrm{KS}_{\mathcal{L}}$ and $\mathcal{K}' = (S, R', L') \in \mathrm{KS}_{\mathcal{L}'}$. $T = \{t_{nm} \mid n, m \in \mathbf{N}\}$. $(t_{nm}, t_{kl}) \in R \iff k = n + 1$, $m = 0$. For any $n \in \mathbf{N}$, there is some $a_n, b_n \in \mathbf{N}_\infty$ such that $R(p, t_{n0}) = a_n$ and $R(p, t_{nm}) = b_n$ for any $m > 0$. $S = \{s_{nm} \mid n \in \mathbf{N}, m \in \{0, 1\}\}$. $(s_{nm}, s_{kl}) \in R'(0) \iff k = n + 1, m = l = 0$. $(s_{nm}, s_{kl}) \in R'(\infty) \iff k = n + 1, m = 0$, $l = 1$. L' is defined so that $s_{n0} \in L'(p_0) \iff a_n = 0$, $s_{n0} \in L'(p_\infty) \iff a_n = \infty$, $s_{n1} \in L'(p_0) \iff b_n = 0$, and $s_{n1} \in L'(p_\infty) \iff b_n = \infty$. Figure 5 illustrates a pair of instances of these Kripke structures. It can be shown that there is a $(\varphi_1, \mathrm{Inf})$-simulation between $(\mathcal{K}, t_{00})$ and $(\mathcal{K}', s_{00})$.

Assume $a_n = 1$ for all $n \in \mathbf{N}$. In this case, we have $[\![\varphi_1]\!](t_{00}) = \infty$. (This can be shown as follows: let $F_n = [\![\varphi_1]\!](t_{n0})$. Then, $F_n = [\![p]\!](t_{n0}) + \Sigma_{m \in \mathbf{N}}[\![\varphi_1]\!](t_{nm}) \geq [\![p]\!](t_{n0}) + [\![\varphi_1]\!](t_{n0}) = a_n + F_{n+1} = 1 + F_{n+1}$.) It is not difficult to show that $\mathcal{K}', s_{00} \models \psi'_{1i}$: in the terminology of game expression [17], Player 1 (the refuter) cannot select ψ'_{1p} at the first stage because $\mathcal{K}', s_{00} \models \psi'_{1p}$, then Player 0 (the prover) selects first $\langle 1 \rangle X_{\mathrm{Inf}}$ and then s_{10}. Both players keep selecting in the same way, and finally, because the fixed-point operator is ν, Player 0 wins.

If there exists some $n \in \mathbf{N}$ such that $a_n = \infty$, then both $[\![\varphi_1]\!](t_{00}) = \infty$ and $\mathcal{K}', s_{00} \models \psi'_{1i}$ hold. In this case, Player 0 selects $\neg p_0 \wedge p_\infty$ when he reaches s_{n0}. Similarly, if there exists some $n \in \mathbf{N}$ such that $b_{n+1} > 0$, then both $[\![\varphi_1]\!](t_{00}) = \infty$ and $\mathcal{K}', s_{00} \models \psi'_{1i}$ hold. Player 0 selects $\langle\infty\rangle\psi'_{1p}$ at s_{n0}.

On the other hand, if $a_n < \infty$ for all $n \in \mathbf{N}_\infty$, $b_n = 0$ for all $n \in \mathbf{N}_\infty \setminus \{0\}$, and there exists some $k \in \mathbf{N}_\infty$ such that $a_n = 0$ for all $n \geq k$, then $[\![\varphi_1]\!](t_{00}) < \infty$ and $\mathcal{K}', s_{00} \not\models \psi'_{1i}$. In this case, Player 1 switches to ψ'_{1p} at s_{k0}.

Next example contains the negation symbol: $\varphi_2 = \nu Y(p \wedge \Box \neg\neg Y)$. Let us compute $\psi'_{2i} = \mathrm{tr}(\varphi_2, \mathrm{Inf})$.

$$\psi'_{2i} = \mathrm{tr}(\varphi_2, \mathrm{Inf}, V_\mathrm{I})$$
$$= \mu Y_\mathrm{neg} \nu Y_\mathrm{Inf}(\mathrm{tr}(p \wedge \Box\neg\neg Y, \mathrm{Inf}, V_4) \wedge \mathrm{tr}(\varphi_2, \mathrm{Pos}, V_4)) \tag{4}$$

where $V_4 = V_\mathrm{I}[(Y, \mathrm{Inf}) \mapsto 2]$. The first term:

$$\mathrm{tr}(p \wedge \Box\neg\neg Y, \mathrm{Inf}, V_4)$$
$$= \mathrm{tr}(p, \mathrm{Inf}, V_4) \vee \mathrm{tr}(\Box\neg\neg Y, \mathrm{Inf}, V_4)$$
$$= (\neg p_0 \wedge p_\infty) \vee \langle 1\rangle\mathrm{tr}(\neg\neg Y, \mathrm{Inf}, V_4) \vee \langle\infty\rangle\mathrm{tr}(\neg\neg Y, \mathrm{Pos}, V_4)$$
$$= (\neg p_0 \wedge p_\infty) \vee \langle 1\rangle\mathrm{tr}(\neg Y, \mathrm{Fin}, V_5) \vee \langle\infty\rangle\mathrm{tr}(\neg Y, \mathrm{Fin}, V_5)$$
$$= (\neg p_0 \wedge p_\infty) \vee \langle 1\rangle\mathrm{tr}(Y, \mathrm{Inf}, V_5) \vee \langle\infty\rangle\mathrm{tr}(Y, \mathrm{Inf}, V_5)$$
$$= (\neg p_0 \wedge p_\infty) \vee \langle 1\rangle\mathrm{tr}(\varphi_2, \mathrm{Inf}, V_5) \vee \langle\infty\rangle\mathrm{tr}(\varphi_2, \mathrm{Inf}, V_5)$$
$$= (\neg p_0 \wedge p_\infty) \vee \langle 1\rangle Y_\mathrm{neg} \vee \langle\infty\rangle Y_\mathrm{neg} \tag{5}$$

where $V_5 = V_\mathrm{I}[(Y, \mathrm{Inf}) \mapsto 3]$. When the negation symbol is processed, all the values of the third argument (V_4, in this case) which are now 2 are changed to 3, in order to mark that the remainder is in the scope of the negation symbol. The second term of (4):

$$\mathrm{tr}(\varphi_2, \mathrm{Pos}, V_4)$$
$$= \mu Y_\mathrm{Pos}\,\mathrm{tr}(p \wedge \Box\neg\neg Y, \mathrm{Pos}, V_4)$$
$$= \mu Y_\mathrm{Pos}(\mathrm{tr}(p, \mathrm{Pos}, V_4) \vee \mathrm{tr}(\Box\neg\neg Y, \mathrm{Pos}, V_4))$$
$$= \mu Y_\mathrm{Pos}((p_0 \vee p_\infty) \vee \langle 1\rangle\mathrm{tr}(\neg\neg Y, \mathrm{Pos}, V_4) \vee \langle\infty\rangle\mathrm{tr}(\neg\neg Y, \mathrm{Pos}, V_4))$$
$$= \mu Y_\mathrm{Pos}((p_0 \vee p_\infty) \vee \langle 1\rangle\mathrm{tr}(\neg Y, \mathrm{Fin}, V_5) \vee \langle\infty\rangle\mathrm{tr}(\neg Y, \mathrm{Fin}, V_5))$$
$$= \mu Y_\mathrm{Pos}((p_0 \vee p_\infty) \vee \langle 1\rangle Y_\mathrm{neg} \vee \langle\infty\rangle Y_\mathrm{neg})$$
$$\equiv (p_0 \vee p_\infty) \vee \langle 1\rangle Y_\mathrm{neg} \vee \langle\infty\rangle Y_\mathrm{neg} \tag{6}$$

Therefore, and since (5) implies (6), we have:

$$\psi'_{2i} \equiv \mu Y_\mathrm{neg}\nu Y_\mathrm{Inf}(((\neg p_0 \wedge p_\infty) \vee \langle 1\rangle Y_\mathrm{neg} \vee \langle\infty\rangle Y_\mathrm{neg})$$
$$\equiv \mu Y_\mathrm{neg}(((\neg p_0 \wedge p_\infty) \vee \langle 1\rangle Y_\mathrm{neg} \vee \langle\infty\rangle Y_\mathrm{neg}) \tag{7}$$

In fact, because all finite values become zero by the double negation, the value of φ_2 can be infinite only if a state with infinite value is reachable, which (7) exactly states.

Solving the Implication Problem for XML Functional Dependencies with Properties

Sven Hartmann[1], Sebastian Link[2], and Thu Trinh[1]

[1] Clausthal University of Technology, Germany
[2] Victoria University of Wellington, New Zealand

Abstract. Due to the complex nature of XML, finding classes of integrity constraints for XML data that are both expressive and practical is an important but challenging task. In this paper, we study a class of XML functional dependencies (called pXFDs) defined on the basis of tree homomorphism. We establish a semantic equivalence between the implications problems for pXFDs and for propositional Horn clauses, which guarantees linear time decidability of pXFD implication. Hence, pXFDs cannot only be used to capture relevant data semantics, but also be reasoned about efficiently.

1 Introduction

Functional dependencies were first introduced by Codd together with the relational data model [5]. Since then important applications of functional dependencies have been encountered, e.g., in database design, data management, data security, data mining, and data cleansing. Functional dependencies are a valuable aid for capturing the semantics of data, e.g., to express business rules that hold in the the fragment of reality represented by the database. Once specified at design time of a database they can be exploited during run time, e.g., for enforcing data integrity, avoiding update anomalies, and rewriting queries to optimise response times. Most importantly, functional dependencies are the basis for schema normalisation that aims at generating "well-designed" databases.

More recently, the eXtensible Markup Language (XML) has emerged as a well-accepted and widely used data model for heterogenous or complex data in many application domains, including e-science, business integration and service computing. Today, all major DBMS support the storage and processing of XML data. With the increasing amounts of persistent XML data, there is an acute need for developing concepts, algorithms and techniques for efficiently organising and handling XML data. As XML was originally conceived as the W3C standard for exchanging data over the web, it provides only limited capabilities for specifying the semantics of data. Consequently, the study of functional dependencies and other integrity constraints has been identified as an important yet challenging topic of XML research [8,14,17,21].

For the relational data model there is a single ubiquitous notion of functional dependency that can be found in most database textbooks: a *functional dependency (FD)* $X \to Y$ states that whenever two tuples in a database table agree

A. Dawar and R. de Queiroz (Eds.): WoLLIC 2010, LNAI 6188, pp. 161–175, 2010.

on each attribute in X then they must also agree on each attribute in Y. In contrast, the complex nature of XML has sparked a multitude of proposals for *XML functional dependency (XFD)*, including [1,9,18,20]. The varying proposals deviate in their expressiveness, but are all justified by natural occurrence in XML data. Roughly speaking, there are several reasonable options how to generalise the notions of "tuple", "attribute", and "agreement" to XML.

The successful application of functional dependencies in relational databases has been based on a thorough investigation of their logical and computational characteristics. As for relational databases, being able to reason about a class of XFDs efficiently will be critical in our ability to apply XFDs for tasks such as integrity enforcement, query optimisation, and schema normalisation. So far, only very few classes of XFDs are known to have tractable logical implication and, even then, only under certain conditions. Thus the search for practical formalisms of XML functional dependency that can be reasoned about efficiently remains a challenge.

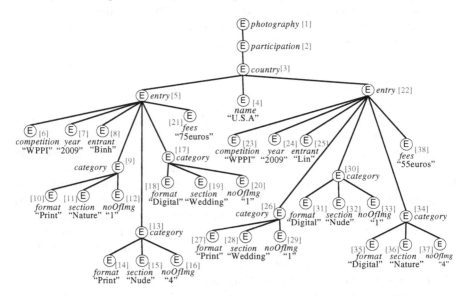

Fig. 1. An XML data tree T'_{photo} with photographic entries

Example 1.1. In this paper, we are concerned with a class of XFDs that extend a proposal in [9]. For motivation, consider an XML document with data on images entered into a photography competition[1], depicted as a data tree in Fig. 1. It is regular practice for the competition organisers to fix the pricing plan every year based on the number of images entered per section per format.

Suppose, for example, the entry fees charged for the WPPI[1] competition 2009 were as follows:

	format:	**Digital**	**Print**
1 image in 1 section		10 euros	15 euros
4 images in 1 section		30 euros	50 euros

---

[1] cf. Wedding & Portrait Photographers International, http://www.wppionline.com/

In T'_{photo} only the total fees paid by each entrant are recorded, as the pricing schedule is stored in a separate place. It is easy to see that we have the following integrity constraint:

Constraint 1. *For every competition and year, the collection of information about the number of images entered into each section in each format determines the total fees of an entry.*

Using a path-based XFD as proposed, e.g., in [1,18,22], the closest that we come to expressing the constraint above is as follows:

$$\left\{ \begin{array}{l} photography/participation/country/entry/competition, \\ photography/participation/country/entry/year, \\ photography/participation/country/entry/category/format, \\ photography/participation/country/entry/category/section, \\ photography/participation/country/entry/category/noOfImg \end{array} \right\}$$

$$\rightarrow \{ photography/participation/country/entry/fees \}$$

But this is not what we want to express: In the data tree T'_{photo}, there are two entrants for WPPI 2009 having the same collection of formats, the same collection of sections, and the same collection of numbers of images, but the fees charged to them are different. This means that the path-based XFD above is violated in T'_{photo}. On the other hand, however, the data tree T'_{photo} satisfies Constraint 1 as it complies with the given pricing schedule.

Constraint 1 helps to pinpoint two limitations of most XFD proposals in the literature: agreement is decided by *i)* comparing singular data items (rather than collections), and *ii)* considering paths independently from one another (rather than jointly as a tree structure). Both issues motivated the XFD proposal in [9] which is capable of expressing integrity constraints like Constraint 1: it allows subtrees of the schema tree to occur as "attributes" in the left and right hand side of an XFD. Here, we extend this idea further by considering an even wider notion of "attributes". For motivation, take the following integrity constraint:

Constraint 2. *For every entry, the information about the format and section determines the category.*

In other words, the constraint states that no entry has multiple categories with the same format and section. Such a functional dependency stipulates a uniqueness constraint that allows one to identify specific nodes within the data tree. This is particularly useful when looking for a syntactic characterisation for the absence of data redundancy - an important indicator of a well-designed schema.

Contribution. We study a class of XFDs that extend the proposal in [9]. We prove the associated implication problem to be equivalent to that of propositional Horn clauses, thus generalising an important result of Fagin for relational FDs. This gives rise to a linear-time algorithm for deciding implication for these XFDs. Thus we have found a new class of XFDs that are both expressive and practical. Incidentally, our proof of semantic equivalence also shows that finite and unrestricted implication coincides for the class of XFDs under inspection.

Organisation. Section 2 surveys related work, and Section 3 assembles basic terminology. In Section 4 we define the class of XFDs considered in this paper. Section 5 contains our major result on the semantic equivalence of logical implication for these XFDs and propositional Horn clauses. We give an example in Section 6 and conclude in Section 7 with consequences and future work plans.

2   Related Work

The efficiency with which we are able to reason about functional dependencies (i.e., decide implication) plays an important role in our ability to capitalise on their applications. The implication problem for relational FDs has been well-studied: The first axiomatisation for the implication of relational FDs was given by Armstrong [2]. Thus FD implication can be tackled by examining the enumeration of possible derivations. Several algorithmic approaches have emerged, often based on the Armstrong axioms. One of the earliest is due to Beeri and Bernstein [3]. The implication problem for relational FDs turned out to be solvable in linear time. This complexity result can also be concluded from the seminal work of Fagin [7] who related the implication of relational FDs to propositional logic. In fact, he proved that the implication problems for relational FDs and for propositional Horn clauses coincide. For propositional Horn clauses, however, the implication problem is equivalent to the well-studied satisfiability problem which can be solved in linear time, e.g., through unit propagation [4,6].

In the case of XML, the implication problem has been studied for a few selected classes of XFDs. Arenas and Libkin [1] showed that for their "tree-tuple" XFDs the implication problem can be solved in polynomial time in the presence of two restricted kinds of DTDs. In particular, for simple DTDs which corresponds to our schema trees, they obtained a quadratic time algorithm. In the presence of two other kinds of DTDs they prove the implication problem for "tree-tuple" XFDs to be coNP-complete. In general, however, they notice that the implication of "tree-tuple" XFDs is not finitely axiomatisable due to a non-trivial interaction with DTDs. Hartmann and Trinh [11,15] gave a finite axiomatisation for the implication of "tree-tuple" XFDs in the presence of schema trees, while Kot and White [12] found a finite axiomatisation for the implication of "tree-tuple" XFDs in the absence of a DTD and in the presence of some special kinds of DTDs. An axiomatisation for "pre-image" XFDs proposed in [9] was sketched in [10]. Vincent et al. [18] gave a sound set of inference rules for the implication of their class of "closest node" XFDs which, however, is only complete for the special case where the left hand sides contain no more than a single path. The relationship of "closest node" XFDs and "tree-tuple" XFDs has been discussed in [19]: both XFD proposals only coincide under very strong assumptions that severely detract from the syntactic flexibility of XML.

The XFDs studied in this paper complement the expressive power of existing classes of path-based XFDs, in particular "tree-tuple" and "closest node" XFDs. There are meaningful functional dependencies that can be expressed as the former but not the latter, and vice versa.

3   Preliminaries

An *XML tree* is a rooted tree T with finite node set V_T, arc set A_T, root r_T, and mappings *name* $: V_T \rightarrow Names$ and *kind* $: V_T \rightarrow \{E, A\}$. In an XML tree, the symbols E and A indicate elements and attributes, with attributes only appearing as leaf nodes. An *XML data tree* is an XML tree T' with a mapping *valuation* $: L_{T'} \rightarrow String$ assigning string values to leaves. An *XML schema tree* is an XML tree T with frequencies $?, 1, *, +$ assigned to its arcs, where $i)$ arcs to attribute nodes may only have frequency $?$ or 1 and, $ii)$ no two siblings have the same name and kind.

We use XML schema trees as structural summaries for collections of XML data trees. The notion of *compatibility* conveys that a particular XML data tree conforms to the structural summary given by an XML schema tree T at hand. We say that an XML data tree T' is T-*compatible* whenever there is a homomorphism $\phi : V_{T'} \rightarrow V_T$ (i.e., root-preserving, name-preserving, kind-preserving and arc-preserving mapping) such that for every vertex v' of T' and every arc $a = (\phi(v'), w)$ of T, the number of arcs $a' = (v', w')$ mapped to a is at most one if a has frequency label $?$, exactly one if a has frequency label 1, at least one if a has frequency label $+$, and arbitrarily many if a has frequency label $*$.

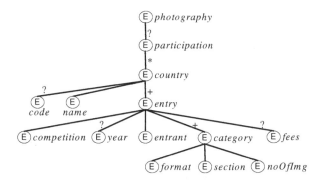

Fig. 2. The data tree T'_{photo} is compatible to the XML schema tree T_{photo} shown here

For every node v in an XML tree there is a unique path from the root to v. In an XML schema tree T we call a path *simple* iff it contains no arcs with frequency other than $?$ and 1. Furthermore, we call a node v in T *simple* iff the path from the root to v is simple. Given a node v, a node n which has a (possibly empty) path to v is called a v-*ancestor*. We can also say v is a *descendant* of n or n is an *ancestor* of v. By $\check{A}_T(v)$ we denote the set of all v-ancestors of T. Furthermore, n is a *simple ancestor* of v (or equivalently v is a *simple descendant* of n) iff the path connecting n with v is simple. Clearly, each node is also its own (simple) ancestor and (simple) descendant, and each simple node is a simple descendant of the root node. We use v_{lbl} to refer to a node with name *lbl*.

Let T be an XML tree, and $L_T \subseteq V_T$ be a given set of leaves of T. A *walk* of T is a path from the root of T to a member of L_T and every walk containing v is called a *v-walk*. A *subgraph* W of T is a (possibly empty) set of walks of T and, a subgraph of T is a *v-subgraph* iff each of its walks contains v. By $\check{S}_T(v)$ we denote the set of all *v*-subgraphs of T. It is easy to see that $\check{S}_T(v)$ contains the empty set and is closed under the union, intersection and difference operators. Clearly a walk or subgraph of T is again an XML tree.

For convenience, we made an effort to use only XML schema trees whose leaves have mutually distinct names as examples in this paper. This saves space as it allows us to refer to a walk by the name of its leaf, and correspondingly we refer to a subgraph by a set of leaf names. Moreover, for a subgraph $\mathcal{X}$ consisting of a single walk B we tend to write B instead of $\{B\}$. Note that we use these abbreviations due to space limitations and do not exclude other cases.

The *total v-subgraph*, denoted by $T(v)$, is the set of all *v*-walks of XML tree T. The homomorphism ϕ between a T-compatible data tree T' and schema tree T induces a mapping of the total subgraphs of T' to the total subgraphs of T. For a fixed node v of T, a *pre-image tree of v* in T' is just a total w-subgraph with $\phi(w) = v$. Suppose every node in a data tree has a unique node id, then the node id for a node w in the data tree also identifies the total w-subgraph in the data tree. By $P_{T'}(v)$ we denote the set of all pre-image trees of v in T'.

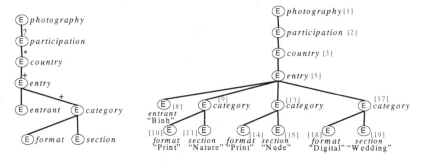

Fig. 3. A subgraph $\{\texttt{entrant}, \texttt{format}, \texttt{section}\}$ of T_{photo} and the projection of the pre-image tree i_2 of v_{entry} to this subgraph

4   XML Functional Dependencies with Properties

Next we formally define the class of XFDs investigated in this paper. Throughout let T be an XML schema tree, T' a T-compatible data tree, and v a node of T. As discussed we need to say how we want to generalise the notions of "tuple", "attribute", and "agreement" from the definition of relational FDs. In the subsequent definition, we will use the *v*-pre-image trees as "tuples", while the *v*-ancestors and *v*-subgraphs will be used as "attributes". For short, we will collectively call the members of $\mathring{A}_T(v) \cup \check{S}_T(v)$ the *v-properties* of T.

"Agreement" will be defined on the basis of tree homomorphism. Given two XML trees T_1 and T_2, we say that they are *isomorphic* or *copies* of one another if there is a homomorphism $\phi : V_{T_1} \to V_{T_2}$ which is bijective and ϕ^{-1} is a homomorphism. In particular, we call such a mapping ϕ a *(tree) isomorphism*. A subgraph U of T_1 is a *subcopy* of T_2 if U is isomorphic to some subgraph of T_2.

To explain when two pre-image trees "agree" on a v-property we need to state what the projection of a pre-image tree to a v-property is. Intuitively projecting to a v-property yields either nodes or XML trees depending on whether we consider a v-ancestor or v-subgraph, and thus we have two cases:

Definition 4.1 (projection). *For a v-property X of T, the projection of T' to X, denoted by $T'|_X$, is:*

- *the set of all pre-images of X in T', if X is a v-ancestor of T, or*
- *the union of all subcopies of X in T', if X is a v-subgraph of T.*

In the literature, two notions of agreement are popular when comparing fragments of XML data: node-equality and value-equality. We use node-equality when comparing the projection to v-ancestors, and value-equality when comparing projection to v-subgraphs.

Definition 4.2 (property-equality, $\doteq$). *Property-equality holds as follows:*

- *Two sets p, q of nodes in an XML data tree T' are property-equal iff $p = q$.*
- *Two XML data trees p, q are property-equal iff there exists a valuation-preserving isomorphism $\phi : V_p \to V_q$ between p and q.*

In words, we say "pre-image trees p_1, p_2 agree on X" to mean $p_1|_X \doteq p_2|_X$. Likewise, we say "pre-image trees p_1, p_2 differ on X" to mean $p_1|_X \not\doteq p_2|_X$.

Definition 4.3 (pXFD). *An XML functional dependency with properties (pXFD) over T is an expression $v : \mathcal{X} \to \mathcal{Y}$ where $\mathcal{X}, \mathcal{Y}$ are sets of v-properties of T. Herein, v is called the* target, *$\mathcal{X}$ the* LHS, *and $\mathcal{Y}$ the* RHS.
T' satisfies the pXFD $v : \mathcal{X} \to \mathcal{Y}$, written as $\models_{T'} v : \mathcal{X} \to \mathcal{Y}$, iff for any two pre-image trees $p_1, p_2 \in P_{T'}(v)$ we have $p_1|_X \doteq p_2|_X$ for all $X \in \mathcal{X}$ imply $p_1|_Y \doteq p_2|_Y$ for all $Y \in \mathcal{Y}$. We also say that the pXFD holds in T'.

Note that we *never* omit outer set parentheses for *sets of v-properties*. In particular, a (possibly empty) of v-property is *always* enclosed in set parentheses. $\emptyset$ denotes the empty v-subgraph, while $\{\}$ denotes the empty set of v-properties.

Example 4.1. The data tree T'_{photo} in Fig. 1 satisfies the pXFDs

$$v_{entry} : \{\texttt{competition}, \texttt{year}, \{\texttt{format}, \texttt{section}, \texttt{noOfImg}\}\} \to \{\texttt{fees}\} \quad (1)$$
$$v_{category} : \{v_{entry}, \{\texttt{format}, \texttt{section}\}\} \to \{v_{category}\} \quad (2)$$

which capture Constraints 1 and 2, respectively. But T'_{photo} violates the pXFDs

$$v_{entry} : \{\texttt{competition}, \texttt{year}, \texttt{format}, \texttt{section}, \texttt{noOfImg}\} \to \{\texttt{fees}\}$$
$$v_{entry} : \{\{\texttt{format}, \texttt{section}\}\} \to \{v_{entry}\}.$$

We like to emphasise that the addition of v-ancestors as "attributes" to XML functional dependencies is quite a powerful extension. A v-ancestor in the left hand side of a pXFD (as for example v_{entry} in (2)) may be regarded as a *context* that restricts the validity of a functional dependency to parts of the entire XML data tree (here the pre-image trees of v_{entry}).

A v-ancestor on the right hand side of a pXFD may be used to capture a categorisation or grouping of nodes. For example, the pXFD

$$v_{entry} : \{\text{competition}\} \rightarrow \{v_{country}\}$$

expresses that all entries for the same competition must be grouped under the same country. Probably most interesting is the inclusion of the target v into the right hand side of a pXFD to capture the uniqueness of nodes. For example, $v_{category}$ in the right hand side of the pXFD (2) just reflects the uniqueness constraint stipulated by Constraint 2 in the introduction.

Syntactically, one can specify a large number of pXFDs since the number of subsets of v-properties is exponential in the number of v-properties. In practice, however, we can restrict ourselves to a smaller subclass of pXFDs without loosing expressiveness. We call the pXFDs in this subclass *canonical*. Each pXFD can be rewritten as a canonical pXFD by translating non-essential v-properties into *essential* ones. We give details in the appendix.

Our paper is motivated by the implication problem for XML functional dependencies. A set of pXFDs Σ *implies* a pXFD σ, denoted by $\Sigma \models \sigma$, iff every T-compatible data tree which satisfies all pXFDs in Σ also satisfies σ. The *pXFD implication problem* is to decide, given any set $\Sigma \cup \{\sigma\}$ of pXFDs, whether $\Sigma \models \sigma$.

5   The Semantic Equivalence Theorem

Our objective is to establish a semantic equivalence between the implication of pXFDs and propositional Horn clauses that generalises the seminal result of Fagin for relational FDs to XML. For that, we need a *Horn encoding* that uses propositional horn clauses for encoding the given pXFDs but also the inherent structural properties associated with the underlying XML tree. We assume some familiarity with propositional logic, cf. [13]. A *Horn clause* over some given set of literals $\mathcal{V}$ is a *clause* (i.e., a disjunction of literals) with at most one *positive* (i.e., non-negated) literal.

Let $\varphi : \mathbf{E}_T^{\check{S}}(v) \cup \mathbf{E}_T^{\mathring{A}}(v) \rightarrow \mathcal{V}$ be a mapping that assigns propositional variables to the essential v-properties of T. If σ is a canonical pXFD $v : \{X_1, \ldots, X_j\} \rightarrow \{Y_1, \ldots, Y_k\}$ then, let

$$H_\sigma = \{\varphi(X_1) \wedge \ldots \wedge \varphi(X_j) \Rightarrow \varphi(Y_1), \ldots, \varphi(X_1) \wedge \ldots \wedge \varphi(X_j) \Rightarrow \varphi(Y_k)\}$$

be the Horn encoding of σ. For a set Σ of pXFDs, let H_Σ be the union of the sets H_σ for all $\sigma \in \Sigma$. Furthermore, we capture information about inherent inter-relationships among essential v-properties by the *base translation*:

$$\begin{aligned}
H_T = \ & \{\varphi(W) \Rightarrow \varphi(Z) \mid W, Z \in \mathbf{E}_T^{\check{S}}(v) \text{ and } W \text{ covers } Z \text{ and } Z \neq \emptyset\} \\
& \cup \{\varphi(n) \Rightarrow \varphi(m) \mid n, m \in \mathbf{E}_T^{\mathring{A}}(v) \text{ and } m \text{ is an immediate essential} \\
& \qquad\qquad\qquad\qquad \text{ancestor of } n \text{ and } n \neq r_T\} \\
& \cup \{\varphi(n) \Rightarrow \varphi(U) \mid \{n\} = \vartheta(\{v\}) \text{ and } U \text{ is a } v\text{-unit}\} \\
& \cup \{\varphi(\emptyset), \varphi(r_T)\}
\end{aligned}$$

where a v-subgraph W is said to *cover* a v-subgraph Z iff W is the union of Z and just one additional v-walk of T, and an essential v-ancestor m is an *immediate essential ancestor* of another essential v-ancestor n iff n is the next essential v-ancestor which can be reached from m.

An example for the Horn encoding is given in Section 6. To decrease the size of the base translation, we made use of the transitive nature of logical implication to consider only *covering* v-subgraphs and *immediate essential* ancestor/descendant essential v-ancestors. It is, of course, possible to use the more general notion of subgraph containment and ancestor/descendant relationship but this is likely to result in a considerably larger set of Horn clauses for the base translation.

Using the Horn encoding above we state our main result in this paper:

Theorem 5.1 (Semantic Equivalence Theorem for pXFDs). *The following statements are equivalent:*

1. Σ *implies* σ,
2. Σ *implies* σ *in the world of two-v-pre-image data trees,*
3. $H_\Sigma \cup H_T$ *logically implies* H_σ.

Σ is said to *imply* σ *in the world of two-v-pre-image data trees* iff every T-compatible data tree containing precisely two pre-image trees of v that satisfies all pXFDs in Σ also satisfies σ. To prove *(1.⇔2.)* we show that every T-compatible data tree that witnesses $\Sigma \models \sigma$ to be *false* contains a two-v-pre-image data tree that already witnesses the same fact.

The proof of *(2.⇔3.)* relies on a special connection between boolean assignment for propositional variables and the agreement of two pre-image trees of v. With this connection, it is possible to determine a boolean (truth) assignment witnessing a logical implication of Horn clauses from a two-v-pre-image T-compatible XML data tree witnessing the corresponding canonical pXFD implication, and vice versa. We use proof by the contrapositive. One direction follows easily from the characteristics of such representative boolean assignments, while the other direction additionally relies on the ability to construct a two-v-pre-image data tree from some input boolean assignment $\mathbb{B}$ such that the the resulting data tree has $\mathbb{B}$ as a representative boolean assignment.

For the proof of *(2.⇔3.)* we need to relate boolean assignments to two-v-pre-image data trees in such a way that pXFDs are satisfied in T' precisely when their corresponding Horn clauses evaluate to *true* under the boolean assignment:

Definition 5.1 (representative boolean assignment). *Let T be an XML schema tree and $\varphi : \mathbf{E}_T^{\mathbb{S}}(v) \cup \mathbf{E}_T^{\mathbb{A}}(v) \to \mathcal{V}$ be a mapping assigning propositional variables to the essential v-properties of T. Further, let $\mathbb{B}$ be a boolean assignment of all propositional variables in $\mathcal{V}$. The boolean assignment $\mathbb{B}$ is said to be* representative *of a given T-compatible two-v-pre-image data tree T' where $P_{T'}(v) = \{p_1, p_2\}$ iff the equivalence $\mathbb{B}(\varphi(W)) = \text{true}$ iff $p_1|_W \doteq p_2|_W$ holds for every essential v-property $W \in \mathbf{E}_T^{\mathbb{S}}(v) \cup \mathbf{E}_T^{\mathbb{A}}(v)$.*

Two important characteristics of boolean assignments $\mathbb{B}$ representing two-v-pre-image data trees are crucial here. The first lemma is analogous to the Semantic Lemma of Fagin [7] and relates the satisfaction of pXFDs in T' to the truth value of the corresponding Horn clauses under $\mathbb{B}$. The second lemma affirms that every Horn clause belonging to base translation H_T evaluates to *true* under $\mathbb{B}$. This attests to the fact that the base translation only encodes inherent inter-relationships among essential v-properties with respect to property-equality.

Lemma 5.1 (Semantic Lemma). *Let $\mathbb{B}$ be a boolean assignment which is representative of some T-compatible two-v-pre-image data tree T'. Let σ be a canonical pXFD $v : \mathcal{X} \to \mathcal{Y}$ over T. Then σ holds in T' iff every Horn clause in the set H_σ evaluates to* true *under $\mathbb{B}$.*

Lemma 5.2 (Triviality Lemma). *Let $\mathbb{B}$ be a boolean assignment which is representative of some T-compatible data tree T'. Then every Horn clause in H_T evaluates to* true *under $\mathbb{B}$.*

For the proof of ($2.\Leftrightarrow 3.$) we further need to construct a T-compatible two-v-pre-image data tree having some specified representative boolean assignment. That is, we create a T-compatible two-v-pre-image data tree whose pre-image trees of v agree precisely on some given set of v-properties. From the triviality lemma and our earlier observations about property-equality when identifying essential v-properties, it is clear that the input set of v-properties cannot be arbitrary, rather it must possess certain characteristics:

Definition 5.2 (equality set). *An equality set $\mathcal{E}_T$ is a subset of v-properties such that the following conditions all hold:*

- *The subset of v-ancestors (i.e., ${}^{\mathbb{A}}\mathcal{E}_T = \mathcal{E}_T \cap \mathring{\mathbb{A}}_T(v)$) must contain the root node r_T; be complete (i.e., if a v-ancestor is in the set then all of its ancestors are also in the set); if a v-ancestor is in the set then all of its simple descendants are also in the set; and not contain the target node v.*
- *The subset of v-subgraphs (i.e., ${}^{\mathbb{S}}\mathcal{E}_T = \mathcal{E}_T \cap \mathring{\mathbb{S}}_T(v)$) must contain the empty subgraph $\emptyset$; be complete (i.e., if a v-subgraph is in the set then all v-subgraph contained in it are also in the set); and if two v-reconcilable v-subgraph X, Y are in the set then also v-subgraph $X \cup Y$ is in the set.*

We use a two-phase combinatorial approach for constructing a two-v-pre-image data tree that agrees precisely on the v-properties in a given equality set:

1. Firstly, we construct two distinct T-compatible pre-image trees of v which *agree precisely on v-subgraphs in the given input equality set.*
2. Secondly, we merge the constructed pre-image trees to form a T-compatible data tree in which the pre-image trees *share precisely the v-ancestors in the given input equality set.*

There is no conflict between the two phases since the former deals exclusively with descendants of v and the latter only with nodes not descended from v. An outline of the construction is given in the appendix. For a complete proof of Theorem 5.1 we refer the interested reader to [16].

6   An Example for Applying the Semantic Equivalence

The following example demonstrates how Theorem 5.1 can be used to decide implication of pXFDs. Recall the XML schema tree T_{photo} in Fig. 2 and consider its node v_{entry}. The essential v_{entry}-properties are $v_{participation}$, $v_{country}$, v_{entry}, competition, year, entrant, and all subgraphs contained in {format,section,noOfImg}.

We study an instance of the pXFD implication problem. Let σ be the pXFD $v_{entry} : \{\texttt{competition}, \texttt{year}, \texttt{entrant}\} \rightarrow \{\texttt{fees}\}$, and let Σ consist of the pXFDs $v_{entry} : \{\texttt{competition}, \{\texttt{format}, \texttt{section}, \texttt{noOfImg}\}\} \rightarrow \{\texttt{fees}\}$, and $v_{entry} : \{\texttt{competition}, \texttt{year}, \texttt{entrant}\} \rightarrow \{v_{entry}\}$.

For a fixed mapping φ from the set of essential v_{entry}-properties to propositional variables, the Horn encoding introduced above yields the following:

$$H_\sigma = \{\, \varphi(\texttt{competition}) \wedge \varphi(\texttt{year}) \wedge \varphi(\texttt{entrant}) \Rightarrow \varphi(\texttt{fees}) \,\}$$

$$H_\Sigma = \left\{ \begin{array}{l} \varphi(\texttt{competition}) \wedge \varphi(\{\texttt{format}, \texttt{section}, \texttt{noOfImg}\}) \Rightarrow \varphi(\texttt{fees}), \\ \varphi(\texttt{competition}) \wedge \varphi(\texttt{year}) \wedge \varphi(\texttt{entrant}) \Rightarrow \varphi(v_{entry}) \end{array} \right\}$$

$$H_{T_{photo}} = \left\{ \begin{array}{l} \varphi(\{\texttt{format}, \texttt{section}, \texttt{noOfImg}\}) \Rightarrow \varphi(\{\texttt{format}, \texttt{section}\}), \\ \varphi(\{\texttt{format}, \texttt{section}, \texttt{noOfImg}\}) \Rightarrow \varphi(\{\texttt{format}, \texttt{noOfImg}\}), \\ \varphi(\{\texttt{format}, \texttt{section}, \texttt{noOfImg}\}) \Rightarrow \varphi(\{\texttt{section}, \texttt{noOfImg}\}), \\ \varphi(\{\texttt{format}, \texttt{section}\}) \Rightarrow \varphi(\texttt{format}), \\ \varphi(\{\texttt{format}, \texttt{section}\}) \Rightarrow \varphi(\texttt{section}), \\ \varphi(\{\texttt{format}, \texttt{noOfImg}\}) \Rightarrow \varphi(\texttt{format}), \\ \varphi(\{\texttt{format}, \texttt{noOfImg}\}) \Rightarrow \varphi(\texttt{noOfImg}), \\ \varphi(\{\texttt{section}, \texttt{noOfImg}\}) \Rightarrow \varphi(\{\texttt{section}\}), \\ \varphi(\{\texttt{section}, \texttt{noOfImg}\}) \Rightarrow \varphi(\{\texttt{noOfImg}\}), \\ \\ \varphi(v_{entry}) \Rightarrow \varphi(v_{country}), \\ \\ \varphi(v_{entry}) \Rightarrow \varphi(\texttt{competition}), \\ \varphi(v_{entry}) \Rightarrow \varphi(\texttt{year}), \\ \varphi(v_{entry}) \Rightarrow \varphi(\texttt{entrant}), \\ \varphi(v_{entry}) \Rightarrow \varphi(\{\texttt{format}, \texttt{section}, \texttt{noOfImg}\}), \\ \varphi(v_{entry}) \Rightarrow \varphi(\texttt{fees}), \\ \\ \varphi(\emptyset), \\ \varphi(v_{participation}) \end{array} \right\}$$

To decide whether σ is implied by Σ, one can check whether there is a boolean assignment which makes all formulas in $H_\Sigma \cup H_{T_{photo}}$ become *true* and the single formula $h \in H_\sigma$ becomes *false*. To make h become *false*, we need to set $\mathbb{B}(\varphi(\texttt{competition})) = true$, $\mathbb{B}(\varphi(\texttt{year})) = true$, $\mathbb{B}(\varphi(\texttt{entrant})) = true$, and $\mathbb{B}(\varphi(\texttt{fees})) = false$. Then, to make the second formula in H_Σ become *true* we must further set $\mathbb{B}(\varphi(v_{entry})) = true$. Further, to make the formulas in $H_{T_{photo}}$ become *true*, we need to set $\mathbb{B}(\varphi(\{\texttt{format}, \texttt{section}, \texttt{noOfImg}\}) = true$.

However, the resulting assignment $\mathbb{B}$ is invalid as it causes the first formula in H_Σ to become *false*. Hence, we cannot find a boolean assignment as required.

That is, H_σ is a logical consequence of $H_\Sigma \cup H_{T_{photo}}$ and we can correspondingly conclude that Σ implies σ.

7   Conclusion and Future Directions

The Semantic Equivalence Theorem enables us to solve the pXFD implication problem via Horn satisfiability: $\Sigma \models \sigma$ holds unless H_σ is *not* a logical consequence of $H_\Sigma \cup H_T$. This corresponds to the question: For some $h \in H_\sigma$, is there a boolean assignment $\mathbb{B}$ of the propositional variables such that each propositional formula in the set $H_\Sigma \cup H_T \cup \{\neg h\}$ evaluates to *true*? This is the Horn Satisfiability problem (Horn-SAT) which is decidable in linear time [4,6].

Corollary 7.1. *The problem of whether Σ implies σ can be decided in time linear in the total number of essential v-properties of T.*

Thus, this paper identifies a new class of XFDs for which implication can be decided efficiently. This makes it practical for XML data architects to use our XFDs as integrity constraints in XML design to capture relevant data semantics. This contributes to the general objective of studying the trade-off between expressiveness and tractability of integrity constraints for XML.

The Semantic Equivalence Theorem has some immediate applications: we successfully used it for identifying and proving an axiomatisation for pXFDs, and for decision support in constraint acquisition, cf. [16]. We further record:

Corollary 7.2. *The finite and the unrestricted (i.e., when considering infinite XML data trees, too) implication problem of pXFDs coincide.*

Several areas emerge as possible directions for future work. It would be helpful to establish a similar semantic equivalence for other classes of XFDs, but also for pXFDs in the presence of further classes of DTDs such as #-DTDs or DTDs with a small number of disjunctions. The study of XML functional dependencies is motivated by the large number of potential applications, e.g., in database design, database tuning, or query optimisation as for relational FDs. The investigation of such opportunities will further justify the practicality of the class of pXFDs. We have started investigating XML normal forms based on pXFDs, cf. [16].

References

1. Arenas, M., Libkin, L.: A normal form for XML documents. ACM ToDS 29, 195–232 (2004)
2. Armstrong, W.W.: Dependency structures of data base relationships. In: IFIP Congress, pp. 580–583 (1974)
3. Beeri, C., Bernstein, P.A.: Computational problems related to the design of normal form relational schemas. ACM ToDS 4, 30–59 (1979)
4. Chang, C., Lee, R.: Symbolic Logic and Mechanical Theorem Proving. Academic Press, London (1987)
5. Codd, E.F.: Further normalization of the data base relational model. IBM Research Report RJ909 (1971)
6. Dowling, W.F., Gallier, J.H.: Linear-time algorithms for testing the satisfiability of propositional Horn formulae. J. Log. Program. 1, 267–284 (1984)

7. Fagin, R.: Functional dependencies in a relational data base and propositional logic. IBM J. Research Dev. 21, 543–544 (1977)
8. Fan, W.: XML constraints: Specification, analysis, and applications. In: Andersen, K.V., Debenham, J., Wagner, R. (eds.) DEXA 2005. LNCS, vol. 3588, pp. 805–809. Springer, Heidelberg (2005)
9. Hartmann, S., Link, S.: More functional dependencies for XML. In: Kalinichenko, L.A., Manthey, R., Thalheim, B., Wloka, U. (eds.) ADBIS 2003. LNCS, vol. 2798, pp. 355–369. Springer, Heidelberg (2003)
10. Hartmann, S., Link, S., Trinh, T.: Efficient reasoning about XFDs with pre-image semantics. In: Kotagiri, R., Radha Krishna, P., Mohania, M., Nantajeewarawat, E. (eds.) DASFAA 2007. LNCS, vol. 4443, pp. 1070–1074. Springer, Heidelberg (2007)
11. Hartmann, S., Trinh, T.: Axiomatising functional dependencies for XML with frequencies. In: Dix, J., Hegner, S.J. (eds.) FoIKS 2006. LNCS, vol. 3861, pp. 159–178. Springer, Heidelberg (2006)
12. Kot, L., White, W.M.: Characterization of the interaction of XML functional dependencies with DTDs. In: Schwentick, T., Suciu, D. (eds.) ICDT 2007. LNCS, vol. 4353, pp. 119–133. Springer, Heidelberg (2006)
13. Rautenberg, W.: A Concise Introduction to Mathematical Logic. Springer, Heidelberg (2006)
14. Suciu, D.: On database theory and XML. SIGMOD Rec. 30, 39–45 (2001)
15. Trinh, T.: Axiomatising functional dependencies for XML with frequencies. Master's thesis, Massey University (2004)
16. Trinh, T.: XML Functional Dependencies based on Tree Homomorphisms. PhD thesis, Clausthal University of Technology (2009)
17. Vianu, V.: A Web odyssey: from Codd to XML. SIGMOD Rec. 32, 68–77 (2003)
18. Vincent, M.W., Liu, J., Liu, C.: Strong functional dependencies and their application to normal forms in XML. ACM ToDS 29, 445–462 (2004)
19. Vincent, M.W., Liu, J., Mohania, M.K.: On the equivalence between FDs in XML and FDs in relations. Acta Inf. 44, 207–247 (2007)
20. Wang, J., Topor, R.W.: Removing XML data redundancies using functional and equality-generating dependencies. In: ADC 2005, pp. 65–74 (2005)
21. Widom, J.: Data management for XML: Research directions. IEEE Data Eng. Bull. 22, 44–52 (1999)
22. Yu, C., Jagadish, H.V.: XML schema refinement through redundancy detection and normalization. VLDB J. 17, 203–223 (2008)

Appendix

We use the appendix to assemble some more technical details that may provide further insight into the results presented in this paper.

Canonical XFDs. Firstly, we explain when a v-property is essential, and how the proposed translation ϑ into canonical pXFDs works. Let $\mathbf{E}_T^{\mathring{A}}(v)$ be the set of all v-ancestors whose incoming arc has frequency other than ? or 1. We call the members of $\mathbf{E}_T^{\mathring{A}}(v)$ *essential v-ancestors*. To check property-equality of a set $\mathcal{X}^{\mathring{A}}$ of v-ancestors, it is sufficient to consider the *lowest* v-ancestor in this set. Instead of such a v-ancestor, it is equivalent to consider its *highest* simple ancestor, which is still essential. Thus, if $\mathcal{X}^{\mathring{A}}$ is non-empty then $\vartheta(\mathcal{X}^{\mathring{A}})$ denotes the singleton set containing the highest simple ancestor of the lowest contained node $\mathtt{lca}(\mathcal{X}^{\check{A}}) \in \mathcal{X}^{\check{A}}$. Otherwise, if $\mathcal{X}^{\mathring{A}}$ is empty, then $\vartheta(\mathcal{X}^{\mathring{A}}) = \{\}$.

We also consider essential v-subgraphs. It is clear that two pre-image trees which agree on some v-subgraph X must also agree on all v-subgraphs contained in X. On the other hand, two pre-image trees may agree on two v-subgraphs X, Y but still differ on the union v-subgraph $X \cup Y$. For example, recall the XML data tree T'_{photo} and its v_{entry}-walks format and section. Can we say when agreement on two v-subgraphs X, Y forces agreement on their union $X \cup Y$? We found the following condition: Two distinct v-subgraphs X, Y are v-reconcilable iff X contains every w-walk in Y or Y contains every w-walk in X, whenever X, Y share some arc (u, w) of frequency other than ? and 1 where w is a proper descendant of v. For an example, take the v_{entry}-walks entrant and year.

Given two v-reconcilable v-subgraphs X, Y and any two pre-image trees p, q we can show that $p_1|_X \doteq p_2|_X$ and $p_1|_Y \doteq p_2|_Y$ iff $p_1|_{X \cup Y} \doteq p_2|_{X \cup Y}$.

Let $\mathbf{E}_T^{\check{\mathbb{S}}}(v)$ be the smallest subset of $\check{\mathbb{S}}_T(v)$ such that the empty v-subgraph and every singleton v-subgraph consisting of a single v-walk belong to $\mathbf{E}_T^{\check{\mathbb{S}}}(v)$ and such that, if two v-subgraphs $X, Y \in \mathbf{E}_T^{\check{\mathbb{S}}}(v)$ are not v-reconcilable then $X \cup Y \in \mathbf{E}_T^{\check{\mathbb{S}}}(v)$. We call the members of $\mathbf{E}_T^{\check{\mathbb{S}}}(v)$ *essential v-subgraphs*. For a set $\mathcal{X}^{\check{\mathbb{S}}}$ of v-subgraphs take all all essential v-subgraphs that are contained in some member of $\mathcal{X}^{\check{\mathbb{S}}}$, and among these take only the ones that are maximal with respect to subgraph containment. This gives us $\vartheta(\mathcal{X}^{\check{\mathbb{S}}})$.

There is a practical way of finding all essential v-subgraphs: A v-*unit* is a v-subgraph U that consists of $i)$ a single v-walk in which every proper descendant of v has an incoming arc of frequency ? or 1; or $ii)$ all w-walks where w is the proper descendant of v whose incoming arc is the only arc in the path from v to w with frequency $*$ or $+$. Note that each v-walk belongs to exactly one v-unit. We can prove that a v-subgraph is essential iff it is contained in a v-unit.

Given a set $\mathcal{X}$ of v-properties, let $\mathcal{X}^{\mathbb{A}}$ be the v-ancestors and $\mathcal{X}^{\check{\mathbb{S}}}$ the v-subgraphs in it. Then the translation is $\vartheta(\mathcal{X}) = \vartheta(\mathcal{X}^{\check{\mathbb{S}}}) \cup \vartheta(\mathcal{X}^{\mathbb{A}})$.

Definition 7.1 (canonical pXFD). *A pXFD* $v : \mathcal{X} \to \mathcal{Y}$ *is a* canonical pXFD *iff* $\mathcal{X} = \vartheta(\mathcal{X})$ *and* $\mathcal{Y} = \vartheta(\mathcal{Y})$.

We can prove that a data tree T' satisfies $v : \mathcal{X} \to \mathcal{Y}$ if and only if T' satisfies $v : \vartheta(\mathcal{X}) \to \vartheta(\mathcal{Y})$. That is, it is indeed sufficient to study canonical pXFDs.

Construction of two-pre-image data trees. Next, we briefly outline the two-phase approach proposed in Section 5 for constructing a two-v-pre-image data tree which will agree precisely on the v-properties in some given equality set $\mathcal{E}_T$. For our purposes here, we found an alternative form of input beneficial. For that, an equality set of v-properties is transformed into a corresponding set of v-properties on which the two pre-image trees must *minimally differ*:

Definition 7.2 (non-equality set). *Given an equality set of v-properties $\mathcal{E}_T$, the corresponding* non-equality set *$\mathcal{NE}_T$ is given by*

$$\mathcal{NE}_T = \{n \in \mathring{\mathbb{A}}_T(v) \mid n \notin \mathcal{E}_T \text{ and } \not\exists \text{ a proper ancestor } m \text{ of } n \text{ s.t. } m \notin \mathcal{E}_T\}$$
$$\cup_{\subseteq - \min}(\{W \in \check{\mathbb{S}}_T(v) \mid W \notin \mathcal{E}_T\})$$

where $\subseteq_{-\min}(\mathcal{S})$ *denotes the subset of v-subgraphs belonging to set* $\mathcal{S}$ *which are minimal with respect to subgraph containment.*

Non-equality sets observe some nice characteristics: The members of a non-equality set are pairwise incomparable with respect to ancestor/descendant relationships and subgraph containment. All v-subgraphs in a non-equality set are essential, and a non-empty non-equality set contains precisely one essential v-ancestor with an incoming arc of frequency other than ? and 1.

For the construction under discussion, we look for two pre-image trees p_1, p_2 that differ on a *single essential v-subgraph* $W \in \mathcal{NE}_T$ but agree on every v-subgraph properly contained in W. For a data tree T' in which leaves are assigned the value "0" or "1", let the *ones-subgraph* X be the largest v-subgraph for which $val(T'|_B) = $ "1" iff the v-walk B is contained in X. In the first phase, we can consider each v-unit independently and use the following construction steps:

---

proc construct-pre-image-trees_one-subgraph(W, U)

Initialise p_1^W, p_2^W as empty XML trees
for all (possibly empty) v-subgraph X which is contained in W **do**
    Create a copy c^X of U whose ones-subgraph is X
    if $|X|$ is odd **then**
        $p_1^W =$Merge c^X with p_1^W on $\eta(U)$
    else
        $p_2^W =$Merge c^X with p_2^W on $\eta(U)$
    end if
end for
return p_1^W, p_2^W

By "merging" two data trees on some node w we mean that the merged data trees must share every node except their respective pre-images of w and its descendants. Observe that a data tree cannot contain multiple copies of U unless U itself contains more than one walk. If U is a singleton then there is only one copy of U to merge with the empty tree, which trivially returns the copy of U. If U is not a singleton, then it has an identifying node $\eta(U)$ whose incoming arc is the only arc on the path from v to $\eta(U)$ having frequency other than ? and 1 which is shared by all walks in U.

By repeating the previous construction and merging the resulting data trees, we obtain for each v-unit U two U-compatible pre-image trees of v which minimally differ on every v-subgraph in $\mathcal{NE}_T|_U = \subseteq_{-\min}(\{W \in \check{\mathcal{S}}_T(v) \mid W$ is contained in U and $W \in \mathcal{NE}_T\})$. Note that $\mathcal{NE}_T|_U$ can only have more than one member when U consists of more than one v-walk, and we have again some proper descendant $\eta(U)$ of v with incoming arc of frequency other than ? and 1. Thus, we can merge the pre-image trees $p_i^{W_j}$ ($i = 1, 2$, $W_j \in \mathcal{NE}_T|_U$) such that they share as many nodes as possible except their pre-images of $\eta(U)$ and its descendants.

Finally, we combine the subtrees constructed for the individual v-units to form a T-compatible data tree containing precisely two pre-image trees which agree on precisely those v-properties belonging to the given equality set $\mathcal{E}_T$.

On Anaphora and the Binding Principles in Categorial Grammar

Glyn Morrill[1] and Oriol Valentín[2]

[1] Universitat Politècnica de Catalunya
morrill@lsi.upc.edu
http://www-lsi.upc.edu/~morrill/
[2] Universitat Pompeu Fabra
oriol.valentin@upf.edu

Abstract. In type logical categorial grammar the analysis of an expression is a resource-conscious proof. Anaphora represents a particular challenge to this approach in that the antecedent resource is multiplied in the semantics. This duplication, which corresponds logically to the structural rule of contraction, may be treated lexically or syntactically. Furthermore, anaphora is subject to constraints, which Chomsky (1981)[1] formulated as Binding Principles A, B, and C. In this paper we consider English anaphora in categorial grammar including reference to the binding principles. We invoke displacement calculus, modal categorial calculus, categorial calculus with limited contraction, and entertain addition of negation as failure.

1 Introduction

Principles A, B and C of Chomsky (1981)[1] identify conditions on reflexive and personal pronouns in English. Principle A points to contrasts such as the following:[1]

(1) a. John$_i$ likes himself$_i$.
 b.*John$_i$ thinks Mary likes himself$_i$.

According to Principle A a reflexive requires a local c-commanding antecedent. Principle B refers to contrasts such as:

(2) a.*John$_i$ likes him$_i$.
 b. John$_i$ thinks Mary likes him$_i$.

According to Principle B a personal pronoun must not have a local c-commanding antecedent. Principle C filters examples such as:

(3) a.*He$_i$ likes John$_i$.
 b.*He$_{i/j}$ thinks Bill$_i$ likes John$_j$.

According to Principle C a personal pronoun cannot c-command its antecedent.

---

[1] The research reported in the present paper was supported by DGICYT project SESAAME-BAR (TIN2008-06582-C03-01).

A. Dawar and R. de Queiroz (Eds.): WoLLIC 2010, LNAI 6188, pp. 176–190, 2010.

In categorial grammar the duplication of the antecedent semantic resource can be performed lexically or syntactically. We consider treating anaphora lexically by assignment of pronouns to higher-order types with lexical semantic contraction in displacement calculus (Morrill and Valentín 2010)[8], and syntactically with the limited syntactic contraction of Jaeger (2005)[5]. In Section 2 we define the displacement calculus $\mathbf{D}$, a calculus which deals with discontinuous phenomena. Like the Lambek calculus $\mathbf{L}$, which it subsumes, $\mathbf{D}$ is a sequence logic without structural rules which enjoys Cut-elimination, the subformula property, and decidability. In Section 3 we look at reflexives and Principle A. In Section 4 we consider personal pronouns and Principle B. In Section 5 we look at Principle C.

2   Displacement Calculus

The types of the calculus of displacement $\mathbf{D}$ classify strings over a vocabulary including a distinguished placeholder 1 called the *separator*. The sort $i \in \mathcal{N}$ of a (discontinuous) string is the number of separators it contains and these punctuate it into $i+1$ maximal continuous substrings or *segments*. The types of $\mathbf{D}$ are sorted into types $\mathcal{F}_i$ of sort i by mutual recursion as follows:

$$
\begin{aligned}
(4) \quad & \mathcal{F}_j := \mathcal{F}_i \backslash \mathcal{F}_{i+j} && \text{under} \\
& \mathcal{F}_i := \mathcal{F}_{i+j}/\mathcal{F}_j && \text{over} \\
& \mathcal{F}_{i+j} := \mathcal{F}_i \cdot \mathcal{F}_j && \text{product} \\
& \mathcal{F}_0 := I && \text{product unit} \\
& \mathcal{F}_j := \mathcal{F}_{i+1} \downarrow_k \mathcal{F}_{i+j}, 1 \le k \le i+1 && \text{infix} \\
& \mathcal{F}_{i+1} := \mathcal{F}_{i+j} \uparrow_k \mathcal{F}_j, 1 \le k \le i+1 && \text{extract} \\
& \mathcal{F}_{i+j} := \mathcal{F}_{i+1} \odot_k \mathcal{F}_j, 1 \le k \le i+1 && \text{discontinuous product} \\
& \mathcal{F}_1 := J && \text{discontinuous product unit}
\end{aligned}
$$

Where A is a type we call its sort sA. The set $\mathcal{O}$ of *configurations* is defined as follows, where Λ is the empty string and $[]$ is the metalinguistic separator:

$$
(5) \quad \mathcal{O} ::= \Lambda \mid [] \mid \mathcal{F}_0 \mid \mathcal{F}_{i+1}\underbrace{\{\mathcal{O} : \ldots : \mathcal{O}\}}_{i+1 \ \mathcal{O}'s} \mid \mathcal{O}, \mathcal{O}
$$

Note that the configurations are of a new kind in which some type formulas, namely the type formulas of sort greater than one, label mother nodes rather than leaves, and have a number of immediate subconfigurations equal to their sort. This signifies a discontinuous type intercalated by these subconfigurations. Thus $A\{\Delta_1 : \ldots : \Delta_n\}$ interpreted syntactically is formed by strings $\alpha_0 + \beta_1 + \cdots + \beta_n + \alpha_n$ where $\alpha_0 + 1 + \cdots + 1 + \alpha_n \in A$ and $\beta_1 \in \Delta_1, \ldots, \beta_n \in \Delta_n$. We call these types *hyperleaves* since in multimodal calculus they would be leaves. We call these configurations *hyperconfigurations*. The sort of a (hyper)configuration is the number of separators it contains. A *hypersequent* $\Gamma \Rightarrow A$ comprises an antecedent hyperconfiguration Γ of sort i and a succedent type A of sort i. The *vector* $\overrightarrow{A}$ of a type A is defined by:

$$(6) \quad \vec{A} = \begin{cases} A & \text{if } sA = 0 \\ A\underbrace{\{[] : \ldots : []\}}_{sA \, []'_s} & \text{if } sA > 0 \end{cases}$$

Where Δ is a configuration of sort at least k and Γ is a configuration, the *k-ary wrap* $\Delta|_k\Gamma$ signifies the configuration which is the result of replacing by Γ the kth separator in Δ. Where Δ is a configuration of sort i and $\Gamma_1, \ldots, \Gamma_i$ are configurations, the *generalized wrap* $\Delta \otimes \langle \Gamma_1, \ldots, \Gamma_i \rangle$ is the result of simultaneously replacing the successive separators in Δ by $\Gamma_1, \ldots, \Gamma_i$ respectively. In the hypersequent calculus we use a discontinuous distinguished hyperoccurrence notation $\Delta\langle\Gamma\rangle$ to refer to a configuration Δ and continuous subconfigurations $\Delta_1, \ldots, \Delta_i$ and a discontinuous subconfiguration Γ of sort i such that $\Gamma \otimes \langle\Delta_1, \ldots, \Delta_i\rangle$ is a continuous subconfiguration of Δ. That is, where Γ is of sort i, $\Delta\langle\Gamma\rangle$ abbreviates $\Delta(\Gamma \otimes \langle\Delta_1, \ldots, \Delta_i\rangle)$ where $\Delta(\ldots)$ is the usual distinguished occurrence notation. Technically, whereas the usual distinguished occurrence notation $\Delta(\Gamma)$ refers to a context containing a *hole* which is a leaf, in hypersequent calculus the distinguished hyperoccurrence notation $\Delta\langle\Gamma\rangle$ refers to a context containing a hole which may be a hyperleaf, a *hyperhole*.

The hypersequent calculus for the calculus of displacement is given in Figure 1. Observe that the rules for both the concatenating connectives $\backslash, \cdot, /$ and the wrapping connectives $\downarrow_k, \odot_k, \uparrow_k$ are just like the rules for Lambek calculus except for the vectorial notation and hyperoccurrence notation; the former are specified in relation to the primitive concatenation represented by the sequent comma and the latter are specified in relation to the defined operations of k-ary wrap.

Abbreviating here and throughout $\uparrow_1$ and $\downarrow_1$ as $\uparrow$ and $\downarrow$ respectively, an extensional lexicon for examples of this paper is as follows:

(7) **a** : $((S\uparrow n(_110))\downarrow S)/cn(_110) : \lambda A \lambda B \exists C[(A\ C) \wedge (B\ C)]$
    about : $PP/n(_98) : \lambda A A$
    before : $(S/S)/S : before$
    buys : $(n(_101)\backslash S)/(n(_106) \bullet n(_108)) : \lambda A((buys\ \pi_1 A)\ \pi_2 A)$
    coffee : $n(n) : coffee$
    every : $((S\uparrow n(_110))\downarrow S)/cn(_110) : \lambda A \lambda B \forall C[(A\ C) \rightarrow (B\ C)]$
    he : $n(m)|n(m) : \lambda A A$
    he : $(((S\uparrow n(m))\uparrow n(m))\&\neg(J\bullet((n(m)\backslash S)\uparrow n(m))))\downarrow(S\uparrow n(m)) :$
        $\lambda A \lambda B((\pi_1 A\ B)\ B)$
    himself : $((n(m)\backslash S)\uparrow n(m))\downarrow(n(m)\backslash S) : \lambda A \lambda B((A\ B)\ B)$
    himself : $(((n(_118)\backslash S)\uparrow n(m))\uparrow n(m))\downarrow_2((n(_133)\backslash S)\uparrow n(m)) :$
        $\lambda A \lambda B((A\ B)\ B)$
    john : $n(m) : j$
    loves : $(n(_101)\backslash S)/n(_103) : loves$
    man : $cn(m) : man$
    mary : $n(f) : m$
    says : $(n(_101)\backslash S)/S : says$
    smiles : $n(_98)\backslash S : smiles$
    talks : $((n(_104)\backslash S)/PP)/PP : talks$

$$\frac{}{\overrightarrow{A} \Rightarrow A} \, id \qquad \frac{\Gamma \Rightarrow A \qquad \Delta\langle \overrightarrow{A} \rangle \Rightarrow B}{\Delta\langle \Gamma \rangle \Rightarrow B} \, Cut$$

$$\frac{\Gamma \Rightarrow A \qquad \Delta\langle \overrightarrow{C} \rangle \Rightarrow D}{\Delta\langle \Gamma, \overrightarrow{A \backslash C} \rangle \Rightarrow D} \, \backslash L \qquad \frac{\overrightarrow{A}, \Gamma \Rightarrow C}{\Gamma \Rightarrow A \backslash C} \, \backslash R$$

$$\frac{\Gamma \Rightarrow B \qquad \Delta\langle \overrightarrow{C} \rangle \Rightarrow D}{\Delta\langle \overrightarrow{C/B}, \Gamma \rangle \Rightarrow D} \, /L \qquad \frac{\Gamma, \overrightarrow{B} \Rightarrow C}{\Gamma \Rightarrow C/B} \, /R$$

$$\frac{\Delta\langle \overrightarrow{A}, \overrightarrow{B} \rangle \Rightarrow D}{\Delta\langle \overrightarrow{A \cdot B} \rangle \Rightarrow D} \, \cdot L \qquad \frac{\Gamma_1 \Rightarrow A \qquad \Gamma_2 \Rightarrow B}{\Gamma_1, \Gamma_2 \Rightarrow A \cdot B} \, \cdot R$$

$$\frac{\Delta\langle \Lambda \rangle \Rightarrow A}{\Delta\langle \overrightarrow{I} \rangle \Rightarrow A} \, IL \qquad \frac{}{\Lambda \Rightarrow I} \, IR$$

$$\frac{\Gamma \Rightarrow A \qquad \Delta\langle \overrightarrow{C} \rangle \Rightarrow D}{\Delta\langle \Gamma |_k \overrightarrow{A \downarrow_k C} \rangle \Rightarrow D} \, \downarrow_k L \qquad \frac{\overrightarrow{A} |_k \Gamma \Rightarrow C}{\Gamma \Rightarrow A \downarrow_k C} \, \downarrow_k R$$

$$\frac{\Gamma \Rightarrow B \qquad \Delta\langle \overrightarrow{C} \rangle \Rightarrow D}{\Delta\langle \overrightarrow{C \uparrow_k B} |_k \Gamma \rangle \Rightarrow D} \, \uparrow_k L \qquad \frac{\Gamma |_k \overrightarrow{B} \Rightarrow C}{\Gamma \Rightarrow C \uparrow_k B} \, \uparrow_k R$$

$$\frac{\Delta\langle \overrightarrow{A} |_k \overrightarrow{B} \rangle \Rightarrow D}{\Delta\langle \overrightarrow{A \odot_k B} \rangle \Rightarrow D} \, \odot_k L \qquad \frac{\Gamma_1 \Rightarrow A \qquad \Gamma_2 \Rightarrow B}{\Gamma_1 |_k \Gamma_2 \Rightarrow A \odot_k B} \, \odot_k R$$

$$\frac{\Delta\langle [] \rangle \Rightarrow A}{\Delta\langle \overrightarrow{J} \rangle \Rightarrow A} \, JL \qquad \frac{}{[] \Rightarrow J} \, JR$$

Fig. 1. Calculus of displacement **D**

to $: PP/n(_98) : \lambda AA$
walks $: n(_98)\backslash S : walks$
woman $: cn(f) : woman$

The first digit in the identifier names of feature variables appear as subscripts, which is the way LaTeX interprets the intial underscore of the variable names of the Prolog implementation used for the derivations in this paper. Atomic types which are unstructured appear in upper case; atomic types with arguments appear all in lower case.

By way of illustration of the displacement calculus consider the example:

(8) **every+man+loves+a+woman** $: S$

Lexical lookup yields the following semantically labelled sequent:

(9) $((S{\uparrow}n(_305)){\downarrow}S)/cn(_305) : \lambda A\lambda B\forall C[(A\ C) \rightarrow (B\ C)], cn(m) : man,$
$(n(_369)\backslash S)/n(_371) : loves, ((S{\uparrow}n(_396)){\downarrow}S)/cn(_396) : \lambda A\lambda B\exists C[(A\ C) \wedge (B\ C)], cn(f) : woman \Rightarrow S$

This has the following derivations and readings:

(10)

$$
\cfrac{
  \cfrac{
    \cfrac{
      \cfrac{
        \cfrac{
          \cfrac{
            \cfrac{
              \cfrac{n(m) \Rightarrow n(m) \quad S \Rightarrow S}{n(f) \Rightarrow n(f) \quad\quad n(m), n(m)\backslash S \Rightarrow S}\ \backslash L
            }{n(m), (n(m)\backslash S)/n(f), n(f) \Rightarrow S}\ /L
          }{[\,], (n(m)\backslash S)/n(f), n(f) \Rightarrow S{\uparrow}n(m)}\ {\uparrow}R \quad\quad S \Rightarrow S
        }{(S{\uparrow}n(m)){\downarrow}S, (n(m)\backslash S)/n(f), n(f) \Rightarrow S}\ {\downarrow}L
      }{(S{\uparrow}n(m)){\downarrow}S, (n(m)\backslash S)/n(f), [\,] \Rightarrow S{\uparrow}n(f)}\ {\uparrow}R \quad\quad S \Rightarrow S
    }{cn(f) \Rightarrow cn(f) \quad\quad (S{\uparrow}n(m)){\downarrow}S, (n(m)\backslash S)/n(f), (S{\uparrow}n(f)){\downarrow}S \Rightarrow S}\ {\downarrow}L
  }{cn(m) \Rightarrow cn(m) \quad\quad (S{\uparrow}n(m)){\downarrow}S, (n(m)\backslash S)/n(f), ((S{\uparrow}n(f)){\downarrow}S)/cn(f), cn(f) \Rightarrow S}\ /L
}{((S{\uparrow}n(m)){\downarrow}S)/cn(m), cn(m), (n(m)\backslash S)/n(f), ((S{\uparrow}n(f)){\downarrow}S)/cn(f), cn(f) \Rightarrow S}\ /L
$$

(11) $\exists C[(woman\ C) \wedge \forall G[(man\ G) \rightarrow ((loves\ C)\ G)]]$

(12)

$$
\cfrac{
  \cfrac{
    \cfrac{
      \cfrac{
        \cfrac{
          \cfrac{
            \cfrac{
              \cfrac{n(m) \Rightarrow n(m) \quad S \Rightarrow S}{n(f) \Rightarrow n(f) \quad\quad n(m), n(m)\backslash S \Rightarrow S}\ \backslash L
            }{n(m), (n(m)\backslash S)/n(f), n(f) \Rightarrow S}\ /L
          }{n(m), (n(m)\backslash S)/n(f), [\,] \Rightarrow S{\uparrow}n(f)}\ {\uparrow}R \quad\quad S \Rightarrow S
        }{cn(f) \Rightarrow cn(f) \quad\quad n(m), (n(m)\backslash S)/n(f), (S{\uparrow}n(f)){\downarrow}S \Rightarrow S}\ {\downarrow}L
      }{n(m), (n(m)\backslash S)/n(f), ((S{\uparrow}n(f)){\downarrow}S)/cn(f), cn(f) \Rightarrow S}\ /L
    }{[\,], (n(m)\backslash S)/n(f), ((S{\uparrow}n(f)){\downarrow}S)/cn(f), cn(f) \Rightarrow S{\uparrow}n(m)}\ {\uparrow}R \quad\quad S \Rightarrow S
  }{cn(m) \Rightarrow cn(m) \quad\quad (S{\uparrow}n(m)){\downarrow}S, (n(m)\backslash S)/n(f), ((S{\uparrow}n(f)){\downarrow}S)/cn(f), cn(f) \Rightarrow S}\ {\downarrow}L
}{((S{\uparrow}n(m)){\downarrow}S)/cn(m), cn(m), (n(m)\backslash S)/n(f), ((S{\uparrow}n(f)){\downarrow}S)/cn(f), cn(f) \Rightarrow S}\ /L
$$

(13) $\forall C[(man\ C) \rightarrow \exists G[(woman\ G) \wedge ((loves\ G)\ C)]]$

3   Reflexives and Principle A

A subject-oriented reflexive may be assigned type $((N\backslash S)\uparrow N)\downarrow(N\backslash S)$ with semantics $\lambda x \lambda y((x\ y)\ y)$. This generates example (1a) *John$_i$ likes himself$_i$* as follows:

$$(14)\quad \dfrac{\dfrac{\dfrac{N \Rightarrow N \quad N\backslash S \Rightarrow N\backslash S}{(N\backslash S)/N, N \Rightarrow N\backslash S}/L}{(N\backslash S)/N, [\,] \Rightarrow (N\backslash S)\uparrow N}\uparrow R \quad \dfrac{N \Rightarrow N \quad S \Rightarrow S}{\dfrac{N, N\backslash S \Rightarrow S}{}}\backslash L}{N, (N\backslash S)/N, ((N\backslash S)\uparrow N)\downarrow(N\backslash S) \Rightarrow S}\downarrow L$$

Thanks to the accommodation of discontinuity in **D**, the assignment also generates non-peripheral subject-oriented reflexivization as in the following example (something not possible in the Lambek calculus):

(15) **john+buys+himself+coffee** : S

Lexical lookup yields the semantically labelled sequent:

(16) $n(m) : j, (n(_197)\backslash S)/(n(_202)\bullet n(_204)) : \lambda A((buys\ \pi_1 A)\ \pi_2 A),$
     $((n(m)\backslash S)\uparrow n(m))\downarrow(n(m)\backslash S) : \lambda A \lambda B((A\ B)\ B), n(n) : coffee \Rightarrow S$

This has the following derivation:

$$(17)$$

This derivation delivers the lexical semantics:

(18) $(((buys\ j)\ coffee)\ j)$

Consider further object-oriented reflexivization:

(19) **mary+talks+to+john+about+himself** : S

Lexical lookup for our secondary wrap object-oriented reflexivization type assignment yields the semantically labelled sequent:

(20) $n(f) : m, ((n(_256)\backslash S)/PP)/PP : talks, PP/n(_269) : \lambda A A, n(m) : j,$
     $PP/n(_298) : \lambda A A, (((n(_337)\backslash S)\uparrow n(m))\uparrow n(m))\downarrow_2((n(_352)\backslash S)\uparrow n(m)) :$
     $\lambda A \lambda B((A\ B)\ B) \Rightarrow S$

$$\dfrac{\dfrac{n(m) \Rightarrow n(m) \quad PP \Rightarrow PP}{PP/n(m), n(m) \Rightarrow PP}\,/L}{PP/n(m), n(m) \Rightarrow PP}\,/L$$

$$\dfrac{n(m) \Rightarrow n(m) \quad PP \Rightarrow PP}{PP/n(m), n(m) \Rightarrow PP}\,/L \qquad \dfrac{n(_2576) \Rightarrow n(_2576) \quad S \Rightarrow S}{\dfrac{n(_2576), n(_2576)\backslash S \Rightarrow S}{n(_2576), (n(_2576)\backslash S)/PP, PP/n(m), n(m) \Rightarrow S}\,/L}\,\backslash L$$

$$\dfrac{n(_2576), ((n(_2576)\backslash S)/PP)/PP, PP/n(m), n(m), PP/n(m), n(m) \Rightarrow S}{((n(_2576)\backslash S)/PP)/PP, PP/n(m), n(m), PP/n(m), n(m) \Rightarrow n(_2576)\backslash S}\,\backslash R$$

$$\dfrac{((n(_2576)\backslash S)/PP)/PP, PP/n(m), n(m), PP/n(m), [\,] \Rightarrow (n(_2576)\backslash S)\!\uparrow\! n(m)}{((n(_2576)\backslash S)/PP)/PP, PP/n(m), n(m), [\,], PP/n(m), [\,] \Rightarrow ((n(_2576)\backslash S)\!\uparrow\! n(m))\!\uparrow\! n(m)}\,\uparrow R$$

$$\dfrac{n(m) \Rightarrow n(m) \qquad \dfrac{n(f) \Rightarrow n(f) \quad S \Rightarrow S}{n(f), n(f)\backslash S \Rightarrow S}\,\backslash L}{n(f), (n(f)\backslash S)\!\uparrow\! n(m)\{n(m)\} \Rightarrow S}\,\uparrow L$$

$$n(f), (((n(_2576)\backslash S)/PP)/PP, PP/n(m), n(m), PP/n(m), (((n(_2576)\backslash S)\!\uparrow\! n(m))\!\uparrow\! n(m))\!\downarrow_2((n(f)\backslash S)\!\uparrow\! n(m))) \Rightarrow S \quad \downarrow_2 L$$

Fig. 2. Object-oriented reflexivization

This has the proof given in Figure 2. This delivers semantics:

(21) $(((talks\ j)\ j)\ m)$

However, such extensional types will also allow Principle A violation such as (1b). Modal categorial calculus can be employed to rectify this.

Whatever the details of temporal semantics may turn out to be, it seems clear that the semantics of each lexical item is evaluated at a temporal index bound in the minimal tensed S within which it occurs. Morrill (1990)[7] proposed to characterize such intensionality by adding a modality to Lambek calculus. Let us extend the set of types as follows:

(22) $\mathcal{F}_i := \Box\mathcal{F}_i$

The semantic type map τ will be such that $\tau(\Box A) = T \to \tau(A)$ where T is the set of time indices, i.e. expressions of type $\Box A$ are to have as semantics the functional abstraction of the corresponding extensional semantics of the expression of type A. Thus, we assume the following semantically annotated rules of S4 modality where $\hat{\ }$ and $\check{\ }$ represent temporal intensionalisation and extensionalisation respectively:

(23)
$$\frac{\Box\Gamma \Rightarrow A : \phi}{\Box\Gamma \Rightarrow \Box A : \hat{\ }\phi}\Box R \qquad \frac{\Gamma\langle \overrightarrow{A} : x\rangle \Rightarrow B : \phi(x)}{\Gamma\langle \overrightarrow{\Box A} : y\rangle \Rightarrow B : \phi(\check{\ }y)}$$

Then assuming the lexical type assignments indicated, *John thinks Mary left* is derived as shown in (24) with semantics (25).

(24)
$$\frac{\dfrac{\dfrac{\dfrac{N \Rightarrow N}{\Box N \Rightarrow N}\Box L \qquad S \Rightarrow S}{\dfrac{\Box N, N\backslash S \Rightarrow S}{\dfrac{\Box N, \Box(N\backslash S) \Rightarrow S}{\Box N, \Box(N\backslash S) \Rightarrow \Box S}\Box R}\Box L}\backslash L \qquad \dfrac{\dfrac{N \Rightarrow N}{\Box N \Rightarrow N}\Box L \qquad S \Rightarrow S}{\Box N, N\backslash S \Rightarrow S}\backslash L}{\dfrac{\Box N, (N\backslash S)/\Box S, \Box N, \Box(N\backslash S) \Rightarrow S}{\Box N, (N\backslash S)/\Box S, \Box N, \Box(N\backslash S) \Rightarrow S}/L}}{\underset{\substack{\text{John} \quad\quad \text{thinks} \quad\quad \text{Mary} \quad\quad \text{left} \\ \Box N, \Box((N\backslash S)/\Box S), \quad \Box N, \Box(N\backslash S) \Rightarrow S}}{}\Box L}$$

(25) $((\check{\ }thinks'\ \hat{\ }(\check{\ }left'\ \check{\ }Mary'))\ \check{\ }John')$

Such modality, independently motivated for categorial intensional semantics, provides a handle on Principle A.

The requirement on $\Box R$ that every antecedent type be $\Box$-ed automatically sensitizes higher order functors to temporal domains according to whether ot not a hypothetical subtype is modalized. A modal reflexive type in which the hypothetical subtype is modalized, $\Box(((N\backslash S)\uparrow\Box N)\downarrow(N\backslash S))$, would generate both of (1a) and (1b); the type $\Box(((N\backslash S)\uparrow N)\downarrow(N\backslash S))$ succeeds in generating (1a), as shown in (26), but not (1b), as shown in (27). Here and henceforth we may abbreviate $N\backslash S$ as VP.

(26)
$$\cfrac{\cfrac{\cfrac{\cfrac{N \Rightarrow N \quad VP \Rightarrow VP}{VP/N, N \Rightarrow VP}\,{/L}}{\Box(VP/N), N \Rightarrow VP}\,{\Box L}}{\Box(VP/N), [\,] \Rightarrow VP{\uparrow}N}\,{\uparrow R} \qquad \cfrac{\cfrac{\cfrac{N \Rightarrow N \quad S \Rightarrow S}{N, VP \Rightarrow S}\,{\backslash L}}{\Box N, VP \Rightarrow S}\,{\Box L}}{}}{\cfrac{\Box N, \Box(VP/N), (VP{\uparrow}N){\downarrow}VP \Rightarrow S}{\underset{\substack{\text{John}\qquad\text{likes}\qquad\qquad\text{himself}}}{\Box N, \Box(VP/N), \Box((VP{\uparrow}N){\downarrow}VP) \Rightarrow S}}\,{\Box L}}\,{\downarrow L}$$

(27)
$$\cfrac{\cfrac{\cfrac{\cfrac{\cfrac{\Box N, \Box(VP/N), N \Rightarrow \Box S}{}\,{*\Box R}\quad VP \Rightarrow VP}{VP/\Box S, \Box N, \Box(VP/N), N \Rightarrow VP}\,{/L}}{\Box(VP/\Box S), \Box N, \Box(VP/N), N \Rightarrow VP}\,{\Box L}}{\Box(VP/\Box S), \Box N, \Box(VP/N), [\,] \Rightarrow VP{\uparrow}N}\,{\uparrow R} \qquad \cfrac{\vdots}{\Box N, VP \Rightarrow S}}{\cfrac{\Box N, \Box(VP/\Box S), \Box N, \Box(VP/N), (VP{\uparrow}N){\downarrow}VP \Rightarrow S}{\underset{\substack{\text{John}\quad\text{thinks}\quad\text{Mary}\quad\text{likes}\quad\qquad\text{himself}}}{\Box N, \Box(VP/\Box S), \ \Box N, \Box(VP/N), \Box((VP{\uparrow}N){\downarrow}VP) \Rightarrow S}}\,{\Box L}}\,{\downarrow L}$$

An intensional lexicon for examples of this paper is as follows:

(28) **after** : $\Box((S/\Box S)/\Box S) : {}^{\vee}\lambda A\lambda B((^{\vee}after\ A)\ B)$
  arrives : $\Box(n(_1 00)\backslash S) : arrives$
  debbie : $\Box n(f) : {}^{\wedge}d$
  everyone : $\Box((S{\uparrow}n(_1 09)){\downarrow}S) : {}^{\wedge}\lambda A\forall B[(^{\vee}person\ B) \to (A\ B)]$
  herself : $\Box(((n(f)\backslash S){\uparrow}n(f)){\downarrow}(n(f)\backslash S)) : {}^{\wedge}\lambda A\lambda B((A\ B)\ B)$
  herself : $\Box(((((n(_1 22)\backslash S){\uparrow}n(f)){\uparrow}_2 n(f)){\downarrow}_2((n(_1 37)\backslash S){\uparrow}n(f))) :$
    ${}^{\wedge}\lambda A\lambda B((A\ B)\ B)$
  likes : $\Box((n(_1 03)\backslash S)/n(_1 05)) : likes$
  she : $\Box n(f)|n(f) : \lambda A{}^{\wedge}A$
  she : $\Box(((S{\uparrow}\Box n(f)){\uparrow}\Box n(f)){\downarrow}(S{\uparrow}\Box n(f))) : {}^{\wedge}\lambda A\lambda B((A\ B)\ B)$
  sings : $\Box(n(_1 00)\backslash S) : sings$
  someone : $\Box((S{\uparrow}\Box n(_1 11)){\downarrow}S) : {}^{\wedge}\lambda A\exists B[(^{\vee}person\ B) \wedge (A\ {}^{\wedge}B)]$
  suzy : $\Box n(f) : {}^{\wedge}s$
  thinks : $\Box((n(_1 03)\backslash S)/\Box S) : thinks$

4 Personal Pronouns and Principle B

Jaeger (2005)[5] presents a syntactic type logical categorial grammar treatment of anaphora inspired by the combinatory categorial grammar treatment of Jacobson (1999)[4]. This uses a type constructor $B|A$ for an expression of type B requiring an antecedent of type A. This was in turn inspired by the syntactic treatment of Hepple (1990)[3] which assigns pronouns the identity function as lexical semantics. Jaeger gives the following left rule for |:

(29)
$$\frac{\Gamma \Rightarrow A : \phi \qquad \Delta_1, A : x, \Delta_2, B : y, \Delta_3 \Rightarrow D : \omega(x,y)}{\Delta_1, \Gamma, \Delta_2, B|A : z, \Delta_3 \Rightarrow D : \omega(\phi, (z\,\phi))}\,|L$$

Thus in an extensional grammar there is the analysis:

(30) **john+says+he+walks** : S

(31) $n(m) : j, (n(_197)\backslash S)/S : says, n(m)|n(m) : \lambda A A, n(_231)\backslash S : walks \Rightarrow S$

(32)
$$\cfrac{n(m) \Rightarrow n(m) \quad \cfrac{\cfrac{n(m) \Rightarrow n(m) \quad S \Rightarrow S}{n(m), n(m)\backslash S \Rightarrow S}\backslash L \quad \cfrac{n(m) \Rightarrow n(m) \quad S \Rightarrow S}{n(m), n(m)\backslash S \Rightarrow S}\backslash L}{\cfrac{n(m), (n(m)\backslash S)/S, n(m), n(m)\backslash S \Rightarrow S}{}/L}}{n(m), (n(m)\backslash S)/S, n(m)|n(m), n(m)\backslash S \Rightarrow S}\,|L$$

(33) $((says\ (walks\ j))\ j)$

Intensionally, and with a quantified antecedent:

(34) **everyone+thinks+she+sings** : S

(35) $\square((S{\uparrow}n(_195))){\downarrow}S) : {}^{\wedge}\lambda A \forall B[({}^{\vee}person\ B) \to (A\ B)], \square((n(_251)\backslash S)/\square S) :$
     $thinks, \square n(f)|n(f) : \lambda A{}^{\wedge}A, \square(n(_295)\backslash S) : sings \Rightarrow S$

(36)
$$\cfrac{n(f) \Rightarrow n(f) \quad \cfrac{\cfrac{\cfrac{\cfrac{\cfrac{n(f) \Rightarrow n(f) \quad S \Rightarrow S}{n(f), n(f)\backslash S \Rightarrow S}\backslash L}{n(f), \square(n(f)\backslash S) \Rightarrow S}\square L}{\square n(f), \square(n(f)\backslash S) \Rightarrow S}\square L}{\square n(f), \square(n(f)\backslash S) \Rightarrow \square S}\square R \quad \cfrac{n(f) \Rightarrow n(f) \quad S \Rightarrow S}{n(f), n(f)\backslash S \Rightarrow S}\backslash L}{n(f), (n(f)\backslash S)/\square S, \square n(f), \square(n(f)\backslash S) \Rightarrow S}/L}{\cdots}}{\cdots}$$

$$\cfrac{n(f), (n(f)\backslash S)/\square S, \square n(f)|n(f), \square(n(f)\backslash S) \Rightarrow S}{\cfrac{\cfrac{[\,], (n(f)\backslash S)/\square S, \square n(f)|n(f), \square(n(f)\backslash S) \Rightarrow S{\uparrow}n(f) \qquad S \Rightarrow S}{(S{\uparrow}n(f)){\downarrow}S, (n(f)\backslash S)/\square S, \square n(f)|n(f), \square(n(f)\backslash S) \Rightarrow S}{\downarrow}L}{\cfrac{(S{\uparrow}n(f)){\downarrow}S, \square((n(f)\backslash S)/\square S), \square n(f)|n(f), \square(n(f)\backslash S) \Rightarrow S}{\square((S{\uparrow}n(f)){\downarrow}S), \square((n(f)\backslash S)/\square S), \square n(f)|n(f), \square(n(f)\backslash S) \Rightarrow S}\square L}\square L}\,{\uparrow}R$$

(37) $\forall B[({}^{\vee}person\ B) \to (({}^{\vee}thinks\ {}^{\wedge}({}^{\vee}sings\ B))\ B)]$

This account has the benefit of great simplicity; it is difficult to see how an account of anaphora could be more simple. But it does not respect Principle B and we do not see any way to sensitize it to principle B or antilocality. Perhaps the following could be said. As reflected in Principles A (locality) and B (antilocality), the distributions of reflexives and personal pronouns are largely complementary, and when a reflexive is used the resolution of the anaphora is less nondeterministic since only local antecedents are allowed. Therefore, perhaps Principle B violation readings are unavailable because our use of language conforms to the facilitative principle that if the local interpretation had been intended, the less ambiguous, or unambiguous, reflexive pronoun form would have been used. Perhaps, therefore, Principle B is not a grammatical principle but a pragmatic principle (cf. Grodzinsky and Reinhart 1993)[2]. In that case, it could be argued, we need not expect our grammar to be able to express antilocality since it is a 'transgenerational' pragmatic effect.

This view may well be the right one, and would allow us to preserve the minimality of the Jaeger account. However, we consider as another possibility the lexical contraction treatment of personal pronouns in displacement calculus, which will provide us with a grammatical handle on antilocality in terms of negation as failure.

Let us extend the calculus with linear additives as follows (cf. Kanazawa 1992[6]):

(38) $\mathcal{F}_i := \mathcal{F}_i \& \mathcal{F}_i \mid \mathcal{F}_i + \mathcal{F}_i$

$$(39) \quad \frac{\Gamma\langle \overrightarrow{A} \rangle \Rightarrow C}{\Gamma\langle \overrightarrow{A\&B} \rangle \Rightarrow C} \&L_1 \qquad \frac{\Gamma\langle \overrightarrow{B} \rangle \Rightarrow C}{\Gamma\langle \overrightarrow{A\&B} \rangle \Rightarrow C} \&L_2$$

$$\frac{\Gamma \Rightarrow A \qquad \Gamma \Rightarrow B}{\Gamma \Rightarrow A\&B} \&R$$

$$\frac{\Gamma\langle \overrightarrow{A} \rangle \Rightarrow C \qquad \Gamma\langle \overrightarrow{B} \rangle \Rightarrow C}{\Gamma\langle \overrightarrow{A+B} \rangle \Rightarrow C} +L$$

$$\frac{\Gamma \Rightarrow A}{\Gamma \Rightarrow A+B} +L_1 \qquad \frac{\Gamma \Rightarrow B}{\Gamma \Rightarrow A+B} +L_2$$

We propose to introduce into type logical categorial grammar a negation, interpreted in the succedent as non-provability (strong negation, as for example in autoepistemic logic, and Prolog):

(40) $\mathcal{F}_i := \neg \mathcal{F}_i$

$$(41) \quad \frac{\not\vdash \Gamma \Rightarrow A}{\Gamma \Rightarrow \neg A} \neg R$$

Thus, to express that *walk* is a non-third person present tense form we might assign it type $(\exists a N(a) \& \neg N(3(sg)))\backslash S$.

Treating pronouns by secondary wrap in modal displacement calculus, generating an example like (2b) requires a pronoun type $\Box(((S{\uparrow}N){\uparrow}_2 \Box N){\downarrow}_2(S{\uparrow}N))$ in which the pronoun hypothetical subtype is modalized to allow the pronoun in a subordinate clause. But this would also overgenerate (2a). Our proposal is to enforce Principle B by employing the negation:

(42) **him** : $\Box((((S{\uparrow}N){\uparrow}_2\Box N)\&\neg((J{\cdot}(N{\backslash}S)){\uparrow}_2 N)){\downarrow}_2(S{\uparrow}N)) = \Box\alpha$

Then (2a) is filtered because the negative goal in Figure 3 succeeds; here and henceforth we may abbreviate $(N{\backslash}S)/N$ as TV. succeeds. Example (2b) is allowed however because the negative goal in Figure 4 fails as required.

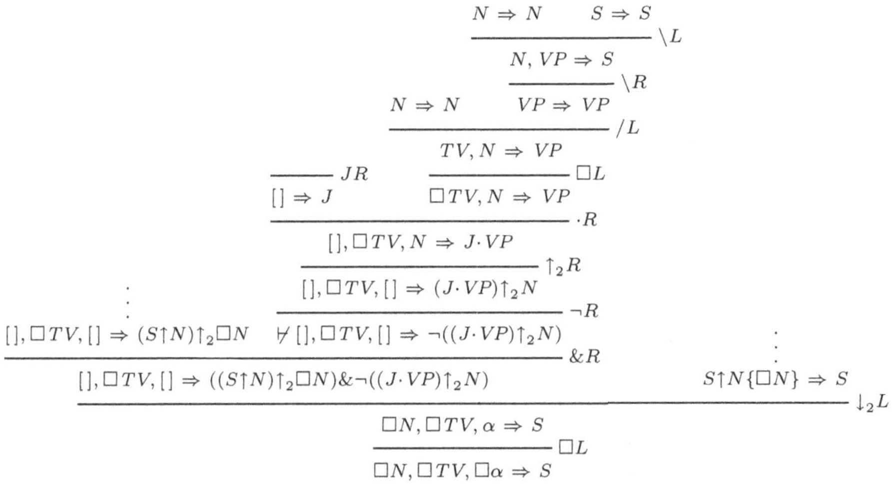

$$
\begin{array}{c}
\cfrac{
  \cfrac{
    \cfrac{
      \cfrac{
        N \Rightarrow N \qquad S \Rightarrow S
      }{N, VP \Rightarrow S}\backslash L
    }{VP \Rightarrow VP}\backslash R
  }{}
\end{array}
$$

Fig. 3. Blocking of *John$_i$ likes him$_i$* in accordance with Principle B because of the provability of the subgoal which is required to be not provable

5 Principle C

We can adopt a similar strategy in order to block Principle C violations in cataphora. The analysis of the following, where the pronoun does not c-command its antecedent, goes through since the negative subgoal fails as required.

(43) **before+he+walks+every+man+smiles** : S

Lexical lookup yields the semantically labelled sequent:

(44) $(S/S)/S$: *before*, $(((S{\uparrow}n(m)){\uparrow}n(m))\&\neg(J{\bullet}((n(m){\backslash}S){\uparrow}n(m)))){\downarrow}(S{\uparrow}n(m))$:
$\lambda A\lambda B((\pi_1 A\ B)\ B), n(341){\backslash}S$: *walks*, $((S{\uparrow}n(366)){\downarrow}S)/cn(366)$:
$\lambda A\lambda B\forall C[(A\ C) \to (B\ C)], cn(m)$: *man*, $n(427){\backslash}S$: *smiles* $\Rightarrow S$

The derivation delivers semantics:

(45) $\forall C[(man\ C) \to ((before\ (walks\ C))\ (smiles\ C))]$

But as required, Principle C violations such as the following will be blocked.

(46) a.*He$_i$ likes John$_i$.
      b.*He$_i$ thinks Mary likes John$_i$.

$$
\cfrac{
\cfrac{\cdots}{
\cfrac{\Box N, \Box TV, \Box N \Rightarrow S}{\Box N, \Box TV, \Box N \Rightarrow \Box S}\ \Box R
}\quad
\cfrac{
\cfrac{N \Rightarrow N \quad S \Rightarrow S}{N, N\backslash S \Rightarrow S}\ \backslash L
}{
\cfrac{[], N\backslash S \Rightarrow S\!\uparrow\!N}{}
}\ /L
}{}
$$

$$
\cfrac{[], VP/\Box S, \Box N, \Box TV, \Box N \Rightarrow S\!\uparrow\!N}{
\cfrac{[], \Box(VP/\Box S), \Box N, \Box TV, \Box N \Rightarrow S\!\uparrow\!N}{
[], \Box(VP/\Box S), \Box N, \Box TV, [] \Rightarrow (S\!\uparrow\!N)\!\uparrow_2\!N
}\ \uparrow_2 R
}\ \Box L
$$

$$
\cfrac{
\cfrac{\Box N, \Box TV, N \Rightarrow \Box S\ {}^{*\Box R} \quad VP \Rightarrow VP}{VP/\Box S, \Box N, \Box TV, N \Rightarrow VP}\ /L
}{
\cfrac{\Box(VP/\Box S), \Box N, \Box TV, N \Rightarrow VP}{}
}\ \Box L
$$

$$
\cfrac{[] \Rightarrow J}{}\ JR \qquad
\cfrac{[], \Box(VP/\Box S), \Box N, \Box TV, N \Rightarrow VP}{[], \Box(VP/\Box S), \Box N, \Box TV, N \Rightarrow J\cdot VP}\ \Box L
$$

$$
\cfrac{[], \Box(VP/\Box S), \Box N, \Box TV, N \Rightarrow J\cdot VP}{
\forall\ [], \Box(VP/\Box S), \Box N, \Box TV, [] \Rightarrow (J\cdot VP)\!\uparrow_2\!N
}\ \uparrow_2 R
$$

$$
\cfrac{\forall\ [], \Box(VP/\Box S), \Box N, \Box TV, [] \Rightarrow (J\cdot VP)\!\uparrow_2\!N}{
[], \Box(VP/\Box S), \Box N, \Box TV, [] \Rightarrow \neg((J\cdot VP)\!\uparrow_2\!N)
}\ \neg R
$$

$$
\cfrac{[], \Box(VP/\Box S), \Box N, \Box TV, [] \Rightarrow ((S\!\uparrow\!N)\!\uparrow_2\!N)\&\neg((J\cdot VP)\!\uparrow_2\!N)}{}\ \&R
$$

$$
\cfrac{\Box N, \Box(VP/\Box S), \Box N, \Box TV, \alpha \Rightarrow S}{\Box N, \Box(VP/\Box S), \Box N, \Box TV, \Box\alpha \Rightarrow S}\ \Box L
$$

$$
\cfrac{\cdots \quad S\!\uparrow\!N\{\Box N\} \Rightarrow S}{}\ \downarrow_2 L
$$

Fig. 4. Derivation of $John_i$ $thinks$ $Mary$ $likes$ him_i in accordance with Principle B because of the nonproveability of the subgoal which is required to be not proveable

6   Conclusion

This paper offers two innovations in relation to anaphora and the binding principles: we consider the possible application of the generalized discontinuity of the displacement calculus to various forms of anaphora, and we make the technical innovation of introducing negation as failure into categorial logic, and apply this to the capture of binding principles.

As regards the Cut rule and negation as failure, note that by using them both together we would get undesirable derivations such as the following:

$$
(47)\ \dfrac{N \Rightarrow S/(N\backslash S)\quad \dfrac{\nvdash S/(N\backslash S) \Rightarrow N}{S/(N\backslash S) \Rightarrow \neg N}\ \neg R}{N \Rightarrow \neg N}\ Cut
$$

Adding the negation as failure (right) rule brings our categorial logic to the realms of non-monotonic reasoning where the transitivity of the consequence relation must be dropped. The other connectives used in this paper, the displacement connectives, S4 modality, and additives, enjoy Cut-elimination. But in the presence of negation as failure, the Cut rule must be considered not just eliminable, but inadmissable. However, the subformula property holds of all the connectives used here: the sequent presentation is such that for every rule, the formula occurrences in the premises are always subformulas of those in the conclusion. Given this state of affairs, the Cut-free backward chaining sequent search space turns out to be finite and hence the categorial logic used in this paper is decidable. Thus the system considered here is *implementable*; indeed some derivation examples used in this document have been generated automatically from a Prolog implementation.

Concerning the negation connective, let us remark the following aspects. On the one hand, as far as we are aware, no left sequent rule for negation as failure is known. This seems to be an open problem. On the other hand, as the reader may have noticed, the polarity of the negated subtypes in our applications is always positive, consistent with the absence of a left rule.

Much remains to be said and done on anaphora and the binding principles in English and other languages and we have only been able to touch on a few points here. The account of Principle A in terms of modal categorial logic was introduced twenty years ago but it appears that no other categorial account of locality has been developed in detail. Here we have suggested that parts of Principles B (antilocality) and C may be treated in the grammar by means of negation, in particular negation as failure. We hope this may be a first indication of how categorial approaches may be sensitized to these negative conditions directly in the grammar while preserving as much as possible the good theoretical properties of the logic.

References

1. Chomsky, N.: Lectures on Government and Binding: The Pisa Lectures. Foris Publications, Dordrecht (1981)
2. Grodzinsky, Y., Reinhart, T.: The Innateness of Binding and Coreference. Linguistic Inquiry 24(1), 69–101 (1993)
3. Hepple, M.: The Grammar and Processing of Order and Dependency. PhD thesis, University of Edinburgh (1990)
4. Jacobson, P.: Towards a variable-free semantics. Linguistics and Philosophy 22(2), 117–184 (1999)
5. Jäger, G.: Anaphora and Type Logical Grammar. Trends in Logic – Studia Logica Library, vol. 24. Springer, Heidelberg (2005)
6. Kanazawa, M.: The Lambek calculus enriched with additional connectives. Journal of Logic, Language and Information 1, 141–171 (1992)
7. Morrill, G.: Intensionality and Boundedness. Linguistics and Philosophy 13(6), 699–726 (1990)
8. Morrill, G., Valentín, O.: Displacement Calculus. To appear in the Lambek Festschrift, special issue of *Linguistic Analysis* (2010), http://arxiv.org/abs/1004.4181

Feasible Functions over Co-inductive Data

Ramyaa Ramyaa and Daniel Leivant

Indiana University
{ramyaa,leivant}@cs.indiana.edu

Abstract. Proof theoretic characterizations of complexity classes are of considerable interest because they link levels of conceptual abstraction to computational complexity. We consider here the provability of functions over co-inductive data in a highly expressive, yet proof-theoretically weak, variant of second order logic $\mathbf{L}_*^+$, which we believe captures the notion of feasibility more broadly than previously considered pure-logic formalisms.

Our main technical result is that every basic feasible functional (i.e. functional in the class **BFF**, believed to be the most adequate definition of feasibility for second-order functions) is provable in $\mathbf{L}_*^+$.

1 Introduction

Relations between the complexity of program-termination proofs and the computational complexity of the programs considered go back at least to Parson's [28] characterization of primitive recursion in terms of existential induction. Frameworks for characterizing computational complexity classes without any reference to resources have been developed over the last dozen odd years, jointly referred to as *Implicit Computational Complexity*. Included are, among others, ramified functional programs, ramified first order proof systems, higher order logics with restricted set-existence, structural restrictions on applicative terms and proofs, and modal and linear type systems and proof systems. Such formalisms are particularly attractive for delineating notions of feasibility in higher type: they are based on concepts that do not refer directly to functions and computations, and consequently they lift seamlessly to higher type computing. The proof-theoretic strand of implicit computational complexity is of particular interest, since it unravels underlying concepts in particularly stark terms, and often relates those directly to complexity of type systems for applicative programs via Curry-Howard morphisms. Within the proof-theoretic approach, second-order logic offers a useful combination of a powerful descriptive machinery, and of allowing very weak proof formalisms by drastically restricting the Comprehension Principle (i.e. admitting only restricted forms of set-definitions as legitimate). For example, in [21] we gave a characterization of PTime by limiting set-existence to positive-existential first-order formulas.

In this paper we consider the proof-theoretic characterization of feasible computing over the set $\mathbb{S}(\mathbb{N})$ of streams over natural numbers, and the set $\mathbb{T}(\mathbb{W})$ of infinite binary trees over $\mathbb{W} = \{0,1\}^*$. We adopt a restricted second-order logic,

A. Dawar and R. de Queiroz (Eds.): WoLLIC 2010, LNAI 6188, pp. 191–203, 2010.

$\mathbf{L}_*^+$, and prove that every functional in the class **BFF** (basic feasible functionals) [12, 19, 30], when expressed as a function over $\mathbb{T}(\mathbb{W})$, is provably productive (i.e. fair) in $\mathbf{L}_*^+$. We strongly conjecture that the converse holds as well.

Since the elements of $\mathbb{T}(\mathbb{W})$ are complex objects, obtained by nesting inductive data within co-inductive data, our logic $\mathbf{L}_*^+$ must support fairly complex arguments, considerably more than for $\mathbb{N}$ and $\mathbb{W}$ for example. At the same time the logic must remain computationally feasible (PTime in an appropriate sense). The restrictions that define $\mathbf{L}_*^+$ are all natural, germane to computational complexity, and known from related works. To start, we take ramified second-order logic, in which relational variables are assigned levels, and comprehension is required to respect those levels.[1] We further restrict the comprehension formulas with two requirements. First, they have to be "positive", in the sense of having no object $\exists$ or relational $\forall$ in negative positions, and dually for object $\forall$ and relational $\exists$. (Even slight relaxation of this restriction yields the provability of all PSpace functions.) Further, we require comprehension formulas to be *separated*, in the sense that a quantifier of a relational variable R cannot have other variables free in its scope.[2]

2   Background

2.1   Equational and Relational Programs

A *constructor-vocabulary* is a finite set $\mathcal{C}$ of function identifiers, referred to as *constructors*, each assigned an *arity* $\geqslant 0$. (Constant constructors have arity 0.) We posit an infinite set $\mathcal{X}$ of *variables*, and an infinite set $\mathcal{F}$ of *function-identifiers*, dubbed *program-functions*, and assigned arities $\geqslant 0$ as well. The sets $\mathcal{C}$, $\mathcal{X}$ and $\mathcal{F}$ are, of course, disjoint.

If $\mathcal{E}$ is a set consisting of function-identifiers and (possibly) variables, we write $\bar{\mathcal{E}}$ for the terms generated from $\mathcal{E}$ by application: if $\mathbf{g} \in \mathcal{E}$ is a function-identifier of arity r, and $t_1 \dots t_r$ are terms, then so is $\mathbf{g} \, t_1 \, \cdots \, t_r$. We use informally the parenthesized notation $\mathbf{g}(t_1, \dots, t_r)$ when convenient. We refer to $\bar{\mathcal{C}}$, $\overline{\mathcal{C} \cup \mathcal{X}}$ and $\overline{\mathcal{C} \cup \mathcal{X} \cup \mathcal{F}}$ as the *data-terms*, *base-terms* and *program-terms*, respectively.

As in [22, 23], we use an equational computation model, in the style of Herbrand-Gödel, familiar from the extensive literature on algebraic semantics of programs. There are easy translations between equational programs and the program-terms of Moschovakis's $\mathbf{FLR_0}$ [27]; however, equational programs integrate easily into logical calculi, because they be construed as equational theories; codifying them as terms is a redundancy, since the computational behavior of such terms is itself spelled out using equations or rewrite-rules.

A *program-equation* is an equation of the form $\mathbf{f} t_1 \dots t_k = q$, where $\mathbf{f}$ is a program-function of arity k, $t_1 \dots t_k$ are base-terms, and q is a program-term.

---

[1] Compare e.g. [20], or even Charles Parson's 1961's PhD Dissertation.

[2] This restriction alone reduces the complexity of full second-order logic to (at most) the theory of iterated inductive definitions, as shown in [1], and the complexity of Gödel's system **T** to the Kalmar-elementary functions [2].

The identifier $\mathbf{f}$ is dubbed the *lead-function* of the equation, and the tuple $\langle t_1 \ldots t_k \rangle$ its *case*. Two program-equations are *compatible* if they have distinct lead functions, or else have cases that cannot be unified. A *program-body* is a finite set of pairwise-compatible program-equations. A program $(P, \mathbf{f})$ consists of a program-body P and a program-function $\mathbf{f}$, dubbed the program's *principal-function*. We identify a program with its program-body when in no danger of confusion. We write V_P for the vocabulary of P, i.e. $\mathcal{C}$ augmented with the program-functions used in P.

It is easy to define the denotational semantics of an equational program for (the algebraic interpretation of) inductive data, since such data is finite. For example, if $(P, \mathbf{f})$ is a program for a unary function over $\mathbb{N}$, then it computes the partial function $f : \mathbb{N} \upharpoonright \mathbb{N}$ where $f(p) = q$ just in case the equation $\mathbf{f}(\bar{p}) = \bar{q}$ is derivable from P in equational logic, where $\bar{n}$ is the n'th numeral, i.e. $\mathbf{ss} \cdots \mathbf{s0}$ with n occurrences of the identifier $\mathbf{s}$ (the successor).

Since co-inductive data is (in general) infinite, defining the semantic of equational programs must refer to finite information about the output. It must also refer to the data-objects not as syntactic terms that can be present in equations, but as values bound to variables. The underlying idea is obvious, and to simplify its articulation, we will formulate our semantics using fresh auxiliary variables, one variable $\mathbf{v}_a$ for each $a \in [\![\mathcal{S}]\!]$. (In fact only countably many variables will be needed, and only finitely many will be present at any given step.)

The *diagram* of $\mathcal{S}$ is the theory

$$Diag(\mathcal{S}) \quad = \quad \{\mathbf{v}_a = \mathbf{c}\mathbf{v}_{b_1} \cdots \mathbf{v}_{b_r} \mid a = \mathbf{c}_{\mathcal{S}} b_1 \cdots b_r\}$$

That is, the diagram describes, for each constructor $\mathbf{c}$, its interpretation $\mathbf{c}_{\mathcal{S}}$ in $\mathcal{S}$. We say that a program $(P, \mathbf{f})$ computes, over $[\![\mathcal{S}]\!]$, the k-ary partial function f iff for every $a_1, \ldots, a_k, b \in [\![\mathcal{S}]\!]$, we have $f(a) = b$ just in case the equation $\mathbf{f}(\mathbf{v}_{a_1}, \ldots, \mathbf{v}_{a_k}) = \mathbf{v}_b$ is derivable in equational logic from $P \cup Diag(\mathcal{S})$.

Note that this is a *global* semantic, referring to arbitrary semantic interpretations of the underlying vocabulary (i.e the constructors). It is not a canonical structure obtained from categorical considerations. Moreover, in this semantics bi-simulation between co-inductive data does not guarantee true equality (though it does imply observational equality in an appropriate sense). For example, in a non-standard model of arithmetic, the non-standard elements are all starting points for an infinite chain of predecessors; they all represent then the stream $s(s(s(s(\cdots \cdots$, and have identical computational behavior, and yet they are distinct elements of the model.

2.2   A Logical Characterization of Correct Computability

In our present semantic approach, the correct typing of a function f computed by a program $(P, \mathbf{f})$ is not attached to the object consider (ontological, i.e. Church-style typing), but is obtained as a semantic property of the objects (semantic, i.e. Curry-style, typing). Namely, typing is expressed using data-preservation formulas.

For example, the following second-order formula $N[x]$ defines, uniformly in all structures, the denotations of the numerals:

$$N[x] \equiv \quad \forall R \ Cl[R] \ \rightarrow R(x)$$

where

$$Cl_N[R] \equiv \quad R(\mathbf{0}) \wedge \forall z \ R(z) \rightarrow R(\mathbf{s}z)$$

Then, to state that a function f, computed by the program above, is total over the natural numbers, we would write $\forall x \ N[x] \rightarrow N[\mathbf{f}x]$. This formula expresses, in terms of validity in all structures, the convergence of the program P for all input in $\mathbb{N}$: if the program terminates, then its execution can be emulated in any structure in which program P, understood as a set of equations, is true. And if the program does not terminate for input n, then there is a model of P in which the value of the term $\mathbf{f}(\bar{n})$ is not equal to the value of any numeral. In fact, the construction in [23] uses a single canonical model for that purpose, namely the quotient of the term model over the provable-equality of terms using the program. The latter is necessary to guarantee that the structure constructed is a model of the program.

It is of interest to consider the analog of that construction for co-inductive data. For streams we posit a ground object ϵ, the binary constructor : (the cons function), and the corresponding destructor functions hd and tl, with the equations

$$\mathsf{hd}(x : y) = x \qquad \mathsf{hd}(\epsilon) = \epsilon$$
$$\mathsf{tl}(x : y) = y \qquad \mathsf{tl}(\epsilon) = \epsilon$$

(the status of correct typing will be clarified momentarily).

The formula defining the streams of natural numbers is then

$$S[x] \equiv \quad \exists R \ Pl_S[R] \ \wedge \ R(x) \ \wedge \neg R(\epsilon)$$

where

$$Pl_S[R] \equiv \quad \forall z (R(z) \rightarrow N[\mathsf{hd}(z)] \wedge R(\mathsf{tl}(z)))$$

The formula $\forall x \ S[x] \rightarrow S[\mathbf{f}x]$ expresses that the process of computation of the successive entries of the output of $\mathbf{f}$ for an input stream a will be a stream, i.e. the production of the output will be fair.

The binary trees of words are defined using a ternary constructor $\mathbf{t}$ intended to be a double cons, with the first entry containing a string in $\mathbb{W} = \{0, 1\}^*$), and latter two the immediate subtrees. The corresponding destructors are nd, tl_0 and tl_1, with the obvious defining equations. Thus, the formula defining the binary trees of 01-words is

$$T[x] \equiv \quad \exists R \ Pl_T[R] \ \wedge \ R(x) \ \wedge \neg R(\epsilon)$$

where

$$Pl_T[R] \equiv \quad \forall z (R(z) \rightarrow W[\mathsf{hd}(z)] \wedge R(\mathsf{tl}_0(z)) \wedge R(\mathsf{tl}_1(z)))$$

In analogy to [25, Theorem 2], we have

THEOREM 1. *Let $(P, \mathbf{f})$ be a program over $\mathbb{N}$ and $\mathbb{S}(\mathbb{N})$, say $\mathbf{f}$ binary. A program $(P, \mathbf{f})$ computes a partial-function that maps inputs $n \in \mathbb{N}$ and $\alpha \in \mathbb{S}(\mathbb{N})$ to an output in $\mathbb{S}(\mathbb{N})$, iff the formula*

$$\models \forall x, y \; N[x] \wedge S[y] \rightarrow S[\mathbf{f}(x, y)] \tag{1}$$

i.e. the formula is true in all structures.

And similarly for functions of other types, as well as for functions over $\mathbb{W}$ and $\mathbb{T}(\mathbb{W})$.

In considering the particular data-types $\mathbb{S}(\mathbb{N})$ and $\mathbb{T}(\mathbb{W})$ we are motivated by their computational nature. The set $\mathbb{N}$ provides addresses in streams, whereas $\mathbb{W}$ provides addresses in $\mathbb{T}$. While $\mathbb{S}(\mathbb{N})$ is simpler, and better understood, it corresponds to computing over unary functions, thus falling short of capturing the computational machinery underlying **BFF**. The latter is better captured by $\mathbb{T}(\mathbb{W})$.

3 Formal Reasoning about Inductive and Coinductive Data

3.1 Coinduction

A common reasoning tool for coinductive data is the coinduction rule (e.g. [3, 29]). For streams over $\mathbb{N}$, using relational identifiers S and N for streams and for natural numbers respectively, the coinduction rule for eigen-predicate $\lambda z.\varphi[z]$ (φ a formula) can be given as[3]

$$\frac{\{\varphi[x]\} \qquad \{\varphi[x]\}}{\varphi[\mathbf{t}] \quad N(\mathsf{hd}(x)) \quad \varphi[\mathsf{tl}(x)]}{S(\mathbf{t})}$$

In [25] we defined a generic first-order framework for reasoning about equational programs over "data-systems" with data-types built up inductively as well as co-inductively. The rule of Coinduction plays there a central role, and we showed that the functions over streams of booleans defined by corecursion are precisely those that are provable using coinduction over "data-positive" formulas (in analogy to a similar result in [24] for primitive-recursion).

Here we tackle the subtler issue of an implicit characterization of *feasible* computing over streams. Cook and kapron have shown [13] that a higher-order computation model may have only PTime as first-order fragment and yet be inadequate for capturing feasibility for infinite-objects such as functions and streams[4].

---

[3] The generic rule for a coinductive type C needs an additional premise, which is dispensable for streams; see [25, §2.2].

[4] This point is ignored in some recent works on feasibility in higher type, such as [4].

Theorem 1 provides the justification for our concept of *provable* correctness of programs: $(P, \mathbf{f})$ is *provable correct* in a second-order logic $\mathbf{L}$ if the formula (1) above is not merely valid, but is provable. The logic we consider here is a ramified second-order logic, with restricted comprehension. We refer to Prawitz's natural deduction formalism for second-order logic [31] (or see [21]). Second-order quantifiers bind relational-variables, each of a fixed arity, and the Comprehension Rule is conveyed via the relational (second-order) $\forall$-elimination and $\exists$-introduction rules.

In our ramified formalism each relational variable R is assigned a *level*, $level(R) \in \mathbb{N}$. The level of formulas φ without program-functions is defined then by structural recurrence. That is, the level of atomic formulas without relational variables is 0; the level of formulas $R(\mathbf{t})$ is $level(R)$; $level(\neg\varphi) = level(\varphi)$; $level(\varphi \star \psi) = \max(level(\varphi), level(\psi))$ for each binary connective $\star$; $level(Qx)\varphi) = level(\varphi)$ for first order quantifiers Qx; and for relational quantifiers, $level(QR\,\varphi) = \max(1 + level(R),\ level(\varphi))$. The levels are designed to break the impredicativity inherent in second-order logic: the relational $\forall$-elimination and $\exists$-introduction rules are restricted by requiring that their eigen-formula be of level not exceeding the level of the quantified variable. In particular, one cannot infer from $\forall R\varphi[R]$ (R unary say) the formula $\varphi[\lambda z.\forall R.\varphi]$, because $level(\forall R, \varphi) > level(R)$.

In the presence of program functions the use of levels should also account for the fact that the interpretation in a structure of the program-functions is itself less determined than the interpretation of the constructors. We therefore distinguish between two sorts: definite, and virtual, with the definite sort a subset of the virtual sort. Our intent is that data-terms are definite, and terms with program-functions are virtual. We thus start by distinguishing between variables ranging over the two sorts, writing x, y, z for definite variables and v, u, w for virtual variables. The sorts of definite and virtual terms are then generated inductively: the definite variables are definite terms, and all variables are virtual terms; both sorts are closed under the constructors, but only the virtual terms are closed under program-functions. An equation $\mathbf{t} \approx \mathbf{q}$ is then considered well-formed only if both terms $\mathbf{t}$ and $\mathbf{q}$ are of the same sort. The first-order quantifier rules are sorted accordingly: eigen-terms must be of the same sort as the variable they replace.

We now extend our definition above of the level of formulas, to allow for the presence of program-functions (and virtual terms). The level of an atomic formula $R(\mathbf{t})$ is $level(R)$ if no program-function is present in $\mathbf{t}$, but is $1 + level(R)$ otherwise.

Our logic $\mathbf{L}_*^+$ is ramified second-order logic, as defined above, with the additional restriction that comprehension formulas (i.e. the eigen-formulas of the $\forall$E and $\exists$I rules for relations) satisfy the following two additional requirements.

1. *Positive:* No object $\exists$ or relational $\forall$ in negative positions, and no object $\forall$ and relational $\exists$ in negative position.
2. *Separated:* A relational-quantifier QR does not have relational variables other than R free in its scope.

3.2   Functional Representation in $\mathbf{L}_*^+$

When computational feasibility is of interest we must distinguish between unary and binary representations of natural numbers. Modulo unary representation a function $f : \mathbb{N} \to \mathbb{N}$ is represented by a stream of natural numbers, $\sigma_f \in \mathbb{S}(\mathbb{N})$, which at position n has the number $f(n)$; i.e. $\mathsf{hd}(\mathsf{tl}^{[n]}(\sigma_f)) = f(n)$. However, modulo binary representation we actually consider the function $f' : \mathbb{W} \to \mathbb{W}$ given by $f'([n]_2) = [f(n)]_2$, whose coinductive representation is a tree of words $\tau \in \mathbb{T}(\mathbb{W})$, which for each binary address $w = [n]_2$ has the entry $\tau_w = [f(n)]_2 \in \mathbb{W}$. Here τ_w is $val(\tau, w)$, i.e. the entry of τ at address w. This is defined recursively by $val(\tau, \epsilon) = \mathsf{hd}(\tau)$, $val(\mathsf{t}(\tau, \mathsf{d}w) = val(\mathsf{tl}_d(\tau), w)$ $(\mathsf{d} = 0, 1)$.

Since **BFF** is formulated in terms of computing over $\mathbb{W}$, our proof-theoretic analysis of **BFF** will refer to $\mathbb{T}(\mathbb{W})$. The second-order definition (global and uniform for all structures $\mathcal{S}$) of the set $\mathbb{T}(\mathbb{W})$ of binary trees over binary words is analogous to the second-order definition above of $\mathbb{S}(\mathbb{N})$. That is,

$$T[x] \equiv \exists R \; Pl_T[R] \wedge R(x) \wedge \neg R(\epsilon)$$

where

$$Pl_S[R] \equiv \forall z(R(z) \to W[\mathsf{hd}(z)] \wedge R(\mathsf{tl}(z))$$

Here W is itself a universal second-order formula, defining the free word-algebra isomorphic to $\{0,1\}^*$; that is, using $\mathbf{0}$ and $\mathbf{1}$ as unary functions:

$$W[x] \equiv \forall Q \; Cl_W[Q] \to Q(x)$$

where

$$Cl_W[Q] \equiv Q(\epsilon) \wedge \forall z Q(z) \to Q(\mathbf{0}z) \wedge Q(\mathbf{1}z)$$

This is in fact a template for a family of formulas $T^{i,j}$, one for each choice of levels i and j for R and Q, respectively:

$$T^{i,j}[x] \equiv \exists R^i \; Pl_T^j[R] \wedge R(x) \wedge \neg R(\epsilon)$$

where

$$Pl_S^j[R] \equiv \forall z(R(z) \to W^j[\mathsf{hd}z] \wedge R(\mathsf{tl}z)$$

and

$$W^j[x] \equiv \forall Q^j \; Cl_W[Q] \to Q(x)$$

We focus on *admissible* definitions, which we define to be those where $i > j$. This is quite natural, since one must assume that the basic objects used are understood before building infinite object out of them.

We say that a program $(P, \mathbf{f})$ (with $\mathbf{f}$ binary) is *provable in $\mathbf{L}_*^+$ to be of type* $(W \to W) \times W \to W$ if for some ℓ and m the formula

$$T^\star[x] \wedge W^\ell[y] \to W^m[\mathbf{f}(x, y)]$$

is provable in $\mathbf{L}_*^+$ from the (universal closure of) the equations in P, where $T^\star[x]$ is the conjunction of formulas of the form $T^{i,j}$ with $i > j$.

3.3   Examples

In each of the following examples, we give an equational program, and discuss its provability in $\mathbf{L}_*^+$.

1. (Addition) $\mathsf{sum} : N \times N \to N$ is computed by the program consisting of the two equations $\mathsf{sum}(0, x) = y$; $\mathsf{sum}(sx, y) = s(\mathsf{sum}(x, y))$,
   We have $N^1[x] \wedge N^0[y] \to N^0[\mathsf{sum}(x, y)]$, as in [21].
2. (Polynomials) Consider the functions over $\mathrm{Ntp}_k(x_1 \ldots x_k, y)$ $=_{\mathrm{df}}$ $x_1 x_2 \cdots x_k + y$ $(k \geqslant 1)$ defined by

$$\mathsf{tp}_0(y) = sy;$$
$$\mathsf{tp}_{k+1}(0, x_2 \ldots x_k, y) = y,$$
$$\mathsf{tp}_{k+1}(sx, x_2 \ldots x_k, y) = \mathsf{tp}_k(x_2 \ldots x_k, \mathsf{tp}_{k+1}(x, x_2 \ldots x_k, y))$$

We prove in $\mathbf{L}_*^+$ that

$$\wedge_{i=1..k} N^1[x_i] \wedge N^0[y] \to N^0[\mathsf{tp}_k(x_1 \ldots x_k, y)] \tag{2}$$

The proof is by (discourse level) induction on k. For $k = 0$ (2) is trivial. Assume (2) for k, and towards proving it for $k+1$ assume $\wedge_{i=1..k+1} N^1[x_i] \wedge N^0[y]$. Let R be a unary relational variable of level 0, and assume $Cl_N[R]$, and consider the formula $\varphi[z] \equiv_{\mathrm{df}} R(\mathsf{tp}_{k+1}(z, x_2, \ldots, x_{k+1}, y))$, which is of level 1. From $N^1[x_1]$ we conclude $Cl_N[\varphi] \to \varphi[x_1]$.

But we have $Cl_N[\varphi]$: $\varphi[0]$ since $\mathsf{tp}_{k+1}(0, x_2, \ldots, x_{k+1}, y) = y$, whereas $N^0[y]$ and $Cl_N[R]$ imply $R(y)$, and $\varphi[z]$ implies $\varphi[sz]$, i.e. $R(\mathsf{tp}_{k+1}(z, x_2, \ldots, x_{k+1}, y))$ implies $R(\mathsf{tp}_{k+1}(sz, x_2, \ldots, x_{k+1}, y))$, by IH for k and the definition of tp_{k+1}. This yields $\varphi[x_1]$, concluding the proof.

We can similarly define functions on $\mathbb{W}$ that on inputs x, y return an output of length $(\prod_i |x_i|) + |y|$.
3. (Exponentiation) We showed above that multiplication is provably of type $N^1 \times N^1 \to N^0$. More generally, we could show that it is of type $N^i \times N^j \to N^k$ provided $i, j > k$. The latter constraint prevents the provability of programs for exponentiation.
4. (Subtree) Consider the function $\mathsf{sbtree} : W, T \to T$ that on input x, y return the subtree of y rooted at address x. This is computed by the program consisting of the equations

$$\mathsf{sbtree}(\epsilon, y) = y; \quad \mathsf{sbtree}(dx, y) = \mathsf{tl}_d(\mathsf{sbtree}(x, y)) \quad (d = 0, 1)$$

We prove in $\mathbf{L}_*^+$ that

$$W^2[x] \wedge T^{1,0}[y] \to T^{1,0}[\mathsf{sbtree}(x, y)] \tag{3}$$

Assume $W^2[x]$, as well as $T^{1,0}[y]$, i.e. $P_T^0[P] \wedge P(\mathsf{sbtree}(y))$ where P is a relational variable of level 1.

Consider the formula $\varphi[z] \equiv_{\mathrm{df}} P(\mathsf{sbtree}(z, y))$, which is of level 2. From $W[x]$ we obtain $Cl_W[\varphi] \to \varphi[x]$. But $Cl_W[\varphi]$ is straightforward from the definition of sbtree using $Pl_T[P]$, so we obtain $\varphi[x]$, that is $P(\text{sbtree}(x,y))$. Now consider the formula $\psi[z] \equiv_{\text{df}} P(\text{sbtree}(x,z))$. From $Pl_T[P]$ and the definition of sbtree we have $Pl_T[\psi]$, whence $Pl_T[\psi] \wedge \psi[y]$, which is of level 1; so $\exists R\, Pl_T[R] \wedge R(y)$ (with R of level 1), i.e. $T^{1,0}[\text{sbtree}(x,y)]$.

Defining the function entry : $W, T \to W$ by $\text{entry}(x,y) = \text{hd}(\text{sbtree}(x,y))$, i.e. the node of tree y at address x, we conclude that entry is provable in $\mathbf{L}_*^+$ to be of type $W^2 \times T^{1,0} \to W^0$.

5. (Tree composition) Consider the function compose : $T \times T \to T$ that on input x, y returns the tree whose entry at an address w is y's entry at address z, where z is x's entry at address w. That is, compose is computed by the single equation program $\text{compose}(\mathbf{t}(w, x_0, x_1), y) = \mathbf{t}(\text{entry}(w,y), \text{compose}(x_0, y), \text{compose}(x_1, y))$. Or equivalently, using a core-cursive style, by the program consisting of the three equations

$$\text{nd}(\text{compose}(x,y)) = \text{entry}(\text{nd}x, y)$$
$$\text{tl}_0(\text{compose}(x,y)) = \text{compose}(\text{tl}_0 x, y))$$
$$\text{tl}_1(\text{compose}(x,y)) = \text{compose}(\text{tl}_1 x, y))$$

We prove in $\mathbf{L}_*^+$ that $T^{3,2}[x] \wedge T^{1,0}[y]$ implies $T^{3,0}[\text{compose}(x,y)]$. Assume $T^{3,2}[x] \wedge T^{1,0}[y]$, that is $Pl_T^2[Q]\&Q(x)$ for a relational variable Q of level 2, and $Pl_T^0[P]\&P(y)$ for P of level 1. Consider the level 3 formula

$$\varphi[u] \quad \equiv_{\text{df}} \quad \exists x, y\, Q(x) \wedge Py \wedge u = \text{compose}(x,y)$$

We prove $Pl^0[\varphi] \wedge \varphi[\text{compose}(x,y)]$ as in the proof above, using $Pl_T^0[P]$ and $Pl_T^2[Q]$.

4   The Basic Feasible Functionals Are Provable in Ramified Second Order Logic

4.1   Basic Feasible Functionals

Computable higher type functionals have been studied for about a century, for several intertwined reasons. One of the first to explicitly consider *feasibility* of functionals was Robert Constable, who in [9] introduced a machine model for functionals, and considered the definability of the functionals computable therein in a certain function algebra.[5] Melhorn [26] refined Constable's algebraic approach by lifting to second order types the characterization given by Cobham [8] of the class FP of functions computable in polynomial time. A corresponding machine model was defined by Kapron and Cook in [17], and shown to be equivalent to Mehlhorn's class.

Another thread in the evolution of the subject was concerned with functional interpretation of proofs in Buss's Bounded Arithmetic. In [5] Buss introduced a system IS_2^1 of arithmetic and showed that its definable functions form precisely FP. In [6] Buss considered the intuitionistic variant of IS_2^1, and defined

---

[5] See [7] for a correction.

a functional interpretation which yields a poly-time instantiation theorem for the system. This approach was substantially refined and simplified by Cook and Urquhart in [14, 15], where they defined a system **BFF** (for *Basic Feasible Functionals*), based on the typed lambda calculus, and which supports a functional interpretation of IS_1^2, analogous to Gödel's functional interpretation of first order arithmetic [16].[6] In [18] Cook and Kapron showed that the second order fragment **BFF**$_2$ of **BFF** contains precisely the functionals defined in Mehlhorn's system, viz. the same as the functionals computable by the machine model of [17].

It is not immediately clear that **BFF**$_2$ should be admitted as a canonical delineation of the feasible second order functionals. Indeed, Cook exhibited in [10] a functional L that might be considered feasible, and yet falls outside **BFF**$_2$. Cook stated three conditions that any proposed definition of type 2 feasibility must satisfy, and those are in fact satisfied by **BFF**$_2$ appropriately augmented with L. However, Seth showed [32] that when two additional and quite natural conditions are imposed, then **BFF**$_2$ emerges as the only admissible notion of feasibility for second order functionals. Nonetheless, it is useful to lift doubts about the robustness of **BFF**$_2$, and more generally of the class **BFF**, by providing additional natural characterizations.

Functional feasibility is best understood via oracle Turing machines (OTMs) that use input functions as function-oracles. These machines are Turing transducers (using input, work and output tapes) augmented with a *query tape*, and with two distinguished states *query* and *answer*. When in state *query*, the machine overwrites the entire contents w of the query tape by the string $f(w)$, and switches to the *answer* state. This operation is counted as a single computation-step in counting the time complexity of the computation.

To define the time complexity of an OTM M we need to refer to the size of the input, which now includes a function. One plausible definition, dubbed the *PTime oracle Turing machines (POTM)*, admits OTMs M for which there is a polynomial p such that the runtime of M on inputs (w, f) is bounded by by $p(n)$, where n is the larger of $|w|$ and max $\{f(y) \mid y$ is one of the computation's queries $\}$. The class of functionals computed by POTM's is denoted by OPT.

OPT gives an upper bound on reasonable notions of functional feasibility [11], but OPT has non-feasible properties [32, 33]. Indeed, large query answers may boost dramatically the allowable run time, and such boosts may occur an unbounded number of times during computation, depending on the string and the function inputs. Such a boost is dubbed *change of space* by Pelozzi [30]. Given a polynomial $p(x)$, an OTM M makes a *change of space* during its computation for inputs w, f when M enters a query for some string u, and $f(u)$ is longer than $p(|w|)$ as well as $p(|f(v)|)$ for all preceding queries v. Pezzoli proved that **BFF** consists exactly of the functionals computed by POTMs, with polynomial p, for which there is a $k \geqslant 0$ that bounds the number of M's changes of space for all input.

---

[6] Initially the system was denoted PV^ω.

4.2   BFF Is Provable in Ramified Second Order Logic

As noted above, functions of type $W \to W$ can be represented by trees of strings, $\mathbb{T}(\mathbb{W})$. Thus functionals of type $(\mathbb{W} \to \mathbb{W}) \times \mathbb{W} \to \mathbb{W}$ can be construed as *first-order* functions of type $\mathbb{T}(\mathbb{W}) \times \mathbb{W} \to \mathbb{W}$.

THEOREM 2. *Every functional in* **BFF**$_2$ *is computed by an equational program which is provable in* $\mathbf{L}_*^+$ *to be of type* $\mathbb{T}(\mathbb{W}) \times \mathbb{W} \to \mathbb{W}$.

Proof. Given an OTM M, and an oracle f, represented by a tree $\tau \in \mathbb{T}(\mathbb{W})$, consider the configuration-update functions

$$G_i : \mathbb{T}(\mathbb{W}) \times (\mathbb{W})^9 \to \mathbb{W} \quad i = 0..8$$

for M. That is, for configuration $c = (q, u_0, v_0, u_1, v_1, u_2, v_2, u_3, v_3)$, with state q and the cursor-split contents of the input, work, output and query tapes, the functions G_i's $(i = 0..8)$ output the corresponding components of the next configuration. The definition of the G_i's by simultaneous recurrence is routine for non-query transitions of M. For a query, G_8 outputs $\mathsf{entry}(v_3, \tau)$.[7]

Note that all G_i's can be easily proved in $\mathbf{L}_*^+$ to be of type $T^{j+1,j} \times W^j \to W^j$, for all j.

We show that if M is a POTM, and reaches configuration c' from a configuration c as above, with at most k changes of space, then $\mathbf{L}_*^+$ proves, for all j:

$$(\wedge_{i \leqslant k} T^{j+2i+1, j+2i}(\tau)) \wedge \wedge_{m=0..8} W^{j+2k+2}(c_m) \quad \to \quad \wedge_{m=0..8} W^j(c'_m) \qquad (4)$$

where c_m is the m'th component of configuration c.

The proof is by induction on k. For the base case $k = 0$, i.e. where the oracle is not invoked, we have the assumption $W^{j+3}(c)$, from which we obtain, that $W^{j+1}(p(|c|)$ for any polynomial p, as in example (ii) above (compare [21] for detail).

For the induction step we invoke Example (iv) above, showing that entry is provable in $\mathbf{L}_*^+$ for type $W^2 \times T^{1,0} \to W^0$, and more generally for type $W^{j+2} \times T^{j+1,j} \to W^j$ for any j.

This conclude the proof of (4), from which the Theorem follows outright.   □

References

[1] Aehlig, K.: Parameter-free polymorphic types. Ann. Pure Appl. Logic 156(1), 3–12 (2008)
[2] Beckmann, A., Weiermann, A.: Characterizing the elementary recursive functions by a fragment of gödel's t. Arch. Math. Log. 39(7), 475–491 (2000)
[3] Bertot, Y., Komendantskaya, E.: Inductive and coinductive components of corecursive functions in coq. Electron. Notes Theor. Comput. Sci. 203(5), 25–47 (2008)

---

[7] We stipulate here that the cursor is at leftmost position at the time of a query. Also, G_7 reinitializes to the empty string.

[4] Burrell, M.J., Cockett, R., Redmond, B.F.: Pola: a language for PTIME programming. Logic Computational Complexity, Logic in Computer Science (2009)

[5] Buss, S.: Bounded Arithmetic. Bibliopolis, Naples (1986)

[6] Buss, S.: The polynomial hierarchy and intuitionistic bounded arithmetic. In: Wiedermann, J., Gruska, J., Rovan, B. (eds.) MFCS 1986. LNCS, vol. 233, pp. 77–103. Springer, Heidelberg (1986)

[7] Clote, P.: A note on the relation between polynomial time functionals and constable's class k. In: Kleine-Büning, H. (ed.) CSL 1995. LNCS, vol. 1092, pp. 145–160. Springer, Heidelberg (1996)

[8] Cobham, A.: The intrinsic computational difficulty of functions. In: Bar-Hillel, Y. (ed.) Proceedings of the International Conference on Logic, Methodology, and Philosophy of Science, pp. 24–30. North-Holland, Amsterdam (1962)

[9] Constable, R.: Type 2 computational complexity. In: Fifth Annual ACM Symposium on Theory of Computing, pp. 108–121. ACM, New York (1973)

[10] Cook, S.: Computability and complexity of higher type functions. In: Moschovakis, Y. (ed.) Logic from Computer Science, pp. 51–72. Springer, New York (1991)

[11] Cook, S.A.: Computability and complexity of higher type functions. In: Chern, Singer, Kaplansky, Mooreand, Moschovakis (eds.) Logic from Computer Science, Springer, New York (1989)

[12] Cook, S.A., Kapron, B.M.: Characterizations of the basic feasible functionals of finite type. In: FOCS, pp. 154–159. IEEE, Los Alamitos (1989)

[13] Cook, S.A., Kapron, B.M.: Characterizations of the Basic Feasible Functionals of Finite Type. In: Feasible Mathematics: A Mathematical Sciences Institute Workshop, pp. 71–95 (1990)

[14] Cook, S.A., Urquhart, A.: Functional interpretations of feasible constructive arithemtic (extended abstract). In: Proceedings of the 21st ACM Symposium on Theory of Computing, pp. 107–112 (1989)

[15] Cook, S.A., Urquhart, A.: Functional interpretations of feasible constructive arithemtic. Annals of Pure and Applied Logic 63, 103–200 (1993)

[16] Gödel, K.: Über eine bisher noch nicht benutzte erweiterung des finiten standpunktes. Dialectica 12, 280–287 (1958)

[17] Kapron, B.M., Cook, S.A.: A new characerization of type-2 feasibility. SIAM Journal of Computing 25, 117–132 (1996)

[18] Kapron, B., Cook, S.: Characterizations of the basic feasible functionals of finite type. In: Buss, S., Scott, P. (eds.) Feasible Mathematics, pp. 71–95. Birkhauser, Boston (1990)

[19] Kapron, B., Cook, S.A.: A new characterization of type-2 feasibility. SIAM J. on Computing 25(1), 117–132 (1996)

[20] Leivant, D.: Finitely stratified polymorphism. Inf. Comput. 93(1), 93–113 (1991)

[21] Leivant, D.: A foundational delineation of poly-time. Information and Computation 110, 391–420 (1994); (Special issue of selected papers from LICS'91, edited by Kahn, G.). Preminary report: A foundational delineation of computational feasibility, In: Proceedings of the Sixth IEEE Conference on Logic in Computer Science. IEEE Computer Society Press, Los Alamitos (1991)

[22] Leivant, D.: Intrinsic theories and computational complexity. In: Leivant, D. (ed.) LCC 1994. LNCS, vol. 960, pp. 177–194. Springer, Heidelberg (1995)

[23] Leivant, D.: Intrinsic reasoning about functional programs I: First order theories. Annals of Pure and Applied Logic 114, 117–153 (2002)

[24] Leivant, D.: Intrinsic reasoning about functional programs ii: unipolar induction and primitive-recursion. Theor. Comput. Sci. 318(1-2), 181–196 (2004)

[25] Leivant, D., Ramyaa, R.: Implicit complexity for coinductive data: a proof-theoretic characterization of primitive corecursion. In: Conference submission (2010), see current draft as
http://www.cs.indiana.edu/~leivant/corecursion.pdf

[26] Mehlhorn, K.: Polynomial and abstract subrecursive classes. J. Comput. Syst. Sci. 12(2), 147–178 (1976)

[27] Moschovakis, Y.N.: The formal language of recursion. J. Symb. Log. 54(4), 1216–1252 (1989)

[28] Parsons, C.: On a number-theoretic choice schema and its relation to induction. In: Kino, A., Myhill, J., Vesley, R. (eds.) Intuitionism and Proof Theory, pp. 459–473. North-Holland, Amsterdam (1970)

[29] Paulson, L.C.: Mechanizing coinduction and corecursion in higher-order logic. Journal of Logic and Computation 7 (1997)

[30] Pezzoli, E.: On the computational complexity of type 2 functionals. In: Nielsen, M., Thomas, W. (eds.) CSL 1997. LNCS, vol. 1414, pp. 373–388. Springer, Heidelberg (1998)

[31] Prawitz, D.: Natural Deduction. Almqvist and Wiksell, Uppsala (1965)

[32] Seth, A.: Some desirable conditions for feasible functionals of type~2. In: LICS, pp. 320–331 (1993)

[33] Seth, A.: Complexity theory of higher type functionals. PhD thesis, University of Bombay, PhD Thesis (1994)

Interval Valued Fuzzy Coimplication

Renata H.S. Reiser[1], Benjamin C. Bedregal[2], and Gesner A.A. dos Reis[1]

[1] Programa de Pós-Graduação em Informática,
Universidade Católica de Pelotas
Rua Felix da Cunha 412, 96010-000 Pelotas, Brazil
reiser@ucpel.tche.br, gesner@ucpel.tche.br
[2] Depto de Informática e Matemática Aplicada,
Universidade Federal do Rio Grande do Norte
Campus Universitário s/n, 59072-970 Natal, Brazil
bedregal@dimap.ufrn.br

Abstract. The aim of this paper is to introduce the dual notion of interval implications, the interval coimplications, as interval representations of fuzzy coimplications. Using the canonical representation, this paper considers both the correctness and the optimality criteria, in order to provide interpretation for fuzzy coimplications as the non-truth degree of conditional rule in expert systems. It is proved that ℕ-dual interval coimplications satisfy the main properties of interval implications discussed in the literature. Lastly, border and model interval fuzzy coimplications are also considered.

1 Introduction

Fuzzy logic provides the theoretical foundation for reasoning about imprecise propositions, such reasoning has been referred to as approximate reasoning, using the fundamental idea of fuzzy set membership function to deal with partial truths. The membership function of ordinary fuzzy sets are often precise, requiring each element of the universal set be assigned to a real number. However, in some concepts and context the value of membership degree might include uncertainty. It may be able to define membership function only approximately, identifying meaningful lower and upper bounds of membership grades of an element in the universal set. In such approach, a membership function is assigned to a closed interval of real numbers between the identified lower and upper bounds. Fuzzy sets identified by such membership functions are called interval-valued fuzzy sets. It was first proposed by Sambuc [38] under the name ϕ-fuzzy sets. Interval-valued fuzzy sets appear in the literature in many ways [42,40,41,9,43,27,28].

Interval-valued fuzzy sets are a particular case of type-2 fuzzy sets, which have been studied by Zadeh [47] and others authors (e.g., [22,23]) since the 70's, allowing to deal not only with vagueness (lack of sharp class boundaries), but also with uncertainty (lack of information) [18,30]. Since then, the integration of fuzzy theory with interval mathematics considers different viewpoints, as properly pointed out by Lodwick [30] (see, e.g., in [18,30,12,16,17,20,26,31,33,32,45,46]) generating several different approaches. This paper follows the approach first introduced in Bedregal and Takahashi's works [3,4], applied in other papers, where interval extensions for some

A. Dawar and R. de Queiroz (Eds.): WoLLIC 2010, LNAI 6188, pp. 204–217, 2010.

fuzzy connectives were provided (see, e.g., [2,7,5,15,36]), considering both correctness (accuracy) and optimality aspects [39].

Let $\mathbb{U} = \{[a, b] | 0 \le a \le b \le 1\}$. In this work we will consider the following two partial orders on $\mathbb{U}$:

Product order: $X \le Y \Leftrightarrow \underline{X} \le \underline{Y} \wedge \overline{X} \le \overline{Y}$;

Inclusion order: $X \subseteq Y \Leftrightarrow \underline{Y} \le \underline{X} \wedge \overline{X} \le \overline{Y}$.

Let X be a crisp set. An interval fuzzy set $\mathbb{A}$ on X is given by $\mathbb{A} = \{\langle x, \mu_{\mathbb{A}}(x)\rangle \mid x \in X\}$, where $\mu_{\mathbb{A}}:X \to \mathbb{U}$.

Let $\mathbb{A}$ and $\mathbb{B}$ be interval fuzzy sets on X and Y, respectively. The intervals $\mu_{\mathbb{A}}(x)$ and $\mu_{\mathbb{B}}(y)$ denote, respectively, the interval membership degree of the element x in $\mathbb{A}$ and of the element y in $\mathbb{B}$.

Let x and y be variables taking values in X and Y, respectively. A conditional rule in expert systems has the following form

$$if \ x \ is \ \mathbb{A} \ then \ y \ is \ \mathbb{B} \tag{1}$$

and it is interpreted as an interval fuzzy relation using an interval implication function $\mathbb{I} : X \times Y \to \mathbb{U}$, associating to each $(x, y) \in X \times Y$, $\mathbb{I}(\mu_{\mathbb{A}}(x), \mu_{\mathbb{B}}(y))$, which is always interpreted as the interval truth degree of the conditional rule (1). In order to analyse the non-truth degree of such conditional rule, the definition of valued interval fuzzy coimplication has been considered [8,1]. Thus, in a fuzzy dual-based approach, when $\mathbb{J} : X \times Y \to \mathbb{U}$ is an interval implication function, $\mathbb{J}(\mu_{\mathbb{A}}(x), \mu_{\mathbb{B}}(y))$ provides an interpretation to the interval non-truth degree of such antecedent-consequent form of conditional rule[21,19]. While a fuzzy implication is an extension of the Boolean implication ($p \Rightarrow q$), meaning that p is sufficient for q, a coimplication is an extension of the Boolean coimplication ($p \not\Leftarrow q$), meaning that p is not necessary for q.

Although the fuzzy coimplications can be used in a dual approach of fuzzy implications, they have been less discussed in the literature. However, the coimplications also play an important role in classical logic, fuzzy logic and intuitionistic fuzzy logic. See [8,1,11,14,37,44,13,34,35]. The concept of fuzzy coimplication was introduced as a new approach to approximate reasoning of expert systems using the equivalence relation for Modus Ponens in the inference in fuzzy expert systems instead of fuzzy implication. Thus, it seems natural to extend this notion of fuzzy coimplication to interval valued fuzzy theory.

The paper is organized as follows. Firstly, compressing preliminaries, Section 2.1 presents the main concepts of interval representations of real functions. The canonical representation of fuzzy negations and triangular norms and conorms are discussed in Sect. 2.2 and Sect. 2.3, respectively. The definition and related properties of interval fuzzy coimplications are presented in Sect. 3. Section 5 considers the duality between interval valued implications and coimplications, which is preserved by canonical representation and the main related results. Some properties preserved by duality relationships are studied in Section 4. Model (border) interval coimplications are introduced in Sect. 6. Section 7 is the Conclusion, with some final remarks on related work.

2   Preliminary Studies

In this section, we recall some basic concepts and results of the canonical representation of real function applied to negation functions and triangular norms and conorms.

2.1   Best Interval Representation

Let U be the unit interval, i.e. $U = [0, 1]$. The set of intervals $\mathbb{U}$ has the *projection functions* $\pi_1, \pi_2 : \mathbb{U} \rightarrow U$, defined by $\pi_1([x_1, x_2]) = x_1$ and $\pi_2([x_1, x_2]) = x_2$, respectively, for any $[x_1, x_2] \in \mathbb{U}$. For each $X \in \mathbb{U}$, the projections $\pi_1(X)$ and $\pi_2(X)$ are also denoted by $\underline{X}$ and $\overline{X}$, respectively.

Let X and Y be interval representations of a real number α, that is, $\alpha \in X$ and $\alpha \in Y$. Thus, X is said to be a better representation of α than Y whenever $X \subseteq Y$.

Definition 1. *[2, Definition 2] A function $F : \mathbb{U}^n \longrightarrow \mathbb{U}$ is an interval representation of a real function $f : U^n \longrightarrow U$ if, for each $X \in \mathbb{U}^n$ and $x \in X$, $f(x) \in F(X)$.* [1]

Let $F, G : \mathbb{U}^n \longrightarrow \mathbb{U}$ be interval representations of $f : U^n \longrightarrow U$. F is a *better interval representation* of f than G $(G \sqsubseteq F)$ if, for each $X \in \mathbb{U}^n$, $F(X) \subseteq G(X)$.

Definition 2. *[2, Definition 3] $\widehat{f} : \mathbb{U}^n \longrightarrow \mathbb{U}$ is the* best interval representation *(canonical representation) of a real function $f : U^n \longrightarrow U$, defined by:*

$$\widehat{f}(X) = [\inf\{f(x) \mid x \in X\}, \sup\{f(x) \mid x \in X\}]. \tag{2}$$

2.2   Interval Fuzzy Negations

$\mathbb{N} : \mathbb{U} \longrightarrow \mathbb{U}$ is an *interval fuzzy negation* if, for all X, Y in $\mathbb{U}$, the properties hold:

N1 $: \mathbb{N}([0, 0]) = [1, 1]$ and $\mathbb{N}([1, 1]) = [0, 0]$;
N2a $:$ If $X \leq Y$ then $\mathbb{N}(Y) \leq \mathbb{N}(X)$;
N2b $:$ If $X \subseteq Y$ then $\mathbb{N}(X) \subseteq \mathbb{N}(Y)$.

If $\mathbb{N}$ also satisfies N3, then $\mathbb{N}$ is an *interval strong fuzzy negation*:

N3 $: \mathbb{N}(\mathbb{N}(X)) = X$ (involutive property).

A typical example of a strong interval fuzzy negation is $\mathbb{N}_S : \mathbb{U} \rightarrow \mathbb{U}$, defined by $\mathbb{N}_S(X) = [1, 1] - X$, i.e. $\mathbb{N}_S(X) = [1 - \overline{X}, 1 - \underline{X}]$. $\mathbb{N}_S$ is the interval version of the Zadeh fuzzy negation $(N_S(x) = 1 - x)$.

The interval function $\widehat{N} : \mathbb{U} \rightarrow \mathbb{U}$ of a negation $N : U \longrightarrow U$ can be expressed as:

$$\widehat{N}(X) = [N(\overline{X}), N(\underline{X})]. \tag{3}$$

Definition 3. *Let $\mathbb{N} : \mathbb{U} \rightarrow \mathbb{U}$ be a strong interval fuzzy negation and $\mathbb{F} : \mathbb{U}^n \longrightarrow \mathbb{U}$ be an interval function. The $\mathbb{N}$-dual interval function of $\mathbb{F}$ is the interval function*

$$\mathbb{F}_{\mathbb{N}}(X_1, X_2, \ldots X_n) = \mathbb{N}(\mathbb{F}(\mathbb{N}(X_1), \mathbb{N}(X_2), \ldots, \mathbb{N}(X_n))). \tag{4}$$

---

[1] Other authors, e.g., [25,10,24], also consider this definition but with other name and purpose.

When $\mathbb{N} = \mathbb{N}_S$ then Eq. 4 is given by:

$$\mathbb{F}_{\mathbb{N}_S}(X_1, X_2, \ldots, X_n) = [1, 1] - (\mathbb{F}([1, 1] - X_1, [1, 1] - X_2, \ldots, [1, 1] - X_n)). \quad (5)$$

Thus, $\mathbb{F}$ and $\mathbb{F}_{\mathbb{N}_S}$ are called interval functions mutually dual of each other.

2.3 Interval Fuzzy t-Norms and t-Conorms

A *triangular norm (conorm)*, *t-norm (t-conorm)* for short, is a function $T(S) : U^2 \to U$ that is commutative, associative, monotonic and has 1 (0) as the neutral element. Its generalization introduced in [4], fits the idea: *interval membership degrees as approximations of exact degrees*. Applying the principles discussed in previous sections, the so-called *interval t-norm (interval t-conorm)* is defined as an interval representation of a t-norm (t-conorm), including its $\mathbb{N}$-dual interval function.

Definition 4. [4] *A function* $\mathbb{T}(\mathbb{S}) : U^2 \to U$ *is an* interval t-norm *(*interval t-conorm*), whenever it is commutative, associative, monotonic with respect to the product and inclusion orders, and* $[1, 1]$ *(*$[0, 0]$*) is the identity element.*

The following proposition shows the main result about interval t-norms and t-conorm.

Proposition 1. *[4, Theorem 5.1 and 5.2] If T (S) is a t-norm (t-conorm), the canonical representation* $\widehat{T}(\widehat{S}) : U^2 \to U$ *is an interval t-norm (t-conorm) expressed by equations (Eq.6) and (7):*

$$\widehat{T}(X, Y) = [T(\underline{X}, \underline{Y}), T(\overline{X}, \overline{Y})], \quad (6)$$

$$\widehat{S}(X, Y) = [S(\underline{X}, \underline{Y}), S(\overline{X}, \overline{Y})]. \quad (7)$$

Proposition 2. *A function* $\mathbb{T}(\mathbb{S}) : U^2 \to U$ *is an interval t-norm (t-conorm) if and only if* $\mathbb{S}_{\mathbb{N},\mathbb{T}}(\mathbb{T}_{\mathbb{N},\mathbb{S}}) : U^2 \to U$ *defined in Eq.(8) (Eq.(9)) is an interval t-conorm (t-norm) for any strong interval fuzzy negation* $\mathbb{N}$.

$$\mathbb{S}_{\mathbb{N},\mathbb{T}}(X, Y) = \mathbb{N}(\mathbb{T}(\mathbb{N}(X), \mathbb{N}(Y))); \quad (8)$$

$$\mathbb{T}_{\mathbb{N},\mathbb{S}}(X, Y) = \mathbb{N}(\mathbb{S}(\mathbb{N}(X), \mathbb{N}(Y))). \quad (9)$$

3 Interval Fuzzy Coimplications

Since real numbers may be identified with degenerate intervals in the context of interval mathematics, the boundary conditions that must be satisfied by the classical fuzzy implications can be naturally extended to interval fuzzy degrees, whenever degenerate intervals are considered.

Definition 5. *The binary function* $\mathbb{J}(\mathbb{I}) : U^2 \to U$ *is called an interval fuzzy coimplication (implication) if it satisfies the boundary conditions given by* $\mathbb{J}1$ *(*$\mathbb{I}1$*):*

$\mathbb{J}1 : \mathbb{J}([1, 1], [1, 1]) = \mathbb{J}([1, 1], [0, 0]) = \mathbb{J}([0, 0], [0, 0]) = [0, 0]$ *and* $\mathbb{J}([0, 0], [1, 1]) = [1, 1]$;
$\mathbb{I}1 : \mathbb{I}([1, 1], [1, 1]) = \mathbb{I}([0, 0], [1, 1]) = \mathbb{I}([0, 0], [0, 0]) = [1, 1]$ *and* $\mathbb{I}([1, 1], [0, 0]) = [0, 0]$.

In [29, Proposition 3.1], a function $I_N : U^2 \to U$ is a fuzzy coimplication[2] if and only if $I : U^2 \to U$ defined as in Eq.(10) is a fuzzy implication for any strong fuzzy negation N. Dually, a function $J_N : U^2 \to U$ is a fuzzy implication if and only if $J : U^2 \to U$ defined as in Eq.(11) is a fuzzy coimplication for any strong fuzzy negation N.

$$I(x,y) = N(I_N(N(x), N(y)); \tag{10}$$

$$J(x,y) = N(J_N(N(x), N(y)). \tag{11}$$

Thus, fuzzy implications and fuzzy coimplications are dual notions. According to [28], (I, I_N, N) $((J_N, J, N))$ identifies a De Morgan triple, and the functions I and I_N (J_N and J) are dual to each other with respect to the strong fuzzy negation N. This duality can be extended to the interval approach. In Proposition 3, $\mathbb{I}_\mathbb{N}$ ($\mathbb{J}_\mathbb{N}$) denotes the $\mathbb{N}$-dual interval coimplication (implication) of an interval fuzzy implication $\mathbb{I}$ (coimplication $\mathbb{J}$).

Proposition 3. *A function $\mathbb{I}_\mathbb{N}(\mathbb{J}_\mathbb{N}) : \mathbb{U}^2 \to \mathbb{U}$ is an interval fuzzy coimplication (implication) if and only if there exists an interval fuzzy implication (coimplication) $\mathbb{I}(\mathbb{J}) : \mathbb{U}^2 \to \mathbb{U}$ and a strong interval fuzzy negation $\mathbb{N} : \mathbb{U} \to \mathbb{U}$ such that, $\forall X, Y \in \mathbb{U}$, the next equality, described in Eq.(13) (Eq.(12)), holds:*

$$\mathbb{J}_\mathbb{N}(X,Y) = \mathbb{N}(\mathbb{J}(\mathbb{N}(X), \mathbb{N}(Y))); \tag{12}$$

$$\mathbb{I}_\mathbb{N}(X,Y) = \mathbb{N}(\mathbb{I}(\mathbb{N}(X), \mathbb{N}(Y))). \tag{13}$$

Proof. We will present the proof of an interval coimplication $\mathbb{I}_\mathbb{N}$. The proof of $\mathbb{J}_\mathbb{N}$ can be obtained in an analogous way.

($\Rightarrow$) Let $\mathbb{I}$ and $\mathbb{N}$ be an interval implication and an interval negation, respectively. Thus, $\mathbb{I}_\mathbb{N}$ satisfies Definition 5:

$\mathbb{I}_\mathbb{N}([0,0],[0,0]) = \mathbb{N}(\mathbb{I}(\mathbb{N}([0,0]), \mathbb{N}([0,0]))) = \mathbb{N}(\mathbb{I}([1,1],[1,1]) = \mathbb{N}([1,1]) = [0,0].$
$\mathbb{I}_\mathbb{N}([1,1],[0,0]) = \mathbb{N}(\mathbb{I}(\mathbb{N}([1,1]), \mathbb{N}([0,0]))) = \mathbb{N}(\mathbb{I}([0,0],[1,1]) = \mathbb{N}([1,1]) = [0,0].$
$\mathbb{I}_\mathbb{N}([1,1],[1,1]) = \mathbb{N}(\mathbb{I}(\mathbb{N}([1,1]), \mathbb{N}([1,1]))) = \mathbb{N}(\mathbb{I}([0,0],[0,0]) = \mathbb{N}([1,1]) = [0,0].$
$\mathbb{I}_\mathbb{N}([0,0],[1,1]) = \mathbb{N}(\mathbb{I}(\mathbb{N}([0,0]), \mathbb{N}([1,1]))) = \mathbb{N}(\mathbb{I}([1,1],[0,0]) = \mathbb{N}([0,0]) = [1,1].$

($\Leftarrow$)The converse follows from the canonical representation in Definition1.

4   Properties of Interval Coimplications and Duality Relationships

Some properties usually demanded from a fuzzy coimplication J (implication I) can then also be naturally extended to an interval-based approach. For all $X, Y, Z \in \mathbb{U}$, the properties considered in this work are listed below:

---

[2] Notice that in [29] the notion of a fuzzy coimplication (implication) requires some extra properties.

[J2] If $X \leq Z$ then $\mathbb{J}(X,Y) \geq \mathbb{J}(Z,Y)$ [I2] If $X \leq Z$ then $\mathbb{I}(X,Y) \geq \mathbb{I}(Z,Y)$

[J3] If $Y \leq T$ then $\mathbb{J}(X,Y) \leq \mathbb{J}(X,T)$ [I3] If $Y \leq T$ then $\mathbb{I}(X,Y) \leq \mathbb{I}(X,T)$

[J4] $\mathbb{J}([1,1],Y) = [0,0]$ [I4] $\mathbb{I}([0,0],Y) = [1,1]$

[J5] $\mathbb{J}(X,[0,0]) = [0,0]$ [I5] $\mathbb{I}(X,[1,1]) = [1,1]$

[J6] $\mathbb{J}([0,0],Y) = Y$ [I6] $\mathbb{I}([1,1],Y) = Y$

[J7] $\mathbb{J}(X,\mathbb{J}(Y,Z)) = \mathbb{J}(Y,\mathbb{J}(X,Z))$ [I7] $\mathbb{I}(X,\mathbb{I}(Y,Z)) = \mathbb{I}(Y,\mathbb{I}(X,Z))$

[J8] $\mathbb{J}(X,Y) = [0,0]$ if and only if $X \geq Y$ [I8] $\mathbb{I}(X,Y) = [1,1]$ if and only if $X \leq Y$

[J9] $\mathbb{N}_{\mathbb{J}}(X) = \mathbb{J}(X,[1,1])$ is a strong negation   [I9] $\mathbb{N}_{\mathbb{I}}(X) = \mathbb{I}(X,[0,0])$ is a strong negation

[J10] $\mathbb{J}(X,Y) \leq Y$ [I10] $\mathbb{I}(X,Y) \geq Y$

[J11] $[0,0] \in \mathbb{J}(X,X)$ [I11] $[1,1] \in \mathbb{I}(X,X)$

[J12] $\mathbb{J}(X,Y) = \mathbb{J}(\mathbb{N}(Y),\mathbb{N}(X))$ [I12] $\mathbb{I}(X,Y) = \mathbb{I}(\mathbb{N}(Y),\mathbb{N}(X))$

[J13] If $X < [1,1]$ then $\mathbb{J}(X,[1,1]) > [0,0]$ [I13] If $X < [0,0]$ then $\mathbb{I}(X,[0,0]) < [1,1]$

    If $Y > [0,0]$ then $\mathbb{J}([0,0],Y) > [0,0]$ If $Y < [1,1]$ then $\mathbb{I}([1,1],Y) < [1,1]$

Theorem 1. *These properties are not independent.*

(i) If $\mathbb{J}12$ holds, then $\mathbb{J}2$ (first place antitonicity) and $\mathbb{J}3$ (second place isotonicity) are equivalent.

(ii) $\mathbb{J}10$ can be inferred from $\mathbb{J}2$, $\mathbb{J}5$ and $\mathbb{J}6$.

(iii) $\mathbb{J}5$ can be inferred from $\mathbb{J}10$ and $\mathbb{J}12$.

(iv) Sufficient condition of $\mathbb{J}8$ can be inferred from $\mathbb{J}2$ and $\mathbb{J}11$.

Proof. Let $\mathbb{J}$ be an interval fuzzy coimplication and $\mathbb{N}$ a strong interval fuzzy negation. (i) Suppose that $\mathbb{J}$ satisfies $\mathbb{J}12$ and $\mathbb{J}2$. Since, for all $Y, Z \in \mathbb{U}$, when $Y \leq Z$ then $\mathbb{N}(Y) \geq \mathbb{N}(Z)$, it follows that $\mathbb{J}$ satisfies $\mathbb{J}3$:

$$\mathbb{J}(X,Y) = \mathbb{J}(\mathbb{N}(Y),\mathbb{N}(X) \text{ by } \mathbb{J}12$$
$$\leq \mathbb{J}(\mathbb{N}(Z),\mathbb{N}(X)) = \mathbb{J}(X,Z) \text{ by } \mathbb{J}2 \text{ and } \mathbb{J}12.$$

Analogously, suppose that $\mathbb{J}$ satisfies $\mathbb{J}12$ and $\mathbb{J}3$. Since for all $X, Z \in \mathbb{U}$, if $X \leq Z$ then $\mathbb{N}(X) \geq \mathbb{N}(Z)$, it follows that

$$\mathbb{J}(X,Y) = \mathbb{J}(\mathbb{N}(Y),\mathbb{N}(X) \text{ by } \mathbb{J}12$$
$$\geq \mathbb{J}(\mathbb{N}(Y),\mathbb{N}(Z)) = \mathbb{J}(Z,Y) \text{ by } \mathbb{J}3 \text{ and } \mathbb{J}12.$$

and so, $\mathbb{J}$ also satisfies $\mathbb{J}2$. Therefore, when $\mathbb{J}12$ holds, then $\mathbb{J}2$ and $\mathbb{J}3$ are equivalent.

(ii) Suppose that $\mathbb{J}$ satisfies $\mathbb{J}2$ and $\mathbb{J}6$. Then, for all $X, Y \in \mathbb{U}$ it follows that $\mathbb{J}(X,Y) \leq \mathbb{J}([0,0],Y)$ by $\mathbb{J}2$. In addition, $\mathbb{J}([0,0],Y) = Y$ by $\mathbb{J}6$. Thus, $\mathbb{J}(X,Y) \leq Y$.

(iii) For all $Y \in [0,1]$ it follows that $\mathbb{J}([1,1],Y) = \mathbb{J}(\mathbb{N}(Y),[0,0])$ by $\mathbb{J}12$. In addition, $\mathbb{J}(\mathbb{N}(Y),[0,0]) = [0,0]$ by $\mathbb{J}10$. Therefore, $\mathbb{J}(X,Y) = [0,0]$.

(iv) For all $X, Y \in \mathbb{U}$ such that $X \leq Y$, it follows that $\mathbb{J}(X,Y) \leq \mathbb{J}(Y,Y)$ by $\mathbb{J}2$ and $\mathbb{J}(Y,Y) = [0,0]$ by $\mathbb{J}11$. Therefore, $\mathbb{J}(X,Y) = [0,0]$.

Proposition 4. *If an interval fuzzy coimplication $\mathbb{J}$ satisfies the Properties $\mathbb{J}2$ and $\mathbb{J}3$ then $\mathbb{J}$ also satisfies the Properties $\mathbb{J}4$ and $\mathbb{J}5$.*

Proof. Let $\mathbb{J}$ be an interval fuzzy coimplication and $X, Y \in \mathbb{U}$.

(i) Since $Y \leq [1,1]$, it follows that $\mathbb{J}([1,1],Y) \leq \mathbb{J}([0,0],[1,1])$ by $\mathbb{J}3$. In addition, $\mathbb{J}([1,1],[1,1]) = [0,0]$ by the boundary conditions in $\mathbb{J}1$. So, $\mathbb{J}([1,1],Y) \leq [0,0]$. On the other hand, $\mathbb{J}([1,1],Y) \geq \mathbb{J}(Y,Y)$ by $\mathbb{J}2$ and $\mathbb{J}(Y,Y) = [0,0]$ by $\mathbb{J}11$, that means, $\mathbb{J}([1,1],Y) \geq [0,0]$. Therefore, $\mathbb{J}([1,1],Y) = [0,0]$.

(ii) Since $X \geq [0,0]$, it follows that $\mathbb{J}(X,[0,0]) \leq \mathbb{J}([0,0],[0,0])$ by $\mathbb{J}2$. In addition, $\mathbb{J}([0,0],[0,0]) = [0,0]$ by $\mathbb{J}1$. So, $\mathbb{J}(X,[0,0]) \leq [0,0]$. On the other hand, $\mathbb{J}(X,[0,0]) \geq \mathbb{J}(X,X)$ by $\mathbb{J}3$ and $\mathbb{J}(X,X) = [0,0]$ $\mathbb{J}11$, that means $\mathbb{J}(X,[0,0]) \geq [0,0]$. Therefore, $\mathbb{J}(X,[0,0]) = [0,0]$.

In the following, based on Theorem 2, interval fuzzy coimplications hold the corresponding properties to their dual interval fuzzy implications.

Theorem 2. *Let $\mathbb{N}$ be a strong interval fuzzy negation and $\mathbb{I}$ be an interval implication. Then $\mathbb{I}$ satisfies the property $\mathbb{I}i$, for some $i = 1, \ldots, 13$ if and only if $\mathbb{I}_N$ satisfies $\mathbb{J}i$.*

Proof. ($\Rightarrow$) Let $\mathbb{N}$ be a strong interval fuzzy negation, $\mathbb{I}$ be an interval implication and $X, Y, Z \in \mathbb{U}$.

(1) Straightforward.
(2) By $\mathbb{I}2$, if $X \leq Z$, $\mathbb{N}(X) \geq \mathbb{N}(Z)$ then $\mathbb{I}(\mathbb{N}(X), \mathbb{N}(Y))) \leq \mathbb{I}(\mathbb{N}(Z), \mathbb{N}(Y)))$. Therefore, $\mathbb{I}_N(X,Y) = \mathbb{N}(\mathbb{I}(\mathbb{N}(X), \mathbb{N}(Y))) \geq \mathbb{N}(\mathbb{I}(\mathbb{N}(Z), \mathbb{N}(Y)) = \mathbb{I}_N(Z,Y)$.
(3) Suppose $\mathbb{I}$ satisfies $\mathbb{I}3$: if $Y \leq Z$ then $\mathbb{I}(X,Y) \leq \mathbb{I}(X,Z)$, that means, if $\mathbb{N}(Y) \geq \mathbb{N}(Z)$ then $\mathbb{N}(\mathbb{I}(X,Y)) \geq \mathbb{N}(\mathbb{I}(X,Z))$. And so, $\mathbb{I}_N(X,Y) = \mathbb{N}(\mathbb{I}(\mathbb{N}(X), \mathbb{N}(Y))) \leq \mathbb{N}(\mathbb{I}(\mathbb{N}(X), \mathbb{N}(Z)) = (\mathbb{I}_N(X,Z)$.
(4) When $\mathbb{I}$ satisfies $\mathbb{I}4$, $\mathbb{I}_N([1,1],Y) = \mathbb{N}(\mathbb{I}([0,0], \mathbb{N}(Y))) = \mathbb{N}([1,1]) = [0,0]$.
(5) If $\mathbb{I}$ satisfies $\mathbb{I}5$ then $\mathbb{I}_N(X,[0,0]) = \mathbb{N}(\mathbb{I}(\mathbb{N}(X),[1,1])) = \mathbb{N}([1,1]) = [0,0]$.
(6) When $\mathbb{I}$ satisfies $\mathbb{I}6$, $\mathbb{I}_N([0,0],Y) = \mathbb{N}(\mathbb{I}([1,1], \mathbb{N}(Y))) = \mathbb{N}(\mathbb{N}(Y)) = Y$.
(7) Suppose $\mathbb{I}$ satisfies $\mathbb{I}7$. Thus,

$$\mathbb{I}_N(X, \mathbb{I}_N(Y,X)) = \mathbb{N}(\mathbb{I}(\mathbb{N}(X), \mathbb{I}(\mathbb{N}(Y), N(Z)))) = \mathbb{N}(\mathbb{I}(\mathbb{I}(\mathbb{N}(X), N(Y)), \mathbb{N}(Z)))$$
$$= \mathbb{N}(\mathbb{I}_N(\mathbb{N}(\mathbb{I}_N(X,Y)), \mathbb{N}(Z))) = \mathbb{I}_N(\mathbb{I}_N(X,Y), Z).$$

(8) Suppose $\mathbb{I}$ satisfies $\mathbb{I}8$. Thus, when $X \geq Y$, $\mathbb{N}(X) \leq \mathbb{N}(Y)$, the next equality holds: $\mathbb{I}_N(X,Y) = \mathbb{N}(\mathbb{I}(\mathbb{N}(X), \mathbb{N}(Y)))$. Therefore $\mathbb{I}_N(X,Y) = \mathbb{N}([1,1]) = [0,0]$.
(9) Suppose $\mathbb{I}$ satisfies $\mathbb{I}9$. Thus,

$(N1) \mathbb{N}_{\mathbb{I}_N}([0,0]) = \mathbb{I}_N([0,0],[1,1]) = \mathbb{N}(\mathbb{I}(\mathbb{N}([0,0]), \mathbb{N}([1,1]))) = \mathbb{N}([0,0]) = [1,1]$.
$(N2) \mathbb{N}_{\mathbb{I}_N}([1,1]) = \mathbb{I}_N([1,1],[1,1]) = \mathbb{N}(\mathbb{I}(\mathbb{N}([1,1]), \mathbb{N}([1,1]))) = \mathbb{N}([1,1]) = [0,0]$.

(N3) In addition, when $X > Y$, $\mathbb{N}(X) < \mathbb{N}(Y)$ and, by $\mathbb{I}9$, $\mathbb{I}(\mathbb{N}(X), [0,0]) < \mathbb{I}(\mathbb{N}(Y), [0,0])$, that means $\mathbb{N}(\mathbb{I}(\mathbb{N}(X), \mathbb{N}[1,1])) > \mathbb{N}(\mathbb{I}(\mathbb{N}(Y), \mathbb{N}[1,1]))$. Therefore, if $X > Y$ then $\mathbb{N}_{\mathbb{I}_N}(X) = \mathbb{I}_N(X,[0,0]) > \mathbb{I}_N(Y,[0,0]) = \mathbb{N}_{\mathbb{I}_N}(Y)$.
(N4) Since $\mathbb{N}$ and $\mathbb{N}_{\mathbb{I}}$ are both involutive fuzzy negations, it holds that

$$\mathbb{N}_{\mathbb{I}_N}(\mathbb{N}_{\mathbb{I}_N}(X)) = \mathbb{N}_{\mathbb{I}_N}(\mathbb{N}(\mathbb{I}(\mathbb{N}(X), [1,1]))) = \mathbb{N}(\mathbb{I}(\mathbb{I}(\mathbb{N}(X), [1,1]), [1,1])) \text{ by } \mathbb{I}9$$
$$= \mathbb{N}(\mathbb{N}_{\mathbb{I}}(\mathbb{N}_{\mathbb{I}}(\mathbb{N}(X)))) = \mathbb{N}(\mathbb{N}(X)) = X.$$

(10) Suppose that $\mathbb{I}$ satisfies I10, thus $\mathbb{I}(\mathbb{N}(X),\mathbb{N}(Y))\geq \mathbb{N}(Y)$. Therefore, $\mathbb{I}_\mathbb{N}(X,Y)=$
$\mathbb{N}(\mathbb{I}(\mathbb{N}(X),\mathbb{N}(Y)))\leq Y$ and $\mathbb{I}_\mathbb{N}$ satisfies J10.

(11) Since $\mathbb{I}$ satisfies I11, thus $\mathbb{I}_\mathbb{N}(X,X)=\mathbb{N}(\mathbb{I}(\mathbb{N}(X),\mathbb{N}(X)))=\mathbb{N}([1,1])=[0,0]$.

(12) By I12, $\mathbb{I}_\mathbb{N}(\mathbb{N}(X),\mathbb{N}(Y))=\mathbb{N}(\mathbb{I}(X,Y))=\mathbb{N}(\mathbb{I}(\mathbb{N}(X),\mathbb{N}(Y)))=\mathbb{I}(X,Y)$.

(13) Firstly, if $X<[1,1]$, $\mathbb{N}(X)>[0,0]$. By I13, $\mathbb{I}(\mathbb{N}(X),[0,0])<[1,1]$. Therefore,
$\mathbb{I}_\mathbb{N}(X,[1,1])=\mathbb{N}(\mathbb{I}(\mathbb{N}(X),[0,0]))>[0,0]$. Now, when $Y>[0,0]$, $\mathbb{N}(Y)<[1,1]$.
By I13, $\mathbb{I}([1,1],\mathbb{N}(Y))<[1,1]$. So, $\mathbb{I}_\mathbb{N}([0,0],Y)=\mathbb{N}(\mathbb{I}([1,1],\mathbb{N}(X)))>[0,0]$.

($\Leftarrow$) It is obtained in an analogous way.

5   Duality Relationships Preserved by Canonical Representation

Based on Definition 2, while an interval fuzzy implication $\widehat{I}$ can be viewed as a generalization of a fuzzy implication I, an interval fuzzy coimplication $\widehat{J}$ generalizes a fuzzy coimplication J. In the following, it is shown that an interval fuzzy coimplication $\widehat{J}$ (implication $\widehat{I}$) can be obtained from any fuzzy coimplication J (implication I), preserving the optimality principle and the same properties satisfied by the corresponding fuzzy coimplication.

Proposition 5. *Let J (I) be a fuzzy coimplication (implication). Then, $\widehat{J}$ ($\widehat{I}$) is an interval fuzzy coimplication (implication).*

Proof. It is straightforward from Definition 5, analogously to [2, Proposition 16].

Proposition 6. *Let $J(I) : U^2 \longrightarrow U$ be a fuzzy coimplication (implication). $J(I)$ satisfies both properties, J2 (I2) and J3 (I3), if and only if the interval fuzzy coimplication (implication) $\widehat{J}(\widehat{I})$ can be expressed as in Eq.(14) (Eq.(15)):*

$$\widehat{J}(X,Y) = [J(\overline{X},\underline{Y}), J(\underline{X},\overline{Y})];\tag{14}$$

$$\widehat{I}(X,Y) = [I(\overline{X},\underline{Y}), I(\underline{X},\overline{Y})].\tag{15}$$

Proof. We present the proof of Eq. (14), see [2, Proposition 21] to prove Eq.(15).

($\Rightarrow$)By Definition 1, $J(\overline{X},\underline{Y})$ and $J(\underline{X},\overline{Y})$ are both in $\mathbf{J}=\{J(x,y)\,|\,x{\in}X, y{\in}Y\}$ $\subseteq \widehat{J}(X,Y)$. If $\underline{X}\leq x\leq \overline{X}$, $\underline{Y}\leq y\leq \overline{Y}$, then, based on the first place antitonicity and the second place isotonicity of J, it follows that $J(\overline{X},\underline{Y})\leq J(x,y)\leq J(\underline{X},\overline{Y})$, and then $J(\overline{X},\underline{Y})$ and $J(\underline{X},\overline{Y})$ are the infimum and the supremum of $\mathbf{J}$, respectively. Therefore, the Eq. (14) follows.

($\Leftarrow$) Let $x,z,y\in U$ be such that $x\leq z$. By Eq. (14), one has that $\widehat{J}([x,z],[y,y]) = [J(z,y), J(x,y)]$, and so $J(z,y)\leq J(x,y)$, which means J satisfies the first place antitonicity property. Analogously, when $y\leq z$, $\widehat{J}([x,x],[y,z]) = [J(x,y), J(x,z)]$ and $J(x,y)\leq J(x,z)$. So, J satisfies the second place isotonicity property.

Proposition 7. *Let N be a strong fuzzy negation, J (I) be a coimplication (implication) and J_N (I_N) be N-dual implication of J (coimplication of I) satisfying both* properties, the first place antitonicity and the second place isotonicity. Then $\widehat{J_N}$ $(\widehat{I_N})$ is an interval fuzzy implication (coimplication) expressed as in Eq.(16) (Eq.(17)):

$$\widehat{J_N}(X,Y) = [J_N(\overline{X}, \underline{Y}), J_N(\underline{X}, \overline{Y})]; \tag{16}$$

$$\widehat{I_N}(X,Y) = [I_N(\overline{X}, \underline{Y}), I_N(\underline{X}, \overline{Y})]. \tag{17}$$

Proof. It follows from Proposition 6.

Theorem 3. *Let N be a strong fuzzy negation, J (I) be a coimplication (implication) and J_N (I_N) be N-dual function of J (I) given by Eq.(18) (Eq.(19)):*

$$\widehat{J}_{\widehat{N}}(X,Y) = \widehat{N}(\widehat{J}(\widehat{N}(X), \widehat{N}(Y))); \tag{18}$$

$$\widehat{I}_{\widehat{N}}(X,Y) = \widehat{N}(\widehat{I}(\widehat{N}(X), \widehat{N}(Y))). \tag{19}$$

If $J_N(I_N)$ is a first place antitonicity and second place isotonicity function, then the duality is preserved by the canonical representation, that means, Eq(20) (Eq(21)) holds:

$$\widehat{J}_{\widehat{N}}(X,Y) = \widehat{J_N}(X,Y); \tag{20}$$

$$\widehat{I}_{\widehat{N}}(X,Y) = \widehat{I_N}(X,Y). \tag{21}$$

Proof. We will present the proof for $\widehat{J}_{\widehat{N}}$, as the proof of $\widehat{I}_{\widehat{N}}$ is analogous.

$$\begin{aligned}
\widehat{J}_{\widehat{N}}(X,Y) &= \widehat{N}(\widehat{J}(\widehat{N}(X), \widehat{N}(Y))) \quad \text{Eq.(18)} \\
&= \widehat{N}(\widehat{J}([N(\overline{X}), N(\underline{X})], [N(\overline{Y}), N(\underline{Y})])) \quad \text{Eq.(3)} \\
&= \widehat{N}(J(N(\underline{X}), N(\overline{Y})), J(N(\overline{X}), N(\underline{Y}))) \quad \text{Eq.(15)} \\
&= [N(J(N(\overline{X}), N(\underline{Y}))), N(J(N(\underline{X}), N(\overline{Y})))] \quad \text{Eq.(3)} \\
&= [J_N(\overline{X}, \underline{Y}), J_N(\underline{X}, \overline{Y})] = \widehat{J_N}(X,Y) \quad \text{Eq.(16)}
\end{aligned}$$

Denote by $\mathcal{C}(I), \mathcal{C}(J), \mathcal{C}(N), \mathcal{C}(I_N), \mathcal{C}(J_N)$ the classes of implications, coimplications, negations, N-dual coimplications and N-dual implications, respectively. The interval extensions are indicated by $\mathcal{C}(\mathbb{I}), \mathcal{C}(\mathbb{J}), \mathcal{C}(\mathbb{N}), \mathcal{C}(\mathbb{I}_\mathbb{N})$ and $\mathcal{C}(\mathbb{J}_\mathbb{N})$, respectively. The results presented above, together with Theorem 3, state the commutativity of the diagram in Fig. 1. Analogously, the commutative of dual classes: $(\mathcal{C}(I_N), \mathcal{C}(I))$ and $(\mathcal{C}(\mathbb{I}_\mathbb{N}), \mathcal{C}(\mathbb{I}))$ could be also considered.

$$
\begin{array}{ccc}
\mathcal{C}(J) \times \mathcal{C}(N) & \xrightarrow{\ Eq.(11)\ } & \mathcal{C}(J_N) \subseteq \mathcal{C}(I) \\
\Big\downarrow{\scriptstyle Eq.(14),\, Eq.(3)} & & \Big\downarrow{\scriptstyle Eq.(16)} \\
\mathcal{C}(\mathbb{J}) \times \mathcal{C}(\mathbb{N}) & \xrightarrow{\ Eq.(12)\ } & \mathcal{C}(\mathbb{J}_\mathbb{N}) \subseteq \mathcal{C}(\mathbb{I})
\end{array}
$$

Fig. 1. Commutative of dual classes: $(\mathcal{C}(J_N), \mathcal{C}(J))$ and $(\mathcal{C}(\mathbb{J}_\mathbb{N}), \mathcal{C}(\mathbb{J}))$

The concept of interval-valued S-implication as presented in [2], is based on the notions of interval t-conorm and interval fuzzy negation. It shows that interval fuzzy S-implication is representable, satisfying the correctness property and also preserving some properties that are analogous to the ones satisfied by fuzzy S-implications. Proposition 8 considers its interval dual approach, so-called interval fuzzy $\mathbb{S}_\mathbb{N}$-coimplication.

Proposition 8. *Let $\mathbb{N}$ be a strong interval fuzzy negation and $\mathbb{S}_\mathbb{N}$ be the $\mathbb{N}$-dual interval t-norm of the interval t-conorm $\mathbb{S}$. Then, when $\mathbb{I}$ is an interval S-implication given by*

$$\mathbb{I}(X,Y) = \mathbb{S}(\mathbb{N}(X),Y), \tag{22}$$

the $\mathbb{N}$-dual interval coimplication of the interval S-implication $\mathbb{I}$ is given by

$$\mathbb{I}_\mathbb{N}(X,Y) = \mathbb{T}_{\mathbb{N},\mathbb{S}}(\mathbb{N}(X),Y) \tag{23}$$

Proof. Firstly, based on Eq.(3), Eq.(7) and Eq.16, $\mathbb{I}(X,Y)$ is well defined and the boundary conditions of Definition 5, related to the Property $\mathbb{J}1$, are also satisfied. Now,

$$\begin{aligned}
\mathbb{I}_\mathbb{N}(X,Y) &= \mathbb{N}(\mathbb{I}(\mathbb{N}(X),\mathbb{N}(Y))) \quad \text{by Eq.(13)} \\
&= \mathbb{N}(\mathbb{S}(\mathbb{N}(\mathbb{N}(X)),\mathbb{N}(Y))) \quad \text{by Eq.(22)} \\
&= \mathbb{T}_{\mathbb{N},\mathbb{S}}(\mathbb{N}(X),Y) \quad \text{by N3 and Eq.(9).}
\end{aligned}$$

Denote by $\mathcal{C}(\mathbb{S})$ and $\mathcal{C}((\mathbb{I})_\mathbb{S})$ the classes of interval t-conorms, interval S-implications, including their corresponding $\mathbb{N}$-dual interval functions $\mathcal{C}(\mathbb{S}_\mathbb{N})$, $\mathcal{C}((\mathbb{I}_\mathbb{N})_{\mathbb{S}_\mathbb{N}})$, respectively. The results presented in Proposition 8 and Theorem 3, state the commutativity of the diagram in Fig. 2.

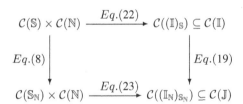

Fig. 2. Commutative of dual classes: $\mathcal{C}((\mathbb{I})_\mathbb{S})$ and $\mathcal{C}((\mathbb{I}_\mathbb{N})_{\mathbb{S}_\mathbb{N}})$

6   Border and Model Interval Fuzzy Coimplications

Extending [1, Definition 6] and [1, Definition 7], an interval fuzzy coimplication (implication) satisfying the left neutrality principle, contraposition property and exchange principle is called a model interval fuzzy coimplication (implication).

Definition 6. *If an interval coimplication $\mathbb{J}$ (implication $\mathbb{I}$) satisfies $\mathbb{J}6$ then it is said to be a* border *interval coimplication (implication).*

Definition 7. *If a border interval coimplication $\mathbb{J}$ (implication $\mathbb{I}$) also satisfies $\mathbb{J}12$ and $\mathbb{J}7$ then it is said to be a* model *interval coimplication (implication).*

In the following, border interval coimplications are contrapositive only in respect to their induced interval fuzzy negation N_J

Proposition 9. *Let N_J be a negation induced by a border interval coimplication J. If J satisfies $J12$ then $N_J = N$. In addition, when N is an interval strong negation, N_J is also an interval strong negation.*

Proof. Since J is an interval coimplication satisfying $J12$, $\forall X \in U$, it holds that, by Definition 7, $N_J(X) = J(X, [1, 1])$. So, by $J12$ and $J6$, it holds that $J([0, 0], N(X)) = N(X)$. And, if N is strong, $N_J(N_J(X)) = N(N(X)) = X$, that means N_J is also strong.

Corollary 1. *Let N be a strong interval fuzzy negation. If I is a (model) border interval implication then I_N is a (model) border interval coimplication.*

Proof. It follows from Theorem 2 and Proposition 9.

Proposition 10. *Let N be a strong interval fuzzy negation and $S_{N,T}$ be the N-dual interval t-conorm of the model (border) interval t-norm T. When $I(X, Y) = S(N(X), Y)$ is a model (border) interval S-implication then the corresponding N-dual interval coimplication $I_N(X, Y) = S_{N,T}(N(X), Y)$ is also a model (border) interval coimplication.*

Proof. It follows from Proposition 8 and Theorem 2.

7   Conclusion and Final Remarks

The main contribution of this paper is the introduction of the canonical representation of fuzzy coimplication functions as an interval extension of N-dual structure of implication functions, and vice-versa.

Additionally, the study of duality relationships preserved by canonical representation remains the idea of representation of interval coimplications as the one that can be obtained from punctual coimplications. It is also able to analyse both the correctness and the optimality criteria, besides considering an approach that was already mentioned in previous work, providing interval extensions for fuzzy connectives (See, e.g. [15,36,3,4,2,6]).

We also show that interval coimplications satisfy the main properties of interval implications discussed in the literature, and, therefore, they may contribute to practical applications, by providing more flexibility in the selection of conditional rule in expert systems. The classes of model (border) coimplications are preserved by the duality relationships and we pointed out the relationships between interval S-implications and related N-dual interval coimplications.

The class of N-dual interval coimplications which is closed under the action of the interval-valued automorphisms is an ongoing study. In addition, we continue investigations into N-dual interval classes of S-implications, extending to R-implications, QL-implications and D-implications, and also including the action of interval automorphisms which preserve main properties of such classes of corresponding punctual functions.

Acknowledgments. This work has been partially supported by CNPq.

References

1. De Baets, B.: Coimplicators, the forgotten connectives. Tatra Mountains Mathematical Publications 12, 229–240 (1997)
2. Bedregal, B.C., Dimuro, G.D., Santiago, R.H.N., Reiser, R.H.S.: On interval fuzzy S-implications. Information Sciences 180, 1373–1389 (2010)
3. Bedregal, B.C., Takahashi, A.: The best interval representation of t-norms and automorphisms. Fuzzy Sets and Systems 157(24), 3220–3230 (2006)
4. Bedregal, B.C., Takahashi, A.: Interval valued versions of t-conorms, fuzzy negations and fuzzy implications. In: Proceedings of the IEEE International Conference on Fuzzy Systems, Vancouver, pp. 1981–1987. IEEE, Los Alamitos (2006)
5. Bedregal, B.R.C., Dimuro, G.P., Reiser, R.H.S.: An approach to interval-valued R-implications and automorphisms. In: Proceedings of International Fuzzy Systems Association World Congress/European Society for Fuzzy Logic and Technology Conference, IFSA/EUSFLAT, Lisboa, pp. 1–6 (2009)
6. Bedregal, B.C.: On interval fuzzy negations. Fuzzy Sets and Systems (2010), doi: 10.1016/j.fss.2010.04.018
7. Bedregal, B.C., Santiago, R.H.N., Reiser, R.H.S., Dimuro, G.P.: Analyzing properties of fuzzy implications obtained via the interval constructor. In: 12th GAMM - IMACS International Symposium on Scientific Computing, Computer Arithmetic and Validated Numerics SCAN 2006 Conference Post-Proceedings, September 26-29, Duisburg IEEE Computer Society, Los Alamitos (2007)
8. Bustince, H., Barrenechea, E., Mohedano, V.: Intuitionistic fuzzy implication operators – an expression and main properties. International Journal of Uncertainty, Fuzziness and Knowledge-Based Systems (IJUFKS) 12(3), 387–406 (2004)
9. Bustince, H., Burillo, P.: Vague sets are intuicionistic sets. Fuzzy Sets and Systems 79, 403–405 (1996)
10. Caprani, O., Madsen, K., Stauning, O.: Existence test for asynchronous interval iteration. Reliable Computing 3(3), 269–275 (1997)
11. Cornelis, C., Deschrijver, G., Kerre, E.E.: Implication in intuitionistic fuzzy and interval-valued fuzzy set theory: Construction, classification, application. International Journal of Approximate Reasoning 35(1), 55–95 (2004)
12. Cornelis, C., Deschrijver, G., Kerre, E.E.: Advances and challenges in interval-valued fuzzy logic. Fuzzy Sets and Systems 157(5), 622–627 (2006)
13. Cross, V.: Compatibility measures using fuzzy truth and co-implication. In: First International Joint Conference of North American Fuzzy Information Processing Society Biannual Conference, Industrial Fuzzy Control and Intelligent Systems Conference and the NASA Joint Technology Workshop on Neural Networks and Fuzzy Logic, San Antonio, TX, December 1994, pp. 455–458 (1994)
14. Deschrijver, G., Cornelis, C., Kerre, E.E.: On the representation of intuitionistic fuzzy t-norms and t-conorms. IEEE Transactions on Fuzzy Systems 12(1), 45–61 (2004)
15. Dimuro, G.P., Bedregal, B.R.C., Reiser, R.H.S., Santiago, R.H.N.: Interval additive generators of interval t-norms. In: Hodges, W., de Queiroz, R. (eds.) Logic, Language, Information and Computation. LNCS (LNAI), vol. 5110, pp. 123–135. Springer, Heidelberg (2008)
16. Dubois, D., Prade, H.: Random sets and fuzzy interval analysis. Fuzzy Sets and Systems 42(1), 87–101 (1991)
17. Dubois, D., Prade, H.: Fuzzy Sets and Systems. Academic Press, New York (1996)
18. Dubois, D., Prade, H.: Interval-valued fuzzy sets, possibility theory and imprecise probability. In: Montseny, E., Sobrevilla, P. (eds.) Proceedings of the Joint 4th Conference of the European Society for Fuzzy Logic and Technology and the 11th Rencontres Francophones sur la Logique Floue et ses Applications, pp. 314–319. Universidad Polytecnica de Catalunya, Barcelona (2005)

19. Fei, Y., Yanbin, F., Hongxing, L.: Fuzzy implication operators and their construction (i): fuzzy implication operators and their properties. Journal of Beijing Normal University (Natural Science) 39, 606–611 (2003)
20. Gehrke, M., Walker, C., Walker, E.: Some comments on interval valued fuzzy sets. International Journal of Intelligent Systems 11, 751–759 (1996)
21. Gera, Z., Dombi, J.: Type 2 implications on non-interative fuzzy truth values. Fuzzy Sets and Systems 159, 3014–3032 (2008)
22. Grattan-Guiness, I.: Fuzzy membership mapped onto interval and many-valued quantities. Z. Math. Logik. Grundladen Math. 22, 149–160 (1975)
23. Jahn, K.U.: Intervall-wertige mengen. Math. Nach. 68, 115–132 (1975)
24. Jaulin, L., Kieffer, M., Didrit, O., Walter, E.: Applied Interval Analisys: with examples in parameter and state estimation, robust control and robotic. Springer, Heidelberg (2001)
25. Kearfott, R.B.: Rigorous Global Search: Continuous problems. Kluwer, Dordrecht (1996)
26. Klir, G.J., Yuan, B.: Fuzzy Sets and Fuzzy Logics: Theory and Applications. Prentice-Hall, Upper Saddle River (1995)
27. Li, P., Fang, S.C.: A note on solution sets of interval-valued fuzzy relational equations. Fuzzy Optimization and Decision Making 8(1), 115–121 (2008)
28. Li, P., Fang, S.C.: A survey on fuzzy relational equations, part i: classification and solvability. Fuzzy Optimization and Decision Making 8, 179–229 (2009)
29. Lin, L., Xia, Z.Q.: Intuicionistic fuzzy implication operators: expressions and properties. Journal of Applied Mathematic and Computing 22(3), 325–338 (2006)
30. Lodwick, W.A.: Preface. Reliable Computing 10(4), 247–248 (2004)
31. Moore, R.E., Lodwick, W.: Interval analysis and fuzzy set theory. Fuzzy Sets and Systems 135(1), 5–9 (2003)
32. Nguyen, H.T., Kreinovich, V., Zuo, Q.: Interval-valued degrees of belief: applications of interval computations to expert systems and intelligent control. International Journal of Uncertainty, Fuzziness, and Knowledge-Based Systems 5(3), 317–358 (1997)
33. Nguyen, H.T., Walker, E.A.: A First Course in Fuzzy Logic. Chapman & Hall/CRC, Boca Raton (1999)
34. Oh, K.W., Kandel, A.: Coimplication and its application to fuzzy expert systems. Information Sciences 56, 59–73 (1991)
35. Oh, K.W., Kandel, A.: A general purpose fuzzy inference mechanism based on coimplication. Fuzzy Sets and Systems 39, 247–260 (1991)
36. Reiser, R.H.S., Dimuro, G.P., Bedregal, B.C., Santiago, R.H.N.: Interval valued QL-implications. In: Leivant, D., de Queiroz, R. (eds.) WoLLIC 2007. LNCS, vol. 4576, pp. 307–321. Springer, Heidelberg (2007)
37. Ruiz, D., Torrens, J.: Residual implications and co-implications from idempotent uninorms. Kybernetika 40(1), 21–38 (2004)
38. Sambuc, R.: Fonctions ϕ-floues. Application l'aide au diagnostic en pathologie thyroidienne. PhD thesis, Univ. Marseille, Marseille (1975)
39. Santiago, R.H.N., Bedregal, B.C., Aciôly, B.M.: Formal aspects of correctness and optimality in interval computations. Formal Aspects of Computing 18(2), 231–243 (2006)
40. Turksen, I.B.: Interval valued fuzzy sets based on normal forms. Fuzzy Sets and Systems 20(2), 191–210 (1986)
41. Turksen, I.B.: Fuzzy normal forms. Fuzzy Sets and Systems 69, 319–346 (1995)
42. Turksen, I.B., Yao, D.W.: Representation of connectives in fuzzy reasoning: The view through normal forms. IEEE Trans. and Systems, Man and yibernetics 14, 146–151 (1984)
43. WagenKnecht, M., Hartmann, K.: Fuzzy modelling with tolerances. Fuzzy Sets and Systems 20, 325–332 (1996)

44. Wolter, F.: On logics with coimplication. Journal of Philosophical Logic 27(4) (1998)
45. Wu, D., Mendel, J.M.: Uncertainty measures for interval type-2 fuzzy sets. Information Sciences 177(23), 5378–5393 (2007)
46. Yager, R.R.: Level sets and the extension principle for interval valued fuzzy sets and its application to uncertainty measures. Information Sciences 178(18), 3565–3576 (2008)
47. Zadeh, L.A.: The concept of a linguistic variable and its application to approximate reasoning - I. Information Sciences 8(3), 199–249 (1975)

Reduction of the Intruder Deduction Problem into Equational Elementary Deduction for Electronic Purse Protocols with Blind Signatures*

Daniele Nantes Sobrinho[1,**] and Mauricio Ayala-Rincón[1,2,***]

Grupo de Teoria da Computação
Departamentos de [1]Matemática e [2]Ciência da Computação
Universidade de Brasília
daniele.nantes@gmail.com, ayala@unb.br

Abstract. The intruder deduction problem for an electronic purse protocol with blind signatures is considered. The algebraic properties of the protocol are modeled by an equational theory implemented as a convergent rewriting system which involves rules for addition, multiplication and exponentiation. The whole deductive power of the intruder is modeled as a sequent calculus that, modulo this rewriting system, deals with blind signatures. It is proved that the associative-commutative (AC) equality of the algebraic theory can be decided in polynomial time, provided a strategy to avoid distributivity law between the AC operators is adopted. Moreover, it is also shown that the intruder deduction problem can be reduced in polynomial time to the elementary deduction problem for this equational theory.

1 Introduction

Cryptographic protocols are programs designed to ensure secure communication over computer networks. A cryptographic protocol involves some cryptographic algorithm, but generally the goal of the protocol is something beyond a simple secrecy. The parties participating of the protocol might want share parts of their secrets to compute a value, jointly generate a random sequence, convince one another of their identity, our simultaneously sign a contract. The objective of using cryptography in a protocol is to prevent or detect eavesdropping and cheating.

By formalizing protocols, one can examine ways in which dishonest parties can subvert them and then develop protocols that are immune to that subversion. These protocols use cryptographic primitives such as public and symmetric encryption, functions that are based on mathematical notions, such as modular

---

* Work supported by the District Federal Research Foundation - FAP-DF 8-004/2007.
** Author supported by the Brazilian Research Council CNPq.
*** Corresponding author partially supported by the Brazilian Research Council CNPq.

A. Dawar and R. de Queiroz (Eds.): WoLLIC 2010, LNAI 6188, pp. 218–231, 2010.

exponentiation and multiplication, and algorithmically hard problems such as the difficulty of calculating discrete logarithms in a finite field.

One of the main challenges in cryptography is to formally verify the security of the cryptographic models taking into account the algebraic properties of the cryptographic primitives. Cryptographic protocols may themselves make use of algebraic properties, which makes it impossible to describe protocols in models that do not handle algebraic properties. A list of algebraic properties used in cryptographic protocols is surveyed in [7]; for instance, the associativity is necessary in Needham-Schoreder-Lowe Modified Protocol, exclusive-or is used in Bull's protocol [5]. Another interesting equational theory, which is the focus of this work is the theory composed by the properties of Abelian groups and modular exponentiation, this is the case of Schnorr's, the Multi-Authority Secret Ballot Election and the Electronic Purse Protocols (EPP) [6, 8].

For studying the EPP, the representation of an execution of the protocol requires the addition of several algebraic properties, which makes its modeling a very complex problem. In order to build the equational theory, one has to consider the Abelian group properties of multiplication and addition and also the properties of modular exponentiation. Unfortunately, a theory having both multiplication and exponentiation properties, together with the distributivity laws, yields undecidability of unification, as was shown by Kapur *et alii* in [9]. In order to obtain decidability of the unification problem, it was necessary to restrict the axioms used in the execution of the protocol. Therefore, to avoid the distributivity axiom, exponentials are not multiplied to each other and an additional homomorphism axiom is included into the equational theory. These changes allows the study of the *intruder deduction problem* for this protocol, which is known to be polynomially decidable [6].

In this work, the EPP is improved allowing blind signatures. Blind signatures are useful to authenticate documents and authorize transactions without knowing their contents as is done, for example, by the election authorities in electronic voting protocols.

In [12] deductive techniques for dealing with a protocol with blind signatures in which mutually disjoint equational theories containing a unique AC operator each are considered. In that paper the intruder capability of deduction is modeled inside a sequent calculus modulo a rewriting system that models the algebraic deductive power following the approach in [3]. The intruder deduction problem can be reduced in polynomial time to the elementary deduction problem (EDP). The restriction on the AC operators to belong to mutually disjoint theories is essential to guarantee polynomiality.

In this work the techniques in [12] are combined with the ones in [6] in order to model an EPP with blind signatures and it is proved, adapting the techniques in these works, that the intruder deduction problem can be also polynomially reduced to the EDP. Instead combining several disjoint equational theories as in [12], the algebraic power is modeled by a unique equational theory, which has more than one AC operator. This is achieved presenting a polynomial algorithm that decides AC equality of the operators used to model the protocol.

Detailed proofs are included in an extended version of this paper available at `http://ayala.mat.unb.br/publications.html`.

Section 2 presents the necessary notions about the considered protocol as well as how it is modeled: firstly, the protocol is described in detail; afterwards, the equational theory and the associated convergent rewriting system are presented; finally, the cut-free sequent calculus that models the intruder deduction is introduced. Before concluding, Section 3 introduces the notion of *normal derivations* that is useful to present a *linear* inference system for the intruder. This system is necessary to prove polynomial reduction to the EDP.

2   Modeling Intruder Deduction for the Electronic Purse Protocol with Blind Signatures

It is assumed basic knowledge on cryptography and rewriting (e.g, [2, 4, 11]). In the following, an important security problem in presence of a passive eavesdropper will be considered, the so-called *intruder deduction problem*: given a finite set of messages Γ and a message M, is it possible for the intruder to retrieve M from Γ by using his deduction capabilities?

2.1   Syntax

The signature adopted consists of a set of function symbols, composed by the union of the set

$$\Sigma_C = \{\mathsf{pub}(\_), \mathsf{sign}(\_,\_), \mathsf{blind}(\_,\_), \{\_\}\_, <\_,\_>\}$$

representing the *constructors*, whose interpretations are:

- $\mathsf{pub}(M)$ gives the public key generated from a private key M;
- $\mathsf{blind}(M, N)$ gives M encrypted with N using blinding encryption;
- $\mathsf{sign}(M, N)$ gives M signed with a private key N;
- $\{M\}_N$ gives M encrypted with the key N using Dolev-Yao symmetric encryption and;
- $\langle M, N \rangle$ constructs a pair of terms from M and N.

In addition, the signature includes the set of symbols Σ_{EP} associated with the equational theory EP. It is also required that $\Sigma_{\mathsf{EP}} \cap \Sigma_C = \emptyset$.

The equational theory EP contains three different AC symbols, which will be denoted by $\{+, \bullet, \star\}$, obeying the standard Abelian group laws and also some axioms for exponentiation. The signature of EP contains three constant symbols for the neutral elements, $e_\circ$, three for the inverse functions, $J_\circ(\_)$, associated with each of the AC symbols: $\circ \in \{+, \bullet, \star\}$. In addition, EP contains two symbols for exponentiation $h(\_)$ and $\exp(\_,\_)$ whose rules will be presented in the Subsection 2.2. Messages are built over countably infinite sets of names N and variables V. As notational convention names will range over the first and variables over the last letters of the Roman alphabet.

Then the grammar of the set of *terms* or messages is given as

$$M, N \quad := \quad a \mid x \mid \mathsf{pub}(M) \mid \mathsf{sign}(M, N) \mid \mathsf{blind}(M, N) \mid \{M\}_N \mid \langle M, N \rangle \mid$$
$$M + N \mid M \bullet N \mid M \star N \mid e_+ \mid e_\bullet \mid e_\star \mid J_+(M) \mid J_\bullet(M) \mid J_\star(M) \mid$$
$$\mathsf{exp}(M, N) \mid h(M)$$

As in [12], some definitions related to terms are necessary, for instance, a term M is said to be an EP-*alien term* if M is headed by a symbol $f \notin \Sigma_{\mathsf{EP}}$. It is a *pure* EP-*term* if it contains only symbols from Σ_{EP}, names and variables.

A *context* is a term with holes. $C^k[\,]$ denotes a context with k-hole(s). An EP-*context* is a context formed using only function symbols in Σ_{EP}.

2.2   The Electronic Purse Protocol: The Equational Theory EP

This protocol, as presented in [6], allows the transaction between an electronic purse and a server. It aims to guarantee a good level of security, using asymmetric cryptography and with a small cost. It involves three agents: the electronic purse EP, a server S and a trusted autority A, which is involved in case of claims of either party only and consequently is not considered here.

Let b and r denote two public positive integers. The public key of EP is $b^s \bmod r$, where s is its private key. Initially, there is a phase during which the server authenticates itself, that is not considered here, since it does not make use of algebraic properties. After this phase, the electronic purse EP authenticates itself with the server S and performs the transaction:

Step 1. EP computes the message $M = \{S, N_S, N_P, M_t\}_{K_A(P)}$ (which is used in case of conflict only);

Step 2. EP sends to the server S: $\mathsf{hash}(b^N \bmod r, S, N_s, M, M_t)$, where M_t is the amount payed;

Step 3. The server S challenges EP sending a nonce N_c;

Step 4. EP sends back $N - s \times N_c, M, M_t$ and subtract M_t from his account;

Step 5. S checks that the the message received at the first step is consistent with the message received at the third step and then increases its account in the amount M_t. S also stores the messages M, N_S, N_P and M_t.

The most important and difficult step is **Step 5**, since S should be able to verifify consistence of the previous steps. For doing it, S shold perform the following operations:

$$\mathsf{hash}((b^s)^{N_c} \times b^{N - s \times N_c} \bmod r, S, N_S, N_P, M, M_t) =$$
$$\mathsf{hash}(b^{s \times N_c} \times b^{N - s \times N_c} \bmod r, S, N_S, N_P, M, M_t) =$$
$$\mathsf{hash}(b^{s \times N_c + N - s \times N_c} \bmod r, S, N_S, N_P, M, M_t) =$$
$$\mathsf{hash}(b^N \bmod r, S, N_S, N_P, M, M_t)$$

In addition to Abelian group properties for both $\times$ and $+$, the following equational properties are used:

$$\exp(\exp(b, y), z) = \exp(b, y \times z) \text{ and } \exp(b, x) \times \exp(b, y) = \exp(b, y + z)$$

This introduces a problem because the properties

(1) $\exp(\exp(x, y), z) = \exp(x, y \times z)$

(2) $\exp(x, y) \times \exp(x, z) = \exp(x, y + z)$

derive distributivity of exponentiation over the multiplication operator. In fact:

$$\begin{aligned}
\exp(\exp(x, y_1) \times \exp(x, y_2), z) &=_2 \exp(\exp(x, y_1 + y_2), z) \\
&=_1 \exp(x, (y_1 + y_2) \times z) \\
&= \exp(x, y_1 \times z + y_2 \times z) \\
&=_2 \exp(x, y_1 \times z) \times \exp(x, y_2 \times z) \\
&=_1 \exp(\exp(x, y_1), z) \times \exp(\exp(x, y_2), z)
\end{aligned}$$

Consequently, the unification and hence security becomes undecidable (*e.g.* [9]). Since exponential needs to be applied to constant bases only, to solve this problem an additional unary function symbol h is adopted, whose meaning is $h(x) = \exp(b, x)$. This adaptation will provide an equational theory EP with decidable unification problem [6].

Actually, the distributivity rule does not need to be considered. The following restriction to a homomorphism axiom is sufficient: $h(x) \bullet h(y) = h(x + y)$.

Thus, the equational theory EP used to model the protocol is composed by the following equational axioms:

$$\begin{array}{ll}
\mathsf{AG}(+, J_+, e_+) & h(x) \bullet h(y) = h(x + y) \\
\mathsf{AG}(\star, J_\star, e_\star) & \exp(h(x), y) = h(x \star y) \\
\mathsf{AG}(\bullet, J_\bullet, e_\bullet) & \exp(\exp(x, y), z) = \exp(x, y \star z)
\end{array}$$

where $\mathsf{AG}(\circ, J_\circ, e_\circ)$ are the axioms of Abelian groups for $\circ \in \{\bullet, +, \star\}$.

These equational axioms are sufficient for modeling the protocol. The following equalities express the main test executed by the server (during **Step 5**):

$$\begin{aligned}
\exp(h(s), N_c) \bullet h(N + J_+(s \star N_c)) &= h(s \star N_c) \bullet h(N + J_+(s \star N_c)) \\
&= h(s \star N_c + N + J_+(s \star N_c)) \\
&= h(N)
\end{aligned}$$

The role of the two multiplication used is to differentiate between the multiplication in the basis of exponentials and the multiplication of exponents.

2.3   The Convergent Rewriting System $\mathcal{R}$ Equivalent to the Equational Theory EP

Standard rewriting notation and notions are used (e.g. [2,4]). A rewriting system is a set $\mathcal{R}$ of oriented equations over terms in a given signature. For terms s and t, $s \rightarrow_\mathcal{R} t$ denotes that s rewrites into t using one application of a rewriting rule in $\mathcal{R}$. The inverse of $\rightarrow_\mathcal{R}$ is denoted by $_\mathcal{R}{\leftarrow}$. The transitive, reflexive-transitive and equivalence closures of $\rightarrow_\mathcal{R}$ are denoted by $\xrightarrow{+}_\mathcal{R}$, $\xrightarrow{*}_\mathcal{R}$ and $\xleftrightarrow{*}_\mathcal{R}$, respectively. Analogously, the transitive and reflexive-transitive closures of $_\mathcal{R}{\leftarrow}$ are denoted by $_\mathcal{R}{\xleftarrow{+}}$ and $_\mathcal{R}{\xleftarrow{*}}$, respectively. The equivalence clousure of the rewriting relation, $\xleftrightarrow{*}_\mathcal{R}$, is also denoted by $\approx_\mathcal{R}$. Composition of relations is denoted by $\circ$.

A term s is in $\mathcal{R}$-normal form if there is no term t such that $s \rightarrow_\mathcal{R} t$; $s \downarrow_\mathcal{R}$ denotes a normal form of s (i.e., a term t such that $s \rightarrow_\mathcal{R} t$ and t is in $\mathcal{R}$-normal form).

$\mathcal{R}$ is said to be convergent whenever it is terminant and confluent, *i.e.*, respectively:

$$\text{there is no infinite chain } s_0 \rightarrow_\mathcal{R} s_1 \rightarrow_\mathcal{R} s_2 \cdots \text{ and}$$

$$(_\mathcal{R}{\leftarrow} \circ \rightarrow_\mathcal{R}) \subseteq (\xrightarrow{*}_\mathcal{R} \circ {}_\mathcal{R}{\xleftarrow{*}})$$

Given an equational theory E, it is said that E is equivalent to $\mathcal{R}$ whenever $\approx_\mathcal{R} = \approx_E$. Subscripts are omitted when they are clear from the context.

The rewriting system $\mathcal{R}$ associated with the equational theory EP, introduced in [6], has as signature

$$\Sigma_{\mathsf{EP}} = \{+, e_+, J_+, \star, e_\star, J_\star, \bullet, e_\bullet, J_\bullet, h, \exp\}$$

and consists of the union of the rewriting systems below.

$\mathcal{R}_{AG(\circ)}$, for $\circ \in \{+, \star, \bullet\}$, denotes the rewriting system modulo AC for $\circ$, given by the set of rules:

$$\mathcal{R}_{AG(\circ)} := \begin{cases} x \circ e_\circ \rightarrow x & x \circ J_\circ(x) \rightarrow e_\circ \\ J_\circ(x) \circ J_\circ(y) \rightarrow J_\circ(x \circ y) & J_\circ(e_\circ) \rightarrow e_\circ \\ J_\circ(J_\circ(x)) \rightarrow x & J_\circ(x) \circ x \circ y \rightarrow y \\ J_\circ(x) \circ J_\circ(y) \circ z \rightarrow J_\circ(x \circ y) \circ z & J_\circ(x \circ y) \circ x \rightarrow J_\circ(y) \\ J_\circ(x \circ y) \circ x \circ z \rightarrow J_\circ(y) \circ z & J_\circ(J_\circ(x) \circ y) \rightarrow x \circ J_\circ(y) \end{cases}$$

$\mathcal{R}_0$ is given by the rules.

$$\mathcal{R}_0 := \begin{cases} \exp(h(x), y) \rightarrow h(x \star y) & J_\bullet(h(x)) \rightarrow h(J_+(x)) \\ \exp(\exp(x, y), z) \rightarrow \exp(x, y \star z) & h(e_+) \rightarrow e_\bullet \\ h(x) \bullet h(y) \rightarrow h(x + y) & J_\bullet(h(x) \bullet y) \rightarrow h(J_+(x)) \bullet J_\bullet(y) \\ h(x) \bullet h(y) \bullet z \rightarrow h(x + y) \bullet z & \exp(e_\bullet, x) \rightarrow h(e_+ \star x) \end{cases}$$

The rewriting system $\mathcal{R} := \mathcal{R}_{\mathsf{AG}(\star)} \cup \mathcal{R}_{\mathsf{AG}(\bullet)} \cup \mathcal{R}_{\mathsf{AG}(+)} \cup \mathcal{R}_0$ was proved convergent modulo AC in [6]. This implies that any equational theorem in EP, namely, $s =_{\mathsf{EP}} t$, can be effectively proved using $\mathcal{R}$, by normalizing s: $s \rightarrow^*_{\mathcal{R}} s\!\downarrow$, and t: $t \rightarrow^*_{\mathcal{R}} t\!\downarrow$, and checking whether $s\!\downarrow =_{AC} t\!\downarrow$.

2.4   Sequent Calculus for the Intruder

The set of inference rules $\mathcal{S}$ for the intruder deduction, presented in Table 1 is essentially the same as in [12], except that the (id) rule considers the equational theory EP and the symbol $=_{AC}$ will be interpreted as equality modulo AC for the operators $\{+, \star, \bullet\}$.

Table 1. System $\mathcal{S}$: Sequent Calculus for the Intruder

$$\frac{\begin{array}{c} M \approx_{\mathsf{EP}} C[M_1,\ldots,M_k] \\ C[\,] \text{ an EP-context, and } M_1,\ldots,M_k \in \Gamma \end{array}}{\Gamma \vdash M}\ (id) \qquad \frac{\Gamma \vdash M \qquad \Gamma, M \vdash T}{\Gamma \vdash T}\ (cut)$$

$$\frac{\Gamma, \langle M, N \rangle, M, N \vdash T}{\Gamma, \langle M, N \rangle \vdash T}\ (p_L) \qquad \frac{\Gamma \vdash M \qquad \Gamma \vdash N}{\Gamma \vdash \langle M, N \rangle}\ (p_R)$$

$$\frac{\Gamma, \{M\}_k \vdash K \qquad \Gamma, \{M\}_k, M, K \vdash N}{\Gamma, \{M\}_k \vdash N}\ (e_L) \qquad \frac{\Gamma \vdash M \qquad \Gamma \vdash K}{\Gamma \vdash \{M\}_k}\ (e_R)$$

$$\frac{\Gamma, \mathsf{sign}(M, K), \mathsf{pub}(L), M \vdash N}{\Gamma, \mathsf{sign}(M, K), \mathsf{pub}(L) \vdash N}\ (\mathsf{sign}_L) K =_{AC} L$$

$$\frac{\Gamma \vdash M \qquad \Gamma \vdash K}{\Gamma \vdash \mathsf{blind}(M, K)}\ (\mathsf{blind}_R) \qquad \frac{\Gamma \vdash M \qquad \Gamma \vdash K}{\Gamma \vdash \mathsf{sign}(M, K)}\ (\mathsf{sign}_R)$$

$$\frac{\Gamma, \mathsf{blind}(M, K) \vdash K \qquad \Gamma, \mathsf{blind}(M, K), M, K \vdash N}{\Gamma, \mathsf{blind}(M, K) \vdash N}\ (\mathsf{blind}_{L_1})$$

$$\frac{\Gamma, \mathsf{sign}(\mathsf{blind}(M, R), K) \vdash R \qquad \Gamma, \mathsf{sign}(\mathsf{blind}(M, R), K), \mathsf{sign}(M, K), R \vdash N}{\Gamma, \mathsf{blind}(M, K) \vdash N}\ (\mathsf{blind}_{L_2})$$

$$\frac{\Gamma \vdash A \qquad \Gamma, A \vdash M}{\Gamma \vdash M}\ (gs), A \text{ is a guarded subterm of } \Gamma \cup \{M\}$$

As in [12], the rule (gs), called *analytic cut*, is necessary to introduce the function symbols in Σ_{EP}. This rule is necessary to "abstract" EP-alien subterms in a sequent in order to prove cut rule *admissibility*.

A sequent $\Gamma \vdash M$ is in *normal form* if M and all the terms in Γ are in normal form. Unless stated otherwise, it is assumed that sequents are in normal form. Moreover, $\Gamma \Vdash_{\mathcal{S}} M$ denotes that the sequent $\Gamma \vdash M$ is derivable in $\mathcal{S}$.

Definition 1 (Admissible rules). *An inference rule R in a proof system $\mathcal{D}$ is admissible for $\mathcal{D}$ if for every sequent $\Gamma \vdash M$ derivable in $\mathcal{D}$, there is a derivation of the same sequent in $\mathcal{D}$ without instances of R.*

Admissibility of the cut rule holds. The proof is based on induction on the height of the left premise derivation immediately above the cut rule as in [12].

Theorem 1 (Admissibility of the cut rule). *The cut rule is admissible for $\mathcal{S}$.*

Proof (Sketch). The cut reduction is driven by the left premise derivation of the cut. The proof is divided in several cases, based on the last rule of the left premise derivation.

For instance, suppose the left premise of the cut ends with the (id)-rule :

$$\frac{\dfrac{}{\Gamma \vdash M}\,(id) \qquad \dfrac{\Pi_1}{\Gamma, M \vdash R}}{\Gamma \vdash R}\,(cut)$$

where $M = C[M_1, \ldots, M_k] \downarrow$, $C[\ldots]$ is an EP-context and $M_1, \ldots, M_k \in \Gamma$. By induction hypothesis $\Gamma, M \vdash R$ is cut-free derivable, hence applying a lemma of preservation of $\mathcal{S}$-derivability on the decomposition of EP-contexts to Π_1 one can obtain a cut-free derivation Π' of $\Gamma \vdash R$.   □

3   Elementary Intruder Deduction under the EP Theory

The decidability of the intruder deduction problem for the EPP without blind signatures is already known to be polynomial [6]. This result was obtained following McAllester's approach which states that there is a polynomial algorithm provided a *locality* property for the inference rules is guaranteed [10]. Here, the techniques in [12] are followed to prove that the decidability result for the EPP with blind signatures can be reduced to the EDP.

For doing this, it is necessary an improvement on the boundary created to guarantee the locality property for the intruder's rules for the EPP in [6], in which all intermediate formulas contained in every derivation were bounded by a notion of subterms involving only terms in the signature Σ_{EP}. Here, since one deals with the system $\mathcal{S}$ and terms headed by constructors are allowed inside the (id) rule, a new bound will be necessary to preserve the subformula property. This bound is built as a combination of the previous notion of subterms and the saturated set of Γ (intruder's knowledge).

Definition 2 (Elementary deduction problem). *The elementary deduction problem for EP, written $\Gamma \Vdash_{\mathsf{EP}} M$, is the problem of deciding whether the (id) rule is applicable to the sequent $\Gamma \vdash M$, by checking whether there exists an EP-context $C[\ldots]$ and terms $M_1, \ldots, M_k \in \Gamma$ such that $C[M_1, \ldots, M_k] \approx_{\mathsf{EP}} M$.*

For $\circ \in \{\star, \bullet, +\}$ define $\mathrm{inv}_\circ(u)$ as the term $J_\circ(u) \downarrow$. The following definitions are essential for the next results.

Definition 3. *Denote by $\mathrm{top}(t)$ the root symbol of the term t. $\mathrm{TOP}(u)$ is defined recursively as*

$$
\mathrm{TOP}(t) := \begin{cases}
\circ, & \textit{if } t = J_\circ(u \circ v), \textit{ for } \circ \in \{\star, \bullet, +\} \\
\bullet, & \textit{if } t = h(v + w) \\
\bullet, & \textit{if } t = h(J_+(v + w)) \\
\mathrm{top}(t), & \textit{otherwise.}
\end{cases}
$$

Definition 4 (EP-decomposition subterms). *Let $\circ \in \{\star, \bullet, +\}$, the set of EP-decomposition subterms, denoted by $\mathrm{DS}_\circ(u)$, is defined as*

1. $\mathrm{DS}_\circ(u \circ v) = \mathrm{DS}_\circ(u) \cup \mathrm{DS}_\circ(v)$,

2. $\mathrm{DS}_\circ(J_\circ(u)) = \{J_\circ(v) | v \in \mathrm{DS}_\circ(u)\}$,

3. $DS_\bullet(h(u)) = \{h(v) | v \in DS_+(u)\}$, *and*

4. $\mathrm{DS}_\circ(u) = \{u\}$ *if $\mathrm{TOP}(u) \neq \circ$.*

Definition 5 (EP-subterms). *Let t be a term in EP-normal form, $\mathrm{Sub}(t)$ is the smallest set of terms such that $t \in \mathrm{Sub}(t)$ and if $u \in \mathrm{Sub}(t)$ then*

1. *either $\circ = \mathrm{TOP}(u) \in \{\star, \bullet, +\}$ and $\mathrm{DS}_\circ(u) \subseteq \mathrm{Sub}(t)$*

2. *or else $u = f(u_1, \ldots u_n)$ and $u_1, \ldots, u_n \in \mathrm{Sub}(t)$.*

If T is a set of terms, $\mathrm{Sub}(T)$ is defined as: $\mathrm{Sub}(T) := \bigcup_{u \in T} \mathrm{Sub}(u)$.

Although the modifications made in the (id) rule, it is possible to see that this rule still preserves the *subformula property*: in any sequent $\Gamma \vdash M$ derivable using the new (id) rule only subformulas of Γ and M occur. In order to obtain this property it is necessary a suitable notion of subterms F, which is a function that associates a term to the set of its subterms.

The function above is basically the same introduced by Bursuc *et alii* in [6] except by a slight alteration in the subset $\{\mathrm{inv}_\circ(t) \mid t \in \mathrm{Sub}(T), \mathrm{TOP}(t) \in \{\star, +, \bullet\}\}$ used in the composition of F.

$F(T) = \mathrm{Sub}(T)$

$\cup \{h(t) \mid t \in \mathrm{Sub}(T), \mathrm{TOP}(t) = +\}$

$\cup \{h(\mathrm{inv}_+(t) \mid t \in \mathrm{Sub}(T), \mathrm{TOP}(t) = +\}$

$\cup \{\mathrm{inv}_\circ(t) \mid t \in \mathrm{Sub}(T), \mathrm{TOP}(t) \in \{\star, +, \bullet\}\}$

$\cup \{h(t) \mid \exists t \in \mathrm{Sub}(T) \text{ s.t. } \mathrm{TOP}(u) = \circ \in \{\star, +\}, t \in \mathrm{DS}_\circ(u)\}$

$\cup \{\mathrm{inv}_\circ(t) \mid \exists u \in \mathrm{Sub}(T) \text{ s.t. } \mathrm{TOP}(u) = \circ \in \{\star, +, \bullet\}, \ t \in \mathrm{DS}_\circ(u)\}$

$\cup \{h(\mathrm{inv}_\circ(t)) \mid \exists u \in \mathrm{Sub}(T) \text{ s.t. } \mathrm{TOP}(u) = \circ \in \{\star, +\}, \ t \in \mathrm{DS}_\circ(u)\}$

Notice that the size of $F(T)$ is linear in the size of T.

Nevertheless the cut-free system $\mathcal{S}$ does not enjoy the *subformula property*, since in (blind_{L_2}) the premisse has a term which is not a subterm of any term in the conclusion. Notice that reading the rules bottom up, the terms introduced are smaller than the terms in the conclusion. Thus a proof search strategy will eventually terminate.

Normal derivations in a deduction system satisfy the following conditions: left rules appear neither above a right rule nor immediately above the left-premise of a branching left rule.

$\Gamma \Vdash_{\mathcal{R}} M$ denotes the fact that the sequent $\Gamma \vdash M$ is provable using only right rules and (id). The system $\mathcal{L}$ given in Table 2 is a linear deduction system for the intruder. The difference with the system in [12] is essentially the new interpretation of the (id) rule and the equality modulo AC used in the rule (sign).

Table 2. System $\mathcal{L}$: a linear proof system for intruder deduction

$$\frac{\Gamma \Vdash_{\mathcal{R}} M}{\Gamma \vdash M} \ (\mathsf{r}) \qquad\qquad \frac{\Gamma, \{M\}_K, M, K \vdash N}{\Gamma, \{M\}_K \vdash N} \ (l_e), \ \text{where } \Gamma, \{M\}_K \Vdash_{\mathcal{R}} K$$

$$\frac{\Gamma, \langle M, N\rangle, M, N \vdash T}{\Gamma, \langle M, N\rangle \vdash T} \ (l_p) \qquad \frac{\Gamma, \mathsf{sign}(M, K), \mathsf{pub}(L), M \vdash N}{\Gamma, \mathsf{sign}(M, K), \mathsf{pub}(L) \vdash N} \ (\mathsf{sign}), \ K =_{AC} L$$

$$\frac{\Gamma, \mathsf{blind}(M, K), M, K \vdash N}{\Gamma, \mathsf{blind}(M, K) \vdash N} \ (\mathsf{blind}_1), \ \Gamma, \mathsf{blind}(M, K) \Vdash_{\mathcal{R}} K$$

$$\frac{\Gamma, \mathsf{sign}(\mathsf{blind}(M, R), K), \mathsf{sign}(M, K), R \vdash N}{\Gamma, \mathsf{sign}(\mathsf{blind}(M, R), K) \vdash N} \ (\mathsf{blind}_2), \ \Gamma, \mathsf{sign}(\mathsf{blind}(M, R), K) \Vdash_{\mathcal{R}} R$$

$$\frac{\Gamma, A \vdash M}{\Gamma \vdash M} \ (ls), \ \text{where } A \text{ is a guarded subterm of } \Gamma \cup \{M\} \text{ and } \Gamma \Vdash_{\mathcal{R}} A$$

Standard DAG representation of Γ with maximum sharing of subterms is assumed (see, e.g. [1]). As in [12], $st(\Gamma)$ denotes the set of subterms of the terms in Γ. A term M is a *proper subterm* of N if M is a subterm of N and $M \neq N$. Denote with $pst(\Gamma)$ the set of proper subterms of Γ, and define

$$sst(\Gamma) = \{\mathsf{sign}(M, N) \mid M, N \in pst(\Gamma)\}.$$

The *saturated* set of Γ with respect to EP, written $St(\Gamma)$, is the set

$$St(\Gamma) = \Gamma \cup pst(\Gamma) \cup sst(\Gamma) \cup F(\Gamma)$$

As in [12], the next complexity results are stated with relation to the size of $St(\Gamma \cup \{M\})$ combined with the notion of EP-subterms.

Definition 6 (Polynomial reducibility to elementary deduction). *Let* $\Gamma \Vdash_{\mathcal{L}} M$ *be a deduction problem and let n be the size of $St(\Gamma \cup \{M\})$. Suppose that the EDP in EP has complexity $\mathcal{O}(f(m))$, where m is the size of the input. The problem $\Gamma \Vdash_{\mathcal{L}} M$ is said to be polynomially reducible to the EDP $\Vdash_{EP}$ if it has complexity $\mathcal{O}(n^k \times f(n))$ for some constant k.*

In order to adapt the proof of the following lemma from [12] it is only necessary to interpret the (id) rule inside the equational theory EP.

Lemma 1 ($\Vdash_{\mathcal{R}}$ reducible polynomially to $\Vdash_{EP}$). *The decidability of the relation $\Vdash_{\mathcal{R}}$ is polynomially reducible to the decidability of elementary deduction $\Vdash_{EP}$.*

Proof. It is enough to assume a simple proof search procedure for $\Gamma \vdash M$ using only right-rules:

1. If $\Gamma \vdash M$ is elementary deducible, then the lemma holds.

2. Otherwise, apply a right-introduction rule (backwards) to $\Gamma \vdash M$ and repeat step 1 for each obtained premise. If no such rules are applicable, then $\Gamma \vdash M$ is not derivable.

Notice that the number of iterations is bound by the number n of distinct subterms of M and that elementary deducibility is checked on problems of size less or equal to n. $\square$

In order to prove the main result, one has to consider the notion of a *principal term* in a left-rule in the proof system $\mathcal{L}$ which was defined in [12]. Given a sequent $\Gamma \vdash M$ and a pair of principal-term and left-rule (N, ρ), the pair (N, ρ) is *applicable* to the sequent if

– ρ is (ls), N is a guarded subterm of $\Gamma \cup \{M\}$, and there is an instance of ρ with $\Gamma, N \vdash M$ as its premise;

– ρ is not (ls), $N \in \Gamma$, and there is an instance of ρ with $\Gamma \vdash M$ as its conclusion.

Assume that the complexity of $\Vdash_E$ is $\mathcal{O}(f(n))$ and let n be the size of $St(\Gamma \cup \{M\})$. Given a sequent $\Gamma \vdash M$ and a pair (N, ρ), observe the following facts:

F1. the complexity of checking whether (N, ρ) is applicable to $\Gamma \vdash M$ is equal to $\mathcal{O}(n^l f(n))$ for some constant l;

F2. if (N, ρ) is applicable to $\Gamma \vdash M$, then there is a unique sequent $\Gamma' \vdash M$ such that the sequent below is a valid instance of ρ:

$$\frac{\Gamma' \vdash M}{\Gamma \vdash M} \; \rho$$

For **F1** it is necessary to assume DAG representation of sequents with maximal sharing of subterms. The complexity of checking if a rule is applicable or not then consists of: pointer comparisons; pattern match a subgraph with a rule; checking equality modulo AC (for the rule sign); checking $\Vdash_{\mathcal{R}}$. Pointer comparisons and pattern matching can be done in polynomial time and checking $\Vdash_{\mathcal{R}}$ is polynomially reducible to $\Vdash_{EP}$ (Lemma 1). The following result shows the polynomiality of the third operation.

Lemma 2 ($=_{AC}$ is polynomially decidable). *Let M, N terms in normal form. The problem whether $M =_{AC} N$ is decidable in polynomial time.*

Proof. By induction on the structure of M. Suppose that $M = f(M_1, \ldots, M_n)$.

1. If $f \notin \{+, \star, \bullet\}$ it is enough to apply induction hypothesis to the subterms $M_1, \ldots, M_n$ of M.

2. Suppose $f \in \{+, \star\}$. To make the computation easier, write: $M = M_1 \circ M_2 \circ \ldots \circ M_n$. Since M is in normal form and according to the rewrite rules,

$$M = M'_1 \circ M'_2 \circ \ldots \circ M'_k \circ J_\circ(M"_1 \circ M"_2 \circ \ldots \circ M"_s)$$

It is possible to count the occurrences of each subterm in M. Hence,

$$M = \alpha_1 M'_1 \circ \alpha_2 M'_2 \circ \ldots \alpha_p \circ M'_p \circ J_\circ(\beta_1 M''_1 \circ \beta_2 M''_2 \circ \ldots \circ \beta_q M''_q)$$

where $\alpha_1, \ldots, \alpha_p, \beta_1, \ldots, \beta_q$ are integers (at least one of them non null) and $p \le k, q \le s$. Hence, $M =_{AC} N$ iff $|M|_{M'_i} = |N|_{M'_i}$ and $|M|_{M''_j} = |N|_{M''_j}$, $1 \le i \le p$ and $1 \le j \le q$. And a simple enumeration gives a polynomial algorithm.

The problematic case happens when

$$N = \gamma_1 N'_1 \circ \gamma_2 N'_2 \circ \ldots \circ \gamma_p N'_p \circ J_\circ(\varphi_1 N''_1 \circ \varphi_2 N''_2 \circ \ldots \circ \varphi_q N''_q),$$

and for each $1 \le i \le p$ (resp. $1 \le j \le q$) there exists a $1 \le l \le p$ (resp. $1 \le r \le q$) such that $M'_i =_{AC} N'_l$ (resp. $M''_j =_{AC} N''_r$). Applying the induction hypothesis, the result follows.

3. Suppose $f = \bullet$. Then, $M = M_1 \bullet \ldots \bullet M_p \bullet J_\bullet(M'_1 \bullet \ldots \bullet M'_q) \bullet h(M''_1 + \ldots + M''_r)$. Reordering the subterms which appear repeatedly,

$$M = \chi_1 M_1 \bullet \ldots \bullet \chi_u M_p \bullet J_\bullet(\mu_1 M'_1 \bullet \ldots \bullet \mu_q M'_q) \bullet h(\rho_1 M''_1 + \ldots + \rho_w M''_w).$$

Analogously to the previous case, a simple enumeration gives a polynomial algorithm.

This completes the proof. □

The polynomial reducibility of $\Vdash_{\mathcal{L}}$ to $\Vdash_{EP}$ can be proved by a deterministic proof search strategy which systematically tries all applicable rules following the same proof methodology as in [12].

Theorem 2 ($\Vdash_{\mathcal{L}}$ reducible polynomially to $\Vdash_{EP}$). *The decidability of the relation $\Vdash_{\mathcal{L}}$ is polynomially reducible to the decidability of elementary deduction $\Vdash_{EP}$.*

Proof (Sketch). Three auxiliary results are used:

- Weakening: if Π is an $\mathcal{L}$-derivation of $\Gamma \vdash M$ and $\Gamma \subseteq \Gamma'$, then there exists an $\mathcal{L}$-derivation Π' of $\Gamma' \vdash M$ such that $|\Pi'| = |\Pi|$.
- Let Π be an $\mathcal{L}$-derivation of $\Gamma \vdash M$. Then for every sequent $\Gamma' \vdash M'$ occurring in Π, $\Gamma' \cup \{M'\} \subseteq St(\Gamma \cup \{M\})$.
- If there is an $\mathcal{L}$-derivation of $\Gamma \vdash M$ then there is an $\mathcal{L}$-derivation of the same sequent whose length is at most quadratic with respect to the size of $\Gamma \cup \{M\}$.

Suppose $\Gamma \vdash M$ is provable in $\mathcal{L}$. Let $M_1, \ldots, M_n$ be an enumeration of the set $St(\Gamma \cup \{M\})$. There is a shortest proof of $\Gamma \vdash M$ where each sequent appears exactly once in each branch of the proof. This also means that there exists a sequence of principal-term and rule pairs

$$(M_{i_1}, \rho_1), \ldots, (M_{i_q}, \rho_q)$$

that is applicable, successively, to $\Gamma \vdash M$. Since no repetitions of sequents are possible, $q \leq n$. Also, it should be noticed that the rules of $\mathcal{L}$ are inversible: one does not lose provability at any point of the proof search. Suppose, both principal-term and rule pairs (N, ρ) and (N', ρ') are applicable to $\Gamma \vdash M$; then if $\Gamma' \vdash M$ is the unique premise determined by either (N, ρ) or (N', ρ'), then, respectively, either (N', ρ') or (N, ρ) applies to $\Gamma' \vdash M$.

A proof search strategy for $\Gamma \vdash M$ is based on repeatedly try all possible applicable pairs (M', ρ') for each possible $M' \in St(\Gamma \cup \{M\})$ and each left-rule ρ' (that is bounded by $6\,n$) and for all generated sequents taking in care elimination of redundancies based on the previous observations and weakening. For all generated sequent $\Delta \vdash M$, before trying possible applicable pairs, one should check whether $\Delta \Vdash_{\mathcal{R}} M$. By Lemma 1, checking $\Vdash_{\mathcal{R}}$ takes $\mathcal{O}(n^a f(n))$ for some constant a. By (**F1**), checking applicability takes $\mathcal{O}(n^l f(n))$ for some constant l. Therefore the whole procedure takes $\mathcal{O}(n^{c+l} f(n))$. □

4   Conclusion

It was shown that the decidability of the intruder deduction problem of an electronic purse protocol with the theory of blind signatures can be polynomially reduced to the elementary intruder deduction problem. For doing this, the techniques used by Bursuc *et alii* in [6] to model the algebraic power of the protocol via a convergent rewriting system were applied together with the techniques introduced by Tiu and Goré in [12] in order to represent the intruder's deduction capacity via a sequent calculus taking into account blind signatures. In the latter work, the equational part is composed by a disjoint combination of equational theories, each one containing at most one AC operator. In this sense, the present paper slightly extends these results since the equational theory considered, which is essential for the execution of the protocol, is composed by three different AC operators and the equational theory cannot be split into disjoint theories. Although the proof techniques were proved to be straightforwardly adaptable, this study is of practical interest since the analysis was extended to EPP in which authority parties can blindly authorize electronic transactions.

As future work, one can consider more complex algebraic equational theories in security analysis of cryptographic protocols (e.g. [7]), using the approach of proof search in sequent calculus and, even more, try to establish similar results for deduction problems in which the constructors interact with the equational theories. Another interesting challenge is to obtain deducibility results with respect to active attacks.

References

1. Abadi, M., Cortier, V.: Deciding knowledge in security protocols under equational theories. Theoretical Computer Science 367(1-2), 2–32 (2006)
2. Baader, F., Nipkow, T.: Term Rewriting and All That. Cambridge University Press, Cambridge (1998)
3. Bernat, V., Comon-Lundh, H.: Normal proofs in intruder theories. In: Okada, M., Satoh, I. (eds.) ASIAN 2006. LNCS, vol. 4435, pp. 151–166. Springer, Heidelberg (2008)
4. Bezem, M., Klop, J.W., de Vrijer, R. (eds.): Term Rewriting Systems by TeReSe. Cambridge Tracts in Theoretical Computer Science, vol. 55. Cambridge University Press, Cambridge (2003)
5. Bull, J., Otwary, D.J.: The authetication protocol. Technical Report CIS3/PROJ/CORBA/SC/1/CSM/436-04/03, Defense Research Agency (1997)
6. Bursuc, B., Comon-Lundh, H., Delaune, S.: In: Comon-Lundh, H., Kirchner, C., Kirchner, H. (eds.) Jouannaud Festschrift. LNCS, vol. 4600, pp. 196–212. Springer, Heidelberg (2007)
7. Cortier, V., Delaune, S., Lafourcade, P.: A survey of algebraic properties used in cryptographic protocols. Journal of Computer Security 14(1), 1–43 (2006)
8. Delaune, S.: Vérification des protocoles cryptographiques et propriétés algébriques. PhD thesis, École Normale Supérieure de Cachan (2006)
9. Kapur, D., Narendran, P., Wang, L.: An E-unification algorithm for analyzing protocols that use modular exponentiation. In: Nieuwenhuis, R. (ed.) RTA 2003. LNCS, vol. 2706, pp. 165–179. Springer, Heidelberg (2003)
10. McAllester, D.: Automatic recognition of tractability in inference relations. Journal of the ACM 40, 284–303 (1990)
11. Schneier, B.: Applied Cryptography. John Wiley & Sons, Inc., Chichester (1996)
12. Tiu, A., Rajeev, G.: A proof theoretic analysis of intruder theories. In: Treinen, R. (ed.) RTA 2009. LNCS, vol. 5595, pp. 103–117. Springer, Heidelberg (2009)

Intersection Type Systems and Explicit Substitutions Calculi

Daniel Lima Ventura[1,*],
Mauricio Ayala-Rincón[1,**], and Fairouz Kamareddine[2]

[1] Grupo de Teoria da Computação, Dep. de Matemática Universidade de Brasília,
Brasília D.F., Brasil
{ventura,ayala}@mat.unb.br
[2] School of Mathematical and Computer Sciences Heriot-Watt University,
Edinburgh, Scotland UK
fairouz@macs.hw.ac.uk

Abstract. The λ-calculus with de Bruijn indices, called λ_{dB}, assembles each α-class of λ-terms into a unique term, using indices instead of variable names. Intersection types provide finitary type polymorphism satisfying important properties like principal typing, which allows the type system to include features such as data abstraction (modularity) and separate compilation. To be closer to computation and to simplify the formalisation of the atomic operations involved in β-contractions, several explicit substitution calculi were developed most of which are written with de Bruijn indices. Although untyped and simply types versions of explicit substitution calculi are well investigated, versions with more elaborate type systems (e.g., with intersection types) are not. In previous work, we presented a version for λ_{dB} of an intersection type system originally introduced to characterise principal typings for β-normal forms and provided the characterisation for this version. In this work we introduce intersection type systems for two explicit substitution calculi: the $\lambda\sigma$ and the λs_e. These type system are based on a type system for λ_{dB} and satisfy the basic property of subject reduction, which guarantees the preservation of types during computations.

1 Introduction

The λ-calculus à la de Bruijn [deBruijn72], λ_{dB} for short, was introduced by the Dutch mathematician N.G. de Bruijn in the context of the project Automath [NGdV94] and has been adopted for several calculi of explicit substitutions ever since, e.g. [deBruijn78, ACCL91, KR97]). Term variables are represented by indices instead of names in λ_{dB}, assembling each α-class of terms in the λ-calculus [Barendregt84] into a unique term with de Bruijn indices, thus making it more *"machine-friendly"* than its counterparts. The $\lambda\sigma$- [ACCL91] and the λs_e- [KR97] calculi have applications in higher order unification, HOU for short

---

* Corresponding author supported by the Brazilian Research Council CNPq.
** Author partially supported by the Brazilian Research Council CNPq and supported by the District Federal Research Foundation - FAP-DF 8-004/2007.

A. Dawar and R. de Queiroz (Eds.): WoLLIC 2010, LNAI 6188, pp. 232–246, 2010.

[DHK2000, AK01]. These explicit substitution calculi with de Bruijn indices have been investigated for both type free and simply typed versions but to the best of our knowledge there is no work on more elaborate type systems such as intersection types.

Intersection types, IT for short, were introduced as an extension to simple types, in order to provide a characterisation of strongly normalising λ-terms [CDC78, CDC80, Pottinger80]. In programming, the IT discipline is of interest because λ-terms corresponding to correct programs not typable in the standard Curry type assignment system [CF58], or in some polymorphic extensions as the one present in ML [Milner78], are typable with IT. Moreover, some IT systems satisfy the principal typing property, PT for short, which means that for any typable term M there is a type judgement $\Gamma \vdash M : \tau$ representing all possible typings $\langle \Gamma' \vdash \tau' \rangle$ of M in the corresponding type system. Principal typings has been studied for some IT systems [CDV80, RV84, Rocca88, Bakel95, KW04] and in [CDV80, RV84] it was shown that for a term M, the principal typing of M's β-normal form, β-nf for short, is principal for M itself.

In [VAK09] we introduced an IT system for the λ_{dB}, based on the type system given in [KN07], and proved it to satisfy the subject reduction property, SR for short, which states that types under β-reduction are preserved: whenever $\Gamma \vdash M : \sigma$ and M β-reduces into N, then $\Gamma \vdash N : \sigma$. Due to the interaction between sequential type contexts and the subtyping relation, the system in [VAK09] is not relevant in the sense of [DG94], whereas the system of [KN07] is. Hence, in [VAK10] we introduce a relevant IT system for λ_{dB}. This system is a de Bruijn version of the system originally introduced in [SM96a], for which we established a characterisation of the syntactic structure of PT for β-nfs.

In this paper we concentrate on the SR property, with a discussion originally presented in [VAK10], and we prove for the first time the property for the β-contraction in λ_{dB} with some considerations. We then propose a variant for the type system, which is a de Bruijn version of the system in [SM97]. We also give the first IT systems for $\lambda\sigma$ and λs_e, which we base on this variant, and we establish that they both have SR for the full rewriting system. As a preliminary step to obtain the system for λs_e, we introduce an IT system for λs [KR95], based on the system of [VAK10], with similar properties such as relevance and SR for the simulation of β-contraction.

Below, we present the untyped versions of the λ_{dB}, λs, λs_e and $\lambda \sigma$ calculi. Section 2 consists of two parts. In Subsection 2.1 we present the IT systems λ_{dB}^{SM} and λ_{dB}^{SMr}, followed by the relevance property and a discussion of the SR property. In Subsection 2.2 we present the new work on the system λ_{dB}^{SM}, introducing some properties related to the proof of SR for β-contraction in the type system, which is discussed at the end of the second part. In Section 3 we introduce the IT system λs^{SM} for λs and the system $\lambda s_e^{\wedge}$ for λs_e, with their respective properties. In Section 4, the IT system for $\lambda \sigma$ is introduced followed by its properties.

1.1 λ-Calculus with de Bruijn Indices

Definition 1 (Set Λ_{dB}). *The set of λ_{dB}-term, denoted by Λ_{dB}, is inductively defined for $n \in \mathbb{N}^* = \mathbb{N} \setminus \{0\}$ by: $M, N \in \Lambda_{dB} ::= \underline{n} \mid (M\ N) \mid \lambda.M$.*

The index $\underline{i}$ is bound if it is inside i λ's and otherwise it is free. We introduce the following subsets in order to present a formal definition of the set of free indices for some term.

Definition 2. *Let $N \subset \mathbb{N}^*$ and $k \geq 0$. We define:*
   1.$N \backslash k = \{n - k \mid n \in N\}$ 3.$N + k = \{n + k \mid n \in N\}$
   2.$N_{>k} = \{n \in N \mid n > k\}$ 4.$N_{\leq k} = \{n \in N \mid n \leq k\}$, $N_{<k} = \{n \in N \mid n < k\}$

Definition 3. *$FI(M)$, the **set of free indices** of $M \in \Lambda_{dB}$, is defined by:*
   $FI(\underline{n}) = \{\underline{n}\}$ $FI(M_1 \ M_2) = FI(M_1) \cup FI(M_2)$ $FI(\lambda.M) = FI(M) \backslash 1$

The free indices correspond to the notion of free variables in the λ-calculus with names, hence M is called closed when $FI(M) \equiv \emptyset$. The greatest value of $FI(M)$ is denoted by $sup(M)$. In [VAK09] we give the formal definitions of those concepts. Terms like $((\ldots((M_1 \ M_2) \ M_3) \ldots) \ M_n)$ are written $(M_1 \ M_2 \cdots M_n)$, as usual. The β-contraction definition in this notation needs a mechanism which detects and updates free indices of terms. Intuitively, the **lift** of M, denoted by M^+, corresponds to an increment by 1 of all free indices occurring in M. Thus, we are able to present the definition of the substitution used by β-contractions, similarly to the one presented in [AK01].

Definition 4. *Let $m, n \in \mathbb{N}^*$. The **β-substitution** for free occurrences of $\underline{n}$ in $M \in \Lambda_{dB}$ by term N, denoted as $\{\underline{n}/N\}M$, is defined inductively by*

1. $\{\underline{n}/N\}(M_1 \ M_2) = (\{\underline{n}/N\}M_1 \ \{\underline{n}/N\}M_2)$ 3. $\{\underline{n}/N\}\underline{m} = \begin{cases} \underline{m-1}, & \text{if } m > n \\ N, & \text{if } m = n \\ \underline{m}, & \text{if } m < n \end{cases}$
2. $\{\underline{n}/N\}(\lambda.M_1) = \lambda.\{\underline{n+1}/N^+\}M_1$

Observe that in item 2 of Definition 4, the lift operator is used to avoid the capture of free indices in N. We define β-contraction as usual (e.g. see [AK01]).

Definition 5. *β-**contraction** in λ_{dB} is defined by $(\lambda.M \ N) \rightarrow_\beta \{\underline{1}/N\}M$.*

Notice that item 3 in Definition 4 is the mechanism which does the substitution and updating of the free indices in M as a consequence of the elimination of the lead abstractor. β-**reduction** is defined to be the λ-compatible closure of β-contraction defined above. A term is in β-**normal form**, β-nf for short, if there is no β-reduction to be done. When $\underline{i} \notin FI(M)$, then we have that $\{\underline{i}/N\}M = M^{-i}$, where M^{-i} is the term M in which indices greater than i are decreased by one. We call this an **empty substitution** because no index is replaced by an instance of term N. The β-contraction $(\lambda.M \ N) \rightarrow \{\underline{1}/N\}M$ is thus called an **empty application**.

1.2   The λs_e-Calculus

The λs-calculus is a proper extension of the λ_{dB}-calculus. Two operators σ and φ are introduced for substitution and updating, respectively, to control the atomisation of the substitution operation by arithmetic constraints.

Definition 6 (Set Λs). *The set of λs-terms, denoted by Λs, is inductively defined for $n, i, j \in \mathbb{N}^*$ and $k \in \mathbb{N}$ by: $M, N \in \Lambda s ::= \underline{n} \mid (M \ N) \mid \lambda.M \mid M \sigma^i N \mid \varphi_k^j M$.*

The term $M\sigma^i N$ represents the procedure to obtain the term $\{\underline{i}/N^{+(i-1)}\}M$; i.e., the substitution of the free occurrences of $\underline{i}$ in M by N with its free indices incremented by $(i-1)$, updating the free indices on both terms. The term $\varphi_k^j M$ represents $j-1$ applications of the k-lift to the term M; i.e., $M^{+k^{(j-1)}}$. Table 1 contains the rewriting rules of the λs_e-calculus as given in [KR97]. The bottom six rules of Table 1 are those which extend the λs-calculus [KR95] to λs_e [KR97]. They ensure the confluence of the λs_e-calculus on open terms and its application to the HOU problem [AK01]. In this paper we work with the same set Λs of terms for both calculi.

Table 1. The rewriting system of the λs_e-calculus

$(\lambda.M\ N)$	$\longrightarrow M\,\sigma^1 N$	$(\sigma\text{-generation})$
$(\lambda.M)\sigma^i N$	$\longrightarrow \lambda.(M\sigma^{i+1}N)$	$(\sigma\text{-}\lambda\text{-transition})$
$(M_1\ M_2)\sigma^i N$	$\longrightarrow ((M_1\sigma^i N)\ (M_2\sigma^i N))$	$(\sigma\text{-app-trans.})$
$\underline{n}\,\sigma^i N$	$\longrightarrow \begin{cases} \underline{n-1}\ \text{if}\ n>i \\ \varphi_0^i N\ \text{if}\ n=i \\ \underline{n}\quad\ \text{if}\ n<i \end{cases}$	$(\sigma\text{-destruction})$
$\varphi_k^i(\lambda.M)$	$\longrightarrow \lambda.(\varphi_{k+1}^i M)$	$(\varphi\text{-}\lambda\text{-trans.})$
$\varphi_k^i(M_1\ M_2)$	$\longrightarrow ((\varphi_k^i M_1)\ (\varphi_k^i M_2))$	$(\varphi\text{-app-trans.})$
$\varphi_k^i\,\underline{n}$	$\longrightarrow \begin{cases} \underline{n+i-1}\ \text{if}\ n>k \\ \underline{n}\qquad \text{if}\ n\le k \end{cases}$	$(\varphi\text{-destruction})$
$(M_1\sigma^i M_2)\sigma^j N$	$\longrightarrow (M_1\sigma^{j+1}N)\sigma^i(M_2\sigma^{j-i+1}N)$ if $i\le j$	$(\sigma\text{-}\sigma\text{-trans.})$
$(\varphi_k^i M)\sigma^j N$	$\longrightarrow \varphi_k^{i-1}M$ if $k<j<k+i$	$(\sigma\text{-}\varphi\text{-trans. 1})$
$(\varphi_k^i M)\sigma^j N$	$\longrightarrow \varphi_k^i(M\sigma^{j-i+1}N)$ if $k+i\le j$	$(\sigma\text{-}\varphi\text{-trans. 2})$
$\varphi_k^i(M\sigma^j N)$	$\longrightarrow (\varphi_{k+1}^i M)\sigma^j(\varphi_{k+1-j}^i N)$ if $j\le k+1$	$(\varphi\text{-}\sigma\text{-trans.})$
$\varphi_k^i(\varphi_l^j M)$	$\longrightarrow \varphi_l^j(\varphi_{k+1-j}^i M)$ if $l+j\le k$	$(\varphi\text{-}\varphi\text{-trans. 1})$
$\varphi_k^i(\varphi_l^j M)$	$\longrightarrow \varphi_l^{j+i-1}M$ if $l\le k<l+j$	$(\varphi\text{-}\varphi\text{-trans. 2})$

$=_{s_e}$ denotes the equality for the associate substitution calculus, denoted as s_e, induced by all the rules except $(\sigma\text{-generation})$. The rewriting system obtained by removing from s_e the bottom six rules presented in Table 1 is called the s-calculus, which is the substitution calculus associated with λs. In order to have a syntactic characterisation related to empty applications and substitutions, as the free indices for λ_{dB}, we present the available indices, a notion analogous to that of available variables introduced in [LLDDvB04].

Definition 7. $AI(M)$, *the* **set of available indices** *of* $M \in \Lambda s$ *is defined by:*
$AI(\underline{n}) = \{\underline{n}\}$ $AI(\lambda.M) = AI(M)\backslash 1$ $AI(M_1\ M_2) = AI(M_1)\cup AI(M_2)$ *and*
$AI(\varphi_k^i M) = AI(M)_{\le k}\cup(AI(M)_{>k}+(i-1))$
$AI(M\sigma^i N) = \begin{cases} AI(M^{-i})\cup AI(\varphi_0^i N), & \text{if}\ i\in AI(M) \\ AI(M^{-i}), & \text{if}\ i\notin AI(M) \end{cases}$
where $AI(M^{-i})$ *denotes* $AI(M)_{<i}\cup(AI(M)_{>i})\backslash 1$.

The greatest value of $AI(M)$ is denoted by $sav(M)$.

1.3   The $\lambda\sigma$-Calculus

The $\lambda\sigma$-calculus is given by a first-order rewriting system, which makes substitutions explicit by extending the language with two sorts of objects: **terms** and **substitutions** which are called $\lambda\sigma$-expressions.

Definition 8 (Set $\Lambda\sigma$). *The set of $\lambda\sigma$-expressions, denoted by $\Lambda\sigma$, is formed by the set $\Lambda\sigma^t$ of terms and the set $\Lambda\sigma^s$ of substitutions, inductively defined by:*
$$M, N \in \Lambda\sigma^t ::= \underline{1} \,|\, (M\ N) \,|\, \lambda.M \,|\, M[S] \qquad S \in \Lambda\sigma^s ::= id \,|\, \uparrow \,|\, M.S \,|\, S \circ S.$$

Substitutions can intuitively be thought of as lists of the form $N/\underline{i}$ indicating that the index $\underline{i}$ ought to be replaced by the term N. The expression id represents a substitution of the form $\{\underline{1}/\underline{1}, \underline{2}/\underline{2}, \dots\}$ whereas $\uparrow$ is the substitution $\{\underline{i+1}/\underline{i} \,|\, i \in \mathbb{N}^*\}$. The expression $S \circ S$ represents the composition of substitutions. Moreover, $\underline{1}[\uparrow^n]$, where $n \in \mathbb{N}^*$, codifies the de Bruijn index $\underline{n+1}$ and $\underline{i}[S]$ represents the value of $\underline{i}$ through the substitution S, which can be seen as a function $S(i)$. The substitution $M.S$ has the form $\{M/\underline{1}, S(i)/\underline{i+1}\}$ and is called the **cons of M in S**. $M[N.id]$ starts the simulation of the β-reduction of $(\lambda.M\ N)$ in $\lambda\sigma$. Thus, in addition to the substitution of the free occurrences of the index $\underline{1}$ by the corresponding term, free occurrences of indices should be decremented because of the elimination of the abstractor. Table 2 lists the rewriting system of the $\lambda\sigma$-calculus, as presented in [DHK2000], without the (Eta) rule.

Table 2. The rewriting system for the $\lambda\sigma$-calculus

$(\lambda.M\ N)$	$\longrightarrow M[N.id]$	$(Beta)$	$(\lambda.M)[S]$	$\longrightarrow \lambda.(M[1.(S \circ \uparrow)])$	(Abs)
$(M\ N)[S]$	$\longrightarrow (M[S]\ N[S])$	(App)	$\uparrow \circ (M.S)$	$\longrightarrow S$	$(ShiftCons)$
$M[id]$	$\longrightarrow M$	(Id)	$(S_1 \circ S_2) \circ S_3$	$\longrightarrow S_1 \circ (S_2 \circ S_3)$	$(AssEnv)$
$1[S].(\uparrow \circ S)$	$\longrightarrow S$	$(Scons)$	$(M.S) \circ T$	$\longrightarrow M[T].(S \circ T)$	$(MapEnv)$
$(M[S])[T]$	$\longrightarrow M[S \circ T]$	$(Clos)$	$1.\uparrow$	$\longrightarrow id$	$(VarShift)$
$id \circ S$	$\longrightarrow S$	(IdL)	$1[M.S]$	$\longrightarrow M$	$(VarCons)$
$S \circ id$	$\longrightarrow S$	(IdR)			

This system is equivalent to that of [ACCL91]. The associated substitution calculus, denoted by σ, is the one induced by all the rules except (Beta), and its equality is denoted as $=_\sigma$.

2   Intersection Type Systems for the λ_{dB}-Calculus

The intersection type systems presented in this paper have the same set of types $\mathcal{T}$, of the so called restricted intersection types. The intersection types in $\mathcal{T}$ do not occur immediately on the right of an $\rightarrow$. Besides that, the intersection is linear thus non idempotent. The type contexts in type systems with de Bruijn indices are sequences of types. Below, we present the definitions of these concepts.

$$\frac{}{1:\langle \tau.nil \vdash \tau\rangle}\ \text{var} \qquad \frac{n:\langle \Gamma \vdash \tau\rangle}{n+1:\langle \omega.\Gamma \vdash \tau\rangle}\ \text{varn} \qquad \frac{M:\langle u.\Gamma \vdash \tau\rangle}{\lambda.M:\langle \Gamma \vdash u\to\tau\rangle}\ \to_i$$

$$\frac{M_1:\langle \Gamma \vdash \omega\to\tau\rangle \qquad M_2:\langle \Delta \vdash \sigma\rangle}{(M_1\ M_2):\langle \Gamma \wedge \Delta \vdash \tau\rangle}\ \to'_e \qquad \frac{M:\langle nil \vdash \tau\rangle}{\lambda.M:\langle nil \vdash \omega\to\tau\rangle}\ \to'_i$$

$$\frac{M_1:\langle \Gamma \vdash \wedge_{i=1}^{n}\sigma_i\to\tau\rangle \qquad M_2:\langle \Delta^1 \vdash \sigma_1\rangle \ \dots \ M_2:\langle \Delta^n \vdash \sigma_n\rangle}{(M_1\ M_2):\langle \Gamma \wedge \Delta^1 \wedge \cdots \wedge \Delta^n \vdash \tau\rangle}\ \to_e$$

Fig. 1. Typing rules of system λ_{dB}^{SM}

Definition 9. *1. Let $\mathcal{A}$ be a denumerably infinite* **set of type variables** *and let α, β range over $\mathcal{A}$.*

2. The set $\mathcal{T}$ of **restricted intersection types** *is defined by:*

$$\tau, \sigma \in \mathcal{T} ::= \mathcal{A} \mid \mathcal{U}\to\mathcal{T} \qquad u \in \mathcal{U} ::= \omega \mid \mathcal{U} \wedge \mathcal{U} \mid \mathcal{T}$$

Types are quotiented by taking $\wedge$ to be commutative, associative and to have ω as the neutral element.

3. **Contexts** *are ordered lists of $u \in \mathcal{U}$, defined by: $\Gamma ::= nil \mid u.\Gamma$. Γ_i denotes the i-th element of Γ and $|\Gamma|$ denotes the length of Γ. We let $\omega^{\underline{n}}$ denote the sequence $\omega.\omega.\cdots.\omega$ of length n, called* **omega context**, *and let $\omega^{\underline{0}}.\Gamma = \Gamma$. The extension of $\wedge$ to contexts is done by taking nil as the neutral element and $(u_1.\Gamma) \wedge (u_2.\Delta) = (u_1 \wedge u_2).(\Gamma \wedge \Delta)$. Hence, $\wedge$ is commutative and associative on contexts.*

4. Let $u' \sqsubseteq u$ if there exists v such that $u = u' \wedge v$ and $u' \sqsubset u$ if $v \neq \omega$. Let $\Gamma' \sqsubseteq \Gamma$ if there exists Δ such that $\Gamma = \Gamma' \wedge \Delta$, where neither Γ' nor Δ are omega contexts and $\Gamma' \sqsubset \Gamma$ if $\Delta \neq nil$.

The set $\mathcal{T}$ defined here is equivalent to the one defined in [SM96a]. Type judgements will be of the form $M:\langle \Gamma \vdash_{\mathfrak{S}} \tau\rangle$, meaning that in system $\mathfrak{S}$, term M has type τ in context Γ (where $FI(M)$ are handled). Briefly, M has type τ with Γ in $\mathfrak{S}$ or $\langle \Gamma \vdash \tau\rangle$ is a typing of M in S. The $\mathfrak{S}$ is omitted whenever its is clear which system is being referred to.

2.1 The System λ_{dB}^{SM}

We present in this section the systems λ_{dB}^{SM} and λ_{dB}^{SMr}, introduced in [VAK10]. The system λ_{dB}^{SMr} is the de Bruijn version of the system presented in [SM96a], used to characterise principal typings (PT) for β-nfs.

Definition 10. *1. The typing rules for system λ_{dB}^{SM} are given in Figure 1.*

2. System λ_{dB}^{SMr} is obtained from system λ_{dB}^{SM}, by replacing the rule var by rule

$$\text{var}_r:\ \frac{}{1:\langle \sigma_1 \to \cdots \to \sigma_n \to \alpha.nil \vdash \sigma_1 \to \cdots \to \sigma_n \to \alpha\rangle}\ (n \geq 0).$$

Proposition 1. λ_{dB}^{SM} *is a proper extension of* λ_{dB}^{SMr}.

Hence, the properties stated for the system λ_{dB}^{SM} are also true for the system λ_{dB}^{SMr}. The following lemma states that λ_{dB}^{SM} is relevant in the sense of [DG94].

Lemma 1 (Relevance for λ_{dB}^{SM} [VAK10]). *If* $M : \langle \Gamma \vdash_{\lambda_{dB}^{SM}} \tau \rangle$, *then* $|\Gamma| = sup(M)$ *and* $\forall 1 \leq i \leq |\Gamma|$, $\Gamma_i \neq \omega$ *iff* $\underline{i} \in FI(M)$.

Note that, by Lemma 1 above, system λ_{dB}^{SM} is not only relevant but there is a strict relation between the free indices of terms and the length of contexts in their typings. In [VAK10] we give a characterisation of PT for β-nfs in λ_{dB}^{SMr}.

Despite the fact that all β-nfs are typable in λ_{dB}^{SMr}, the subject reduction property fails for both λ_{dB}^{SMr} and λ_{dB}^{SM}. In the following, we will give counterexamples to show that neither subject expansion nor reduction holds.

Example 1. In order to have the subject expansion property, we need to prove the statement: If $\{\underline{1}/N\}M : \langle \Gamma \vdash \tau \rangle$ then $(\lambda.M\ N) : \langle \Gamma \vdash \tau \rangle$. Let $M \equiv \lambda.\underline{1}$ and $N \equiv \underline{3}$, hence $\{\underline{1}/\underline{3}\}\lambda.\underline{1} = \lambda.\underline{1}$. We have that $\lambda.\underline{1} : \langle nil \vdash \alpha \rightarrow \alpha \rangle$. Thus, $\lambda.\lambda.\underline{1} : \langle nil \vdash \omega \rightarrow \alpha \rightarrow \alpha \rangle$ and $\underline{3} : \langle \omega.\omega.\beta.nil \vdash \beta \rangle$, then $(\lambda.\lambda.\underline{1}\ \underline{3}) : \langle \omega.\omega.\beta.nil \vdash \alpha \rightarrow \alpha \rangle$.

For subject reduction, we need the statement: If $(\lambda.M\ N) : \langle \Gamma \vdash \tau \rangle$ then $\{\underline{1}/N\}M : \langle \Gamma \vdash \tau \rangle$. Note that if we take M and N as in the example above, we get the same problem as before but the other way round. In other words, we have a restriction on the original context after the β-reduction, since we loose the typing information regarding $N \equiv \underline{3}$. □

One possible solution is to replace rule $\rightarrow'_e$ by: $\dfrac{M : \langle \Gamma \vdash \omega \rightarrow \tau \rangle}{(M\ N) : \langle \Gamma \vdash \tau \rangle}$.

This approach was originally presented in [SM96b]. However, the type system obtained there does not have the property described in Lemma 1 since we would not have the typing information for all the free indices occurring in a term. We present a lemma at the end of the present section, stating the property related to relevance for this variant.

The other way to try to achieve the desired properties is to think about the meaning of the properties themselves. Since, by Lemma 1, the system is related to relevant logic (cf. [DG94]), the notion of expansion and restriction of contexts is an interesting way to talk about subject expansion and reduction. These concepts were presented in [KN07] for environments. We introduce the notion of restriction for sequential contexts in Subsection 2.2. This approach of restriction/expansion for contexts is not sufficient to have the subject expansion property because the rule $\rightarrow'_e$ has the typability of the argument as a premiss. Hence, for any non typable term N, $\{\underline{1}/N\}\underline{2}$ is typable while $(\lambda.\underline{2}\ N)$ is not typable in system λ_{dB}^{SM}. Below, we define the system which is the basis for the IT systems we propose for λs_e and $\lambda\sigma$.

Definition 11 (The system $\lambda_{dB}^{\wedge}$). *The system $\lambda_{dB}^{\wedge}$ is obtained from system* λ_{dB}^{SM}, *replacing the rule $\rightarrow'_e$ by the following rule:* $\dfrac{M : \langle \Gamma \vdash \omega \rightarrow \tau \rangle}{(M\ N) : \langle \Gamma \vdash \tau \rangle} \rightarrow_e^{\omega}$.

The following property is related to relevance in this system.

Lemma 2. *If* $M : \langle \Gamma \vdash_{\lambda_{dB}^{\wedge}} \tau \rangle$ *and* $|\Gamma| = m > 0$ *then* $\Gamma_m \neq \omega$ *and* $\forall 1 \leq i \leq |\Gamma|$, $\Gamma_i \neq \omega$ *implies* $\underline{i} \in FI(M)$.

Proof. By induction on the derivation $M : \langle \Gamma \vdash_{\lambda_{dB}^{\wedge}} \tau \rangle$.

2.2   Subject Reduction for System λ_{dB}^{SM}

We present here the properties of system λ_{dB}^{SM} used in the proof of SR, presented at the end of this part. The generation lemmas for λ_{dB}^{SM} were presented in [VAK10] and we omit them here due to lack of space. Below, we give a lemma which relates typings and the updating operator.

Lemma 3 (Updating). *Let $M : \langle \Gamma \vdash_{\lambda_{dB}^{SM}} \tau \rangle$. If $i \geq |\Gamma|$ then $M^{+i} : \langle \Gamma \vdash_{\lambda_{dB}^{SM}} \tau \rangle$. Otherwise, if $0 \leq i < |\Gamma|$ then $M^{+i} : \langle \Gamma_{\leq i}.\omega.\Gamma_{>i} \vdash_{\lambda_{dB}^{SM}} \tau \rangle$.*

Observe that when $i \geq |\Gamma|$ then by the relevance of system λ_{dB}^{SM} we have that $i \geq sup(M)$ thus $M^{+i} = M$ (cf. [VAK09]). Otherwise, the free indices of M greater then i are incremented by one, then we need to add the ω at the $(i+1)$-th position on the sequential context to guarantee the typability for term M^{+i}. We now can introduce the substitutions lemmas.

Lemma 4 (Substitution). *Let $M : \langle \Gamma \vdash_{\lambda_{dB}^{SM}} \tau \rangle$.*

1. *If $i > |\Gamma|$ then, for any $N \in \Lambda_{dB}$, $\{\underline{i}/N\}M : \langle \Gamma \vdash_{\lambda_{dB}^{SM}} \tau \rangle$.*
2. *If $\Gamma_i = \omega$ where $0 < i < |\Gamma|$, then $\{\underline{i}/N\}M : \langle \Gamma_{<i}.\Gamma_{>i} \vdash_{\lambda_{dB}^{SM}} \tau \rangle$.*
3. *Let $\Gamma_i = \wedge_{j=1}^m \sigma_j$, where $0 < i \leq |\Gamma|$, and $\forall 1 \leq j \leq m$, $N : \langle nil \vdash_{\lambda_{dB}^{SM}} \sigma_j \rangle$. If $sup(M) = i$ then $\{\underline{i}/N\}M : \langle \Gamma_{<k}.nil \vdash_{\lambda_{dB}^{SM}} \tau \rangle$ for $k = sup(\{\underline{i}/N\}M)$. Otherwise, $\{\underline{i}/N\}M : \langle \Gamma_{<i}.\Gamma_{>i} \vdash_{\lambda_{dB}^{SM}} \tau \rangle$.*
4. *Let $\Gamma_i = \wedge_{j=1}^m \sigma_j$, where $0 < i \leq |\Gamma|$, and $N \in \Lambda_{dB}$ s.t. $sup(N) \geq i$. If $\forall 1 \leq j \leq m$, $N : \langle \Delta^j \vdash_{\lambda_{dB}^{SM}} \sigma_j \rangle$ then $\{\underline{i}/N\}M : \langle (\Gamma_{<i}.\Gamma_{>i}) \wedge \Delta^1 \wedge \cdots \wedge \Delta^m \vdash_{\lambda_{dB}^{SM}} \tau \rangle$.*

Hence, we have the relation between M and N typings and the typing for term $\{\underline{i}/N\}M$. Note that, whenever N is typable, items 1 and 2 represent the loss of its type information. Therefore, we need the restriction property for sequential contexts, introduced below, to establish the SR property.

Definition 12 (FI restriction). *Let $\Gamma\!\restriction_M$ be a $\Gamma' \sqsubseteq \Gamma$ such that $|\Gamma'| = sup(M)$ and that $\forall 1 \leq i \leq |\Gamma'|$, $\Gamma'_i \neq \omega$ iff $\underline{i} \in FI(M)$.*

Now we state the subject reduction property for β-contraction, using the concept introduced above.

Theorem 1 (SR for β-contraction in λ_{dB}^{SM}). *If $(\lambda.M\ N) : \langle \Gamma \vdash_{\lambda_{dB}^{SM}} \tau \rangle$ then $\{\underline{1}/N\}M : \langle \Gamma\!\restriction_{\{\underline{1}/N\}M} \vdash_{\lambda_{dB}^{SM}} \tau \rangle$.*

Proof. By case analysis of $(\lambda.M\ N) : \langle \Gamma \vdash_{\lambda_{dB}^{SM}} \tau \rangle$. Note that there are only two possibilities for the last inference step, the rules $\rightarrow'_e$ and $\rightarrow_e$. We present here the case when $\rightarrow'_e$ is the last rule applied. Hence, $\lambda.M : \langle \Gamma \vdash \omega \rightarrow \tau \rangle$ and $N : \langle \Delta \vdash \sigma \rangle$ for some context Δ and type σ. If $\Gamma = nil$ then $M : \langle nil \vdash \tau \rangle$. Hence, by a substitution lemma one has that $\{\underline{1}/N\}M : \langle nil \vdash \tau \rangle$. Note that $FI(\{\underline{1}/N\}M) = FI(M) = \emptyset$ thus $(nil \wedge \Delta)\!\restriction_{\{\underline{1}/N\}M} = nil$. The proof when $\Gamma \neq nil$ is similar.

Since the type information lost during β-contraction can affect the type as well, we would need a subtyping relation, and an associated inference rule, in order to obtain the SR property for β-reduction.

$$(\omega\text{-}\varphi) \ \frac{M:\langle \Gamma \vdash \tau\rangle}{\varphi_k^i M:\langle \Gamma_{\le k}.\omega \xrightarrow{i-1}.\Gamma_{>k} \vdash \tau\rangle}, |\Gamma| > k \qquad (\omega\text{-}\sigma) \ \frac{N:\langle \Delta \vdash \rho\rangle \qquad M:\langle \Gamma \vdash \tau\rangle}{M\sigma^i N:\langle \Gamma_{<i}.\Gamma_{>i} \vdash \tau\rangle}, \Gamma_i = \omega$$

$$(nil\text{-}\varphi) \ \frac{M:\langle \Gamma \vdash \tau\rangle}{\varphi_k^i M:\langle \Gamma \vdash \tau\rangle}, |\Gamma| \le k \qquad (nil\text{-}\sigma) \ \frac{N:\langle \Delta \vdash \rho\rangle \qquad M:\langle \Gamma \vdash \tau\rangle}{M\sigma^i N:\langle \Gamma \vdash \tau\rangle}, |\Gamma| < i$$

$$(\wedge\text{-}nil\text{-}\sigma) \ \frac{N:\langle nil \vdash \sigma_1\rangle \dots N:\langle nil \vdash \sigma_m\rangle \qquad M:\langle \omega \xrightarrow{i-1}. \wedge_{j=1}^m \sigma_j.nil \vdash \tau\rangle}{M\sigma^i N:\langle nil \vdash \tau\rangle}$$

$$(\wedge\text{-}\omega\text{-}\sigma) \ \frac{N:\langle nil \vdash \sigma_1\rangle \dots N:\langle nil \vdash \sigma_m\rangle \qquad M:\langle \Gamma \vdash \tau\rangle}{M\sigma^i N:\langle \Gamma_{<(i-k)}.nil \vdash \tau\rangle}, \Gamma_i = \wedge_{j=1}^m \sigma_j \ (*)$$

$$(\wedge\text{-}\sigma) \ \frac{N:\langle \Delta^1 \vdash \sigma_1\rangle \dots N:\langle \Delta^m \vdash \sigma_m\rangle \qquad M:\langle \Gamma \vdash \tau\rangle}{M\sigma^i N:\langle (\Gamma_{<i}.\Gamma_{>i}) \wedge \omega \xrightarrow{i-1}.(\Delta^1 \wedge \cdots \wedge \Delta^m) \vdash \tau\rangle}, \Gamma_i = \wedge_{j=1}^m \sigma_j \ (**)$$

$(*) \ \Gamma = \Gamma_{<(i-k)}.\omega \xrightarrow{k}. \wedge_{j=1}^m \sigma_j.nil$ and $\Gamma_{(i-k-1)} \ne \omega$ $\ (**) \ \Delta^k \ne nil$, for some $1 \le k \le m$, or $\Gamma_{>i} \ne nil$

Fig. 2. Typing rules of the system λs^{SM}

3 An Intersection Type System for λs_e

In order to have an intersection type system for the λs_e-calculus, we introduce a system for λs as a first step. While the type system for λs is based on the system λ_{dB}^{SM}, the system proposed for λs_e is based on the system $\lambda_{dB}^{\wedge}$.

3.1 The System λs^{SM}

Definition 13 (The system λs^{SM}). *The system λs^{SM} is the extension of system λ_{dB}^{SM}, introduced in Definition 10, by the rules presented in Figure 2.*

Observe that, compared with the simple type system for λs and λs_e, which introduces one type inference rule for each operator (cf. [AK01]), there are multiple rules introduced in Figure 2 for the σ and φ operators. This multiplicity reproduces the cases for the updating and substitution lemmas for λ_{dB}^{SM}. For instance, the rule $(nil\text{-}\varphi)$ maintains the same context, since the updating operator will not affect any of the available indices of the corresponding term. Hence, we have a relevance property related to $AI(M)$ instead of $FI(M)$, as stated below.

Lemma 5 (Relevance for λs^{SM}). *If $M:\langle \Gamma \vdash_{\lambda s^{SM}} \tau\rangle$, then $|\Gamma| = sav(M)$ and $\forall 1 \le i \le |\Gamma|, \ \Gamma_i \ne \omega$ iff $\underline{i} \in AI(M)$.*

Proof. By induction on the derivation of $M:\langle \Gamma \vdash_{\lambda s^{SM}} \tau\rangle$. We present the case for the application of the rule $(nil\text{-}\varphi)$. Hence, $\varphi_k^i M:\langle \Gamma \vdash \tau\rangle$ where $M:\langle \Gamma \vdash \tau\rangle$ and $|\Gamma| \le k$. By the induction hypothesis (IH) one has that $|\Gamma| = sav(M)$ and $\forall 1 \le j \le |\Gamma|, \ \Gamma_j \ne \omega$ iff $\underline{j} \in AI(M)$. Observe that $AI(\varphi_k^i M) = AI(M)_{\le k} \cup (AI(M)_{>k} + (i-1)) = AI(M)$ thus $sav(\varphi_k^i M) = sav(M)$.

Despite the fact that the type system is relevant, we have SR for the full s-calculus.

Theorem 2 (SR for s in λs^{SM}). *Let $M : \langle \Gamma \vdash_{\lambda_s SM} \tau \rangle$. If $M \rightarrow_s M'$, then $M' : \langle \Gamma \vdash_{\lambda_s SM} \tau \rangle$.*

Proof. By the verification of SR for each rewriting rule of the s-calculus.

Observe that the type information associated to the empty application disappears when it becomes an empty substitution, since the rules $(nil$-$\sigma)$ and $(\omega$-$\sigma)$ discard the corresponding contexts. Therefore, we need a restriction notion similar to the one introduced in Definition 12, which is related to the available indices, to have an SR statement for the simulation of β-contraction.

Definition 14 (AI restriction). *Let $\Gamma \restriction_M$ be a $\Gamma' \sqsubseteq \Gamma$ such that $|\Gamma'| = sav(M)$ and that $\forall 1 \leq i \leq |\Gamma'|$, $\Gamma'_i \neq \omega$ iff $i \in AI(M)$.*

Theorem 3 (SR for simulation of β-contraction in λs^{SM}). *If $(\lambda.M\ M')$: $\langle \Gamma \vdash_{\lambda_s SM} \tau \rangle$, then $\{\underline{1}/M'\}M : \langle \Gamma \restriction_{\{\underline{1}/M'\}M} \vdash_{\lambda_s SM} \tau \rangle$, for any $(\lambda.M\ M') \in \Lambda_{dB}$.*

Proof. The proof consists in the verification of SR with context restriction for $(\lambda.M\ M') : \langle \Gamma \vdash_{\lambda_s SM} \tau \rangle$ when the rule (σ-generation) is applied and then of SR for the s-calculus.

3.2   The System $\lambda s_e{}^{\wedge}$

While the λs-calculus has the preservation of strong normalisation property [KR95], PSN for short, the rules allowing the composition of substitution in the λs_e-calculus invalidate this property for the calculus. B. Guillaume presents in [Guillaume2000] a counter example of some simply typed term in λs_e which has an infinite reduction strategy. We present an example below, to give an intuition on how to change the system λs^{SM} to have an intersection type system for λs_e with the subject reduction property.

Example 2. Let $A \equiv (\underline{1}\ \underline{1})$, $M \equiv (\underline{3}\,\sigma^1 A)\,\sigma^1 \lambda.A$, $M' \equiv (\underline{3}\,\sigma^2 \lambda.A)\,\sigma^1 (A\,\sigma^1 \lambda.A)$. We have that $M \rightarrow_{\lambda s_e} M'$, where M is typable in λs^{SM} and M' is not typable. Observe that one cannot obtain M' from M in λs and that M is obtained from the term $M_0 \equiv (\lambda.(\lambda.\underline{3}\ A)\ \lambda.A)$ in both calculi.   □

The non typability of the term M_0 above in the system $\lambda s^{\varepsilon M}$ is due to the inclusion of type information from the context of an argument to an empty application. Note that the typability of both M_0 and $A\,\sigma^1 \lambda.A$ reduces to the typability of $\Omega \equiv (\lambda.A\ \lambda.A)$ which has no type in systems like the Barendregt et al. [BCD83] other then the universal ω type. Hence, we drop the typability requirement on rules $\rightarrow'_e$, $(nil$-$\sigma)$ and $(\omega$-$\sigma)$, obtaining the system $\lambda s_e{}^{\wedge}$ below.

$$\frac{}{\underline{1}:\langle \tau.nil \vdash \tau\rangle}\ var \qquad \frac{\underline{n}:\langle \Gamma \vdash \tau\rangle}{\underline{n+1}:\langle \omega.\Gamma \vdash \tau\rangle}\ varn \qquad \frac{M:\langle u.\Gamma \vdash \tau\rangle}{\lambda.M:\langle \Gamma \vdash u\to\tau\rangle}\ \to_i$$

$$\frac{M_1:\langle \Gamma \vdash \omega\to\tau\rangle}{(M_1\ M_2):\langle \Gamma \vdash \tau\rangle}\ \to_e^\omega \qquad \frac{M:\langle nil \vdash \tau\rangle}{\lambda.M:\langle nil \vdash \omega\to\tau\rangle}\ \to_i'$$

$$\frac{M_1:\langle \Gamma \vdash \wedge_{i=1}^n \sigma_i \to\tau\rangle \quad M_2:\langle \Delta^1 \vdash \sigma_1\rangle\ \ldots\ M_2:\langle \Delta^n \vdash \sigma_n\rangle}{(M_1\ M_2):\langle \Gamma \wedge \Delta^1 \wedge \cdots \wedge \Delta^n \vdash \tau\rangle}\ \to_e$$

$$(nil\text{-}\sigma)\ \frac{M:\langle \Gamma \vdash \tau\rangle}{M\sigma^i N:\langle \Gamma \vdash \tau\rangle},\ |\Gamma| < i \qquad (\omega\text{-}\sigma)\ \frac{M:\langle \Gamma \vdash \tau\rangle}{M\sigma^i N:\langle \Gamma_{<i}.\Gamma_{>i} \vdash \tau\rangle},\ \Gamma_i = \omega$$

$$(\wedge\text{-}nil\text{-}\sigma)\ \frac{N:\langle nil \vdash \sigma_1\rangle\ \ldots\ N:\langle nil \vdash \sigma_m\rangle \quad M:\langle \omega^{\underline{i-1}}.\wedge_{j=1}^m \sigma_j.nil \vdash \tau\rangle}{M\sigma^i N:\langle nil \vdash \tau\rangle}$$

$$(\wedge\text{-}\omega\text{-}\sigma)\ \frac{N:\langle nil \vdash \sigma_1\rangle\ \ldots\ N:\langle nil \vdash \sigma_m\rangle \quad M:\langle \Gamma \vdash \tau\rangle}{M\sigma^i N:\langle \Gamma_{<(i-k)}.nil \vdash \tau\rangle},\ \Gamma_i = \wedge_{j=1}^m \sigma_j\ (*)$$

$$(\wedge\text{-}\sigma)\ \frac{N:\langle \Delta^1 \vdash \sigma_1\rangle\ \ldots\ N:\langle \Delta^m \vdash \sigma_m\rangle \quad M:\langle \Gamma \vdash \tau\rangle}{M\sigma^i N:\langle ((\Gamma_{<i}.\Gamma_{>i}) \wedge \omega^{\underline{i-1}}.(\Delta^1 \wedge \cdots \wedge \Delta^m)) \vdash \tau\rangle},\ \Gamma_i = \wedge_{j=1}^m \sigma_j\ (**)$$

$$(\omega\text{-}\varphi)\ \frac{M:\langle \Gamma \vdash \tau\rangle}{\varphi_k^i M:\langle \Gamma_{\leq k}.\omega^{\underline{i-1}}.\Gamma_{>k} \vdash \tau\rangle},\ |\Gamma| > k \qquad (nil\text{-}\varphi)\ \frac{M:\langle \Gamma \vdash \tau\rangle}{\varphi_k^i M:\langle \Gamma \vdash \tau\rangle},\ |\Gamma| \leq k$$

$(*)\ \Gamma = \Gamma_{<(i-k)}.\omega^{\underline{k}}.\wedge_{j=1}^m \sigma_j.nil$ and $\Gamma_{(i-k-1)} \neq \omega$ $(**)\ \Delta^k \neq nil$, for some $1\leq k\leq m$, or $\Gamma_{>i} \neq nil$

Fig. 3. Typing rules of the system $\lambda s_e^\wedge$

Definition 15 (The system $\lambda s_e^\wedge$). *The inference rules for $\lambda s_e^\wedge$ are given by the rules of the system λs_{dB}^{SM} in Figure 1 and the system λs^{SM} in Figure 2, where the inference rule $\to_e'$, $(nil\text{-}\sigma)$ and $(\omega\text{-}\sigma)$ are replaced by the rules below:*

$$\frac{M:\langle \Gamma \vdash \omega\to\tau\rangle}{(M\ N):\langle \Gamma \vdash \tau\rangle}\ \to_e^\omega \qquad (nil\text{-}\sigma)\ \frac{M:\langle \Gamma \vdash \tau\rangle}{M\sigma^i N:\langle \Gamma \vdash \tau\rangle},\ |\Gamma| \leq i$$

$$(\omega\text{-}\sigma)\ \frac{M:\langle \Gamma \vdash \tau\rangle}{M\sigma^i N:\langle \Gamma_{<i}.\Gamma_{>i} \vdash \tau\rangle},\ \Gamma_i = \omega$$

The system $\lambda s_e^\wedge$ is presented in Figure 3.

The system $\lambda s_e^\wedge$ does not have a defined correspondence relating some syntactic characterisation and relevance. However, the system has a property related to relevance, stated below.

Lemma 6. *If $M:\langle \Gamma \vdash_{\lambda s_e^\wedge} \tau\rangle$ for $|\Gamma| = m > 0$, then $\Gamma_m \neq \omega$ and $\forall 1 \leq i \leq m$, $\Gamma_i \neq \omega$ implies $\underline{i} \in AI(M)$.*

Proof. By induction on the derivation of $M:\langle \Gamma \vdash_{\lambda s_e^\wedge} \tau\rangle$ when $\Gamma \neq nil$.

$$\frac{}{\underline{1}:\langle \tau.nil \vdash \tau \rangle}\ (\text{var}) \qquad\qquad \frac{M:\langle u.\Gamma \vdash \tau \rangle}{\lambda.M:\langle \Gamma \vdash u \to \tau \rangle}\ \to_i$$

$$\frac{M_1:\langle \Gamma \vdash \omega \to \tau \rangle}{(M_1\ M_2):\langle \Gamma \vdash \tau \rangle}\ \to_e^\omega \qquad\qquad \frac{M:\langle nil \vdash \tau \rangle}{\lambda.M:\langle nil \vdash \omega \to \tau \rangle}\ \to_i'$$

$$\frac{M_1:\langle \Gamma \vdash \wedge_{i=1}^m \sigma_i \to \tau \rangle \qquad M_2:\langle \Delta^1 \vdash \sigma_1 \rangle \ \ldots \ M_2:\langle \Delta^m \vdash \sigma_m \rangle}{(M_1\ M_2):\langle \Gamma \wedge \Delta^1 \wedge \cdots \wedge \Delta^m \vdash \tau \rangle}\ \to_e$$

$$(\text{clos})\ \frac{S:\langle \Gamma \rhd \Gamma' \rangle \qquad M:\langle \Gamma' \vdash \tau \rangle}{M[S]:\langle \Gamma \vdash \tau \rangle}$$

$$(\wedge\text{-cons})\ \frac{M:\langle \Delta^1 \vdash \sigma_1 \rangle \ \ldots \ M:\langle \Delta^m \vdash \sigma_m \rangle \qquad S:\langle \Delta \rhd \Delta' \rangle}{M.S:\langle \Delta \wedge \Delta^1 \wedge \cdots \wedge \Delta^m \rhd (\wedge_{i=1}^m \sigma_i).\Delta' \rangle}$$

$$(\text{id})\ \frac{\Gamma \neq \Delta.\omega^{\underline{m}}}{id:\langle \Gamma \rhd \Gamma \rangle} \qquad\qquad (\text{comp})\ \frac{S:\langle \Gamma \rhd \Gamma'' \rangle \qquad S':\langle \Gamma'' \rhd \Gamma' \rangle}{S' \circ S:\langle \Gamma \rhd \Gamma' \rangle}$$

$$(\textit{nil}\text{-shift})\ \frac{}{\uparrow:\langle nil \rhd nil \rangle} \qquad\qquad (\textit{nil}\text{-cons})\ \frac{S:\langle \Delta \rhd nil \rangle}{M.S:\langle \Delta \rhd nil \rangle}$$

$$(\omega\text{-shift})\ \frac{\Gamma \neq \Delta.\omega^{\underline{n}}}{\uparrow:\langle \omega.\Gamma \rhd \Gamma \rangle} \qquad\qquad (\omega\text{-cons})\ \frac{S:\langle \Delta \rhd \Delta' \rangle}{M.S:\langle \Delta \rhd \omega.\Delta' \rangle},\ \Delta' \neq \omega^{\underline{n}}$$

Fig. 4. The inference rules for the system $\lambda\sigma^\wedge$

We can prove the subject reduction property for the λs_e-calculus in a standard way, proving some generation lemmas first, where only the $\Gamma_m \neq \omega$ piece of the statement above is needed. Below, we present the subject reduction theorem.

Theorem 4 (SR for $\lambda s_e^\wedge$). *If $M : \langle \Gamma \vdash_{\lambda s_e^\wedge} \tau \rangle$ and $M \to_{\lambda s_e} M'$, then $M' : \langle \Gamma \vdash_{\lambda s_e^\wedge} \tau \rangle$.*

Proof. By the verification of SR for each λs_e rewriting rule.

4   An Intersection Type System for $\lambda\sigma$

Similar to the intersection type system proposed for λs_e, the type system for $\lambda\sigma$ discards any type information from contexts of terms which are related to empty applications.

Definition 16 (The system $\lambda\sigma^\wedge$). *The typing rules for the system $\lambda\sigma^\wedge$ are presented in Figure 4, where $m > 0$ and $n \geq 0$.*

The next lemma states the property of the system $\lambda\sigma^\wedge$ related to relevance.

Lemma 7. *If $M : \langle \Gamma \vdash_{\lambda\sigma^\wedge} \tau \rangle$ and $|\Gamma| = m > 0$, then $\Gamma_m \neq \omega$. In particular, if $S:\langle \Gamma \rhd_{\lambda\sigma^\wedge} \Gamma' \rangle$ and $|\Gamma|=m>0$ then $\Gamma_m \neq \omega$ and if $|\Gamma'|=m'>0$ then $\Gamma'_{m'} \neq \omega$.*

Proof. By induction on the derivation of $M : \langle \Gamma \vdash_{\lambda\sigma^\wedge} \tau \rangle$ when $\Gamma \neq nil$, with subinduction on the derivation of $S : \langle \Gamma \rhd_{\lambda\sigma^\wedge} \Gamma' \rangle$ when $\Gamma \neq nil$ or $\Gamma' \neq nil$.

Now we establish the SR property for the $\lambda\sigma$-calculus in this system.

Theorem 5 (SR for $\lambda\sigma^\wedge$). *If $M : \langle \Gamma \vdash_{\lambda\sigma^\wedge} \tau \rangle$ and $M \rightarrow_{\lambda\sigma} M'$ then $M' : \langle \Gamma \vdash_{\lambda\sigma^\wedge} \tau \rangle$. In particular, if $S : \langle \Gamma \rhd_{\lambda\sigma^\wedge} \Gamma' \rangle$ and $S \rightarrow_{\lambda\sigma} S'$ then $S' : \langle \Gamma \rhd_{\lambda\sigma^\wedge} \Gamma' \rangle$.*

Proof. By the verification of SR for each $\lambda\sigma$ rewriting rule.

5   Conclusion

In this paper, we proved the subject reduction property for β-contraction in the system λ_{dB}^{SM} [VAK10], using an adaptation for sequential contexts of the restricted environments, introduced in [KN07] to prove SR in a relevant intersection type system. Then, we introduced intersection type systems for two explicit substitution calculi, the $\lambda\sigma$ and the λs_e, and established that our two new systems satisfy the SR property. The simply typed version of these calculi have applications on the HOU problem [DHK2000, AK01] and, to the best of our knowledge, the IT systems presented here are the first polymorphic type systems proposed for them.

We intend to use the systems presented here as the basic system for studying the PT property in IT systems for both calculi. The PT property allows one to include features in a type system which include separate compilation, data abstraction and smartest recompilation [Jim96]. The system $\lambda_{dB}^\wedge$, briefly mentioned at the end of Subsection 2.1, is a de Bruijn version of the system in [SM97], were the PT property for β-nfs described in [SM96a] is extended for any normalisable term. Hence, as a first step towards the PT for explicit substitutions, we need to extend the results presented in [VAK10] to normalisable terms in λ_{dB}. Besides that, we believe that the systems λ_{dB}^{SM} and λs^{SM} are able to provide a characterisation for strongly normalising terms in λ_{dB} and λs, respectively. On the other hand, it seems that $\lambda_{dB}^\wedge$, $\lambda s_e^\wedge$ and $\lambda\sigma^\wedge$ can provide a characterisation of weak normalisation for λ_{dB}, λs_e and $\lambda\sigma$, respectively.

References

[ACCL91]   Abadi, M., Cardelli, L., Curien, P.-L., Lévy, J.-J.: Explicit Substitutions. J. func. program. 1(4), 375–416 (1991)

[AK01]   Ayala-Rincón, M., Kamareddine, F.: Unification via the λs_e-Style of Explicit Substitution. Logical Journal of the IGPL 9(4), 489–523 (2001)

[Bakel95]   van Bakel, S.: Intersection Type Assignment Systems. Theoret. comput. sci. 151, 385–435 (1995)

[BCD83]   Barendregt, H., Coppo, M., Dezani-Ciancaglini, M.: A filter lambda model and the completeness of type assignment. J. symbolic logic 48, 931–940 (1983)

[Barendregt84]   Barendregt, H.: The Lambda Calculus: Its Syntax and Semantics. North-Holland, Amsterdam (1984)

[deBruijn72]   de Bruijn, N.G.: Lambda-Calculus Notation with Nameless Dummies, a Tool for Automatic Formula Manipulation, with Application to the Church-Rosser Theorem. Indag. Mat. 34(5), 381–392 (1972)

[deBruijn78]   de Bruijn, N.G.: A namefree lambda calculus with facilities for internal definition of expressions and segments. T.H.-Report 78-WSK-03, Technische Hogeschool Eindhoven, Nederland (1978)

[CDC78]   Coppo, M., Dezani-Ciancaglini, M.: A new type assignment for lambda-terms. Archiv für mathematische logik 19, 139–156 (1978)

[CDC80]   Coppo, M., Dezani-Ciancaglini, M.: An Extension of the Basic Functionality Theory for the λ-Calculus. Notre dame j. formal logic 21(4), 685–693 (1980)

[CDV80]   Coppo, M., Dezani-Ciancaglini, M., Venneri, B.: Principal Type Schemes and λ-calculus Semantics. In: Seldin, J.P., Hindley, J.R. (eds.) To H.B. Curry: Essays on combinatory logic, lambda calculus and formalism, pp. 536–560. Academic Press, London (1980)

[CF58]   Curry, H.B., Feys, R.: Combinatory Logic, vol. 1. North-Holland, Amsterdam (1958)

[DG94]   Damiani, F., Giannini, P.: A Decidable Intersection Type System based on Relevance. In: Hagiya, M., Mitchell, J.C. (eds.) TACS 1994. LNCS, vol. 789, pp. 707–725. Springer, Heidelberg (1994)

[DHK2000]   Dowek, G., Hardin, T., Kirchner, C.: Higher-order Unification via Explicit Substitutions. Information and Computation 157(1/2), 183–235 (2000)

[Guillaume2000]   Guillaume, B.: The λse-calculus does not preserve strong normalisation. J. of func. program. 10(4), 321–325 (2000)

[Jim96]   Jim, T.: What are principal typings and what are they good for? In: Proc. of POPL 1995: Symp. on Principles of Programming Languages, pp. 42–53. ACM, New York (1996)

[KN07]   Kamareddine, F., Nour, K.: A completeness result for a realisability semantics for an intersection type system. Annals pure and appl. logic 146, 180–198 (2007)

[KR95]   Kamareddine, F., Ríos, A.: A λ-calculus à la de Bruijn with Explicit Substitutions. In: Swierstra, S.D. (ed.) PLILP 1995. LNCS, vol. 982, pp. 45–62. Springer, Heidelberg (1995)

[KR97]   Kamareddine, F., Ríos, A.: Extending a λ-calculus with Explicit Substitution which Preserves Strong Normalisation into a Confluent Calculus on Open Terms. J. of Func. Programming 7, 395–420 (1997)

[KW04]   Kfoury, A.J., Wells, J.B.: Principality and type inference for intersection types using expansion variables. Theoret. comput. sci. 311(1-3), 1–70 (2004)

[LLDDvB04]   Lengrand, S., Lescanne, P., Dougherty, D., Dezani-Ciancaglini, M., van Bakel, S.: Intersection types for explicit substitutions. Inform. and comput. 189(1), 17–42 (2004)

[Milner78]   Milner, R.: A theory of type polymorphism in programming. J. comput. and system sci. 17(3), 348–375 (1978)

[NGdV94]   Nederpelt, R.P., Geuvers, J.H., de Vrijer, R.C.: Selected papers on Automath. North-Holland, Amsterdam (1994)

[Pottinger80]   Pottinger, G.: A type assignment for the strongly normalizable λ-terms. In: Seldin, J.P., Hindley, J.R. (eds.) To H. B. Curry: Essays on combinatory logic, lambda calculus and formalism, pp. 561–578. Academic Press, London (1980)

[RV84]   Ronchi Della Rocca, S., Venneri, B.: Principal Type Scheme for an Extended Type Theory. Theoret. comput. sci. 28, 151–169 (1984)

[Rocca88]   Ronchi Della Rocca, S.: Principal Type Scheme and Unification for Intersection Type Discipline. Theoret. comput. sci. 59, 181–209 (1988)

[SM96a]   Sayag, E., Mauny, M.: Characterization of principal type of normal forms in intersection type system. In: Chandru, V., Vinay, V. (eds.) FSTTCS 1996. LNCS, vol. 1180, pp. 335–346. Springer, Heidelberg (1996)

[SM96b]   Sayag, E., Mauny, M.: A new presentation of the intersection type discipline through principal typings of normal forms. Tech. rep. RR-2998, INRIA (1996)

[SM97]   Sayag, E., Mauny, M.: Structural properties of intersection types. In: Proc. of LIRA 1997, pp. 167–175, Novi Sad, Yugoslavia (1997)

[VAK09]   Ventura, D., Ayala-Rincón, M., Kamareddine, F.: Intersection Type System with de Bruijn Indices. In: The many sides of logic. Studies in logic, vol. 21, pp. 557–576. College publications, London (2009)

[VAK10]   Ventura, D., Ayala-Rincón, M., Kamareddine, F.: Principal Typings in a Restricted Intersection Type System for Beta Normal Forms with de Bruijn Indices. In: Proc. of WRS 2009. EPTCS, vol. 15, pp. 69–82 (2010)

[Ventura10]   Ventura, D.: Cálculos de Substituições Explícitas à la de Bruijn com Sistemas de Tipos com Interseção. PhD Thesis Departamento de Matemática, Universidade de Brasília (2010), Online version (in Portuguese), http://ventura.mat.unb.br (March 5, 2010)

Generalising Conservativity

Richard Zuber

Rayé des cadres du CNRS
Richard.Zuber@linguist.jussieu.fr

Abstract. A constraint on functions from sets and relations to sets is studied. This constraint is a generalisation of the constraint of conservativity known from the study of generalised quantifiers in natural languages. It is suggested that this generalised constraint constitutes a semantic universal.

1 Introduction

Progress in the study of the logical properties of natural languages (NLs) is closely related to the study of various constraints that must be satisfied by functions interpreting functional expressions in NLs. We know that such expressions do not denote arbitrarily and thus that functions interpreting them obey various specific logic constraints. The most prominent results obtained in this context are obtained in generalised quantifier theory and concern functions corresponding to various types of quantifiers. The constraint on quantifiers which has been extensively studied from theoretical and empirical points of view is the constraint of conservativity, which concerns the denotations of various determiners found in NLs. Conservativity is generally considered as a language universal. Even though some non-conservative determiners are known, it appears that they are rare and not arbitrary since they are systematically related to conservative determiners (cf. Zuber 2004).

In this paper I generalise the notion of conservativity so that it can apply not only to quantifiers but also to some functions having sets as results. Furthermore, I suggest that the constraint of conservativity thus generalised also constitutes a language universal.

Let me make first some notational and definitional preliminaries which will allow us to define the properties and functions which we are going to discuss. We will be interested in sets and relations over a given universe E. If R is a $k + n$-ary relation and $a_1, ..., a_k \subset E$ then $a_1...a_k R$ is the n-ary relation defined as follows:

$$a_1...a_k R = \{\langle a_{k+1}, ..., a_n \rangle \in E^n : \langle a_1...a_{k+n} \rangle \in R\}$$

The functions in which we will be interested are functions which have as inputs (arguments) sets and relations. If the output of such a function is a truth-value then this function is a (generalised) quantifier. A type $\langle 1 \rangle$ quantifier is a function from sets to truth-values. It is a denotation of a noun phrase (used in subject position in a sentence). Type $\langle 1, 1 \rangle$ quantifiers are functions from binary

A. Dawar and R. de Queiroz (Eds.): WoLLIC 2010, LNAI 6188, pp. 247–258, 2010.

relations between sets to truth values or just binary relations between sets. Type $\langle 1, 2 \rangle$ quantifiers are binary relations between sets and binary relations (that is relations whose domains are sets and co-domains - binary relations between sets). Finally type $\langle 1, 1, 2 \rangle$ (or type $\langle 1^2, 2 \rangle$) quantifiers are ternary relations whose first two "arguments" are sets and the third argument is a binary relation between sets.

We will discuss basically functions which are not quantifiers though they can be seen as related to quantifiers. They are not quantifiers because their co-domains are not truth-values but sets (or relations in a more general case). The type of function which takes n sets and one k-ary relation and gives a i-ary relation (for $i < k$) as result will be noted $\langle 1^n, k : i \rangle$, for $n \geq 1$. The type of function taking a n-ary relation and giving as result an i-ary relation (for $i < k$) will be noted $\langle n : i \rangle$. These functions will be called *arity reducers*.

A special class of *arity reducers* is obtained from quantifiers. Since type $\langle m \rangle$ quantifiers are functions from m-ary relations to truth-values, in order to consider them more generally as arity reducers we need to define their extensions, that is to extend theirs domains so that they can apply to relations of any arity (higher than m). This can be done in two steps in the following way (cf. Keenan and Westerståhl 1997):

D1: Let R_n be the set of n-ary relations (over E). Then F is a reducer of arity by k, noted $F \in [\bigcup_n R_{n+k} \to \bigcup R_n]$ is in $AR(-k)$, if $\forall R \in R_{n+k}$, $F(R) \in R_n$, $(n \geq 0)$.

Every type $\langle k \rangle$ quantifier extends to a function in $AR(-k)$ in the following way:

D2: A type $\langle k \rangle$ quantifier Q extends to a function in $AR(-k)$, also noted Q, by letting, for $R \in R_{n+k}$, $Q(R) = \{\langle a_1, ..., a_n \rangle \in E^n : Q(a_1...a_n R) = 1\}$.

Thus by D2 any type $\langle k \rangle$ quantifier can be considered as a type $\langle n + k : n \rangle$ function, that is a function which applies to relations of arity $n + k$ and which gives as a result a relation of arity n.

Of course there are functions which are arity reducers but which are not extensions of quantifiers. Extended type $\langle 1 \rangle$ quantifiers are characterised by the following property (Keenan and Westerståhl 1997):

Proposition 1. Let $F \in AR(-1)$. F is extended type $\langle 1 \rangle$ quantifier iff $\forall n, m \geq 0$, $\forall R \in R_{n+1} \forall S \in R_{m+1} \forall a_1, ..., a_n, b_1, ..., b_m \in E$, we have

$$a_1...a_n R = b_1...b_m S \Rightarrow (\langle a_1, ..., a_n \rangle \in F(R) \Leftrightarrow \langle b_1, ..., b_m \rangle \in F(S))$$

From now on we will be interested in the particular case when $k = 2$, $n \leq 2$ and $i = 1$ and thus we will study basically functions of type $\langle 2 : 1 \rangle$, of type $\langle 1, 2 : 1 \rangle$ and to a lesser extend functions of type $\langle 1^2, 2 : 1 \rangle$.

Let me illustrate some of the above notions. We are interested in the interpretation of simple sentences of the form NP_1 TVP NP_2. In such sentences the noun phrase NP_1 is interpreted by a type $\langle 1 \rangle$ quantifier, which is a set of sets, and the transitive verb phrase TVP is interpreted by a binary relation. Concerning NP_2 there are two possibilities: it can be interpreted either by a function which is an extension of a type $\langle 1 \rangle$ quantifier or by a function (from binary relations to sets) which is not an extension of a type $\langle 1 \rangle$ quantifier. When such a function is an extension of a quantifier we will call it *accusative extension* (since it occurs in the direct object position of a sentence) and note it Q_{acc}. It is an instance of D2 and is specified in D3:

D3: If Q is a type $\langle 1 \rangle$ quantifier, then $Q_{acc}(R) = \{a : Q(aR) = 1\}$.

Obviously accusative case extensions satisfy the invariant condition given in Proposition 1 and which for the case we consider (k=2) will be called the accusative extension condition (AEC):

AEC: A function F from binary relations to sets satisfies the AEC iff for R and S binary relations, and $a, b \in E$, if $aR = bS$ then $a \in F(R)$ iff $b \in F(S)$.

Thus type $\langle 1 \rangle$ quantifiers become type $\langle 2 : 1 \rangle$ functions by accusative extension. It is also true, however, that any type $\langle 2 : 1 \rangle$ function which satisfies the AEC condition uniquely determines a type $\langle 1 \rangle$ quantifier. Indeed the following proposition holds:

Proposition 2. If a type $\langle 2 : 1 \rangle$ function F satisfies the AEC and the type $\langle 1 \rangle$ quantifier Q is defined as $Q(X) = 1$ iff $a \in F(\{a\} \times X)$ then $Q_{acc}(R) = F(R)$.

Proof: Type $\langle 1 \rangle$ quantifiers and type $\langle 2 : 1 \rangle$ functions satisfying AEC form complete atomic Boolean algebras. For any set $A \subseteq E$, the function F_A such $F_A(X) = 1$ iff $X = A$ is an atom of the algebra of type $\langle 1 \rangle$ quantifiers. Similarly, the function F_A such that $F_A(R) = \{x : xR = A\}$ is an atom of the second algebra. These two algebras are isomorphic (the mapping given in D3 establishes the isomorphism). Given that $F_A(\{a\} \times A) = A$ if $a \in A$ and $F_A(\{a\} \times A) = \emptyset$ if $a \notin A$, we get the needed result.

The following example illustrates Proposition 2. Consider a type $\langle 2 : 1 \rangle$ function F_A defined as follows: $F_A(R) = \{x : |xR \cap A| > |xR' \cap A|\}$ (for a fixed $A \subseteq E$ and E finite). Since $aR = bS$ iff $aR' = bS'$ the function F_A satisfies AEC. It is easy to see that $F_A = (MOST(A))_{acc}$ (where $MOST(A)(Y) = 1$ iff $|A \cap Y| > |A \cap Y'|$).

The following two simple conditions can be used to decide whether functions from binary relations to sets satisfy or not the AEC condition:

Fact 1: A type $\langle 2 : 1 \rangle$ function F does not satisfy the AEC if there exists a set B and $a, b \in B$ such that $a \in F(E \times B) \wedge b \notin F(E \times B)$.

Fact 2: If a type $\langle 2 : 1 \rangle$ function F satisfies AEC then for any $A \subseteq E$ one has $F(E \times A) = \emptyset$ or $F(E \times A) = E$.

In the next section we consider two classes of functions which need not satisfy the AEC condition.

2 Some Arity Reducers

Not every function from binary relations to sets used in NLs semantics satisfies AEC. The best known example is the function $SELF$ defined as $SELF(R) = \{x : \langle x, x \rangle \in R\}$; $SELF$ can be used to interpret the reflexive pronoun *him/herself*.

Among functions not satisfying AEC one can distinguish two sub-classes (cf. Keenan and Westerståhl 1997), according to whether they satisfy one of the two conditions which are strictly weaker than AEC. Because such functions are most frequently found in the semantics because they are necessary for the interpretation of various expressions in NLs, I briefly introduce them.

The function $SELF$ satisfies the the so-called *anaphor condition* AC:

AC: A function F from binary relations to sets satisfies the anaphor condition iff for R and S binary relations, and $a \in E$, if $aR = aS$ then $a \in F(R)$ iff $a \in F(S)$.

Obviously, functions which satisfy AEC also satisfy AC. Functions which satisfy AC but do not satisfy AEC will be called anaphoric functions.

One can check (Keenan 2007) that $SELF$ is an anaphoric function of type $\langle 2 : 1 \rangle$ as is the function $NOBODY\text{-}EXCEPT\text{-}SELF$ needed to interpret sentence (1):

(1) Leo hates everybody except himself.

The AC applies to functions of type $\langle 2 : 1 \rangle$. We need a similar condition for type $\langle 1, 2 : 1 \rangle$ functions (which in NLs are basically denotations of anaphoric determiners):

ACD1: A function F of type $\langle 1, 2 : 1 \rangle$ satisfies anaphor condition (ACD1) iff for any $a \in E$, $X \subseteq E$ and R, S binary relations, if $a(E \times X \cap R) = a(E \times X \cap S)$ then $a \in F(X, R)$ iff $a \in F(X, S)$.

To illustrate ACD1 consider the following example:

(2) Leo trusts no philosopher except himself.

In this example the function $NO\text{-}EXCEPT\text{-}SELF$ of type $\langle 1, 2 : 1 \rangle$ defined in (3) is involved:

(3) $F(X, R) = NO(X)\text{-}EXCEPT\text{-}SELF(R) = \{y : yR \cap X = \{y\}\}$

One can check that this function satisfies ACD1.

The following property gives a justification of the condition ACD1:

Fact 3: If the function F of type $\langle 1, 2 : 1 \rangle$ satisfies ACD1 then the function G^A of type $\langle 2 : 1 \rangle$ defined as $G^A(R) = F(A, R)$ satisfies AC.

What fact 3 informally says is that functions satisfying ACD1 are those from which we get functions satisfying AC when fixing their set argument.

We can use the same method of fixing "nominal" arguments to define anaphoric functions of type $\langle 1, 2 : 1 \rangle$. Thus we have:

D4: A function F of type $\langle 1, 2 : 1 \rangle$ is anaphoric iff it satisfies the condition ACD1 and the function G^A of type $\langle 2 : 1 \rangle$ defined as $G^A(R) = F(A, R)$ is anaphoric for any non-trivial A.

Using fact 1 one can show that the function defined in (3) is anaphoric.

In the above definitions, anaphoricity of type $\langle 1, 2 : 1 \rangle$ functions is reduced to anaphoricity of type $\langle 2 : 1 \rangle$ functions. The condition of non-triviality for A and B is necessary because obviously for values of A or B making F constant such that we get functions which also satisfy AEC.

Let us consider now the second weakening of the AEC, the so-called argument invariance (Keenan and Westerståhl 1997):

D5: A type $\langle 2 : 1 \rangle$ function F is argument invariant iff whenever $aR = bR$ then $a \in F(R)$ iff $b \in F(R)$.

The above definition obviously generalises to type $\langle 1, 2 : 1 \rangle$ functions:

D6: A type $\langle 1, 2 : 1 \rangle$ function F is argument invariant iff whenever $a(E \times X \cap R) = b(E \times X \cap R)$ then $a \in R(X, R)$ iff $b \in F(X, R)$.

As an example consider the function involved in the interpretation of the numerical superlative *the greatest number of* as it occurs in (4a) with the intended meaning given in (4b). This superlative is interpreted by the function given in (5):

(4a) Leo knows the greatest number of languages.
(4b) Leo knows more languages than anybody else.
(5) $NSUP(X, R) = \{x : \forall y (y \neq x \rightarrow |xR \cap X| > |yR \cap X|\}$

It is easy to check that $NSUP$ is argument invariant and that it does not satisfy the AEC1 condition.

3   Conservativity

Conservativity is a property of some classes of quantifiers. It has been basically studied in connection with type $\langle 1, 1 \rangle$ quantifiers but a non-trivial notion of conservativity applies to many classes of quantifiers which take at least two arguments. In particular quantifiers denoted by unary and n-ary determiners can be said to be conservative. Moreover Westeståhl 2004 shows how to define conservativity for type $\langle 1^m, k \rangle$ quantifiers. Conservativity of some other classes of quantifiers is defined in Keenan and Westerståhl (1997).

Conservativity of quantifiers denoted by unary or n-ary determiners (that is determiners taking n common nouns to form a noun phrase) can be easily defined, as we will see. We have seen that anaphoric functions (that we consider here) are systematically related to quantifiers (of type $\langle 1, 1 \rangle$). Simularly, "comparative" functions which are argument invariant (and which interpret comparative constructions such as the one a in (5)), seem to be related to quantifiers. So it is quite natural to ask whether and in what sense anaphoric functions are conservative.

Let us recall first the notion of conservativity for type $\langle 1, 1 \rangle$ quantifiers. A now well-known definition is given in D5:

D5: $F \in CONS$ iff for any property X, Y one has $F(X)(Y) = F(X)(X \cap Y)$.

Given D5 it is easy to show that the type $\langle 1, 1 \rangle$ quantifier F defined as $F(X)(Y) = 1$ iff $X = Y$, is not conservative.

Conservativity of type $\langle 1, 1 \rangle$ quantifiers can additionally be formulated in two different ways:

Fact 5 (cf. Keenan and Faltz 1986): F is conservative or $F \in CONS$ iff for any property X, Y and Z if $X \cap Y = X \cap Z$ then $F(X)(Y) = F(X)(Z)$.

Fact 6 (Zuber 2005): $F \in CONS$ iff for any property X, Y one has $F(X)(Y) = F(X)(X' \cup Y)$.

It is also possible to define conservativity for the whole class of type $\langle 1, 1, 2 \rangle$ quantifiers. In this case we have the following definition, an instance of the general definition proposed in Westerståhl 2004:

D6: A type $\langle 1, 1, 2 \rangle$ quantifier F is conservative iff for any sets A, B and any binary relation R one has $F(A, B, R) = F(A, B, A \times B \cap R)$.

As in the case of "simple" type $\langle 1, 1 \rangle$ quantifiers it is possible to give an equivalent defining condition for conservativity of type $\langle 1, 1, 2 \rangle$ quantifiers to hold. Thus we have:

Proposition 3. A type $\langle 1, 1, 2 \rangle$ quantifier is conservative iff $F(A, B, R_1) = F(A, B, R_2)$ whenever $A \times B \cap R_1 = A \times B \cap R_2$.

Clearly none of the above definitions of conservativity applies directly to an anphoric function. However, proposition 3 and fact 5 give us a hint as to what form the definition of conservativity of type $\langle 1, 2 : 1 \rangle$ functions should take. Here is the definition:

D7: Let F be a type $\langle 1, 2 : 1 \rangle$ function. Then F is conservative iff for all $X \subseteq E$ and R_1, R_2 binary relations, if $E \times X \cap R_1 = E \times X \cap R_2$ then $F(X, R_1) = F(X, R_2)$.

By analogy with fact 1 and definition D1 conservativity of type $\langle 1, 2 : 1 \rangle$ functions can be defined equivalently as the following proposition shows:

Proposition 4. A function F of type $\langle 1, 2 : 1 \rangle$ is conservative iff $F(X, R) = F(X, E \times X \cap R)$.

It is easy to check that the anaphoric type $\langle 1, 2 : 1 \rangle$ function *EVERY-EXCEPT-SELF* defined above, is conservative.

The following property gives additional plausibility to the above definitions of generalised conservativity:

Proposition 5. Let D be a type $\langle 1, 1 \rangle$ quantifier and F a type $\langle 1, 2 : 1 \rangle$ function defined as: $F(X, R) = D(X)_{acc}(R)$. Then F is conservative iff D is conservative.

Proof: Suppose *a contrario* that F is conservative and D is not. Thus for some $X, Y \in E$, $D(X)(Y) \neq D(X)(X \cap Y)$. Let $R = E \times Y$. Then:

$F(X, R) = D(X)_{acc}(R) = \{a : D(X)(aR) = 1\} = \{a : D(X)(a(E \times Y)) = 1\}$
$F(X, E \times X \cap R) = D(X)_{acc}(E \times (X \cap Y)) = \{a : D(X)(a(E \times (X \cap Y))) = 1\}$
Since $D(X)(a(E \times Y)) = D(X)(Y)$ and $D(X)(a(E \times (X \cap Y))) = D(X)(X \cap Y)$, this means that $F(X, R) \neq F(X, E \times X \cap R)$, which is impossible given that F is conservative.

Suppose now that D is conservative. Then:

$F(X, R) = D(X)_{acc}(R) = \{a : D(X)(aR) = 1\} =$
$= \{a : D(X)(X \cap aR) = 1\}$, since D is conservative
$= \{a : D(X)(a(E \times X \cap R) = 1\}$, since $X = a(E \times X)$ and $a(R \cap S) = aR \cap aS$)
$= D(X)_{acc}(E \times X \cap R) = F(X, E \times X \cap R)$

Thus the generalised conservativity of functions induced by type $\langle 1, 1 \rangle$ quantifiers, when they are used in the accusative extension of a type $\langle 1 \rangle$ quantifier, is strictly related to the "classical" conservativity of the inducing quantifier.

Given the example of non-conservative type $\langle 1, 1 \rangle$ quantifier given above it follows from Proposition 5 that the type $\langle 1, 2 : 1 \rangle$ function F defined as $F(X, R) = \{y : X = yR\}$ is not conservative.

Let us recall now some properties of denotations of binary determiners, that is quantifiers of type $\langle \langle 1, 1 \rangle 1 \rangle$. We have the following definition of conservativity (Keenan and Moss 1985, Zuber 2005):

D8: A type $\langle \langle 1, 1 \rangle 1 \rangle$ quantifier is conservative iff for any $X_1, X_2, Y_1, Y_2 \subseteq E$, if $X_1 \cap Y_1 = X_1 \cap Y_2$ and $X_2 \cap Y_1 = X_2 \cap Y_2$ then $F(X_1, X_2)(Y_1) = F(X_1, X_2)(Y_2)$.

The following proposition shows the equivalent way to define conservativity for type $\langle \langle 1, 1 \rangle 1 \rangle$ quantifiers:

Proposition 6. A type $\langle \langle 1, 1 \rangle 1 \rangle$ quantifier is conservative iff for any $X_1, X_2, Y \subseteq E$ one has $F(X_1, X_2)(Y) = F(X_1, X_2)(Y \cap (X_1 \cup X_2))$.

Definition D8 and proposition 6 can be used as basis for generalising conservativity to type $\langle 1^2, 2 : 1 \rangle$ functions:

D9: A type $\langle 1^2, 2 : 1 \rangle$ function F is conservative iff for any $X_1, X_2 \subseteq E$ and any binary relations R_1 and R_2, if $E \times X_1 \cap R_1 = E \times X_1 \cap R_2$ and $E \times X_2 \cap R_1 = E \times X_2 \cap R_2$ then $F(X_1, X_2, R_1) = F(X_1, X_2, R_2)$.

The corresponding equivalent property is indicated in the following proposition:

Proposition 7. A type $\langle 1^2, 2 : 1 \rangle$ function F is conservative iff for any $X_1, X_2 \subseteq E$ and binary relation R one has $F(X_1, X_2, R) = F(X_1, X_2, (E \times (X_1 \cup X_2)) \cap R)$.

Let us see some examples. As we know the type $\langle \langle 1, 1 \rangle 1 \rangle$ quantifier $MORE(X_1\text{-}THAN(X_2)$ is denoted by the binary determiner *more...than....* This determiner may form a noun phrase with two common names. This noun phrase can occur in object position as in (6):

(6) Leo knows more logicians than philosophers.

One can consider that in this case the type $\langle \langle 1, 1 \rangle 1 \rangle$ quantifier $MORE(X_1)\text{-}THAN(X_2)$ gives rise to a type $\langle 1^2, 2 : 1 \rangle$ function F defined in (7):

(7) $F(X_1, X_2, R) = (MORE(X_1)\text{-}THAN(X_2))_{acc}(R) = \{y : |yR \cap X_1| > |yR \cap X_2|\}$.

This function is conservative. This is not surprising since $MORE(X_1)\text{-}THAN(X_2)$ is conservative and we have:

Proposition 8. Let D be a type $\langle \langle 1, 1 \rangle 1 \rangle$ quantifier. Then the type $\langle 1^2, 2 : 1 \rangle$ function $F(X_1, X_2, R) = (D(X_1, X_2))_{acc}(R)$ is conservative iff D is conservative.

Proof of Proposition 8 is similar to that of Proposition 5.

One can consider that Proposition 8 "justifies" D9.

There are obviously type $\langle 1^2, 2 : 1 \rangle$ functions which are not obtained by the accusative extension of type $\langle \langle 1, 1 \rangle 1 \rangle$ quantifiers. Consider the example in (8) which involves the type $\langle 1^2, 2 : 1 \rangle$ function given in (9):

(8) Leo knows more languages than Adam (knows) theorems.
(9) $F_a(X_1, X_2, R) = \{y : |yR \cap X_1| > aR \cap X_2|\}$

The function F_a is conservative (and comparative).

4   Other Constraints

Generalised conservativity as introduced in the previous section in D7 and D9 concerns type $\langle 1, 2 : 1 \rangle$ and type $\langle 1^2, 2 : 1 \rangle$ functions in general and not only anaphoric or comparative functions. Moreover generalised consevativity is independent of anaphor conditions ACD1 and ACD2 for anaphoric functions. It is also independent of argument invariance. What is interesting is the fact that some anaphoric functions satisfy also other constraints, some of which are stronger than generalised conservativity.

Observe that type $\langle 1, 2 : 1 \rangle$ anaphoric functions discussed above, for instance the function given in (3), are used to interpret various constructions in which the reflexive pronoun *him/her-self* occurs. such functions satisfy the constraint given in (8):

(8) $F(A, R) \subseteq A$.

Interestingly, the anaphoric condition ACD1, (generalised) conservativity and the condition given in (8) entail a specific version of conservativity, *anaphoric conservativity* (or a-conservativity) , specific to *self*-type anaphoric determiners. It is defined in D10:

D10: A type $\langle 1, 2 : 1 \rangle$ function F is a-conservative iff $F(X, R) = F(X, X \times X \cap R)$.

Thus we have the following proposition:

Proposition 9. A type $\langle 1, 2 : 1 \rangle$ anaphoric and conservative function F such that $F(X, R) \subseteq X$ is a-conservative.

Proof: Suppose *a contrario* that for some $X \subseteq E$, $F(X, R) \neq F(X, X \times X \cap R)$ and thus that (by conservativity) $F(X, E \times X \cap R) \neq F(X, X \times X \cap R)$. This means that for some $a \in X$, $a \in F(X, E \times X \cap R)$ and $a \notin F(X, X \times X \cap R)$ (or $a \notin F(X, E \times X \cap R)$ and $a \in F(X, X \times X \cap R)$). This is, however, impossible given that F is anaphoric and the fact that in this case $a(E \times X \cap R) = a(X \times X \cap R)$.

It follows from the observations made above that *self*-type anaphoric functions described above are a-conservative. There are also anaphoric functions which are not a-conservative (Zuber 2010).

It is well-known that various natural language quantifiers can satisfy stronger constraints than conservativity (Keenan 1993) . In particular they can be inter-sective or co-intersective. These sub-classes of quantifiers are theoretically im-portant for various reasons. For instance Keenan 1993 shows that conservative type $\langle 1, 1 \rangle$ quantifiers are Booleanly generated by intersective and co-intersective quantifiers. They are also of empirical interest since they lead to various linguis-tically relevant generalisations (cf. Peters and Westerståhl 2006, Kuroda 2008).

The question thus arises whether one can generalise the notion of intersectivity or co-intersectivity to some functions which are not quantifiers. In what follows I show briefly how it can be done.

Recall that a type $\langle 1, 1 \rangle$ quantifier D is intersective (resp. co-intersective) iff $D(X_1, Y_1) = D(X_2, Y_2)$ whenever $X_1 \cap Y_1 = X_2 \cap Y_2$ (resp. $X_1 \cap Y_1' = X_2 \cap Y_2'$). This leads to the following definitions of intersective or co-intersective anaphoric functions:

D11: A type $\langle 1, 2 : 1 \rangle$ function is intersective (resp. co-intersective) iff $F(X_1, R_1) = F(X_2, R_2)$ whenever $E \times X_1 \cap R_1 = E \times X_2 \cap R_2$ (resp. $E \times X_1 \cap R_1' = E \times X_2 \cap R_2'$).

The following proposition, similar to Proposition 5, can be considered as jus-tifying the above definition:

Proposition 10. Let D be a type $\langle 1, 1 \rangle$ quantifier and F a type $\langle 1, 2 : 1 \rangle$ function defined as: $F(X, R) = D(X)_{acc}(R)$. Then F is intersective (resp. co-intersective) iff D is intersective (resp. co-intersective).

It is easy to see that the function $NO(X)$-BUT-$SELF(R)$ as defined in (3) above is intersective. Similarly, the function F_a, for $a \in E$, defined in (9) and which is necessary to interpret (10), is an intersective function:

(9) $F_a(X, R) = \{y : |yR \cap X| \geq |aR \cap X|\}$
(10) Leo knows at least as many languages as Adam.

Concerning co-intersective functions it is easy to show that the function $EVERY(X)$-BUT-$SELF(R)$ defined in (11) is co-intersective:

(11) $EVERY(X)$-BUT-$SELF(R) = \{x : X \cap xR' = \{x\}\}$

It is also possible to generalise other sub-properties of conservativity. Consider so-called cardinal quantifiers. A type $\langle 1, 1 \rangle$ quantifier F is cardinal iff $F(X_1)(Y_1) = F(X_2)(Y_2)$ whenever $|X_1 \cap Y_1| = |X_2 \cap Y_2|$. For instance numerals denote cardinal quantifiers.

In order to generalise the property of cardinality (of quantifiers) to type $\langle 1, 2 : 1 \rangle$ functions observe first the following equivalence:

(12) $E \times X_1 \cap R_1 = E \times X_2 \cap R_2$ iff $\forall y(X_1 \cap yR_1 = X_2 \cap yR_2)$

This means that the condition in D11 can be replaced by the right hand side expression in (12). This leads to the following definition:

D12: A type $\langle 1, 2 : 1 \rangle$ function is cardinal iff $F(X_1, R_1) = F(X_2, R_2)$ whenever $\forall y(|X_1 \cap yR_1| = |X_2 \cap yR_2|)$.

For cardinal functions we have the following proposition, similar to proposition 5 and proposition 10:

Proposition 11. Let D be a type $\langle 1, 1 \rangle$ quantifier and F a type $\langle 1, 2 : 1 \rangle$ function defined as: $F(X, R) = D(X)_{acc}(R)$. Then F is cardinal iff D is cardinal.

The function given in (9) is a cardinal function which is not obtained by the accusative case extension. Similarly, the comparative function F_a given in (13) needed to interpret (14) is a cardinal function (not obtained by the accusative case extension of a cardinal quantifier):

(13) $F_a(X, R) = \{y : |yR \cap X| > |aR \cap X|\}$
(14) Leo proved more theorems than Adam.

Obviously, cardinal functions are conservative. This means that the function $F(X, R) = \{y : X = yR\}$ is not cardinal.

5   Conclusion

After having recalled the various properties of anaphoric and comparative functions which represent the biggest class of type $\langle 1, 2 : 1 \rangle$ functions found in NLs, I have proposed a generalisation of the notion of conservativity classically used in the context of quantifiers. Moreover, some notions stronger than conservativity, that is intersectivity and cardinality (of quantifiers) are also generalised to specific functions. Conservativity is a very natural property. In simple cases it has empirical and theoretical justification (Peters and Westerståhl 2006). In the domain of determiners, that is expressions denoting, roughly speaking, quantifiers, it is considered as a language universal. This means that one has enough empirical data to consider that all determiners, defined syntactically, in all natural languages denote only conservative quantifiers.

Even if in any serious (composional) semantics the (complex) expressions discussed here will automatically get the generalised conservativity (if at least the (simple) quantifiers that are used as building blocks are conservative), it is very tempting to make a similar universalistic claim about the generalised conservativity of specific functions from sets and relations to sets studied in this article. In other words, one would like to suggest, roughly, that NLs expressions denoting type $\langle 1, 2 : 1 \rangle$ or type $\langle 1^2, 2 : 1 \rangle$ functions always denote conservative functions.

Any serious defence of such a claim should be preceded by additional research along the following two lines. First, obviously, more empirical research should be done. The notion of generalised conservativity proposed here applies to all type $\langle 1, 2 : 1 \rangle$ functions, not only anaphoric ones or comparative ones. It has been supposed here that the functions which are not obtained by a case extension and known to be needed in the semantics of NLs are either anaphoric (cf. Zuber 2010) or comparative. This supposition should be empirically substantiated. Second, a syntactic description of expressions denoting conservative functions should be provided. The underlying idea in this article is that such functions are denotations of anaphors or of comparatives and superlatives. Thus the precise syntactic status of such constructions should be provided. This syntactic part of the enterprise is considered as being outside the scope of this article.

References

1. Keenan, E.L.: Natural Language, Sortal Reducibility and Generalised Quantifiers. Journal of Symbolic Logic 58(1), 314–325 (1993)
2. Keenan, E.L.: On the denotations of anaphors. Research on Language and Computation 5(1), 5–17 (2007)
3. Keenan, E.L., Faltz, L.M.: Boolean Semantics for Natural Language. D. Reidel Publishing Company, Dordrecht (1985)
4. Keenan, E.L., Moss, L.: Generalized quantifiers and the expressive power of natural language. In: van Benthem, J., ter Meulen, A. (eds.) Generalized Quantifiers, Foris, Dordrecht, pp. 73–124 (1985)
5. Keenan, E.L., Westerståhl, D.: Generalized Quantifiers in Linguistics and Logic. In: van Benthem, J., ter Meulen, A. (eds.) Handbook of logic and language, pp. 837–893. Elsevier, Amsterdam (1997)
6. Peters, S., Westerståhl, D.: Quantifiers in Language and Logic. Clarendon Press, Oxford (2006)
7. Kuroda, S.-Y.: Head Internal Relative Clauses, Quantifier Float, the Definiteness Effect and the Mathematics of Determiners. San Diego Linguistics Papers 3, 126–183 (2008)

8. Westerståhl, D.: Iterated Quantifiers. In: Kanazawa, M., Pinon, C. (eds.) Dynamics, Polarity and Quantification, CSLI, Stanford University, pp. 173–209 (1994)
9. Zuber, R.: A class of non-conservative determiners in Polish. Linguisticae Investigationes XXVII(1), 147–165 (2004)
10. Zuber, R.: More Algebras for Determiners. In: Blache, P., Stabler, E.P., Busquets, J.V., Moot, R. (eds.) LACL 2005. LNCS (LNAI), vol. 3492, pp. 363–378. Springer, Heidelberg (2005)
11. Zuber, R.: Semantics of Slavic anaphoric possessive determiners. In: Proceedings of SALT, vol. 19 (2010)

Author Index